DATE DUE

			PRINTED IN U.S.A.

THE VITALITY OF JAPAN

ST ANTONY'S SERIES

General Editor: Alex Pravda, Fellow of St Antony's College, Oxford

Recent titles include:

Craig Brandist
CARNIVAL CULTURE AND THE SOVIET MODERNIST NOVEL

Jane Ellis
THE RUSSIAN ORTHODOX CHURCH: Triumphalism and Defensiveness

Y Hakan Erdem
SLAVERY IN THE OTTOMAN EMPIRE AND ITS DEMISE, 1800–1909

Dae Hwan Kim and Tat Yan Kong (editors)
THE KOREAN PENINSULA IN TRANSITION

Jill Krause and Neil Renwick (editors)
IDENTITIES IN INTERNATIONAL RELATIONS

Jaroslav Krejcí and Pavel Machonin
CZECHOSLOVAKIA, 1918–92: A Laboratory for Social Change

Iftikhar H. Malik
STATE AND SOCIETY IN PAKISTAN: Politics of Authority, Ideology and Ethnicity

Barbara Marshall
WILLY BRANDT: A Political Biography

Javier Martínez-Lara
BUILDING DEMOCRACY IN BRAZIL: The Politics of Constitutional Change, 1985–95

Joseph Nevo
KING ABDALLAH AND PALESTINE: A Territorial Ambition

William J. Tompson
KHRUSHCHEV: A Political Life

St Antony's Series
Series Standing Order ISBN 0–333–71109–2
(outside North America only)

You can receive future titles in this series as they are published by placing a standing order. Please contact your bookseller or, in case of difficulty, write to us at the address below with your name and address, the title of the series and the ISBN quoted above.

Customer Services Department, Macmillan Distribution Ltd
Houndmills, Basingstoke, Hampshire RG21 6XS, England

The Vitality of Japan

Sources of National Strength and Weakness

Edited by

Armand Clesse
Director, Luxembourg Institute for European and International Studies
Luxembourg

Takashi Inoguchi
Senior Vice-Rector
United Nations University
Tokyo

E. B. Keehn
President, Japan–America Society
Los Angeles

and

J. A. A. Stockwin
Nissan Professor of Modern Japanese Studies
University of Oxford

in association with
LUXEMBOURG INSTITUTE FOR EUROPEAN AND
INTERNATIONAL STUDIES
and
ST ANTONY'S COLLEGE, OXFORD

First published in Great Britain 1997 by
MACMILLAN PRESS LTD
Houndmills, Basingstoke, Hampshire RG21 6XS and London
Companies and representatives throughout the world

A catalogue record for this book is available from the British Library.

ISBN 0–333–64820–X

First published in the United States of America 1997 by
ST. MARTIN'S PRESS, INC.,
Scholarly and Reference Division,
175 Fifth Avenue, New York, N.Y. 10010

ISBN 0–312–17313–X

Library of Congress Cataloging-in-Publication Data
The vitality of Japan : sources of national strength and weakness /
edited by Armand Clesse . . . [et al.].
p.   cm. — (St. Antony's series)
Includes bibliographical references and index.
ISBN 0–312–17313–X (cloth)
1. Japan—Politics and government—1989—Congresses.   2. Japan–
–Foreign economic relations—Congresses.   3. Japan—Relations–
–Foreign countries—Congresses.   4. Japan—Social conditions—1945–
–Congresses.   I. Clesse, Armand.   II. Series.
DS891.V58 1997
957.03'3—dc21   96–37768
                                                            CIP

This book is printed on paper suitable for recycling and made from fully managed and
sustained forest sources.

10   9   8   7   6   5   4   3   2   1
06   05   04   03   02   01   00   99   98   97

Printed in Great Britain by
The Ipswich Book Company Ltd
Ipswich, Suffolk

Contents

Annex: Excerpts from the Discussions at the Conference

Contributors

David ARASE is an associate Professor, Department of Politics, Pomona College, Claremont, California. He is the author of *Buying Power: The Political Economy of Japan's Foreign Aid.*

Kent E. CALDER is currently the Director of the Program on US-Japan Relations at Princeton University and a tenured Professor of Political and International Affairs at its Woodrow Wilson School. He specialised in East Asian Political Economy. His most recent publication was *Strategic Capitalism: Private Business and Public Purpose in Japanese Industrial Finance.*

Armand CLESSE is the Director of the Luxembourg Institute for European and International Studies.

Kenneth S. COURTIS is a Professor and First Vice-President of Deutsche Bank Group Asia. He also lectures at Keio and Tokyo Universities, and is Visiting Professor at the Stockholm School of Economics. He is a Honorary Councillor of the Atlantic Council. His recent publication is entitled in Japanese, *Miezaru Tomi no Teikoku (Japan: so much to lose, so much to gain).*

George A. DE VOS is a psychologist and Professor emeritus of Anthropology at the University of California, Berkeley. He is the author of numerous books and articles documenting his forty-five years of cross-cultural field experience and research in the United States, East Asia and Western Europe. He is the author of *Social Cohesion and Alienation: Minorities in the United States and Japan.*

Robert GILPIN is the Dwight D. Eisenhower Professor of International Affairs at Princeton University. He has written primarily in the area of the relationships between international economics and international politics. Among his numerous publications is *The Political Economy of International Relations.*

David D. HALE is the Chief Economist and Senior Vice-President of Kemper Financial Companies. He is a member of the National Association of Business Economists and the New York Society of Security Analysts and a variety of government and private-sector economic policy research groups in Washington, Tokyo and Bonn. He writes on a broad range of economic subjects and his articles have appeared in various journals.

Ivan P. HALL was a Professor at Tsukuba, Keio and Gakushuin Universities. His most recent publication is *Japan's Asia Card in the National Interest*.

Donald C. HELLMANN is Professor of International Studies and Political Science at the Henry M. Jackson School of International Studies and Seattle Director of the APEC Study Centre, both at the University of Washington and Chair of the United States Consortium of APEC Study Centres. His most recent book is *Sharing World Leadership: A New Era for Japan and the United States* (with John Makin).

Takashi INOGUCHI is Professor and a Senior Vice-Rector of the United Nations University (UNU), Tokyo. He has published widely, writing and editing some 23 books in Japanese and English in the area of world affairs and international relations. His most recent publication is *Japan's Foreign Policy in an Era of Global Change*.

E.B. KEEHN is currently the President of the Japan-America Society, based in Los Angeles, and a visiting researcher at the University of Southern California. Between 1991 and 1995 he was the Fuji Bank University Lecturer in Japanese Politics at Cambridge University (England) and Visiting University Lecturer in Japanese Politics at the School for Oriental and African Studies, University of London, 1993-94. He has been published in *The Harvard Business Review*, *Foreign Affairs*, *The National Interest*, and *The Times* (London).

Gavan McCORMACK is Professor of Japanese History in the Division of Pacific and Asian History in the Research School of Pacific Studies, Australian National University. He has written a dozen books on aspects of modern Japanese, Korean and Chinese history and Australian-Asian relations, and his work has also been translated and published in Chinese, Korean, Thai, Arabic. His latest book is *Japan at Century's End: The Emptiness of Affluence*.

J.A.A. STOCKWIN has been Nissan Professor of modern Japanese Studies and Director of the Nissan Institute of Japanese Studies at the University of Oxford since 1982 and General Editor of the Nissan Institute/Routledge Japanese Studies Series. He is also a Fellow of St Antony's College, Oxford. He is the author of various books on Japanese politics.

Takeyuki TSUDA is a Ph.D. candidate in anthropology at the University of California at Berkeley. Currently, he is writing up his dissertation as a Visiting Research Fellow at the Centre for US-Mexican Studies at the University of California at San Diego on the return migration of the Japanese-Brazilians from Brazil to Japan. He has also published a paper entitled "The Psychosocial Functions of Liminality: The Japanese University Experience" in the *Journal of Psychohistory*.

Acknowledgements

This volume is part of a long-term project which included a conference organised by the Luxembourg Institute for European and International Studies in Tokyo on 26-27 March 1992. The subject of this project, which is both multidisciplinary and multinational in scope, is 'the vitality of nations'. A wide-ranging array of scholars gathered for the conference in Tokyo, including specialists from Japan, other Asian countries, the United States, and Western Europe.

The conference was made possible by the financial assistance of the Luxembourg government, as well as the support of Luxembourg's Prime Minister at that time, Jacques Santer. In addition, the event would not have been a success without the partnership of the Japan Institute of International Affairs (JIIA), and in particular the efforts of its director, Itaru Umezu, as well as those of Haruhisa Takeuchi, director for research coordination, and Toshihiko Naito and Maki Arai, research assistants who proved to be invaluable in organising the logistical aspects of the conference.

There would not have been such a rich and stimulating exchange of ideas without the cooperation of Karel van Wolferen, who helped to find at least twenty of the conference participants. Both the substance of the discussions and the list of participants benefited from the advice offered by Professor Seizabro Sato, research director at the Tokyo-based International Institute for Global Peace. From the beginning, the endeavour received the support of Ambassador Hisashi Owada, then Vice-Minister of Foreign Affairs; he also offered a splendid reception at the Foreign Ministry for all the participants. Luxembourg's then ambassador to Japan, Jean-Louis Wolzfeld, also gave very good advice and hosted a dinner following the conference.

Regarding the actual editorial work, I would like to thank first and foremost Ms Denise Schauls for her overall supervision; Abey Hailu, who coordinated the preparations at the Institute and prepared the camera-ready copy; several assistants and interns who contributed at various stages in the preparation of the conference and the publication of the book: André Gillissen, Didier Clémens, Tania Berchem, Philippe Théate, Julia Schimmelmann, Miriam Holbe, Sneja Dobrosavljevic, and Anne Maas; Laurie Charles Baillie, who proofread the texts, and T.M. Farmiloe, the publishing editor. Finally, I would like to express my gratitude to my three co-editors, E.B. Keehn, T. Inoguchi, and J.A.A. Stockwin. E.B. Keehn played a key role in shaping the book's structure, and he also wrote the introduction.

Unfortunately, a number of technical constraints have delayed the publication of this book. Nevertheless, I am confident that the contributions retain their original interest. Although Japanese society has undergone tremendous changes in recent years, the papers in the pages that follow will contribute to providing the reader with a deeper understanding of those aspects that have shaped, and continue to shape, the vitality of that nation.

A. Clesse

Introduction

This volume grew out of a conference held in Tokyo in 1992, generously sponsored by the Luxembourg Institute for European and International Studies in association with the Japan Institute of International Affairs (JIIA). All of the chapters included in this volume were written before the Liberal Democratic Party lost its 38-year hold on power in the summer of 1993. As a result, this book is not the place to look for updates on the current Japanese political and economic system. Rather, it is the place to find interesting forms of analysis on Japan just as it was embarking on potentially the most important changes in its political system since 1955, when the Liberal Democratic Party was created through a merger of Japan's two dominant conservative parties of that era.

Like the 1950s, the 1990s will be remembered as an era in which Japan once again had to redefine its party lines, but in a much more difficult domestic and international environment than it faced in the 1950s. With the old Cold War verities no longer in place, new challenges arose for the Japanese government and Japanese corporations. The challenges of the 1990s include a protracted domestic economic downturn, and the need to begin redefining Japan's international profile in the face of an increasingly powerful China, an ever more desperate North Korea, and shifts in the shared responsibilities built into the US-Japan security treaty.

There is no question that the political and economic changes which are occurring in Japan in the 1990s are immense. And many of these changes have become more striking since the chapters which appear in this book were first written. Normally, when such huge changes occur, the editors would demand a series of updates from the contributors. However, we decided against this for two reasons.

First, repeated revisions would have allowed the contributors to alter their original views and analyses of Japan, rather than face up to the test of subsequent historical evidence. Social scientists tend to become uncomfortable when they do not engage in *post-hoc* updating to maintain a reputation for accurate analysis. As a result, rewrites become an important device for the hedging of rhetorical bets by allowing authors to soften strongly held positions or alter previous predictions. Resort to this device may seem no more than reasonable, especially when the publication schedule allows it and when a nation is undergoing changes as varied as

Japan has been experiencing in the 1990s. But this was not done in the case of this book. Chapters written before momentous events occurred in Japan have largely been retained in their original form, leaving it to the reader to evaluate the subsequent accuracy and relevance of each writer's position.

Second, this volume demonstrates that what were deemed controversial views about Japan a few short years ago are today's commonly accepted facts. No one any longer doubts the policy and leadership weaknesses inherent in Japan's system of political parties. The power of the central state bureaucracy, especially the Ministry of Finance, is now so obvious to even occasional students of Japan that it is simply no longer seriously debated, except by a few intellectually isolated academics more committed to theory than reality. To call the Japanese bureaucracy powerful, however, is not to suggest it is efficient or even particularly good at what it does, or is supposed to do. This was tragically demonstrated in the aftermath of the Kobe earthquake of January 1995 when the central government's response was, on its own admission, both slow and inadequate. The emergence of a more independent Japanese foreign policy is also no longer in question. These topics, which were regarded as highly controversial in 1992, are now the normal repertory of Japan's own opinion leaders when discussing their nation's likely future course.

Also unusually for a conference volume, we have included a transcript of the proceedings. There were frank and confrontational exchanges. At other times discussion was not as free-wheeling or as incisive as it could or should have been. This is also part of the record and has not been excised or papered over.

Much of what appears in this book holds up relatively well to the passage of time. Yet, as we head into the last third of this decade, it is impossible for any serious student of Japan to feel satisfied with how we study and perceive this great nation. Both scholars and governments, intellectuals and policymakers, are aware that fundamental changes are underway in Japan - as they are everywhere at the close of the millennium - even if the true nature and extent of these changes remain opaque to the keenest observers.

It is true that records of the past, such as those contained in this book, are imperfect tools for building a better understanding of the future. But it is also true that, in the study of human affairs, there are few tools that have proven more consistently useful. It is as such an imperfect yet serviceable tool that we bring this volume to publication.

Los Angeles, April 1996   E. B. Keehn

Part I
Issues in Economic Strategy

1 Japan: The Course Ahead

Kenneth S. Courtis

The Choice

Today Japan is at an historic crossroads. The interplay of forces unleashed in the domestic economy and politics, together with forces at work in the international economy and political system, have placed Japan in a policy impasse. As pressures build, the temptation to reach, almost reflexively, for measures that have worked so well in the past has been great. Yet today Japan faces an unprecedented situation, and to reverse the course will require unprecedented measures.

It will take an uncustomary exercise of political vision, will and leadership, a demonstration of rare policy creativity and a sustained ability to innovate across a broad front to break the deepening impasse. To do less or to do otherwise would result in a sharp increase in tensions between Japan and the country's principal economic partners.

Indeed, tensions are already set to climb sharply. Unless they are diffused, it will prove increasingly difficult to avoid a risky spillover of these tensions to world financial markets and to areas beyond traditional economic relations. In the unfortunate case that it is unable to find within itself the will and the means to break the policy impasse, both Japan and the world economy would face risks of a dimension that few yet fully understand.

The time has come for Japan to strike a new course. In doing so, the country would not only open for itself a positive resolution to its present difficulties, but would also steer away from an increasingly destabilising clash with North America and Europe. Should Japan not now begin to steer to a new course, the resulting tensions cutting through the international economy would also bring havoc to the blossoming economies of East Asia, that part of the world which is more dependent on trade than any other.

To take a less ambitious or a less demanding course, to choose the *status quo* or to believe that the policies that have worked so well in the past are what is required for the present will lead to a still more problematic situation than Japan confronts today. A business-as-usual approach will lead to most unusual and unfavourable results. With an economy now almost three-quarters the size of that of the United States or about the size of the economies of Germany, France, and Britain combined, Japan is also the primary source of excess global savings and the catalyst for much of the dynamism that characterises the Asia Pacific, and difficulties for Japan, therefore, mean difficulties for the world economy.

The choices facing the country are as clear in their implications as they are demanding in their requirements. Failure to break the growing impasse carries the increasing possibility of unleashing a vicious cycle of deflation, economic dislocation, political instability, financial market disruption, and still further currency market volatility. In embracing a new policy paradigm designed to address the new challenges the country faces, Japan would set itself on course for a period of still more powerful expansion through the end of the decade. To do otherwise or to adopt a less ambitious agenda would open a course that would be increasingly problematic.

Although the options are clear, however, the right choices may not be taken. History is made of promise unfulfilled. Rather, the course ahead depends very much on the political transition that has now begun. Hesitant, fragile and full of contradictions, the transition team will soon find that neither time nor the forces at work in the broader international political economy are on its side. Against this background, markets - witness the manner in which the European currency system was torn asunder - have very little tolerance for policy measures that are inconsistent or, worse, inconsequential.

A New Context

Initially triggered by a policy-induced purge of the excesses of the 1980s, the slide of the economy sharply accelerated in 1993. While short-term factors are at work in this renewed decline, more central to the dynamics driving the economy are profound changes in Japan's international environment and in the forces which have been central in the country's unprecedented expansion of the past four decades. It is only in thinking through these changes and their implications that it will be possible to create the new policy paradigm that Japan now so urgently requires. Indeed, the failure to get Japan moving again - despite some $300 billion in supplementary spending in less than a year and a half - illustrates the need for profound structural change.

Japan is not alone in this regard. This same urgent necessity for policy innovation and the renewal of leadership are critical conditions that both Europe and North America must meet in order to reverse the present course.

At the same time, the changes that have steered Japan into an impasse also require that East Asia reassess the basis for its continued expansion, centred largely on export-driven growth. In the conditions that are likely to characterise the world economy during the period ahead, it is unlikely that it will be possible for East Asia to continue the pace of export expansion to North America and Europe that the region has known over the past two decades. Will Japan be able and willing to fill the gap? If only from this perspective, developments in Japan will be critical to the continued prosperity of East Asia and to the world economy. But more, much more, is at stake.

The Old Paradigm

The Cold War provided for Japan a very particular policy context. After an initial phase of New-Deal-type economic and political changes in the years immediately following 1945, America's policy prescripts for Japan fundamentally reversed course. The reversal was essentially driven by critical international developments: the success of Mao and of Chinese Communism in seizing power in Peking, developments on the Korean peninsula and later the humbling of France at Dien Bien Phu.

These events, together with developments in Eastern Europe and the emergence of the doctrine of Containment, led the United States to see Japan not as a fallen rival, but as being in a position of central strategic importance. In this new international strategic paradigm it became critical to stabilise Japan, to assure the rapid rebuilding of its devastated economy and to transform the country from a vanquished belligerent into a robust model of capitalist economic success and social stability. In return, America needed from Japan what amounted to the strategic free-run of the country. In the words of a latter-day Japanese prime minister, Japan was to become America's unsinkable aircraft carrier in the Pacific. In the process, the United States opened its market to Japan as it had previously opened its heart and industrial hearth to a Europe caught in a desperate struggle with Fascism.

At the same time, important political changes were occurring in Japan. After much labour turmoil in the immediate post-war period, by the early 1950s labour and management came to terms on a broad social contract.

The terms of that contract were as coherent as they were dynamic in their economic impact. On one side, management made an implicit commitment to full employment, in return for modest increases in consumption, moderate social welfare and constant increases in productivity, with the value-added going largely to the corporate sector so that it could invest energetically, and in the process maintain its part of this grand bargain.

This social contract, which has remained largely in place, was given political expression with the emergence of the conservative coalition from the mid-1950s. Three core groups were co-opted into the electoral base of the government party: the newly-enfranchised small farmers (who were one of the largest beneficiaries of the American-imposed post-war reforms), the doctors and the small shopkeepers. In the interval, these groups voted obediently for the LDP. In return for their unswerving support, they saw the tax code and the regulatory structure tailor-made for their particular interests.

As all of these elements fell neatly into place, Japan entered a period of unprecedented growth and previously unexperienced prosperity. In 1960, the United States economy was eleven times larger than that of Japan. By 1994, America is only a third larger, but with twice the population. In the interval, Japan has become not only an economic world leader, but today Tokyo shares with America the mantle of economic superpower and is the critical source of excess savings for a capital-starved world.

The Emerging Paradigm

With the changes in the former Soviet Union from the mid-eighties, the fall of the Berlin Wall, the collapse of the Soviet Empire and of European Communism, the commitment to economic transition in China, and the broad reversal in the global security balance, almost all of the critical international conditions of the old paradigm are today no more.

While there remain important security issues on the agenda, such as the situation on the Korean peninsula, they are largely the still-to-be resolved heritage of the Cold War. Because these issues no longer have the same unifying, systemic base, their larger strategic importance is of a nature different from the issues that have so dominated our lives during these past four decades and have been superseded by concerns more fundamentally economic. The reality of the new situation is encapsulated in the simple expression used by President Bill Clinton: 'It's the economy, stupid!'

After four decades of extraordinary economic effort and unswerving political focus and commitment, America finds itself struggling. It can no longer use access to its internal market - nor does it need to - for the strategic pursuits it followed in the past. Indeed, for no other reason than to restore its own sharply deteriorated financial position, to rebuild its melting infrastructure, to create the informational infrastructure of tomorrow, to reverse the decline of its cities and the performance of its education system, America must for a period generate substantial savings surpluses. To do so, it must run trade surpluses rather than widening trade deficits.

Japan's very success has been a further force that has worked to destroy the old paradigm. Should Japan continue to register trade surpluses through the end of the decade as it has in the past couple of years, the accumulated surplus over the decade would exceed the annual GNP of Germany, the world's third largest economy and which provides some 48 million jobs. With so much of the world struggling to create jobs, imbalances of this magnitude carry clearly ominous implications and can only lead at least to a substantial further rise in international economic tensions.

At the same time, deep demographic change in Japanese society is now working to undermine the political basis of the social compromises central to the country's domestic policy paradigm. In short, the electoral base of the conservative coalition that has ruled since the mid-1950s is today in accelerating decline. The average age of Japan's farmers today is close to 60; only six boys for every 10 farms stay on the farm. Similar dynamics are at work for Japan's general practitioners and shopkeepers. To stay in power it would have been necessary for the LDP to attract a new electorate made up of the younger, better educated, more independent, more widely travelled, urban middle-classes. But the vested interest in the *status quo* of the party's traditional electoral base has made it very difficult for the LDP to adopt the type of policies that would have made that possible. While the older, established politicians of the LDP could perhaps weather the next few years as the base of the party weakened further, that is certainly not the case of the younger members of the party. It is in this sense that the transition is in part generational. But it is much more than that.

The Dynamics of Transition

It is the convergence of these forces, both domestic and international, that today places Japan in what is a fundamentally new situation. The transition has begun, but it is still a very fragile one, full of contradiction and ambiguity. As the political system that has been in place for the past four decades unravels, a destabilisation of Japanese politics has begun. Local officials, increasingly fearful of being caught - rightly or wrongly - in a widening web of suspicion and scandal, have become hesitant to spend public works budgets and to use the fiscal levers needed to reverse the slide of the economy.

At the same time, the deflationary process of purging the financial excesses of the 1980s continues apace. As the small, over-levered producers are pushed to the wall, the large, over-capitalised *keiretsu* players, who used the stock market frenzy of the late 1980s to reduce debt, are moving to pick up the pieces on the cheap while paring their own operating structures down to their rock-hard competitive core.

As asset markets have come tumbling down, the unwillingness or inability of the authorities to take in good time the measures necessary to reduce the brutally deflationary burden of the mountain of bad debt weighing on the financial system has intensified the deflationary squeeze gripping the economy. Indeed, recently real bank-lending has actually contracted for the first time in half a century. As the economy has fallen into recession, imports have sagged, and the corporate sector, saddled with oceans of excess capacity, has moved back on to the attack in international markets. The result has been an explosion of Japan's surpluses to previously unheard-of levels.

These are the dynamics that led to the renewed and still-to-be completed revaluation of the yen, which has had a numbing effect on the economy. In short, to break this cycle, which can only lead to more difficulties, Japan must now move to a new course, both at home and in its relations with the world economy.

Breaking the Cycle

A country that has run a trade surplus, year in, year out, for more than quarter of a century is a country that is in fundamental disequilibrium with the world economy. It is a country that is under-consuming. Consumer spending represents some 56 per cent of GNP in Japan, compared with 64 per cent across Europe, and 68.4 per cent for America. That is one of America's problems: the level of consumption suggests that there are very little savings for positive investment. It is only in breaking the barriers that hold back consumer demand that Japan can break the cycle of decline, reverse the increasingly problematic course of confrontation with its principal trading partners and destabilise its own political system.

Analysis indicates that even were Japan to experience 4 per cent annual growth over the next three years, the current account surplus would still be some $80 billion in 1996. Indeed, forces at work in global commodity markets, together with the current strength of the yen, could well lead to still higher trade surpluses before the process of reform begins to have an effect.

With Europe, America and Japan all looking at slow growth ahead, oil prices are on course to test their 1986 lows. Indeed, should oil prices simply average 30 per cent lower over the next 12 months than they have during the past 12 months and the yen remain at its current level, Japan's energy imports would fall by some $30 billion, which, everything else being equal, would be added directly to the surplus. If for only these reasons it is urgent for Japan to move.

A Programme of Reform

To move the economy ahead requires a broad-based programme of economic reform. That programme must include financial reform, thorough fiscal reform, a complete overhaul of the real-estate system, related building codes, zoning regulations and taxes, aggressive deregulation across a broad front and decongestion of the economy through decentralisation.

Also central to a policy that would allow Japan to restore equilibrium and to set the base for renewed expansion is the urgent need to build for the country a modern social infrastructure. There is simply no reason why subways in Tokyo and Osaka should be more crowded than those of Bombay and Calcutta, why the country's highways are frequently transformed into serpentine parking lots, or why Japan has only one international airport with but one runway. This situation is the product of past policy decisions, and its transformation can be effected only by new policy directions.

Although financial authorities remain largely adamant in their refusal to reverse course and to reduce taxes, traditional fiscal spending has proven inadequate and will continue to be insufficient to set the economy on a new course. In large measure, the authorities are right in stating that a tax-cut will not be sufficient to restore growth. They are right, but for the wrong reason, and it is for that reason that the entire approach is wrong.

Fiscal Reform

The position that Japan cannot afford to reduce taxes because the central government is already running a small deficit is both wrong and wrong-headed. The larger picture reveals that even after 24 months of economic weakness, the general government financial balance continues to be in surplus. When the overfunding of the social security system is included, the overall surplus is some 4 per cent of GNP. So the money is there.

But simply more money is not what is required. More urgent is tax reform, including a substantial reduction of marginal tax rates, a widening of the tax base to include large sectors of income earners who today pay virtually no tax, and a move to a value-added or consumption-based tax system. Direct taxation on individuals and corporations represents almost three-quarters of total government revenues, with the urban salaried classes carrying the brunt of the burden. It is in putting funds directly into the hands of the urban consumer that Japan can begin to move towards a period of dynamic, domestic-centred, consumer-driven expansion.

Tax reform would be only a first step to releasing Japan's pent-up demand. Indeed, tax reform in the absence of a more broad-based programme of economic reform could even make the current situation more difficult, for it would create demand that, in expressing itself, would generate much unproductive investment and the same speculative excesses that began to occur at the end of the 1980s.

Land Reform

Another major obstacle to liberating Japan's domestic demand is the pervasive blockages that have worked to keep the land market so inefficient. Indeed, it is often claimed that Japan is land-poor, yet the population density of Tokyo is similar to that of Amsterdam. One-seventh of Tokyo is zoned as agricultural land. The average height of Tokyo buildings is but 1.7 storeys.

The land is there, but it is simply not being put to efficient use. To reverse the course would require thorough reform of the country's building codes, zoning regulations, land-use policies, real-estate taxation and of the laws of land-ownership itself. In creating a more efficient land- and real-estate market, conditions would be in place to allow the modernisation of the country's housing stock. That in turn would lead to a renewal and upgrading of Japan's stock of consumer durables.

Deregulation

Still another area for urgent reform is the country's regulatory structure. From telecommunications to the dress codes of elementary school children, from the lessons of history children read to how financial assets are created and traded, Japan's economy carries a heavy and an increasingly inefficient carcase of smothering regulation. To release pent-up demand across the economy in a sustainable, non-inflationary manner to increase the productivity and quality of daily life, what is further required is wide-gauged deregulation across a broad front.

Realising the type of ambitious reform that is now urgent also means, however, direct confrontation with politically powerful groups with enormous vested interest in the *status quo*. But nothing less is required. To break these interests will require a great act of political leadership.

Leadership

It is here that the challenge confronting Japan resides. Simply stated, it is the challenge of leadership. To reverse the current course, to adjust, to adapt, to reposition Japan for a new phase of expansion will require an uncommon act of leadership. To wait until a deeper crisis develops before acting will lead to an even more problematic situation for Japan and the world economy. It would also, and still more fundamentally, be the act of a debilitating failure of leadership and of will.

The responsibility of leadership is to generate the vision that surmounts the past, that sees beyond the immediate, that represents the future to the present. The failure today to generate the determination to lead, the will to act and the vision to strike a new course could dash for Japan and for much of Asia the promise that is today so close at hand. It would also make it still more difficult for North America and Europe to reverse their present course.

To seize the opportunity that the current crisis offers would allow Japan to move to a new course of open and shared prosperity. What is at stake are not abstract issues of policy, but rather the very prosperity of Japan, of the region, and beyond that of North America and Europe.

Japan's Corporations and Consumers

The future of corporate Japan and the welfare of the country's citizens are also at stake. To continue their development and in order to carry the investment and research budgets that will be required this decade and beyond, corporate Japan must continue to generate a revenue stream that only largely unquestioned access to the markets of North America and Europe will allow. Failure to move now on Japan's new domestic agenda would lead to much more difficulty in accessing these markets in the future than is the case today.

Failure to adopt the type of policies that would allow the healthy liberation of Japan's pent-up domestic demand would inevitably mean continued very high external surpluses. Should that happen, Japan would experience an equally inevitable new cycle of yen strength. Perhaps Japan can adjust to a yen at current levels, but should the currency move much higher any time soon, the country would see the severe dislocation of its prime industrial assets. While all the world would be harmed were such developments to occur, the biggest losers would be corporate Japan itself and the country's consumers who have laboured so hard to produce the prosperity that Japan knows today.

Public Finances

The Japanese state would also gain handsomely from this change of course, for it would result in substantially higher growth rates than any other scenario can offer. That would mean substantially reduced budgetary pressures. In turn, that would allow Japan to finance with ease the social infrastructure investment that is so necessary and to provide for its aging population more readily than would otherwise be the case. It would also allow Japan without strain on financial markets to meet its commitment to spend the three-and-a-half trillion dollars in infrastructure that was made within the Structural Impediments Initiative framework negotiations with the United States in 1990.

Europe and North America

In order to stabilise unemployment at current levels, Europe requires 3 per cent growth. To set unemployment on a course to lower levels would require still higher levels of expansion. Yet the outlook for Europe is average growth of 2.25 per cent to 2.5 per cent during the remainder of this decade. Under these conditions, it will be particularly difficult for Europe's free-traders to keep the Common Market anchored on that side of the divide. It is of more than passing interest in this regard that some have raised the question of just how open Europe's markets should be in stating that countries that do not produce in conditions 'socially equivalent' to those of Europe should not have access to its market.

Similar pressures are at work in North America, where the reversal of the present course requires the smooth recycling of the capital surpluses of Asia. Further disruption of global financial markets and of foreign exchange markets would have the direct consequence of making that less likely, and risk-levels would everywhere climb substantially. Indeed, access to Japan's enormous pools of capital will become one of the great questions at issue between America, Europe and Japan this decade. With the banking sector in both countries already under so much strain and the volume of funds to be recycled so vast, clearly we are dealing here with what will become a major affair of state.

East Asia

The liberalisation of trade has been the primary force for global economic expansion over the past three decades. With the type of export-led growth strategy that has characterised the economic policies of East Asia during that period, the region has been one of the principal beneficiaries of the opening of world markets.

For example, from 1982 to 1992, total world trade increased in real terms by almost half. During the same period, total trade among the core economies of the Common Market - Germany, France, Italy, and the United Kingdom - increased by just under three-fifths, whereas for all of Asia, trade doubled. For Singapore, Hong Kong, Korea, and Taiwan, total trade is today four times larger than it was just 10 years ago. In this expansion of trade, Japan and North America have played opposite, but complementary roles.

Japan: The Supply Side

Through direct investment and its own finely targeted trade expansion, Japan has supplied the region with capital and intermediate goods. Japan's activity has been instrumental in the supply-side development of Asia. The resulting transfer of technology, widening industrial base and increasing competitiveness have been the key to Asia's dynamic expansion of trade. In the process, however, Japan has generated huge trade surpluses with key countries in the region. In 1992, Japan's trade surplus with the principal economies of East Asia was some $40 billion, even larger than Japan's surplus with the entire Common Market, although the economies of East Asia are less than a third the size.

United States: The Demand Side

In contrast, the United States has played the role of market for Asia. For example, in 1992, net exports of manufactured goods from Singapore, Hong Kong, Taiwan and Korea to the United States exceeded $50 billion. While consumer products form the bulk of Asia's manufactured exports to America, intermediate goods and capital equipment are becoming increasingly important. For example, since the mid-1980s, Korea, Taiwan, Hong Kong and Singapore have built an expanding net surplus with the United States for capital equipment. Given the role that it has played on the input side of Asia's growth, Japan has also gained immensely from the expansion of Asia's exports to America. For example, about half of the value-added of Korean car exports to North America is of Japanese origin.

But the Pattern is Not Sustainable

This pattern of relations will not be sustainable during the years ahead, for the simple reason that North America is not and will not grow quickly enough. Indeed, carrying debt levels equivalent to those last seen during the Great Depression in the mid-1930s, America's economic situation is today fragile and precarious. Further, as a base condition for the reversal of its own imbalances, the United States will have to run for a time of external surplus during the period ahead. Pushed on to the defensive, North America is today a less open market than it has been in the past. Although not fundamentally protectionist in intent, to the extent that the proposed North American Trade Agreement contains new and more stringent local content requirements it puts additional constraints on access to the American market.

Where will Asia Turn?

With America unable to absorb an increasing wave of imports, Asian traders have begun to look elsewhere. In the ideal, Japan should become a net importer of manufactured goods from Asia. To do so, however, would require a major reversal of public policy, of corporate strategy and of economic structure. In many ways, that is the agenda that is before Japan today. But even in the best of circumstances such changes will take time, and Asia cannot wait.

Already Asian traders have begun moving aggressively into the lower-end markets of Europe. With the high-end and middle markets of Europe under attack by Japanese producers, this new wave of exports from Asia will lead to further trade conflict. In particular, the new economies of Eastern Europe see as the lever of their growth the same entry-level markets that the Asian producers are targeting. The dynamics of this situation are clear. If they are not handled with great sensitivity, much more protectionism will be the result.

Japan Shifts to Asia

As conditions tighten in Europe and North America, Japan has begun to shift to Asia at a lightning pace. In 1985, Japan traded a third more with America than with Asia. Today, it trades a third more with Asia than it does with America. The same pattern is emerging for investment, development assistance, bank lending, diplomatic policy, and even in areas such as education and culture.

At the same time, the continuing revaluation of the yen is now driving Japan into a new investment blitz to East Asia, as low value-added, labour-intensive production is moved off-shore. This new wave of Japanese investment in Asia will dwarf anything that has yet occurred, such that it is increasingly Japan that sets the tempo and determines the economic rhythm of East Asia.

From Japan, capital and technology flow throughout the region. The countless decisions made by Japanese firms - where to invest, where and what to produce, where to source, and how and what to sell - not only powerfully amplify the broader dynamics at work in the region, but also accelerate the pace of regional integration. But Japan is the master of the process. With their complex Asian production capacity, Toyota and Nissan already produce the ASEAN car.

But the power of Japan is so dominant in the region that it also provokes constant anxiety. Occurring in the context of the relative strategic retreat of America and Europe from Asia, these trends work to strengthen still further Japan's dominance in Asia. This shift in turn substantially reduces the options open to countries in the region. Who controls much of the excess capital? Where increasingly is the technology? The answer is Japan.

Yet much of Asia remains reluctant to see Japan exercise the role of spokesman for the region. These divisions reduce the weight of Asia in international councils. Further, they contribute to an increasingly unstable situation, whereby the global shift of economic and financial power to Asia has no commensurate political expression.

Regional Security

Nowhere is this situation more problematic than in the area of regional security. During the Cold War, America's unquestioned commitment to Asia's stability and its equally unquestioned economic might set limits to the extent of conflict in the region. But with America's hegemony waning in the region, new dimensions of security and power are beginning to express themselves in Asia.

However, Asia cannot continue to count on America playing forever the role of stabiliser. Asia will have to come to terms with the new security issues that economic weight and a shifting global balance of power create. To do so, much depends on decisions made in Japan.

Towards a New International Economic Framework

After every major war, the leading powers of the new era have come together to reformulate the policies and institutions of the pre-war period, and to redesign the international institutional framework for managing the new balance of economy and political power that emerges. Such was the purpose of the Congress of Vienna in 1815, which set in place a half-century of prosperity. That was also the purpose of the Treaty of

Versailles, but the result was a failure. That failure contributed to the subsequent nightmare of the 1930s and 1940s.

In the period 1945-50, we again worked to redesign the international institutional structure for managing the world economy. That is when the IMF, GATT, the World Bank, and Bretton Woods were all set in place. During the following four decades, the world was locked in the Cold War. The Cold War is now behind us, as are the economics of that period, such that the multilateral institutions we have today to manage the world economy are based on a balance of economic, financial, and industrial power that no longer exists. It is now urgent to create the new structures we need to manage the new balance of power that has emerged from the Cold War.

Given Japan's weight and position in the world economy, its role in creating these new structures and in managing this new balance of power, where it is one of the two lone superpowers, is critical. But to play that role, Japan must first engage the change at home that is now at the very top of the country's policy agenda. In doing so, Japan would open for itself and for the world economy a new phase of healthy and powerful expansion. To hesitate now, to do less or to do otherwise would mean for Japan, for the Asia-Pacific and indeed for the world economy that the promise which is now so close at hand would slip irreparably from our grasp.

That is the dimension of the opportunity Japan faces today. It is also the dimension of the challenge.

2 The Yen's Role in World Financial Diplomacy: Should we Focus on Trade Flows or Investment Flows?

David D. Hale

During the past 100 years the value of the yen has fluctuated widely in response to changes in Japan's international economic status. In the late 19th century the yen was considered a heavy currency. In 1874 it was worth more than one dollar and in London it traded at four shillings and two pence while the pound itself was worth about $4.88. As Japan opened its economy to more trade, the yen weakened and by 1900 it was worth only about 50 cents. This value held until the Great Depression of the early 1930s, when the yen was devalued in order to promote faster export growth. By the time Japan began its war against China in 1937 the yen was worth only about 29 cents or 6 pence against the British pound. As Japanese prices rose nearly sixfold during the Second World War, the yen's value fell sharply and it was finally stabilised in 1949 at a rate of 360 to the dollar. The 1949 exchange rate persisted until the breakdown of the Bretton Woods fixed exchange rate system in 1971, when the yen re-emerged for the first time in nearly 100 years as a strong currency. Despite large multi-year fluctuations in response to oil price shocks and global business upheavals, the yen has risen by nearly 70 per cent against the US dollar since 1971 and many analysts believe it will continue to be a strong currency through the mid-1990s.

The arguments for the yen to remain a strong currency centre on both Japan's macroeconomics and trade performance.

First, the country has a large trade surplus with both the US and Europe as well as many developing countries in east Asia. In 1992 the current account surplus was $118 billion or 3.2 per cent of GDP. In 1993, it could rise to $140 billion.

Secondly, *Japan has enjoyed a healthy export performance during the past two decades despite the strength of the currency*. Although the yen has appreciated by 70 per cent since 1970, Japanese export prices have increased by only about 45 per cent. Japanese firms have tried to maintain their external competitiveness by absorbing currency appreciation into their profit margins. Depending upon the status of profit margins at the time of the yen's appreciation, Japanese firms have absorbed anywhere from 25 per cent to 100 per cent of the effects of exchange rate appreciation on their export prices. Despite the magnitude of Japan's recent recession, there has so far been no change in corporate pricing behaviour during the current cycle. Between June 1992 and May 1993, for example, the price of Japanese imports to the US increased by only 5.7 per cent while the yen rose by nearly 20 per cent against the dollar.

Thirdly, during the past decade there has been a major change in the composition of Japanese trade which has made it easier for the country to adjust to exchange-rate appreciation. *Since 1977, the share of Japanese exports in the high-tech R&D intensive sector has increased from 29.5 per cent to 50.9 per cent of the total while the shares of labour intensive exports have shrunk from 17.8 per cent to 6.5 per cent and mid-tech capital-intensive exits have slid from 46.9 per cent to 38.0 per cent.* The new R&D-intensive exports tend to have lower price and higher income elasticities than the mid-tech exports. As a result, yen appreciation has not had as depressing an effect on demand for such products as it has had on demand for Japanese cars or other durable goods. In fact, the sharp rise in exports of high-tech R&D-intensive goods has played a major role in sustaining Japan's trade growth in the face of both protectionism and yen appreciation. In 1991 such items accounted for 48.7 per cent of Japanese exports to the US and 56.0 per cent of Japanese exports to Europe, compared with only about 30 per cent during the late 1970s.

Despite the increasingly high-tech character of Japanese exports, the country is not insensitive to changes in currency values. According to the OECD, Japanese export growth underperformed the growth of Japan's export markets by 3.7 per cent and 8.4 per cent during 1991 and 1992. American exports, by contrast, outperformed the growth of their markets by 1.2 per cent and 0.1 per cent respectively. But Japan has been able to sustain some export growth in the face of a strong yen because of its shift away from labour-intensive or middle technology products which would be highly vulnerable to price increase. The yen's strength also has helped to reduce the cost of imports and many Japanese firms have used the benefits of such import cost savings to offset reduced profit margins on exports. As a result, yen appreciation has produced fewer reductions in import costs for Japanese consumers than would be the case in other countries.

The final argument for a strong yen is that Japan's high level of savings relative to investment will continue to produce large current account surpluses even when the economy recovers. The surplus may decline to 2.0 per cent of GDP from the 3.0-4.0 per cent range of 1993, but such a correction would still leave an imbalance in the $60-90 billion range. If

Japan's capital outflows suddenly take off again, the yen could weaken despite the large current account surplus. But since other countries often criticise the Japanese trade surplus, the financial markets will tend to regard it as an argument for the yen to remain strong.

What remains to be seen is how the yen will behave if there is an agreement on GATT and a lessening of tensions over other trade issues. The yen rose sharply during May and early June 1993 because investors feared that during the summer there would be highly-publicised trade disputes with the US which would encourage policymakers to talk up the yen. Investors perceived that Japan would be unable to satisfy American trade demands and that yen appreciation would therefore emerge as the only policy alternative for correcting trade imbalances. The yen then slumped when the Miyazawa government fell because it called into question both the outlook for Japanese domestic policy and the ability of the US even to launch an aggressive trade initiative.

The yen's performance during June and early July 1993 suggests that it will remain sensitive to political developments which might open the door to trade adjustment through channels other than exchange rate appreciation, such as liberalisation of regulatory policies, which are perceived to inhibit imports or political reforms which would strengthen the position of Japanese consumer interest groups over producer groups. As a result, the upcoming Japanese election and the renewed attempt at political reform which will follow could have an important impact on investor attitudes. Will political reform produce a major change in the distribution of political power? Will the new political equilibrium alter economic policies which influence the level of consumption and private savings? Will the enlarged delegation of urban-based Diet members demand a change in the trade policies which have inflated the price of food and other goods with import barriers?

The dominant issue on the agenda of the new government will be political reform, so it is unlikely that there will be any substantive changes in economic policy until after the next Japanese election. While the LDP will still have 200-220 seats after the election, it will not be able to enact any legislation without the support of smaller parties and it is far from clear how cooperative they will be. As with Italy's Christian Democrats, it is possible to construct a variety of scenarios in which the LDP remains Japan's dominant party but is constantly rotating cabinets because of the need to accommodate smaller parties in either formal or informal coalitions.

The American government will not abandon its trade demands because of Japan's political upheavals but it will tone down its rhetoric and focus its requests more carefully in order to give *de facto* support to the reform groups which might help liberalise the Japanese economic system. The major risk posed by the election is that it will cripple Japan's ability to play a substantive role in concluding the GATT negotiations. Japan was not playing a major leadership role even before the political crisis and the loss of the LDP's parliamentary majority will make it even more difficult for Japan to offer major trade concessions, especially on agriculture.

The Case Against Yen Appreciation

The arguments against further yen appreciation centre on the nature of Japan's trade surplus and the impact of a strong yen on foreign investment in Japan's asset markets.

First, as the Japanese government itself argues, the recent expansion of the trade surplus has not resulted from robust exports but from the effects of the domestic recession on import demand as well as the effects of the global recession on commodity prices. There was a sharp improvement in Japan's terms of trade last year as commodity prices fell. At present, food and natural resources account for over half of Japanese imports while resource-intensive manufactured goods account for another 8 per cent.

Secondly, Japanese manufacturing firms have already experienced such a severe profit recession since 1990 that further yen appreciation could force them to reduce employment and wages to levels which would only prolong the recession in domestic demand itself. Corporate profits are currently about 70 per cent below their 1989 peak and most analysts were projecting little or no growth this year even when the yen was in the 115-120 range. In the 1992 MITI survey of exporters, fewer than 3 per cent of Japanese firms felt that they would be able to compete if the yen rose into the 100-110 range.

The G-7 countries have rejected such arguments on the grounds that Japan has ample potential to stimulate domestic spending through more expansionary fiscal and monetary policies. Japan has a structural budget surplus and its ratio of government debt to GDP is only about 6 per cent compared with 40-80 per cent in most other industrial countries. As a result of the deflation which has occurred in Japanese asset markets since 1990, coupled with the impact of the recession and the strong yen on consumer prices, there also is a good case for the BOJ to reduce interest rates an additional 50-75 basis points. In fact, the recent US-Japan trade negotiations focused heavily on the need for a more expansionary macroeconomic policy in Japan, not just sectoral trade problems. What remains to be seen is how further interest rate declines would affect Japan's capital account and the value of the yen itself. In the late 1980s, Japan pursued an easy monetary policy in order to slow the yen's appreciation, and the low interest rates which resulted from that policy helped to nurture an asset inflation. The domestic asset inflation ultimately set the stage for a yen decline by discouraging foreign investment in the Japanese stock market as well as encouraging large capital outflows from Japan in order to purchase foreign assets. *The US Treasury wants Japan to put more emphasis on fiscal rather than monetary stimulus this time in order to lessen the risk of renewed asset inflation and capital outflows depressing the yen again.*

As a result of the damage done to Japan's banking system by the real-estate boom and bust of 1986-92, it is difficult to imagine lower interest rates having as dramatic an impact on asset prices and capital outflows as they did during the late 1980s. In the short term, a rally in the stock market might even bolster the yen by attracting an influx of foreign capital. But as the strong yen will increase the incentive for Japanese firms to shift production offshore, there is likely to be a rebound of Japanese foreign direct investment during 1994 and 1995 after a slump from $48 billion to $17 billion between 1990 and 1992. While such capital outflows will not by themselves depress the yen, they will help to bolster the competitiveness of Japanese firms by providing new low-cost sources of component manufacturing in Southeast Asia and elsewhere.

The direction of Japan's next wave of foreign direct investment also will influence exchange-rate relationships. If the investment is heavily targeted on North America and Latin America, it will tend to bolster the dollar. Conversely, if it is targeted primarily on East Asia, it could encourage the emergence of a circular flow of capital and trade within the region that would be both yen-denominated and yen-financed. In such a scenario, the yen could emerge as a more important reserve currency and thus tend to rise in value because of a new demand for it among official institutions, not just private investors.

The final argument against encouraging further yen appreciation is that it will reduce the potential which Japan's recent asset deflation has created for encouraging more foreign direct investment in the country. In recent years, there has been considerable academic work done on the relationship between foreign direct investment and trade. This work suggests that the low level of FDI in Japan has inhibited foreign access to the Japanese market and magnified trade tensions.

In the modern era, Japan has had the lowest level of foreign direct investment within her borders of any industrial country. Various academic studies have found that foreign investment is equal to only about 1 per cent of Japan's capital stock, compared with 10-20 per cent in many other industrial nations. Japan's stock of inward FDI is about $23 billion compared with her own foreign direct investment of $242 billion. On the basis of per capita comparisons, FDI within Japan is only $180 compared with $800 in Germany, $1600 in the US, and $2000 in Britain. Meanwhile, other studies suggest that the low level of foreign direct investment in Japan has become a barrier to trade. *In the big industrial countries. there is now a high correlation between the trade and investment flows of multinational companies.* The Commerce Department, for example, reports that 45.6 per cent of US imports come from related parties. The shares range from 73 per cent in the case of Japan to 47 per cent in the cases of Europe and Canada. This trend has also been documented in a study by Harvard Business School Professor Dennis Encarnation. He found that the majority-owned foreign subsidiaries of American or Japanese companies import far more from parent firms back home than they procure locally.

In addition to boosting exports directly, foreign investment can also serve as an important complement to external trade. *During 1988, American multinational companies sold nearly three times as much overseas through their majority-owned subsidiaries as the US exported to the world.* As Japan's large outflow of foreign direct investment began much later than America's, her ratio of multinational sales generated locally to exports is only two, or the same level as the US in the late 1950s, but this gap will narrow as Japan further expands her foreign direct investment. *In the case of the US, locally generated sales of Japanese multinationals are already three times greater than Japanese exports to the US.* In Japan, by contrast, the locally generated sales of US multinational firms barely exceed US exports to Japan. Moreover, whereas two-thirds of all US imports from Japan were shipped through intracompany channels, primarily Japanese multinational firms such as Toyota and Matsushita, such intracompany trade accounted for only 50 per cent of US exports to Japan. Much of this export volume also consisted of commodities shipped by Japanese trading companies. As Fred Bergsten and Noland explained in their book about US-Japan trade relations, *Reconcilable Differences*,

> The Japanese trade pattern appears distinctive in at least two other dimensions. The first is the unusually high share of intrafirm trade. Lawrence (1991 a) reports that, while around half of US trade with Europe is intrafirm trade, around three-quarters of US trade with Japan is intrafirm. Furthermore, while in the case of US trade with Europe the

ratio of exports from the United States controlled by the US parent firms to exports controlled by the European parent firms is more than 3:1, in the case of Japan the ratio is reversed. That is, whereas American firms control most of the intrafirm US exports going to Europe, Japanese firms control most of the US exports to Japan. Lawrence attributes this to the prominent role of giant trading companies in Japanese trade, and he argues that this pattern of trade is consistent with imperfectly competitive Japanese domestic markets.

The US trade position in Japan does not merely suffer from the low level of FDI in the country, but also from the structure of the investment. American firms tend to depend more upon joint ventures or minority shareholdings in Japan than they do in other countries. According to research by Dennis Encarnation, minority shareholdings impede the ability of US firms to penetrate the Japanese market. He found that

> While in the United States, the majority Japanese-owned subsidiaries of Honda, Sony, and other such multinationals have generated the same proportion of sales (over 85 per cent) that they recorded worldwide, in Japan the Americans have never seen majority subsidiaries generate their global share (over 75 per cent) of foreign sales. To the contrary, as late as 1988, majority US subsidiaries in Japan - led by IBM - still generated less than two-fifths of the sales recorded by all American multinationals there. Here, Mazda and other minority US affiliates accounted for the remainder, the bulk of multinational sales in Japan, even though their relative position had declined over the previous decade. By this measure, Japan actually has as much in common with developing India, where the dislodging of multinationals represents the national strategy, as with industrialised Germany. For in no other advanced economy do majority US subsidiaries continue to occupy such a lowly position as they do in Japan. By contrast, in Germany, American multinationals own and control some of that country's largest manufacturers, such as GM's Opel subsidiary. In Germany, moreover, as well as in Canada, the United Kingdom, and France - each with an economy less than one-half Japan's size - Opel and other majority US subsidiaries recorded larger dollar sales than they did in Japan. Thus, the lower incidence of majority subsidiaries in Japan worked to deny American multinationals the same market access they otherwise exploited in other industrialised countries.

In 1990, only 34 per cent of FDI in Japan was in majority-owned foreign firms, while in manufacturing the share was even lower at 26 per cent.

The strong correlation between foreign direct investment and trade suggests that one of the most effective ways of reducing the US trade deficit with Japan would be to promote more American direct investment in Japan. This conclusion is also reinforced by a recent study on US business in Japan done by the Wednesday Group, a Republican congressional taskforce. In a survey of American firms in Japan, they found that the major barriers to US business in Japan were not government regulatory policies but the high cost of establishing facilities as well as the Japanese emphasis on nurturing long-term relationships (which can discourage market access for outsiders). During the early 20th century, many US firms had established large market shares in Japan, but their operations were greatly curtailed during the 1930s and 1940s and never recovered during the post-war period because of government restrictions designed to encourage local control over important industries. In recent years the Japanese government has abandoned many of these official restrictions but foreign investment has remained at low levels because of the impact of Japan's high land-prices on the cost of establishing new businesses. The Wednesday group coined the term 'cost protectionism' to describe the adverse effects of high asset prices on US corporate attitudes towards increasing investment in Japan.

In the 1980s, there was a surge of foreign merger and acquisition activity in many industrial countries but the phenomena largely bypassed Japan because of a combination of high asset prices and perceived informal barriers to take-over activity within the Japanese marketplace. Between 1987 and 1990, there were 72 foreign acquisitions of Japanese firms for a sum of about 105 billion yen. Since the asset deflation began in 1990, there have been an additional 55 take-overs worth about 75 billion yen, but this number is still modest compared with the level of M & A activity in other countries. At the peak in the late 1980s, foreign take-overs in the US and Britain reached levels equal to 1.0-2.0 per cent of GDP. Such a number in Japan would be equal to $30-60 billion dollars (4-8 trillion yen).

Despite the large decline in Japanese stock prices since the peak in 1989, it would be difficult to argue that Japanese equity prices are now cheap. As a result of the severe recession in corporate profits, the Tokyo market still sells at a p/e multiple of 60-70 or a level not far below the peak of three years ago. But the market does not appear to be nearly as expensive as it was during the late 1980s when adjustments are made for changes in the level of interest rates and accounting differences. Since their peak in 1991, Japanese short-term interest rates have fallen from nearly 9.0 per cent to 2.5 per cent while bond yields have fallen to about 4.0 per cent. Japan's cash flow multiples also have fallen from a peak of 18 three years ago to about eight recently. Moreover, if corporate earnings enjoy a cyclical recovery of 40-50 per cent during fiscal 1994 and 1995, the p/e multiple of the market will fall back to the 35-40 range while the cash flow multiple will drop to 5-6.

In the English-speaking countries, an asset price correction as great as the one Japan recently experienced would be regarded as an opportunity to launch take-over bids and reorganise companies. While the stock market decline has prompted some adjustments in Japanese shareholdings patterns, the changes so far have been quite modest. Yet, it would be difficult to imagine better circumstances in which to promote increased foreign direct investment within Japan through take-over activity. American firms have stock market multiples of 20 on the basis of ordinary earnings and 10-11 on the basis of cash earnings or the highest levels since the 1960s. On the basis of 1995 profits, Japanese firms are selling at cash flow multiples not much above the levels which encouraged the upsurge in US corporate restructuring during the early 1980s. There also has been a sharp decline in the price of land in many Japanese cities, especially Tokyo, Osaka, and Nagoya, while some Japanese companies now sell for less than book value on the stock market.

As a result of official concern about the low level of FDI in the country, the Japanese government announced a special programme in 1992 to promote more foreign investment. The programme was outlined in a recent edition of the Jetro monitor.

The many special measures taken by the government were spelled out in the Law of Extraordinary Measure for the Promotion of Imports and the Facilitation of Foreign Direct Investment in Japan. The law took effect in July 1992.

One of the new incentives offered under the law is preferential tax treatment to help foreign affiliates recover their investment costs faster than before, enabling them to establish a more solid footing in the market. The specific incentives included accelerated depreciation of buildings, machinery and equipment, and extension of the standard carry-over period for accounting losses, and, with certification from MITI, exemption from special land-holding taxes.

Loan guarantees by the Industrial Structure Improvement fund are provided for up to 95 per cent of liability when a qualified foreign investor borrows funds to acquire facilities and equipment or carry out operations within five years after start-up. Special credit insurance for small and medium-size foreign companies has also been made available.

All special support is available to any company acquiring certification as a 'designated inward investor through MITI.'

The law further provides for the establishment of what is provisionally known as the Foreign Affiliate Business Supporting Company, capitalised at $4 million by the government and supported by private-sector funds. The company will offer reasonably priced services covering orientation, consultation, recruitment support, training and seminars, and for investors without a physical presence in Japan, agent services. Services will be organised around a two-tiered system offering a choice of monthly reports, newsletters and networking opportunities and/or direct links to services providers.

As the programme is less than twelve months old, it is unclear whether it will have a major impact on corporate attitudes toward direct investment in Japan. But the fact that foreign corporations are not yet taking advantage of depressed share prices to expand their investment in Japan suggests that there will probably have to be a sustained government effort, including both special tax incentives and moral suasion, to narrow Japan's FDI gap with other countries.

The failure of the Tokyo stock market crash to trigger more corporate restructuring will probably also revive debate about other unique institutional features of the Japanese financial system and its role in the corporate sector. First, some foreign investors are reluctant to purchase Japanese equities because they perceive that the stock market has been artificially propped up by buying from government pension funds. Secondly, banks continue to own about 24 per cent of all Japanese corporate equity as a result of cross-shareholding relationships which were established during the 1960s and 1970s. In theory, the banks should now be selling some of this equity both because of their large losses on real estate lending and the emergence in Japan of a more securitised lending market (bonds and commercial paper), which should erode main bank relationships. But it does not appear that banks have yet become major sellers of equities both because of moral suasion by the MoF and the fact that they enjoy more flexibility than American or European banks in how they account for non-performing loans. As a result, the supply of 'free equity' in Tokyo continues to be much smaller than in other major stock markets. Private retail investors still account for only about 20 per cent of Japanese share ownership compared with 60-70 per cent during the early 1950s. Finally, *the Japanese fund-management industry continues to have very different competitiveness features from the fund-management industries of other countries.* The government limits the number of firms which are licensed to offer mutual fund or investment trust products.

There are only about sixteen domestic and four foreign firms offering investment trust products to retail investors compared to several hundred in the US. The fund-management affiliates of the big four brokerage houses also control about 75 per cent of investment trust assets, despite the fact that the industry has over $350 billion under its control. Management of pension fund assets is dominated by trust banks and life insurance companies, which have not historically competed on the basis of superior investment performance. In the past they have usually offered a guaranteed return which was the same across the industry. The Japanese fund management industry also abounds with stories about firms allocating their pension fund assets on the basis of criteria which have little to do with portfolio optimisation, such as whether the pension fund management group will be prepared to buy the firm's own shares. As Stephen Cohen of Warburgs noted in a recent report on the Japanese money management industry, attitudes towards performance measurement differ significantly in Tokyo from other centres.

> The underdeveloped state of a performance measurement industry in Japan limits the one way foreign investment advisors can hope to win funds. The Nihon Koshasai Kenkyujo, the Pension Fund Association, Frank Russell and Intersec all have some presence, but the latest proposal for the Trust Bank to measure performance under MoF guidance seems to represent a considerable conflict of interest. The only international precedent of this was in Switzerland, where the Swiss Banking Association measured fund performance. This was not successful, and the responsibility for Swiss fund performance was transferred to Intersec, the independent performance measurement company.

The stock market deflation since 1989 has created more awareness of the need to improve the returns on pension fund assets, but the playing field remains distorted by the ability of the insurance companies to subsidise their pension fund clients with profits from their own equity portfolios. As Christopher Wood explained in his book, *The Bubble Economy*,

> The life insurers' recent success in attracting pension funds has nothing to do with their superior investment skills and everything to do with their ability to pool their pension fund assets in their general accounts, which also contain their conventional life insurance policies. This arrangement allows them, with the Ministry of Finance's approval, to smooth out returns to lean years by taking profits on shares that were bought long ago to back life insurance policies. However legal, this is

another example of the ingrained habit within the Japanese financial world of compensating some at the expense of others. Funds entering the general pool benefit from profits built up over many years. Or, to put it more bluntly, long-standing owners of life insurance policies subsidise new pension fund clients.

This unfairness has only come to light as a result of last year's stock market crash. Traditionally, pension fund management in Japan operated like any good cozy cartel. The return was rigged to meet an agreed-upon rate. The trust banks and life insurers were usually content with an annual cash return of 8 or 9 per cent, which was more than enough to finance current commitments. That return was easily manufactured, since under Japanese accounting law assets are carried at book value (what the fund paid for the investments), not actual current market values. Managers can thus revalue assets almost at will. Unrealised gains and losses can be conveniently ignored.

The accounting for life insurance company investment returns is a controversial subject in many countries, but the heavy concentration of Japanese savings flows in only a few intermediaries, such as insurance companies and trust banks, makes the issue a more pressing problem for new firms trying to enter Japan's fund management industry. As a result of the unique institutional factors governing the allocation of Japanese pension fund assets the nine foreign-owned trust banks manage only 69 billion yen of assets compared with 23 trillion at the trust banks and 16 trillion yen at the large life insurance companies.

There will be no simple way to reverse the long-standing aversion to foreign take-over activity within Japan. Except for the three decades between 1900 and 1930, Japan has had severe restrictions on foreign investment for all its modern history. The Japanese people also do not regard corporate assets and employees to be as fungible a set of commodities as do the Anglo-Saxon societies. *But there is a clear and compelling case for the Japanese government to override these objectives because the low level of foreign direct investment has emerged as a de facto trade issue.* It is now widely perceived that Japanese custom, if not official policy, in the area of foreign direct investment differs significantly from other industrial countries and that the lack of foreign investment has become a trade barrier.

What can Japan do to promote a greater role for the stock market as an agent for corporate control? First, the MoF should permit more competition in the retail fund management industry. There are press reports that the MoF may issue several new licences for domestic and foreign investment trust companies later this year. By the end of the century Japan should have several dozen investment trust managers and it should not have any form of official rationing. The MoF could encourage competition by reducing the licence fee for investment trust managers (currently about $3.0 million) and issuing new rules permitting companies to register automatically as investment trust managers rather than depending upon MoF discretion to obtain a licence. Secondly, there should be far more transparency in the accounting for returns on Japanese investment products, including both investment trusts and pension funds. If there were more comparable data available for determining how performance is measured and assets are allocated, there would be more pressure on companies to select managers on the basis of transparent fiduciary criteria, not as a *quid pro quo* for other relationships. Thirdly, US firms have taken major steps during recent years to give their employees more control over how their investment funds are allocated. As a result of the movement towards more widespread use of defined contribution plans rather than defined benefit plans, employees are increasingly being asked to determine whether their savings should be invested in an equity fund, a bond fund, a money market fund, or some mixture of the three. In Japan, employees have little choice over how their pension funds are allocated and the plans often have hybrid features, which make it difficult to compare performance. Greater choice coupled with increased transparency for Japanese pension fund beneficiaries would help promote further decentralisation of the country's savings flows.

As the stock market scandals of the early 1990s will testify, the transparency problems of the Japanese financial system are not simply the result of custom and historical accidents. Until recently, the system was characterised by a series of cartels which produced such high returns that the brokers were able to compensate institutional investors or wealthy clients who suffered losses in the market. These cartels have been weakened by the asset deflation since 1990 but there is no reason why they could not re-emerge during the next equity bull market unless there are continued government efforts to encourage more competition and transparency in the Japanese financial system. Liberalisation of the asset markets through the creation of a more competitive fund management industry also would help facilitate the large structural changes which are likely to occur to the corporate cross-shareholding system during the next decade as Japan's capital costs converge with other countries, non-bank forms of lending expand further, and both banks and commercial firms find more profitable places to deploy their funds than passive cross-shareholdings. Japanese retail investors have withdrawn from the Tokyo market during recent years because of falling equity prices and the low opinion they have of the existing fund-management industry. The introduction of new players in the industry would provide them with more choices for their savings and thus could help increase the level of retail investment in the market after a long period of decline.

As a result of the linkages between the structure of Japan's asset markets, the low level of foreign investment, and trade tensions, it is not surprising that the recent US-Japan negotiations included discussion of topics such as FDI and the need to encourage more foreign competition in the Japanese fund management industry. Many of the current trade tensions stem from organisational differences in the structures of the Japanese and American forms of capitalism. Japan has few formal barriers to imports. But there are numerous informal barriers as a result of the way Japanese firms develop business relationships, manage cross-shareholdings, and compensate friendly financial institutions for their favours.

The Japanese and American Role in the World Trading System

In recent years, it has been fashionable for political pundits to argue that the erosion of America's share of global GDP and role as hegemony in the western security system would erode her support for free trade and open markets. According to these commentators, America embraced free trade after the Second World War only because of her new role as a global superpower and thus will now gradually revert to protectionism because of her new focus on military rather than economic competition.

The current tensions over trade policy have certainly given this view great credibility but it also represents an overly simplistic interpretation of American history. *The fact is the first great move towards American trade liberalisation occurred in the years before the First World War, not after the Second World War*. In the first decade of the 20th century, the US pursued a series of bilateral trade liberalisation agreements with Latin America which almost immediately boosted exports. As these agreements demonstrated the benefits of trade enhancement through low tariffs rather than high tariffs, support developed for more comprehensive trade liberalisation and in 1913 the Congress enacted a trade bill which slashed US tariffs to 26.8 per cent on dutiable goods from 41.0 per cent while increasing the percentage of imports subject to no duty from 51.3 per cent to 67.5 per cent. *The Economist* described the new US tariff law as the 'heaviest blow that has been aimed against the Protective system since the British legislation of Sir Robert Peel between 1842 and 1846'.

The Americans did not embrace more open markets for altruistic reasons or because of a sudden change in trade ideology. Rather, it was a decision based on a new view of the country's commercial position. There had been a large rise in America's share of world output during the previous three decades, so Americans were increasingly confident they had competitive manufacturing industries. Meanwhile, there was increasing protectionist sentiment in Britain, a country which still consumed about 24 per cent of US exports. As the US had a vested interest in discouraging the rise of protectionism in Britain, there were both defensive and offensive reasons to support more liberal trade policies.

In a 1912 campaign speech, Woodrow Wilson outlined the new thinking on trade policy. As a result of their political base in the agricultural states of the south, the Democrats had long been advocates of low tariffs, but by 1912 they had a more cosmopolitan view of the issue than during the 19th century. Wilson contended,

> After the Spanish War was over we joined the company of nations for the first time... Now we are getting very much interested in foreign markets, but the foreign markets are not particularly interested in us. We have not been very polite, we have not encouraged the intercourse with foreign markets that we might have encouraged, and have obstructed the influence of foreign competition. So these circumstances make the tariff question a new question, our internal arrangements and new combinations of business on one side and on the other our external necessities and the need to give scope to our energy, which is now pent up and confined within our own borders.

Wilson also asserted that

> if prosperity is not to be checked in this country we must broaden our borders and make conquest of the markets of the world. That is the reason why America is so deeply interested in... breaking down... that dam against which all the tides of our prosperity have banked up, the great dam which runs around all our coasts and which we call the protective tariff.

America's early 20th century embrace of more liberal trade policies has been overlooked in recent discussions about how declining superpowers adjust to their new status. But the fact is that there are arguments for liberal trade policies which have nothing to do with strategic military relationships or global hegemony. The growth of trade creates the opportunity for a more beneficial exchange of goods and services on the basis of comparative advantage. Since the US has a large resource endowment of land, labour, capital, and technology, there is no reason why it cannot establish a large number of profitable and high value-added niches in an open global trading system.

The American experience with trade liberalisation in 1913 has two implications for the world economy during the 1990s. First, it serves as a useful reminder that America is capable of pursuing sensible open-market policies even when its share of global GDP is only about 20 per cent and its foreign policy is not driven by a cold war. Secondly, the US movement towards liberal trade policies in order to lessen the upsurge of protectionist sentiments in Britain provides an interesting role model for Japanese trade policy today. *The only country which has ever come close to duplicating the tremendous surge which occurred in the American share of world output between 1870 and 1914 is Japan since 1950.* Between 1870 and 1914, the American share of world output grew from 23 per cent to 36 per cent while between 1950 and 1992 Japan's share has expanded from barely 1.0 per cent to about 17 per cent. As a result, Japan now faces a policy adjustment not dissimilar from the one which confronted the US in 1913. It must now be seen by other countries to be playing a leadership role in promoting open markets in order to lessen the risk they will pursue more protectionist trade policies because of concerns about their own competitiveness. The US is a far more dynamic country today than was Britain in 1913, but many of the arguments which are heard against GATT or free trade in the US today are not dissimilar from the arguments expressed for restrictive trade policies in Britain during the years before the First World War.

Japan joined the GATT in the 1960s and has very low tariffs today. But because of the country's unique economic history, low level of manufactured imports, and Kereitsu corporate structure, there is still a strong perception that the Japanese market is far more restricted than others. Many senior officials in the Clinton administration believe that Japan represents an alternative form of capitalism which poses both an ideological and commercial challenge to the US. As a result of these perceptions, *Japan will have to pursue a policy of trade diplomacy which extends beyond nominal complicity with GATT in order to persuade other countries that its markets are open.* It will have to take highly visible and substantial actions to encourage more foreign investment, liberalise its fund management industry, and ensure that its markets for manufactured imports are accessible without the unrelenting use of political pressure to force them open on a sector-by-sector basis.

The effectiveness with which Japan pursues such trade diplomacy will then have a major influence on the value of the yen. If investors perceive that Japan is capable of pursuing a trade adjustment without significant exchange rate overvaluation, the yen could stabilise near its current level for the next few years. But if G-7 governments, US trade negotiators and multinational companies continue to perceive the Japanese market to be abnormally resistant to imports, there will be recurring upward pressure on the yen without any discouragement from other countries. As a result, *the value of the yen is now emerging as a de facto proxy for trade tension.* If trade problems can be managed amicably and investors perceive that there will be serious policy action to boost FDI in Japan, the yen is likely to trade in a range of 105-115 during the next several months. If trade tensions continue to intensify, the yen could rise into the 90-100 range or even higher. Finally, if the US turns highly protectionist because of frustration over the adverse effects of the Clinton fiscal programme on economic growth and the failure of other countries to offer the trade concessions needed to sell GATT to the US Congress, the yen could rise into the 80-90 range temporarily and then collapse later in the decade because of investors' apprehension about Japan's ability to sustain its prosperity in the face of escalating global protectionism.

The challenge now facing Japanese officials is to limit the risk of these extreme outcomes by pursuing policy changes which will cause foreign companies and governments to regard commercial overvaluation of the yen as a lost investment opportunity rather than as a lever for prodding open the Japanese market-place.

Figure 2.1 *Trade-weighted yen exchange rate.*

The yen has been in an erratic bull market since the breakdown of the Bretton Woods fixed exchange rate system in 1971.

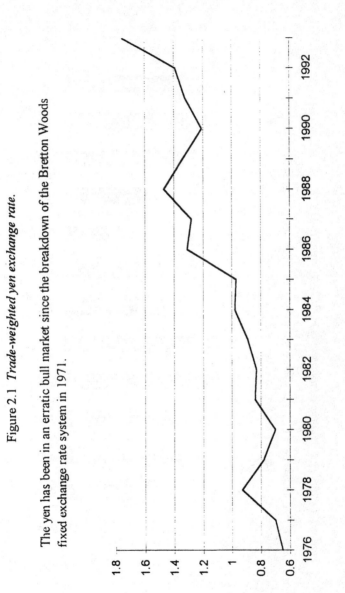

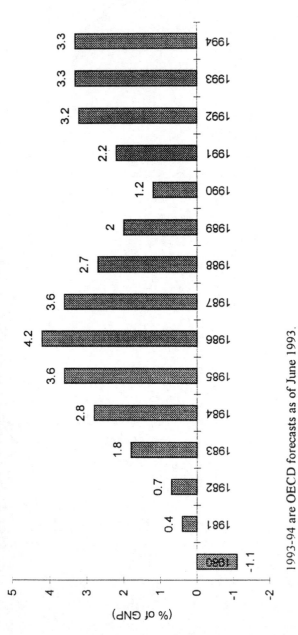

Figure 2.2 *Japan's current account balances 1980-94 (ratio to GNP).*

Japan's current account has been in surplus since the 1979-1980 oil shock because of resilient exports, a high savings rate, and low commodity prices.

1993-94 are OECD forecasts as of June 1993.

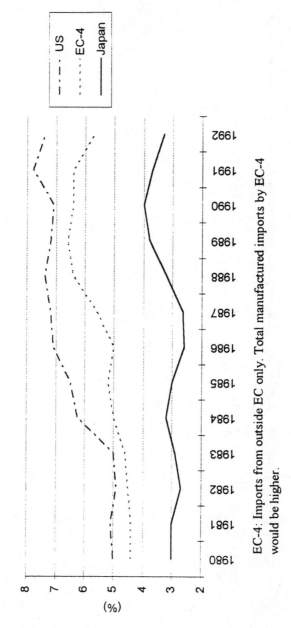

Figure 2.3 *Manufactured imports as ratio of GNP/GDP.*

Japan's ratio of manufactured imports to GDP rose during the strong yen period of 1986-89 but then fell during the recession.

EC-4: Imports from outside EC only. Total manufactured imports by EC-4 would be higher.

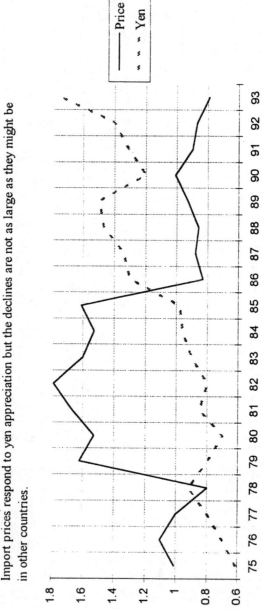

Figure 2.4 *Index of import prices for Japan and the trade-weighted yen.*

Import prices respond to yen appreciation but the declines are not as large as they might be in other countries.

Figure 2.5 *Index of export prices for Japan and the trade-weighted yen.*

Japanese firms often respond to yen appreciation by reducing yen-denominated export prices.

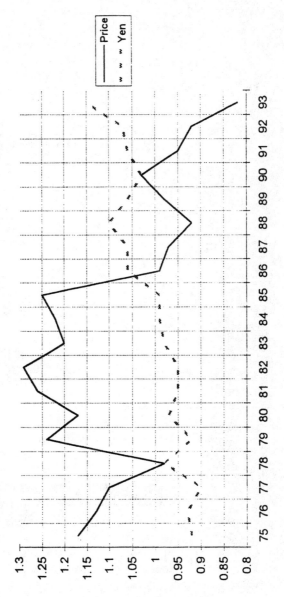

Figure 2.6 G-7: *Foreign direct investment (end of 1990).*

The level of foreign direct investment in Japan is abnormally low compared with other industrial countries.

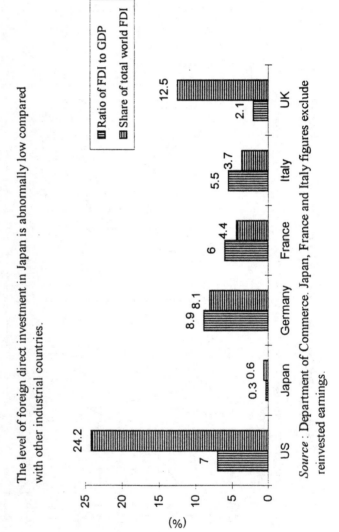

Source: Department of Commerce. Japan, France and Italy figures exclude reinvested earnings.

Table 2.1 *Regional distribution of Japanese trade account (in percentage).*

Japan's dependence upon the US market has shrunk since the mid-1980s while its export position in Southeast Asia has increased significantly, and exports to OPEC have slumped due to falling oil prices.

	1980	1986	1987	1990	1991	1992
1) Exports						
Industrialised regions	47.1	62.7	62.3	59.2	56.3	54.4
US	24.2	38.5	36.5	31.5	29.1	28.2
Western Europe	16.6	17.9	2.0	22.1	21.9	21.2
EC	12.8	14.7	16.4	18.7	18.8	18.4
Developing regions	45.8	30.6	32.5	37.3	39.9	44.8
Southeast Asia	23.8	20.0	23.1	28.8	30.6	34.2
Middle East	11.1	4,7	4.0	3.4	3.9	4.5
Central/South America	6.9	4.5	3.8	3.6	4.1	4.7
Africa	3.8	1.0	1.3	1.2	1.1	1.2
Former Communist bloc	7.1	6.7	5.2	3.4	3.8	4.4
2) Imports						
Industrialised regions	35.0	49.2	47.9	50.8	49.4	48.9
US	17.4	23.0	21.1	22.3	22.5	22.4
Western Europe	7.4	14.3	15.2	18.2	16.6	16.3
EC	5.6	11.1	11.8	14.9	13.4	13.4
Developing regions	60.4	44.3	45.0	42.0	42.6	49.3
Southeast Asia	22.6	23.3	25.8	23.3	24.8	31.9
Middle East	31.7	14.6	13.5	13.3	12.4	12.6
Central/South America	4.1	4.9	4.3	4.2	4.2	3.7
Africa	1.5	1.1	1.0	0.8	0.8	0.7
Former Communist bloc	4.7	6.5	7.1	7.2	8.1	9.1
3) Export/import balance of payments (percentage of contribution)						
Industrialised regions	-112.4	83.3	89.4	97.1	77.2	66.4
US	-64.9	62.1	65.4	72.8	49.1	40.8
Western Europe	-103.2	23.4	-22.8	39.7	38.2	31.9
EC	-82.2	20.2	25.1	35.5	35.2	29.1
Developing regions	235.5	9.7	8.9	16.6	32.0	34.9
Southeast Asia	7.8	14.9	18.0	53.9	48.0	39.0
Middle East	281.1	-10.4	-13.8	-41.1	-21.9	-13.1
Central/South America	-30.0	4.0	3.0	0.8	3.8	6.7
Africa	-25.6	1.0	1.8	2.9	2.2	2.4
Former Communist bloc	-23.2	7.0	1.6	-13.7	-9.2	-5.9

Note: Data for 1992 were obtained through flash reports.
Source: The Bank of Japan, Balance of Payments Monthly, December 1992.

Table 2.2 *Characteristics of Japanese export by product group and by destination.*

Japanese exports of high-tech R&D intensive products have increased significantly while labour-intensive exports have fallen as a share of the total.

1) Export composition by product group (%)

Product group (Classification by relative factor intensities)	To the US 1977	1980	1985	1991	To the EC 1977	1980	1985	1991	Worldwide 1977	1980	1985	1991
Food and natural resources	1.7	1.3	1.0	0.7	2.9	2.1	1.5	0.8	2.6	2.9	1.9	1.6
Manufactured goods	97.4	98.0	97.9	97.9	96.9	97.6	98.1	98.9	96.6	96.1	97.1	96.8
Natural resource-intensive	1.8	2.4	1.5	0.7	2.0	2.4	0.9	0.9	2.4	2.5	1.7	1.4
Unskilled labour-intensive	7.0	4.7	4.3	4.2	18.1	11.2	6.6	5.2	17.8	10.4	8.8	6.5
Capital-cum-mid-tech-intensive	61.7	63.7	57.3	44.2	44.2	47.4	42.0	36.7	46.9	50.1	48.2	38.0
High-tech (R&D-intensive)	27.0	27.2	34.8	48.7	32.6	36.6	48.6	56.0	29.5	33.1	38.5	50.9
Others	0.8	0.7	1.0	1.5	0.2	0.3	0.3	0.4	0.8	1.0	1.0	1.6
Total	100.0	100.0	100.0	100.0	100.0	100.0	100.0	100.0	100.0	100.0	100.0	100.0

2) Percentage destination of US exports by product group (regional dependency ratio)

Product group	To the US 1977	1980	1985	1991	To the EC 1977	1980	1985	1991	Worldwide 1977	1980	1985	1991
Food and natural resources	15.6	11.8	22.5	12.1	14.4	11.0	10.3	8.5	100.0	100.0	100.0	100.0
Manufactured goods	23.7	25.9	41.6	30.5	13.1	15.4	13.0	18.7	100.0	100.0	100.0	100.0
Natural resource-intensive	17.9	24.4	36.0	15.9	10.9	14.6	7.0	11.5	100.0	100.0	100.0	100.0
Unskilled labour-intensive	9.2	11.5	20.4	19.6	13.3	16.4	9.7	14.8	100.0	100.0	100.0	100.0
Capital-cum-mid-tech-intensive	30.9	32.2	49.0	35.2	12.4	14.3	11.2	17.8	100.0	100.0	100.0	100.0
High-tech (R&D-intensive)	21.5	20.8	37.3	28.9	14.5	16.8	16.3	20.2	100.0	100.0	100.0	100.0
Total	23.5	25.4	41.2	30.2	13.1	15.2	12.9	18.4	100.0	100.0	100.0	100.0

David D. Hale 43

3) Average annual rate of increase by product group (%)

Product group	To the US			To the EC			Worldwide		
	1977-80	1980-85	1985-91	1977-80	1980-85	1985-91	1977-80	1980-85	1985-91
Food and natural resources	10.3	6.1	-3.1	10.4	6.1	4.0	20.9	12.0	7.5
Manufactured goods	20.5	11.8	4.6	23.4	13.4	17.0	17.0	9.9	10.1
Natural resource-intensive	32.5	18.4	-6.9	31.5	17.9	16.0	19.4	11.2	6.7
Unskilled labour-intensive	5.4	3.2	4.2	4.9	2.9	12.4	-2.1	-1.3	4.9
Capital-cum-mid-tech-intensive	21.6	12.4	0.2	25.9	14.8	14.3	19.9	11.5	5.9
High-tech (R&D-intensive)	20.6	11.9	10.6	27.9	15.9	19.7	21.8	12.5	15.5
Total	20.3	11.7	4.6	23.1	13.3	16.9	17.2	10.0	10.2

Note: Because 'Others' ('Commodities and transactions not classified elsewhere in SITC') is relatively unimportant in this context, we did not include it under 2) and 3).
Source: OECD Trade Tape.

Table 2.3 *Characteristics of Japanese import by product group and by origin.*

The food and resource share of Japanese imports has been shrinking while manufactured imports are growing.

1) Import composition by product group (%).

Product group (Classification by relative factor intensities)	From the US				From the EC				Worldwide			
	1977	1980	1985	1991	1977	1980	1985	1991	1977	1980	1985	1991
Food and natural resources	63.9	57.6	47.2	36.4	17.5	16.6	17.8	9.1	78.8	78.3	70.6	50.7
Manufactured goods	35.9	42.0	51.7	61.8	81.1	82.2	81.1	89.6	20.8	21.0	28.1	48.2
Natural resource-intensive	3.3	4.9	2.7	4.8	6.6	6.0	5.6	6.8	4.4	4.4	4.7	7.3
Unskilled labour-intensive	2.0	2.3	2.4	4.2	14.0	15.1	14.7	16.4	3.8	3.9	5.0	10.3
Capital-cum-mid-tech-intensive	4.5	4.6	5.3	9.6	15.7	16.7	18.0	28.0	2.8	2.8	3.8	9.6
High-tech (R&D-intensive)	26.1	30.2	41.3	43.2	44.8	44.4	42.9	38.4	9.7	9.9	14.6	21.0
Others	0.2	0.4	1.1	1.8	1.3	1.2	1.1	1.2	0.4	0.6	1.4	1.1
Total	100.0	100.0	100.0	100.0	100.0	100.0	100.0	100.0	100.0	100.0	100.0	100.0

2) Percentage origin of Japanese imports by product group (regional dependency ratio)

Product group	From the US				From the EC				Worldwide			
	1977	1980	1985	1991	1977	1980	1985	1991	1977	1980	1985	1991
Food and natural resources	11.9	10.8	11.3	14.1	1.2	1.0	1.6	1.9	100.0	100.0	100.0	100.0
Manufactured goods	25.4	29.2	31.2	25.1	20.3	18.4	17.9	19.9	100.0	100.0	100.0	100.0
Natural resource-intensive	10.8	16.1	9.7	13.0	7.8	6.4	7.4	10.1	100.0	100.0	100.0	100.0
Unskilled labour-intensive	8.0	8.6	8.1	8.0	19.3	18.2	18.0	17.0	100.0	100.0	100.0	100.0
Capital-cum-mid-tech-intensive	23.4	24.2	23.5	19.5	28.9	28.1	29.4	31.0	100.0	100.0	100.0	100.0
High-tech (R&D-intensive)	39.4	44.5	48.0	40.4	24.0	21.1	18.2	19.5	100.0	100.0	100.0	100.0
Total	14.7	14.6	16.9	19.6	5.2	4.7	6.2	10.7	100.0	100.0	100.0	100.0

[Table 2.3 *Cont.*]

3) Average annual rate of increase by product group (%)

Product group	From the US			From the EC			Worldwide		
	1977-80	1980-85	1985-91	1977-80	1980-85	1985-91	1977-80	1980-85	1985-91
Food and natural resources	21.1	-2.9	8.5	19.3	5.1	8.5	25.4	-3.9	4.7
Manufactured goods	32.1	5.4	16.8	22.1	3.4	23.2	26.2	4.0	21.0
Natural resource-intensive	43.1	-10.3	24.9	17.9	2.0	25.4	25.4	-0.7	19.1
Unskilled labour-intensive	30.0	2.1	24.5	24.4	3.1	23.5	27.0	3.3	24.6
Capital-cum-mid-tech-intensive	26.5	3.7	25.3	24.1	5.2	30.4	25.2	4.3	29.2
High-tech (R&D-intensive)	31.7	7.6	14.2	21.2	2.9	19.0	26.2	6.0	17.6
Total	25.4	1.1	13.4	21.7	3.7	21.1	25.6	-1.8	10.6

Note: Because 'Others' ('Commodities and transactions not classified elsewhere in SITC') is relatively unimportant in this context, we did not include it under 2) and 3).

Source: OECD Trade Tape.

Table 2.4 *Overall trade structure of the US and Japan by product groups, 1985-1991 (Summary).*

This table shows the structure of the US and Japanese trade accounts. The great bulk of Japan's trade surplus is still concentrated in mid-tech products.

(1) The US overall trade structure

Product groups	Trade structure by product (Percentage distribution)		Annual rate of increase (%)		US trade balance of individual product ($billion)	
	US exports 1991	US imports 1991	US exports 1985-91	US imports 1985-91	1985	1991
Food and natural resources	19.0	20.3	6.9	1.8	-42.0	-27.9
Manufactured goods	77.6	76.7	13.2	7.0	-112.8	-82.4
Natural resource-intensive	2.4	3.9	15.3	3.6	-11.8	-10.2
Unskilled labour-intensive	5.4	14.4	18.8	9.0	-36.1	-51.9
Capital-cum-mid-tech-intensive	17.4	26.2	13.3	3.1	-77.9	-64.3
High-tech (R&D-intensive)	52.4	32.1	12.6	10.7	13.0	44.0
Others	3.4	3.0	-	-	-	-
Total	100.0	100.0	11.5	5.9	-153.7	-112.3

(2) Japanese overall trade structure

Product groups	Trade structure by product (Percentage distribution)		Annual rate of increase (%)		Japanese trade balance of individual product ($billion)	
	JA exports 1991	JA imports 1991	JA exports 1985-91	JA imports 1985-91	1985	1991
Food and natural resources	1.6	50.7	7.5	4.7	-13.7	-31.0
Manufactured goods	96.8	48.2	10.1	21.0	-55.9	-74.5
Natural resource-intensive	1.4	7.3	6.7	19.1	70.9	138.0
Unskilled labor-intensive	6.5	10.3	4.9	24.6	-1.3	-12.9
Capital-cum-mid-tech-intensive	38.0	9.6	5.9	29.2	48.1	58.8
High-tech (R&D-intensive)	50.9	21.0	15.5	17.6	0.0	2.2
Others	1.6	1.1	-	-	-	-
Total	100.0	100.0	10.2	10.6	48.1	80.6

Sources: OECD and Long-Term Credit Bank of Japan Institute of Research.

Table 2.5 *Movements in payable yen exchange rate by Japanese industry (January 1992).*

(¥/US$ %)

¥/$	Average	Below 110	110-20	120-30	130-40	140-50	150-60	160 or above 160	Total
All industry	126.2	2.3%	9.9 %	47.1%	29.2%	7.1%	2.5%	2.0%	100.0%
Manufacturing industry	126.2	2.4	9.7	46.3	29.9	7.2	2.8	1.7	100.0%
Material-type	127.2	2.2	7.9	46.0	29.5	7.2	3.6	3.6	100.0%
Processing-type	125.9	1.8	7.4	51.1	31.3	5.9	2.2	0.4	100.0%
Others	125.7	3.9	16.5	36.2	27.6	10.2	3.1	2.4	100.0%
Non-manufacturing industry	126.3	1.4	11.3	53.5	23.9	5.6	-	9.2	100.0%

Note: ¥/US$ in January 1992 was 125.1.

Table 2.6 *Foreign trade prices (average unit values) of selected other OECD countries.*
(Percentage changes, national currency terms)

	Exports					Imports				
	1990	1991	1992	1993	1994	1990	1991	1992	1993	1994
Austria	-2.3	-4.3	-0.6	-0.2	2.3	-2.9	3.3	-1.4	-0.6	2.5
Belgium-Luxembourg	-3.1	-1.9	-1.4	0.4	2.0	-1.8	-1.3	-3.2	0.4	2.2
Denmark	-1.5	-0.4	-1.7	-2.1	1.7	-3.0	0.0	-3.0	-2.2	1.9
Finland	-1.2	0.8	6.0	9.5	8.9	1.7	2.5	10.1	12.5	9.0
Ireland	-8.7	-2.0	1.9	-1.5	-0.3	-5.2	2.3	0.6	-1.7	0.8
Netherlands	-0.9	-0.9	-3.4	1.1	1.9	-2.0	-0.6	-2.5	0.6	1.8
Norway	3.8	-3.5	-8.6	4.7	2.8	1.0	-1.6	-2.4	1.4	2.3
Spain	-2.5	-1.5	0.5	4.7	3.5	-3.2	-2.8	-3.0	8.1	3.0
Sweden	2.0	0.4	-3.1	11.4	4.4	1.7	-0.9	-4.9	12.5	3.6
Switzerland	1.3	2.3	0.9	1.4	2.2	-0.3	0.1	2.1	1.5	1.8
Total of smaller European countries	-0.2	0.3	-0.1	3.6	3.7	-0.1	1.2	0.0	4.3	4.0
Australia	-2.6	-6.2	1.0	7.8	1.1	1.5	-0.5	1.4	10.7	0.3
New Zealand	-1.3	-4.2	8.3	1.5	2.0	0.8	1.0	8.0	0.4	1.9
Total of smaller countries	-0.3	-0.1	0.0	3.8	3.5	0.0	1.1	0.2	4.6	3.7

Sources: Direction of trade data - United Nations Statistical Office, OECD Foreign Trade by Commodities.

Table 2.7 Trade in manufactured goods: export market growth and relative export performance. (Percentage changes from previous year)

	1 Import volume				2 Export market growth				3 Export volume				4 Relative export performance			
	1991	1992	1993	1994	1991	1992	1993	1994	1991	1992	1993	1994	1991	1992	1993	1994
United States	2.0	12.3	8.4	7.0	5.3	6.0	4.8	6.5	6.5	6.2	5.1	7.0	1.2	0.1	0.3	0.5
Japan	3.2	-3.9	0.3	4.1	6.5	9.6	7.2	7.5	2.5	0.4	1.1	3.1	-3.7	-8.4	-5.7	-4.1
Germany	12.3	0.2	-0.4	2.5	0.3	3.2	2.6	5.2	-3.9	2.0	-2.2	2.0	-4.2	-1.2	-4.7	-3.0
France	1.9	0.9	1.1	4.4	5.0	4.4	1.9	4.8	0.0	4.8	0.1	4.0	-0.7	0.4	-1.8	-0.8
Italy	3.1	5.7	-1.2	5.2	4.4	3.8	2.4	4.8	0.0	2.7	4.9	6.7	-4.2	-1.1	2.5	1.8
United Kingdom	-4.4	6.3	5.9	6.0	4.6	5.2	3.0	5.3	2.7	2.6	6.8	7.3	-1.8	-2.5	3.6	1.9
Canada	2.5	7.3	5.5	6.8	2.6	11.2	7.9	6.9	-1.0	10.7	8.6	8.0	-3.5	-0.5	0.6	1.0
Total of the above countries	3.4	5.3	3.8	5.3	3.9	5.8	4.2	6.0	1.6	3.5	2.5	4.9	-2.2	-2.2	-1.7	-1.0
Austria	2.8	2.7	0.0	2.8	4.7	1.7	1.2	4.2	8.3	3.7	-0.7	2.6	3.5	2.1	-1.8	-1.5
Belgium-Luxembourg	3.3	0.6	-2.0	1.9	4.6	3.1	2.1	4.6	2.8	-0.5	-1.7	2.0	-1.8	-3.5	-3.6	-2.5
Denmark	4.8	3.0	-1.0	5.5	2.0	2.8	2.1	4.7	6.1	5.6	-1.0	3.7	4.0	2.7	-3.0	-0.9
Finland	-20.1	-11.6	-9.6	1.2	-2.6	1.2	2.6	5.2	-12.2	8.1	14.2	10.3	-9.8	6.8	11.3	4.9
Ireland	-4.3	7.3	5.9	6.4	1.7	4.2	3.0	5.0	4.1	8.2	4.9	6.0	2.4	3.9	1.9	1.0
Netherlands	5.4	0.3	1.6	3.0	4.5	3.2	1.6	4.4	5.0	2.1	0.6	2.9	0.5	-1.0	-0.9	-1.4
Norway	2.8	5.0	2.6	4.3	2.4	3.5	2.6	5.1	-0.5	3.4	1.6	7.7	-2.9	0.0	-1.0	2.5
Portugal	6.4	12.6	6.3	7.9	3.7	3.1	1.2	4.5	0.5	6.6	1.1	6.7	-3.1	3.4	-0.1	2.0
Spain	11.9	6.3	-3.6	5.5	3.9	4.7	2.8	5.1	11.7	6.3	4.5	7.8	7.6	1.5	1.6	2.6
Sweden	-7.3	-2.1	-0.6	2.2	2.2	3.9	2.4	5.0	-2.8	-0.1	6.5	9.0	-4.9	-3.9	4.0	3.8
Switzerland	-0.1	-6.1	-2.3	2.2	5.0	4.2	2.7	5.1	-0.7	6.1	6.3	2.0	-5.5	1.9	-2.8	-2.9
Total of smaller European countries	2.5	1.5	-0.3	3.6	3.7	3.3	2.1	4.7	2.8	3.2	1.6	4.5	-0.9	-0.1	-0.5	-0.2
Australia	-2.0	7.7	1.4	8.1	4.9	6.1	6.3	7.2	19.8	9.6	7.0	7.1	14.2	3.3	0.7	-0.2
New Zealand	-11.4	8.5	5.0	5.3	2.3	5.7	3.6	7.1	10.2	9.9	9.2	7.5	7.7	4.0	5.3	0.3
Total of smaller countries	2.0	2.0	-0.1	4.0	3.7	3.4	2.2	4.8	3.2	3.5	1.8	4.6	-0.6	0.0	-0.4	-0.2
Total OECD	3.0	4.4	2.7	5.0	3.8	5.3	3.8	5.7	1.9	3.5	2.3	4.8	-1.8	-1.7	-1.4	-0.8
Total of non-OECD of which:	7.5	9.3	8.2	8.4	5.4	7.4	6.0	6.8	8.5	10.2	9.1	10.3	2.9	2.6	2.9	3.3
Developing areas	12.5	11.1	10.1	9.4	5.1	7.7	6.3	7.0	10.9	10.9	9.5	10.9	5.5	3.0	3.0	3.6
Asian NIEs	19.1	12.5	11.7	11.0	5.0	8.3	6.6	7.0	14.0	10.8	9.8	11.8	8.5	2.3	3.0	4.5

a) The calculation of export markets is based on a weighted average of import volumes (panel 1 above) in each exporting country's markets, with weights based on manufacturing trade flows in 1987.

b) Relative export performance (panel 4 above) is derived for each country as the ratio of export volumes (panel 3 above) to export markets (panel 2 above)

Sources: Direction of trade data - United Nations Statistical Office, OECD Foreign Trade by Commodities.

Table 2.8 *US direct foreign investment abroad: majority-owned assets as a share of total assets 1990 (percentages).*

The percentage of US foreign direct investment in Japan represented by majority-owned affiliates is small compared with other countries.

	Percentage of majority-owned assets in total assets	
	All industries	Manufacturing
All countries	78	71
Developed countries	76	73
Canada	91	92
European Communities	81	80
Japan	34	26
Austrl, N. Zeal, & S. Afr.	67	69
Developing countries	82	61
Latin America	88	71
South America	82	80
Central America	69	56
India	14	14
South Korea	18	14

Source: National Trade Data Bank. US Department of Commerce, Bureau of Economic Analysis. Operations of US parent companies & their foreign affiliates.

Table 2.9 *Number of mergers and acquisitions involving Japanese firms, 1981-90.*

This table shows that foreign M&A activity remained subdued during the 1980s compared with activity among Japanese firms.

Year	Japanese firms acquire Japanese firms	Japanese firms acquire foreign firms	Foreign firms acquire Japanese firms	Total
1981	122	48	6	176
1985	163	100	26	289
1986	226	204	21	451
1987	219	228	22	469
1988	223	315	17	555
1989	240	405	15	660
1990	293	440	18	751

Sources: Yamaichi Security Co. Ltd as cited by Japan Economic Institute in *Foreign Direct Investment in Japan*, 1991, No. 35A.

Table 2.10 *US foreign direct investment abroad: majority-owned and minority-interest affiliates.*

This table shows how the ownership structure of US firms in Japan compares with other countries.

JAPAN

	1977			1990			Percentage change 1977-90		
	Employment	Sales	Assets	Employment	Sales	Assets	Employment	Real Sales (1)	Real Assets (1)
Majority-owned	16.83%	25.50%	16.06%	32.41%	37.43%	33.85%	70.40%	12.30%	91.40%
Minority-owned	83.17%	74.50%	83.94%	67.59%	62.57%	66.15%	-28.10%	-35.80%	-28.40%
Total	389 123	$51.9 bil	$41.8 bil	344 300	$113.4 bil	$108.3 bil	-11.50%	-23.50%	-9.20%

DEVELOPED COUNTRIES

	1977			1990		
	Employment	Sales	Assets	Employment	Sales	Assets
Majority-owned	76.70%	75.40%	71.30%	75.10%	77.50%	76.20%
Minority-owned	23.30%	24.60%	28.70%	24.90%	22.50%	23.80%
Total	4 980 691	$449.0 bil	$359.6 bil	4 308 500	$871.1 bil	$843.2 bil

Notes: (1) Sales and assets adjusted for inflation and exchange rate changes. Consumer price index in Japan 1977-90 rose 54%.
In 1977, yen=$268.5 and in 1990 yen=$144.8.
Data on 1990 employment, sales, and assets from national trade data base.
Data on 1977 employment, sales, and assets from 1977 survey of current business, benchmark survey.
Source: Inflation and Exchange Rates from International Financial Statistics.

Table 2.11   *Percentage breakdown of number of manufacturing subsidiaries of US-based companies by subsidiaries' method of entry into foreign country.*

This table shows how US manufacturing firms have entered foreign countries. Direct acquisitions in Japan are low.

Country	Newly formed	Reorgani-sation	Acquired directly	Number of firms
Canada	35.0%	2.8%	62.0%	703
Belgium	49.0%	0.0%	51.0%	103
Denmark	48.0%	0.0%	52.0%	29
France	39.0%	3.5%	57.0%	286
Germany	42.0%	2.3%	56.0%	259
Greece	78.0%	0.0%	22.0%	23
Ireland	45.0%	3.2%	52.0%	31
Italy	50.0%	0.5%	50.0%	200
Luxembourg	49.0%	0.0%	51.0%	
Netherlands	53.0%	1.1%	46.0%	91
United Kingdom	35.0%	3.3%	62.0%	452
Australia	59.0%	0.0%	41.0%	22
Finland	60.0%	0.0%	40.0%	5
Norway	50.0%	0.0%	50.0%	18
Portugal	81.0%	0.0%	19.0%	21
Spain	43.0%	0.8%	57.0%	129
Sweden	62.0%	0.0%	38.0%	39
Switzerland	48.0%	0.0%	52.0%	25
Turkey	86.0%	0.0%	14.0%	14
Japan	64.0%	0.7%	35.0%	142
Australia	47.0%	2.1%	50.0%	236
New Zealand	58.0%	2.3%	30.0%	44
Weighted average	43.3%	2.1%	54.5%	

Time period when US firms entered into the Japanese market

	pre-1946	1946-57	1958-67
Per cent of total	6.4%	16.7%	76.9%

Source: *The World's Multinational Enterprises* by Vaupel and Curhan, Table 13. Data cover subsidiaries formed between 1900 and 1968. The study covers approximately 40% of the total number of all foreign manufacturing subsidiaries of US companies and approximately 70% of the value of US manufacturing investment in subsidiaries. Data include minority-interest and majority-owned affiliates.

Table 2.12 *Foreign direct investment in the United States: method of entry.*

Foreign acquisitions in the US are very common.

	1981	1982	1983	1984	1985	1986	1987	1988	1989	1990
Total	23218	10817	8092	15197	23106	39178	40310	72692	71163	64424
Acquired % of total	78.2	60.7	59.9	77.9	86.9	80.3	84.2	89.2	83.9	88.1
Established % of total	21.8	39.3	40.1	22.1	13.1	19.7	15.8	10.8	16.1	11.9

Source: *Survey of Current Business*, 'Business enterprises acquired or established by foreign direct investors', selected May issues.

Table 2.13 *Foreign direct investment in the United States: method of investment by source country, 1989.*

This table shows FDI in the US by sector and country of investor.

	All countries	Canada	France	Germany	Japan	Netherlands	Switzerland	UK
Mergers & acquisitions	79.21%	86.85%	90.53%	86.72%	56.20%	99.07%	91.68%	97.53%
Equity increases	3.98%	0.51%	0.00%	0.00%	5.45%	0.00%	8.11%	0.02%
Joint-ventures	3.13%	4.33%	1.50%	0.00%	6.47%	0.00%	0.21%	0.66%
New plants	4.94%	4.47%	6.32%	5.24%	10.23%	0.18%	0.00%	1.20%
Plant expansion	3.57%	0.89%	0.00%	7.94%	9.28%	0.00%	0.00%	0.29%
Real estate	4.59%	2.94%	1.44%	0.00%	11.34%	0.74%	0.00%	0.24%
Other	0.57%	0.00%	0.21%	0.10%	1.03%	0.00%	0.00%	0.04%
Total value known (millions)	74 715.4	3 691.3	3 324.8	2 381	22 977.7	3 824.1	4 306.8	24 955.1

Notes: The data include only the investments for which the value of the transaction is known. Foreign direct investment is defined as ownership of 10% or more of a company.

Source: 'Foreign Direct Investment in the United States', 1989 Transactions, US Department of Commerce. International Trade Administration. Office of Trade & Investment Analysis.

Table 2.14 *US direct investment and US exports to 40 nations, 1991.*

This table shows the relationship between US foreign direct investment and exports. In many cases there is a high correlation.

Country	US FDI stock ($ billions)	Rank	US exports ($ billions)	Rank
Canada	33.23	1	75.90	1
UK	20.64	2	20.33	4
Germany	17.49	3	19.44	5
Brazil	11.29	4	5.18	17
France	11.05	5	13.69	6
Japan	10.62	6	31.39	2
Italy	8.53	7	6.38	14
Netherlands	8.14	8	10.33	8
Mexico	7.31	9	28.40	3
Australia	6.06	10	7.77	12
Spain	5.00	11	3.80	19
Ireland	4.89	12	2.40	24
Belgium	4.87	13	7.99	11
Singapore	2.36	14	8.28	10
Argentina	1.57	15	1.90	26
Taiwan	1.45	16	10.03	9
Switzerland	1.18	17	5.31	16
Sweden	1.06	18	3.01	23
Venezuela	0.96	19	4.02	18
Korea	0.92	20	11.13	7
Malaysia	0.86	21	3.67	20
Philippines	0.82	22	1.80	28
Colombia	0.80	23	1.73	29
Hong Kong	0.78	24	6.73	13
Saudi Arabia	0.58	25	5.69	15
India	0.51	26	1.48	32
Thailand	0.46	27	3.33	22
Egypt	0.45	28	1.90	27
South Africa	0.41	29	1.96	25
Panama	0.36	30	0.75	38
New Zealand	0.34	31	0.90	36
Israel	0.31	32	3.41	21
Denmark	0.29	33	1.26	35
Portugal	0.29	34	0.45	40
Chile	0.28	35	1.67	30
Ecuador	0.17	36	0.83	37
Jamaica	0.15	37	0.70	39
Indonesia	0.14	38	1.36	33
Turkey	0.12	39	1.54	31
Norway	0.12	40	1.31	34

Source: US Commerce Department, Bureau of the Census and Bureau of Economic Affairs.

Table 2.15 *Japanese intra-corporation trade by region (1989) (Unit: $ billions).*

This table shows the level of intra-corporation trade by region for Japanese firms. It is very high in case of Japanese imports from the US as well as exports to Asia.

	Exports		Imports		Balance	
	Actual value	% of total exports	Actual value	% of total imports	Actual value	% of total balance
General trade (A)						
World	276.0	100.0	207.4	100.0	68.7	100.0
US	93.7	33.9	48.5	23.4	45.2	65.9
Asia	82.7	30.0	64.7	31.2	18.1	26.3
EC	48.2	17.5	27.9	13.4	20.3	29.6
Intra-corporation trade (B)						
World	65.5	100.0	28.6	100.0	36.9	100.0
US	35.8	54.7	5.6	19.7	30.2	81.9
Asia	7.1	10.8	7.2	25.2	-0.1	-0.3
EC	14.3	21.8	3.0	10.4	11.3	30.7
Intra-corporation trade ratio (B)/(A)						
World	23.7%		13.8%		53.7%	
US	38.2%		11.6%		66.7%	
Asia	8.6%		11.2%		-0.7%	
EC	29.7%		10.7%		55.7%	

Note: 'Intra-corporation trade' indicates transactions that take place between a Japanese parent company and its overseas subsidiaries.

Source 1: Figures under 'General trade' are taken from OECD, *Foreign Trade by Commodities.*

Source 2: Figures for 'Intra-corporation trade' are based on the amounts appearing in the Ministry of International Trade and Industry's *Overview of Overseas Investment*, under the heading 'Transaction occurring within single corporation', which describes the transaction of Japanese overseas subsidiaries (sales and procurement).

Table 2.16 *US intra-corporation trade by region (1989) (Unit: $ billions).*

This table shows the level of intra-corporation trade for US firms. It is very high for Canada as well as for US exports to Europe.

	Exports		Imports		Balance	
	Actual value	% of total exports	Actual value	% of total imports	Actual value	% of total balance
General trade (A)						
World	361.7	100.0	477.4	100.0	-115.7	100.0
Canada	80.7	22.3	89.9	18.8	-9.3	8.0
Mexico	24.7	6.8	27.1	5.7	-2.5	2.1
Japan	43.9	12.1	93.5	19.6	-49.7	42.9
Asia	68.0	18.8	113.8	23.8	-45.8	39.6
EC	84.5	23.4	85.5	17.9	-1.0	0.9
Intra-corporation trade (B)						
World	85.6	100.0	72.4	100.0	13.3	100.0
Canada	32.1	37.4	32.5	44.9	-0.4	-3.0
Mexico	6.0	7.0	6.4	8.9	-0.4	-3.1
Japan	6.0	7.1	2.0	2.7	4.1	30.8
Asia	10.4	12.1	13.3	18.4	-2.9	-22.1
EC	25.0	29.2	11.1	15.3	14.0	105.2
Intra-corporation trade ratio (B)/(A)						
World	23.7 %		15.2 %		-11.5 %	
Canada	39.7 %		36.1 %		4.3 %	
Mexico	24.3 %		23.6 %		16.9 %	
Japan	13.8 %		2.1 %		-8.2 %	
Asia	15.3 %		11.7 %		6.4 %	
EC	29.6 %		13.0 %		-1403.4 %	

Notes:

1) 'Intra-corporation trade' indicates transactions that take place between a US parent company and its overseas subsidiaries.

2) Those appearing under 'Intra-corporation trade' apply to various materials and products traded within each corporation. Therefore, in some cases, intra-corporation trade ratios surpass 100%.

Source 1: Figures under 'General trade' are taken from OECD, *Foreign Trade by Commodities.*

Source 2: Figures under 'Intra-corporation trade' are taken from US Department of Commerce, *US Direct Investment Abroad, 1989 Benchmark Survey, Preliminary Results.*

3 The Japan Problem: Economic Challenge or Strategic Threat?

Robert Gilpin

Japan is the fourth nation in the modern world economy to capture a substantial fraction of world trade in a very short period of time and thereby upset the global economic *status quo*.[1] In the early 19th century, following the conclusion of the Napoleonic Wars and continuing late into the century, British industry and exports expanded rapidly and overwhelmed foreign competitors. Subsequently, towards the end of the century, Germany, following its political unification and industrialisation, rapidly expanded as an industrial and trading power. Almost at the same time and especially in the early 20th century, the United States accelerated its drive to become the world's foremost industrial and trading nation. In each case these aggressive export drives caused immense economic dislocations and adjustment problems in other countries. Denunciation of the predatory trading practices of the British, Germans, and the Americans proliferated under such titles as *The German Problem* and *The American Problem*. These powerful economic and political reactions in other countries intensified economic nationalism, economic conflict and political hostility.

The same type of negative economic and political reaction is occurring today with respect to Japanese economic expansionism. As a consequence of its rapid industrial development, Japan has followed in the footsteps of earlier expanding industrial powers in capturing a substantial fraction of world trade in a relatively short time period. Over almost the entire course of the post-war era, Japan has enjoyed a remarkably high rate of economic growth and has become the world's second largest economic power. In addition Japan has climbed with incredible speed up the ladder of advanced technology and taken the lead in one technological development and industrial sector after another. Japan's dynamic comparative advantage has caused serious dislocations and has imposed heavy adjustment costs on its trading partners. More recently, the rapid overseas expansion of Japanese corporations and financial institutions has greatly accentuated the Japanese competitive challenge. As a result of these developments, Japan's outstanding economic success has become a serious problem for Western Europe, the United States, and other countries.

In increasing numbers, Americans have come to regard Japan as an economic problem and, in some cases, even as a 'security threat' to the United States.[2] Similarly, in Western Europe as well, anti-Japanese sentiment has intensified and protectionist policies directed against goods have increased in recent years. On the Japanese side too, resentment against foreign attacks and especially American pressures to 'open' the Japanese market has led to an intensification of nationalistic outbursts and increasing resistance to being 'pushed around' by the Americans and, to a lesser extent, the West Europeans. In brief, the clash between Japan and the West threatens to become a crucial feature of the post-Cold War era.

The American and West European approaches to the Japan problem, it should be noted, are strikingly different. The American approach is essentially an effort through unilateral pressures and bilateral negotiations to open the Japanese market to American exports and direct investments. Successive American administrations have used different means to achieve this objective. This policy has evolved in the direction of being more comprehensive in its objective and more confrontational in its tone. The Reagan Administration's MOSS talks sought to open a few specific sectors; the Bush Administration's Structural Impediments Initiative (SII) was directed toward the goal of changing certain structural features of the Japanese economy; and the Clinton Administration's 'results-oriented' approach demands that Japan agree to purchase specified amounts of American goods each year. The West Europeans, on the other hand, tend to emphasise control over Japanese access to the European market and place less emphasis on opening the Japanese market; through anti-dumping measures and other protectionist devices, the Europeans are attempting to limit Japanese expansionism in the EC. Setting aside the reasons for these different approaches, the Japanese resent American pressures to make changes in their economy and economic policies far more than they dislike West European protection.

The danger of a serious rupture in American-Japanese relations can no longer be ignored. While few observers on either side of the Pacific foresee a return to the military confrontation of the 1940s, many do worry that economic competition could spill over into serious political conflict. As such a development would have devastating consequences not only for both societies but also for the world economic and political system, a balanced and impartial assessment of the 'Japan problem' has become imperative. In addressing this issue, three fundamental questions must be answered. *The first question* is whether the Japan economy and Japanese economic behaviour differ fundamentally from those of West. *The second question* is whether Japanese society has a long-term economic strategy or whether Japanese overseas economic expansion can be explained entirely as a response to market factors. Depending in part on the answer to the second question, *the third question* is whether Japan constitutes primarily an economic challenge to the West or rather a security threat that must be stopped? While I shall attempt to be as objective as possible in considering these questions, both Japanese and European readers, I am sure, will find many American biases in my analysis.

The place to begin a consideration of these three questions is with the intensifying debate in the United States over the 'Japan problem'. The central issue in this debate is the nature of the Japanese political economy: Do the Japanese behave in accordance with Western economic principles or do they behave in accordance with fundamentally different rules? The two opposed positions in this debate come to very different conclusions on the questions of the existence of a Japanese long-term strategy, the character of the Japanese challenge and the proper response to Japan. Following the presentation of the positions taken by the two sides on key questions, I shall set forth my own interpretation which will attempt to draw insights from both positions.

The American Debate over the Japanese Political Economy

Although many Americans have come to believe that Japan and its rapid economic expansion pose a serious challenge, the extent, nature, and causes of the Japan problem have become matters of intense debate. On one side it is argued that it is greatly exaggerated and, in so far as Japanese economic competition does constitute a problem for the United States at least, the primary source of the problem lies in the United States itself. America's short-sighted economic policies, deteriorating educational system and flabby business culture are held to be chiefly responsible for America's disappointing economic performance. For many adherents of this position, in fact, Japanese experience, investment, and technology are of major benefit to the United States. On the other side are those individuals who regard Japan as a serious threat to American economic prosperity and even to American national security. 'Japan Inc.', the adherents of this position allege, is waging total economic warfare against a divided and essentially defensive United States and the rest of the world. The United States and the rest of the world, they believe, must stop Japanese economic expansionism while it is still possible.

Two fundamentally opposed sets of American opinions can in fact be discerned on these issues. Although it would be a mistake to overlook significant differences among the adherents of each camp, American scholars, business leaders, and public officials generally fall into two schools of thought on the 'Japan problem'. In addition to very different opinions on the nature of the Japanese political economy, each position comes to very different conclusions with respect to appropriate American policy toward Japan. At the time of writing, the debate between these positions has become much more intense. The issues at stake have also become much more important because of the underlying serious problems of the American economy and the belief held by increasing numbers of Americans and the Clinton Administration that Japan is a source of at least some of America's problems.

Despite a recent, significant shift in the direction of 'Japan bashing', the dominant interpretation in the United States of Japanese economic behaviour and the Japanese political economy is what I shall call the *'neo-classical' position* because it is based on the theories of Western neo-classical economics. This position, whose tenets have guided American policy toward Japan and which is strongly represented in the American economics profession, argues that Japanese economic behaviour is explicable almost entirely in terms of the conventional theories of Western economics. According to this position, the extraordinary success of the Japanese economy can be explained almost entirely by market factors. It is not necessary to invoke the uniqueness of Japanese culture or the interventionist policies of the Japanese state. Market rationality, in effect, is the key to Japanese behaviour.[3] The principal policy recommendation of this position is that the United States should continue to pursue a liberal economic policy toward the Japanese.

The second or what has come to be known as the *revisionist position* is that the Japanese political economy and Japanese economic behaviour are fundamentally 'different' from Western economic behaviour and, for at least some but certainly not all adherents of this persuasion, Japan cannot be understood by the theories of Western economics.[4] The revisionist argument, which is held by an influential group of Japan experts and appears to be influential in the Clinton Administration, emphasises the importance of political and non-market factors in explaining Japanese economic success. In particular, the revisionists stress the unique features of Japanese society, the crucial role of the Japanese state in directing economic development through national, industrial and other policies, and the peculiar structure of Japanese business. The United States, they argue, should take the uniqueness of the Japanese into account in the formulation of its trade and other economic policies towards the Japanese.

The neo-classical and revisionist positions set forth fundamentally different interpretations of the Japanese challenge and proper course of action for the United States. If, for example, the arguments of the more extreme proponents of the revisionist school are accepted, Japan is seeking to destroy American industry and poses a major security threat to the United States. In response, the United States should adopt a set of trade, industrial, and other policies to defend the American economy and contain Japanese expansionism. The neo-classical position, on the other hand, regards Japan as a normal economy whose policies are explicable in market terms and whose expansionism will slow as Japan closes the economic and technological gap with the West. For this position, extraordinary policies or measures are not really required to deal with Japan. In the following sections, these conflicting interpretations of the nature of the Japanese problem will be discussed.

The Neo-classical Position

The neo-classical interpretation is that Japanese economic behaviour and outstanding success can be explained almost entirely in rational economic and market terms. The fundamental principles of conventional Western economics such as the law of comparative advantage and the law of supply and demand hold as much for Japan as they do for any other economy. The principal economic actors in Japan, as elsewhere, are individual firms and consumers, motivated by the goal of maximising their economic interests in response to market signals. These interpreters of Japanese economic behaviour reject the idea of a 'Japan Inc.' under the leadership of the Japanese state pursuing an overall economic and political strategy of world economic conquest. Instead, their 'Japan' is an intensely competitive market in which Japanese corporations behave much like their American counterparts. Although the neo-classical position accepts that the Japanese government has provided a very favourable environment for business activities, the credit for Japanese economic success, they believe, belongs almost exclusively to Japanese business.

While the advocates of this position may differ among themselves on the weight they assign to Japanese government policies, uniquely Japanese institutions and Japanese cultural traits in determining economic outcomes, they all agree that impersonal market factors more than anything else account for Japanese economic behaviour and economic success. As one neo-classical authority has put it, it is not the uniqueness of the Japanese political system or Japanese culture that has brought about Japanese economic success but market rationality. In so far as protectionist and similar policies can be attributed to the Japanese, these undesirable forms of economic behaviour are the product of a Japan that is rapidly moving in the same direction as other advanced economies. In time these questionable practices, which they believe have actually been economically detrimental to Japanese economic development, will disappear as Japan becomes a mature, developed economy.

What the Japanese government has wisely done, they emphasise, is to pursue policies that have encouraged a high rate of productivity growth. The Japanese state has pursued stable macroeconomic policies in contrast to the 'stop and go' policies of the United States. The Japanese government has created incentives for the Japanese to enjoy the highest savings and investment rates in the world. The Japanese have invested heavily in technological research and excellent education. Through policies that benefit the overall Japanese economy rather than specific industrial sectors, the Japanese state has created the endowments of inexpensive capital, productive knowledge, and skilled labour that account for Japan's economic success and trading patterns. In short, the rapid accumulation of productive factors and intelligent business leadership have produced the Japanese economic miracle.[5]

In opposition to the revisionists, the neo-classical position denies that Japanese industrial policy and other forms of state intervention in the economy at the microeconomic or industrial sector level have had any significant, positive effect on the overall performance of the Japanese economy. The Japanese state, they believe, has been no more successful than other governments in targeting specific industries for development. On the contrary, they point out, the Ministry for Industry and Investment (MITI), which is responsible for Japanese industrial policy, has made a number of serious errors of omission and commission. For example, MITI has encouraged wasteful investment in industrial sectors such as steel and shipbuilding, where Japan no longer has had a comparative advantage. MITI also gave almost no support to the development of the Japanese automobile industry and even opposed the entry of Honda into the automobile business. Furthermore, the Japanese government has made a fool of itself in supporting dubious projects; the so-called fifth-generation computer project is a notable example. In short, MITI's record of directing industrial development, they contend, does not support the claim that Japanese industrial policy and 'Japan, Inc.' account for Japanese success.

In the opinion of the neo-classical school, cultural factors such as the alleged unique Japanese national character or the Confucian historical tradition are of minor importance in explaining Japanese economic behaviour or the structure of the Japanese economy. For example, Harvard Business School Professor W. Carl Kester in his book *Japanese Takeovers: The Global Contest for Corporate Control* uses essentially two well-established Western economic theories - the theory of transaction costs and agency theory - to provide an excellent explanation of the Japanese system of industrial groupings (*keiretsu*).[6] This type of industrial organisation, characterised by cross-holdings of corporate stocks and stable informal ties among firms, such as Mitsubishi and Mitsui, he demonstrates, is prevalent in Japan because it is remarkably efficient and not, as many foreigners and even Japanese believe, because of some uniquely Japanese cultural traits such as cultural exclusivity and love of social harmony. Moreover, contrary to the arguments of at least some revisionists, he shows that these business organisations have been very dynamic and have changed greatly over a century and more in response to economic, technological, and other developments.[7]

One of the most succinct and persuasive defences of the neo-classical position has been provided by Charles Wolf. In his opinion, the main characteristics of Japanese economic behaviour - rapid economic growth, aggressive development of high-tech industry, and large export surpluses - can be explained in conventional economic terms rather than having to employ the sinister explanations of Japan's critics.[8] While he concedes that there is some validity in the criticisms of Japanese behaviour by the revisionists, the most important explanations of Japanese success, he argues, are four simple factors:

(1) Investment. Japan's rate of domestic investment averaged about 24 per cent of its GNP in the late 1980s compared with only about 16 per cent for the United States;

(2) Savings. Japan's domestic savings rate averaged 28 per cent of GNP in the late 1980s compared with only 13 or 14 per cent for the United States;

(3) Labour. Japan's work-force is highly disciplined, trained, skilled, industrious and literate;

(4) Management. Japanese managers are energetic, experienced, and competent and, through domestic and international competition, have earned to strive continuously to cut production costs and raise the quality of their products.

As Wolf concludes, the high investment rate accounts for nearly all the difference in average annual growth rates - about 2 or 3 per cent - between Japan and the USA. It also explains Japan's strong performance in those sectors - automobiles, consumer electronics, and semiconductors - that are capital-intensive and heavily reliant on research and development. Savings and investment taken together account for Japan's persistent huge trade surplus (i.e. the excess of savings over investment) and the persistent deficits of the USA. The extraordinary quality of Japanese labour and management account for the high rate of productivity growth. In addition, as another observer has pointed out, Japanese business leaders have taken to heart the theories of Joseph Schumpeter regarding the importance of technological innovation and have always been highly entrepreneurial.

The neo-classical position rejects the warning of revisionists that the United States and the rest of the world is threatened by an impending Japanese economic ascendancy. Underlying this generally complacent attitude toward Japanese economic success is what economists call the catching-up or *convergence theory* of Japanese economic success.[9] According to this interpretation, Japan's high rate of productivity growth and overall economic growth have been due to a lag that will slow down and level off as Japan catches up with the West. Japan, they argue, has had the great advantage of economic backwardness. Japanese business has been able to borrow technology and ideas from the more advanced Western economies. In addition, Japanese wage rates have been lower than those of their Western competitors. As Wolf and others believe, in the next few years these advantages will change. The savings rate will fall because of increased consumer demand and the ageing of the population. Investment could fall as a result of tighter capital markets and a relocation of resources from the private to public sectors. Productivity growth could also fall in response to social and economic developments. As Japan catches up with the West and convergence takes place, the challenge posed by the high rate of Japanese growth and international competitiveness will become much less pressing. In the meanwhile, although adherents of this position might advocate one or another reform of the American economy, they believe that there is no pressing need to change America's essentially liberal and multilateral economic policies toward Japan and the rest of the world.

The Revisionist Position

In contrast to the neo-classical position, the core of the revisionist thesis is that the Japanese political economy and Japanese economic behaviour are fundamentally different from Western economies and Western economic behaviour. While the revisionists differ among themselves in their emphasis on cultural, historical or political factors in explaining the peculiarities of Japanese economic behaviour, they argue as a group that the Japanese state, the Japanese private sector, and Japanese consumers have different economic objectives from their Western counterparts and play by fundamentally different rules from those of the West. Because of its uniqueness and many anomalies, the Japanese political economy, they argue, cannot be understood by Western neo-classical economics and its theories based on the assumption of a universal rational economic actor.[10] In fact, they contend, Japan has been so successful precisely because it has defied the teachings of Western economics. The Japanese, they claim, have violated the canons of Western economics such as the belief in free trade and the guiding principle of comparative advantage. Moreover, they claim, it is a very serious error on the part of the West to discount these fundamental differences and to base economic and other policies on the naive assumption that the Japanese are 'just like us'.

Although the number of revisionist writings has reached flood-tide, the most influential and respected statement of the revisionist thesis is Chalmers Johnson's *MITI and the Japanese Miracle* (1982).[11] In this detailed and learned analysis of the causes of Japan's remarkable post-war economic growth, Johnson argues that Japan is an authoritarian 'capitalist development state' whose overriding purpose is to make Japan the dominant economic power in the world. The Japanese, he points out, have different concepts of the state and the market; the relationship of state and market is very different from that of the West. In contrast to the non-interventionist doctrine of the United States in particular, the 'economic high command' of the Japanese state, composed of MITI, the Ministry of Finance, and other agencies, is said to plan and manage the Japanese economy. Through their industrial policies and the technique of 'administrative guidance', government bureaucrats effectively set the course of Japanese economic development. According to the revisionist interpretation, the Japanese market and private corporations are essentially subordinate to the economic and political objectives of the Japanese state. Thus, the guiding and highly visible hand of the Japanese state rather than the invisible hand of the market, according to Johnson and other revisionists, explains Japanese behaviour and the Japanese economic miracle.

According to Johnson and other revisionists, the Japanese have a different concept of the market and economic competition than that which exists in the West, especially the United States. Whereas the objective of Western capitalism is to benefit the consumer, the objective of Japanese capitalism is to benefit Japanese producers and ultimately the Japanese state. As Peter Drucker has made the point, Japan is an investment-driven rather than, as in the United States, a consumption-driven society.[12] The Japanese are also said to have a very different conception of economic competition. Competition in Japan, the revisionists argue, is highly constrained by the Japanese bureaucracy because the Japanese regard too much competition as socially disruptive and economically wasteful. While competition in Japan can be fierce, it is largely cartelised among the *keiretsu* and other major industrial groupings. Moreover, the market is highly segmented with restricted access to particular markets. Outside firms, whether they are Japanese or foreigners, tend to be kept out of these segmented markets. Foreign goods have to pass through a Byzantine system of informal import barriers that restrict imports and keep the prices of foreign goods too high to be really competitive with Japanese products. In crude terms, the revisionists characterise the differences between the two systems in the following terms. In the Western free market system, if it is not explicitly prohibited it is permitted; in Japan's more restricted and regulated market, if it is not explicitly permitted, it is prohibited. Thus, in contrast to the Western commitment to free trade and open markets, Japan is said to be a neo-mercantilist society whose ultimate political goal is Japanese economic and technological superiority.

In addition to their emphasis on the nature of the Japanese state and its guiding hand in the functioning of the economy, the revisionists point to the structure of the Japanese economy and peculiar aspects of Japanese economic behaviour. The structure of the economy and the private economic practices of Japanese business, they argue, make it very difficult for foreigners to penetrate the Japanese market despite the absence of formal trade barriers. Among these non-tariff barriers that serve to keep out foreign goods, the revisionists emphasise complex import regulations, the ancient distribution system of small retail stores frequently tied to particular producers, and the structure of Japanese industry. Moreover, Japanese officials, they point out, have a long tradition of making arbitrary decisions whose purpose is to 'protect' Japanese consumers against foreign goods. Japanese laws favour a distribution system based on 'mom and pop' stores frequently tied to distributors and manufacturers who discriminate against foreign goods. The personal and institutional links among Japanese businesses make it very difficult for the goods and services of foreign firms to reach the Japanese consumer. Other distinctive features that set Japan apart from Western capitalism include the prevalence and toleration of collusive business practices; the highly integrated structure of Japanese business (i.e. the *keiretsu* form of industrial organisation); the existence of a host of informal and non-transparent trade barriers; a docile and subservient labour force; discriminatory regulatory and contractual practices; a powerful bias among consumers against non-Japanese products; unprecedented favouritism toward agricultural and land-holding interests; and a cultural antipathy toward all outsiders. In brief, the Japanese economy functions to advantage Japanese producers and discriminate against foreign producers.

The revisionists reject the convergence theory of the neo-classical position that Japan is changing and becoming more 'like us' as it closes the economic and technological gap with the United States and other Western countries. While revisionists acknowledge that some aspects of the Japanese economy may be adapting to internal and external developments, Japan, they assert, is not fundamentally changing. The purpose of Japanese economic policy continues to be the desire to surpass the West and dominate the world economically; this overriding objective, they argue, will never change and Japan will continue to subordinate all other objectives to its achievement. The nature of the Japanese political economy and especially the directing role of the state will never change. As Karel van Wolferen, one of the doyens of the revisionist school, argues in his best-selling book *The Enigma of Japanese Power*, Japan is really incapable of changing and saving itself from 'its excesses'.[13] Among these excesses is the desire of the Japanese to pursue what the revisionists call Japan's 'adversarial' trade strategy. In the next section, I shall discuss neo-classical and revisionist interpretations of Japanese external economic behaviour and whether Japan has a long-term economic strategy that poses simply an economic challenge or an actual economic threat to the West.

The Issue of Japanese Overseas Economic Expansionism

Three separate issues are involved in the neo-classical-revisionist debate over Japan's economic expansionism and its significance for other countries. The first issue is the huge Japanese trade surplus, especially with the United States, that has persisted since the mid-1980s; the persistence of this large surplus has become a significant irritant in American-Japanese relations. The second issue is what many critics regard as the peculiar or distinctive pattern of Japanese trade; in contrast to other advanced industrial countries, Japan imports a small (albeit growing) fraction of the manufactured goods it consumes. And the third issue is the rapid overseas expansion of Japanese corporations; this development suggests to many critics a deliberate Japanese strategy of economic conquest. However, prior to discussing the neo-classical and revisionist interpretations of these issues, the issues themselves should be discussed briefly.

The Trade Imbalance: The issue of the Japanese trade surplus, especially with the United States, is quite straightforward. Since the early 1980s, the overall Japanese trade surplus has ballooned. Following the Plaza Agreement of September 1985, and the subsequent appreciation of the yen, the Japanese trade surplus dropped considerably. Subsequently, it began to rise again with the slowing of the Japanese economy as a result of the collapse of the so-called 'bubble' economy of the late 1980s. In 1993, the Japan's overall trade surplus with the United States set a new record of over $120 billion. In brief, for the better part of a decade, Japan has had an immense trade surplus with the United States and the rest of the world with almost no prospect that it will go away soon.

The Distinctive Pattern of Japanese Trade: In contrast to other advanced industrialised economies, Japan imports a remarkably small share of the manufactured goods it consumes. Or, to put the matter another way, unlike other advanced economies, a very small fraction of Japanese trade constitutes a two-way flow of trade within particular industries. In more formal terms, whereas a substantial fraction of American and European trade tends to be *intra-industry* trade, Japanese trade is largely *inter-industry* trade. *Intra-industry* trade entails the exporting and importing of goods in the same economic sectors such as exportation of one type of consumer electronics and the importation of another type of consumer electronics. *Inter-industry* trade, on the other hand, entails the exporting and importing of goods in different economic sectors such as the exporting of manufactured goods and the importing of raw materials. Thus Japan imports mainly food, raw materials, and fuels and exports mainly motor vehicles and other manufactures.[14]

The anomaly of Japan's trading pattern may be demonstrated by contrasting it to the more 'normal' German pattern. Germany, which has traditionally been a much more important exporter than Japan and, until reunification, tended to have an overall trade surplus in manufactured goods, also imports many of the manufactured goods it consumes. Moreover, German trade tends to be intra-industry trade; for example, Germany both imports and exports automobiles. In addition, whereas Japanese trade is highly concentrated in a few industrial sectors, especially automobiles, consumer electronics, and auto parts, German exports are highly diversified in terms of products as well as foreign markets. The United States, which is the world's largest exporter, has a trade pattern similar to the German. These fundamental differences between trans-Atlantic and trans-Pacific trade are an important factor in explaining why Americans and Germans, for example, have a low level of trade friction with each other and why many Americans and some Europeans are irritated by Japan's peculiar trading pattern.

Moreover, the fact that some of the industrial sectors affected by Japanese exports are major sources of blue-collar employment, are geographically concentrated in particular regions of the country and are suffering from technological unemployment greatly magnifies the political impact of Japanese exports. Another factor is that, although Japan is making a determined effort to diversify its export markets, the United States has been and will continue to be for some time the major market for its exports; the largest fraction of the overall Japanese trade surplus in fact comes from its bilateral trade with the United States. Lastly, as the Japanese continue to move rapidly up the technological ladder into sectors that American firms regard as their turf, more and more American firms feel threatened by their competitiveness. For all the above reasons, therefore, the reasons for and the legitimacy of the peculiar trading pattern of Japanese trade have become very controversial and a matter of intense debate between the neo-classical and revisionist schools.

The Global Expansion of Japanese Corporations: The third issue irritating American-Japanese relations is the rapid expansion of Japanese direct investment in the American economy and East Asia. This Japanese corporate expansionism into the American economy and, I would add, the European economies began in the late 1980s as an effort to jump over rising trade barriers, as a response to the Plaza Agreement that resulted in a substantial appreciation of the yen, and as a means to reduce trade friction. While Japanese investment in high visibility real estate such as the purchases of Rockefeller Centre and the Pebble Beach Golf Club were highly visible symbols of the Japanese 'takeover' of the American economy, the most significant controversy has been the fear that the Japanese are implanting in the American economy the Japanese system of industrial groupings (*keiretsu*) and are taking over America's high-tech industries. While the most contentious issue is automobiles and auto parts, Japanese investment in other American industries has also become highly controversial.

The Neo-classical Explanation

The neo-classical position regarding these trade and investment issues is quite simple and straightforward: the Japanese trade surplus, the distinctive pattern of Japanese trade, and Japanese overseas investment can be explained by the basic theories of neo-classical economics. For example, the American trade deficit and the Japanese trade surplus are explained almost entirely by the differential savings rates of the two countries. For reasons that will not be elucidated here, the savings rate of a country and its trade balance tend to be equal. The United States traditionally has had a low savings rate that has been lowered even further by the huge federal budget deficit; under these circumstances, it is inevitable that the United States will have a trade deficit, if not with Japan then with some other country or countries. Japan, on the other hand, has an extraordinarily high savings rate and consequently will have a huge trade surplus. Thus, for the neo-classical position, Japan's trade surplus represents Japanese frugality rather than some devious economic machinations.

According to the neo-classical position, Japan's alleged distinctive trading pattern can be explained almost entirely by the conventional theory of comparative advantage. The Heckscher-Ohlin factor endowment theory of trade, they point out, tells us that Japan's pattern of trade is a product of Japan's factor endowments, e.g. a shortage of raw materials, a highly skilled labour force, and low-cost capital. Any other country, such as Italy, for example, with similar factor endowments would exhibit the same trading pattern of exporting manufactured goods and importing primarily raw materials. Thus, it is quite natural for Japan to export automobiles, consumer electronics, and auto parts; it is also quite natural that Japan imports a small percentage of the manufactured goods it consumes. The impact of this trading pattern is magnified because, unlike Germany or the United States, Japan has no large wealthy neighbours with whom it can trade.[15] It is, therefore, ridiculous to suggest, as do the revisionists, that Japan systematically targets for destruction American and other Western high-tech industries.

With respect to Japanese foreign direct investment in the United States, the neo-classical position argues that these overseas activities of Japanese corporations can be explained primarily in terms of market forces. In particular, this new phase of Japanese economic behaviour is due to the substantial appreciation of the yen that followed the Plaza Agreement. In effect, Japanese corporations in pursuing a more aggressive overseas investment strategy are only following in the footsteps and catching up with their American and European rivals. Contrary to alarmist critics, the neo-classical position argues that these Japanese investments benefit the American and other foreign economies. Moreover, they point out that there is no evidence to support the charge that Japanese foreign investment in the United States poses an economic or political threat. The most authoritative study of the subject by Edward M. Graham and Paul R.

Krugman concludes that 'Japanese FDI in the United States does not justify tremendous worry'; in fact, most of the effects are 'beneficial'. Japanese firms, they find, do not behave essentially differently from other foreign firms or American firms for that matter.[16] In brief, the Japanese are behaving in the way that any rational economic actor would behave.

The Revisionist Explanation

For the revisionists, Japan's huge trade surplus and distinctive pattern of trade constitutes *prima-facie* evidence that Japan is an unfair trader and is seeking to destroy American and other foreign competitors. Foreign manufactures, especially those that are directly competitive with domestic Japanese products, revisionists contend, are systemically discriminated against and denied access to the Japanese market. For example, economist Robert Lawrence, currently a professor at Harvard University's Kennedy School, is reported to have characterised Japan as 'the scourge of the world trading system'. Japan, he has charged, deliberately discriminates against American imports and should be importing 40 per cent more manufactured goods.[17] At the same time as Japan pursues a trade offensive against other countries, the Japanese, according to Lawrence and other critics, pursue a strategy of pre-emptive investment. That is to say, Japan excludes foreign goods from its domestic market until Japanese firms have made the necessary investments and have become sufficiently strong to defeat foreign competition anywhere in the world.

Revisionist economist Laura Tyson, who is Chair of President Clinton's Council of Economic Advisers and a principal author of the Administration's 'result-oriented' trade strategy towards Japan, challenges the applicability of conventional trade theory to Japanese behaviour. Instead, she suggests that Japanese policies of protection, preclusive investment and industrial targeting over the post-war period should be looked at. The purpose of these policies, she argues, has been to create Japan's competitive advantage in the targeted sector by keeping foreign competitors out of the targeted sector until Japanese firms have established a stronghold in the sector. Japan, she argues, has consistently pursued market-closing or exclusionary policies in one sector after another. These protectionist policies, through fostering economies of scale and movement down the earning curve, reduce Japan's production costs and thus have a permanent effect on Japanese competitiveness. As a result, when the Japanese market in the targeted sector is finally opened, Japanese firms are strong and competitive enough to resist foreign competition. In brief, she argues, the structure of the Japanese economy and of Japanese trade are a product of the Japanese state and its industrial policies rather than the conventional law of comparative advantage.[18]

The most serious charge of the revisionists is that Japan pursues what Peter Drucker has labelled an *'adversarial' trade policy*. According to Chalmers Johnson, 'adversarial trade means that a country tends not to import any of the products it exports'. This type of trade is in contrast to 'competitive trade', in which firms and consumers in a country manufacture, sell, and purchase a wide range of goods from all over the world depending only on their preferences and comparative shopping'.[19] The purpose of Japan's strategy of 'adversarial trade', e.g. inter-industry trade, the revisionists charge, is to target and destroy deliberately and systematically American industry sector by sector. The two primary components of Japan's alleged policy of adversarial trade are the trade offensive against foreign industry and the combined techniques of import protectionism and preclusive investment strategy. Thus, whereas neo-classical writers regard Japan's distinctive pattern of inter-industry trade as a natural function of the country's factor endowments, the revisionists attribute it to Japan's long-term strategy of industrial conquest.

In opposition to the neo-classicals' favourable opinion regarding Japanese direct investment in the United States, the revisionists believe that this investment is but the most recent manifestation of the Japanese strategy to establish their industrial and technological dominance. The Japanese, revisionists charge, are systematically taking over the 'commanding heights' of the American economy. Moreover, while Japanese firms are free to invest in the United States, American firms are restricted from investing in Japan and thus their access to the Japanese market is greatly restricted. Of particular significance, while Japanese firms and government agencies are unwilling to share their most advanced technology with American firms, Japanese companies are said to be making a concerted effort to buy up American high-tech firms, purchase the basic research output of American universities, and obtain by every conceivable means America's technological secrets. The strategic objective of the Japanese, these critics believe, is to dominate those technologies and industrial sectors that will increasingly determine global economic and military power.

In brief, the revisionists regard the rapid overseas expansion of Japanese corporations as but a continuation of Japan's policy of 'adversarial trade' and attempt to gain control of the so-called 'commanding heights' of the contemporary high-tech economies. Fuelled by the appreciation of the yen, Japan is said to be using its huge capital resources to buy up relatively cheap high-tech industries, technological potential, and other assets of its competitors. The overseas subsidiaries of Japanese firms are held to be mere operations that import their highly-valued components from Japan itself. As the high-paying jobs, research, and high value-added production stays in Japan, these direct investments make only a minor contribution to providing good jobs and high-quality investments in the American economy.[20] In addition, Japan is charged with attempting once again to create an exclusive Co-prosperity Sphere in East and Southeast Asia from which American and other Western corporations will be excluded. Thus, from the perspective of the revisionists, while Japan's expansionist tactics have changed, its overall objective of achieving economic and technological supremacy has not changed.

Does Japan Have a Long-Term Economic and Political Strategy?

The most basic issue raised by the debate between the neo-classical and the revisionist positions is whether or not Japan has a long-range economic strategy. Is Japan, as the neo-classical position argues, a 'normal' economic society where everyone is trying 'to make a buck' (or better a 'yen')? Or is Japan, as the revisionists proclaim, playing a very different game and by very different rules in which national power and global domination is the name of the game? The contrasting answers to these questions, as we shall see below, lead the two positions to draw strongly opposed conclusions regarding how the United States should deal with the Japanese.

The Neo-classical Position

The major representatives of the neo-classical school believe that it is foolish to speak of Japan as such having a long-term economic strategy. While they acknowledge that some Japanese politicians and government officials undoubtedly harbour ambitions of economic conquest, it is impossible, except under very unusual circumstances, e.g. under wartime conditions, and only in the vaguest sort of way, to speak of a state or of a whole society having an economic strategy. States and societies, this position believes, are composed of individuals and groups with very different sets of private interests. Societies are simply too diverse and fragmented in their interests for its members to have a common set of economic objectives other than perhaps that of the pursuit of general economic welfare, and the idea of a unified strategy to achieve this goal or any other goal is absurd. On the other hand, the proponents of the neo-classical position would argue that individual Japanese corporations certainly do have objectives and have developed corporate strategies to achieve them. However, like other corporations throughout the world, that strategic objective is profit maximisation within the constraints of the market. In this respect, there is nothing unique about Japanese corporations. In brief, the revisionist position is that, although Japanese business presents a formidable competitive challenge, Japan itself does not pose a strategic threat to other countries.

The Revisionist Position

In contrast to this benign interpretation of Japanese behaviour, the revisionist school believes the Japanese state and society do have a long-term economic strategy that is inimical to American interests. However, two fundamentally different positions can be discerned within this school on the nature of this strategy and its implication for American policy. One group of revisionists believes Japanese behaviour is essentially defensive: the purpose of Japanese economic strategy is primarily to increase Japan's economic autonomy and political independence. The other group believes Japanese behaviour is offensive: the Japanese are said to be pursuing an aggressive or 'adversarial' trade strategy whose purpose is to destroy systematically the industries of other economies and dominate the world economy.

Among those revisionists who regard Japanese behaviour as essentially 'defensive', Clyde Prestowitz is perhaps the best example.[21] According to Prestowitz, the Japanese state, supported by the Japanese political consensus, has a long-term economic strategy whose overriding objectives are economic self-sufficiency and industrial equality with, if not actual superiority over, the West. This desire for economic equality and strategic rivalry with the West, Prestowitz argues, makes it impossible for the United States and other Western economies to establish a 'normal' working relationship with the Japanese. Japan is singular and plays by very different economic rules that put Americans in a disadvantageous position in all their dealings with the Japanese. Americans do not and never will understand Japanese behaviour, Prestowitz contends. It is, therefore, foolish and even dangerous to try to change Japanese society as, for example, the Structural Impediments Initiative (SII) negotiations attempt to do. The efforts of successive American Administrations to pressurise the Japanese into 'becoming more like us' only give rise to powerful nationalist reactions in Japan and equally dangerous frustrations in the United States. The better approach, Prestowitz believes, is to accept Japan for the mercantilist state that it is and attempt to work out a *modus vivendi* of some kind. Prestowitz and those other revisionists who share his opinion, therefore, advocate a policy of managed trade and similar negotiated arrangements rather than simply leaving trans-Pacific economic relations up to the market.

The other revisionist group believes Japan has a secret long-term strategy of economic conquest and constitutes a 'strategic threat' to the United States.[22] In their opinion, Japan has launched an economic *offensive* against the West. Through its trade and overseas investment, Japan is attempting to achieve economic and eventual political supremacy by systematically destroying the high-tech industries of the United States and other countries. For these critics, Japan's strategy of 'adversarial' trade, patterns of corporate expansionism, and social exclusivity demonstrate that Japan today, as in the 1930s, is once again seeking to dominate the Pacific and the rest of the world. Only the means to implement this strategy of overseas conquest are said to have changed. The Japanese army has been replaced by Japanese corporations as the instrument of foreign conquest. Unless Japan is stopped, they proclaim, Japan will one day attempt an economic Pearl Harbour. Therefore, if the world is to be spared a *Pax Nipponica* the Japanese long-term strategy of economic conquest must be contained and eventually defeated. Thus, for this position, the end of the Cold War between the United States and the Soviet Union has given way to a new Cold War between the two economic superpowers.

The Author's Assessment

Thus far this article has analysed the two dominant and contradictory positions in the United States regarding the nature of the Japan problem. In this concluding section of the article, I shall draw what I consider to be the important insights of each position and set forth what I hope is a more balanced assessment. In brief, my own position is that Japan is different and does pose a serious economic challenge to the United States and the rest of the world. However, I do not find convincing evidence that Japan is a security threat, at least under present circumstances. Of equal importance, recent developments suggest that Japan, as the neo-classical position argues, is changing, although it may not be changing as much as this position would like us to believe. In fact a changed Japan might be an even more formidable economic competitor.

A Late Industrialiser with Japanese Characters

The Japanese political economy is different in important ways from those of the West. Much like Germany in the late 19th century and, to a lesser extent, Russia in the 20th century, the Japanese economy has been shaped by Japan's overwhelming political and economic objective of catching up with the more advanced economies. Like these other late industrialisers, the pursuit of this objective has meant a concerted national effort and a greater role for the state in the development of the economy. As a result, although many of the differences between the Japanese and other capitalist economies are more of degree than of kind, the revisionists are essentially correct that Japan is different, and is different in a number of fundamental ways. These differences include Japan's long-term economic and political strategy, those unique features of the Japanese political economy such as the key role of business groupings and the very high savings rate that distinguish it from other advanced capitalist societies, and the distinctive pattern of Japanese trade and overseas investment.

The Japanese conception of the purpose of economic affairs is more political and 'collective' than that of Western society and, particularly, the American emphasis on the welfare of the consumer and economic individualism. The Japanese do have a more restrictive concept of the market. The central role of the Japanese state in directing the economy is unknown in any other advanced industrial economy outside the former socialist bloc. The overall structure and private practices of Japanese business based on the *keiretsu* and similar industrial groupings are uniquely Japanese. In addition the attitudes of Japanese labour, the Japanese consumer and the Japanese public towards their own society and outsiders most certainly do set Japan apart. In summary, Johnson's conception of Japan as a 'capitalist development state' is a very apt characterisation.

A story told by G. C. Allen, the distinguished British authority on Japanese economic history, provides an important insight into Japanese economic psychology and national ambitions. At the end of the Second World War, American and other economists advised the Japanese to rebuild their war-torn economy on the theory of comparative advantage. Japan's comparative advantage, these economists pointed out, lay with labour-intensive products. The Japanese bureaucratic elite, however, had different ideas and would have nothing to do with what they considered to be an American effort to relegate Japan to the low end of the economic and technological spectrum. Instead, MITI and the other members of the Japanese high command set their sights on making the new Japan into the economic and technological equal, if not actually the superior, of the West. This objective continues to be the driving force of Japanese society.

In fact, ever since the Meiji Restoration of 1868, Japan has had an economic and political strategy of catching up with the more economically advanced West and thereby maintaining its political independence. Most American and Japanese scholars in fact acknowledge that Japan has traditionally had two major goals. As the distinguished Japanese economist Ryutaro Komiya has written, since the Meiji Restoration the overriding goals of Japan have been those of 'making the economy self-sufficient' and 'catching up with the West'.[23] This second ambition in turn once meant building a strong army as well as becoming an industrial power. While the disastrous defeat in the Second World War caused the Japanese people to abandon militarism, the ambition that Japan should became a powerful industrial and technological nation, Komiya points out, was actually strengthened after the war. These ambitions in practice have meant a concerted effort through industrial policy and other forms of state interventionism to challenge and, by implication, surpass the West in one industrial sector after another through a continual ascent up the ladder of ever more advanced technology.

The essence of Japan's post-war economic policy can best be characterised as neo-mercantilism.[24] In the words of Mike Mochizuki, *neo-mercantilism* involves the practice of state assistance, regulation, and protection of specific industrial sectors to enhance their international competitiveness and ultimately to achieve national pre-eminence over the 'commanding heights' of the world economy. The origins of this strategic objective, as we have already noted, lie in Japan's experience as a late developer and its strong sense of economic and political vulnerability. But in addition the source of this powerful drive arises out of the Japanese people's overwhelming belief in their uniqueness, in the superiority of their culture, and in their manifest destiny to lead Asia. In effect, the overall Japanese economic and political strategy has become one of achieving through peaceful means what they failed to achieve through military force.

The revisionists are also correct in contending that the structure of the Japanese economy is different, but in a sense they are right for the wrong reasons. Japanese capitalism is different, but the reasons have as much to do with market rationality and economic factors as they do with the uniqueness of Japanese culture or the role of the state in the economy. Many of the essential features of the Japanese political economy are explicable in terms of Western economics. As Kester demonstrates in his study of Japanese corporate takeovers, the nature and governance of Japanese corporations are fundamentally different from American and, to a somewhat lesser extent, continental European corporations.[25] In borrowing the term 'governance' from the realm of politics, Kester is referring to the unique purposes, organising principles and basic structure of Japanese corporations. In contrast to American capitalism the purpose of the Japanese firm is to serve the interests of the *stakeholders* rather than the stockholders; the stakeholders in the Japanese firm include the firm's banker, component suppliers and other firms in addition to labour, corporate management, and shareholders. The basic organising principle is mutual trust among the stakeholders leading to the establishment of long-term working relationships among business groupings.

As Kester points out, owing to its system of corporate governance, the Japanese firm and the industrial grouping of which they are a part are a highly efficient mode of industrial organisation. Contrary to Western perceptions, it is a market rational institution and not a mysterious product of Japanese culture. As Japanese and foreign observers point out, it has a number of characteristics that make it a formidable competitor in world markets. It is especially adaptable to changing market and technological circumstances. It has tended to enjoy lower capital costs than foreign firms. As it is freed from stockholder pressures, it is able to take a very long view of business and technological opportunities.

The basic problem with the Japanese industrial system and especially the *keiretsu* is that it is a closed system and excludes all 'outsiders'.[26] By 'outsider' I mean everyone who is not a member of the alliance of stakeholders who share the monopolistic rents generated by this oligopolistic form of business organisation. This includes Japanese as well as foreigners. The nature of the Japanese system of corporate governance means that it is very difficult for non-Japanese to become stakeholders. This fact has become a major cause of resentment by non-Japanese as Japanese corporations, even though the motives are defensive, as the neo-classical position argues, take over more and more of the high-tech firms and growth industries of other countries. While others certainly benefit, the Japanese stakeholders are by far the greatest beneficiaries. As Sylvia Ostry, a former Canadian trade official, has pointed out, the resulting problem of asymmetrical access of Japanese and non-Japanese firms to one another's markets and technology has been a major issue in trade negotiations.[27]

For these reasons, the exclusive nature of the Japanese industrial groupings is regarded as especially pernicious by non-Japanese, and with good reason. The fact that Japanese firms can easily take over American and European firms, while the reverse is very difficult, constitutes a very vexing political issue. It means that Japanese firms can establish themselves in foreign markets and gain access to important foreign technology while foreigners cannot do the same in Japan. This situation is a legitimate basis for criticism of the Japanese. Thus, the fact that American firms can invest in German markets and share in that economy's monopolistic rents decreases the tendency of Americans to complain about German economic success. This problem of differential access is one of the most important raised by the overseas expansion of Japanese firms.[28]

Japanese Economic Expansion

With regard to Japanese overseas economic expansionism, both the neo-classical and revisionist positions are partially correct. The neo-classical answer to why Japan has such a huge and continuing trade surplus and, correspondingly, why the United States has such a large and continuing trade deficit is essentially correct, at least at one level of analysis. The trade imbalance, as the neo-classical position argues, is due primarily to the differential saving rates of the two societies. At another and deeper level of analysis, however, why does Japan in fact have such a high savings rate and imports so very few foreign manufactures that compete against domestic products? The answers to these and similar questions can be found in the underlying political interests, governmental policies, and cultural factors that influence and in so many ways determine the structure of the Japanese economy and the economic behaviour of the Japanese people. Or, to put it another way, as the revisionists emphasise, a *political economy* answer must be sought for the reasons for Japan's economic success and trade surplus.

One example may suffice to make the point. As the neo-classical position correctly argues, the high rate of Japanese savings has been a major factor in Japan's export success and equally high rate of business investment. However, these neo-classical writers neglect the crucial question of why Japan has a high savings rate in the first place. They fail to take appropriate account of the role of the Japanese state and Japanese policies in promoting the high rate of Japanese savings that in the past at least lowered the cost of capital for Japanese firms and gave them a definite advantage over foreign competitors. Ironically, the reason for this difference in capital costs was a result of the American occupation and not some inherent frugality embedded in Japanese culture.

Perhaps the most convincing explanation of Japan's unique pattern of trade is Edward Lincoln's *Japan's Unequal Trade*.[29] While using essentially neo-classical economic methods in his analysis of Japanese trade and rejecting the appellation 'adversarial', Lincoln's study largely supports the revisionists' position on the reasons for Japan's peculiar trading pattern while at the same time rejecting the revisionist solutions of managed trade and industrial policy. As he demonstrates in his careful and dispassionate analysis, the answers to the questions why Japan imports a relatively small amount of manufacturing goods and has almost a total absence of intra-industry trade are essentially the same.

The primary reason Japan imports so few manufactured goods and has almost no two-way trade in the same industrial sectors is explained, he argues, principally by the history of Japanese industrialisation with its emphasis on catching up with the West and the overwhelming Japanese concern with economic vulnerability and political independence. The resulting economic behaviour - exclusivity, industrial policies, and trade barriers - have continued to dominate the Japanese political economy even though Japan has caught up with the West and may in fact have surpassed it as an economic and technological power. In the absence of outside pressures, he does not believe Japan will change this inherited mentality.

As has already been noted, several aspects of Japanese economic behaviour and the structure of the Japanese economy set Japan apart and make it exceptionally difficult for foreign firms to export manufactured goods to Japan or to make direct investments in Japan. As Lincoln persuasively demonstrates, Japanese industrial policy, the policy of preclusive investment and outright protectionism deliberately keep out foreign manufactured goods, at least until Japanese firms have gained a strong foothold in the industry. In addition, both the low level of foreign manufactured imports and the low level of intra-industry trade are largely the result of the structure and highly restrictive private practices of Japanese business based, as it is, on very close and highly exclusive linkages among business firms. The *keiretsu* and similar types of integrated business organisations have meant that Japanese firms, through various techniques, have discriminated against foreign manufactures even though this practice is very costly to Japanese consumers.

Moreover, as the level of manufactured imports has increased in recent years largely because of the appreciation of the yen and the movement of Japanese producers to more advanced technologies, Japanese importers have favoured importing manufactured goods made overseas, especially in

East Asia, by the subsidiaries of Japanese corporations. In brief, Japanese firms prefer to import from the low end of the tech spectrum and reserve the high end, high valued-added products, for their home plants. In addition, following a long-established practice, Japanese importers and the Japanese distribution system keep the prices of imports artificially high, thus discouraging consumption. Additional and more subtle impediments to manufactured imports have been the inherited mentality of 'buying Japanese' and the Japanese mercantilist conception of international competition.

Unfortunately, as Lincoln points out, the Japanese seem conceptually unable or at least unwilling to accept the concept of intra-industry trade and that a problem of foreign access to their market even exists. The whole problem, they tend to argue in response to American criticisms regarding the openness of their market, arises because the United States is not 'competitive' or because Americans do not really try hard enough. Frequently, as did some of my Japanese students, they retort to American complaints about Japanese openness that the United States is no longer competitive in manufactured goods. While a particular American industry might no longer be competitive or might not be competitive with respect to a particular product area, it is absurd and runs totally contrary to the concept of comparative advantage, to speak of a national economy as being non-competitive. As neo-classical economists rightly point out, every country has a comparative advantage in something and, for this reason, over the long term international trade is commonly beneficial.

The Japanese, however, appear to accept their lack of intra-industry trade and the low level of foreign manufactured imports as perfectly natural. They apparently cannot conceive of an international economy in which several nations can share comparative advantage and exchange goods in the same industrial sector, that is, a trading world in which each economy has a comparative advantage with respect to particular products in the same industrial sectors and exchanges those goods with one another. This mentality entails a denial of the possibility of intra-industry trade and makes it very difficult for the Japanese to accept the reality of the type of intra-industry trade that characterises so much of the manufacturing trade between the United States and Western Europe.

The Japanese, Lincoln argues, tend to believe that international trade is a zero-sum game in which one nation's gain inevitably means another's loss. Japan, he points out, does not really accept the rationale of an open, liberal trading regime that is commonly beneficial to every nation. Japan's distinctive inter-industry trading pattern is in part a consequence of this belief. This type of trade is harmful to its trading partners and imposes a much higher adjustment cost than if Japanese trade were intra-industry.[30] Japan, however, has deviated from its trading practices and opened its market to the manufactured goods and direct investments of other countries only in response to external pressures. While Lincoln acknowledges that Japan is changing, he concludes his analysis with the observation that unless Japan becomes more willing to import more manufactured goods from other countries and accepts the necessity of intra-industry trade, the possibility of working out a satisfactory trading relationship with other countries seems highly unlikely. While Lincoln is hopeful and believes the West must keep trying to open Japan, his own sober analysis of the roots of the problem is not very encouraging with respect to ultimate success.[31] Until the Japanese recognise the reality of intra-industry trade, serious trade frictions with the United States and other countries will surely persist.

In summary, throughout the whole post-war period, three common and constant elements have defined Japanese policy:
(1) a steady and relentless movement up the technological ladder;
(2) the subordination of all other considerations to the promotion of export markets; and
(3) a remarkable capacity to adapt to changing conditions.

This last aspect of Japanese economic success is what Ronald Dore has paradoxically characterised as the 'flexible rigidities' of Japanese society.[32] In short, while the economic tactics may change, the long-term strategic objective of the Japanese and, so it would appear, the capacity of Japan to adapt successfully to a changing economic and political environment have not. These characteristics of Japan's overall economic strategy make Japan a formidable challenger, but do they add up to the revisionist warning that Japan poses a security threat to the West?

Does Japan Pose a Security Threat to the West?

In official report after official report, alarming evidence is mounting that Japan is taking the lead in one industrial or technological sector after another. As a consequence, many Americans and Europeans fear that Japan will achieve a monopoly in strategic technologies that could be exploited for political and eventually military purposes. Despite these concerns, it is very doubtful that Japan or any nation today could take the type of technological lead that Great Britain enjoyed in the 19th century and the United States has had throughout much of this century. The scope and the expense of modern science and technology are simply too great for any one nation to secure a dominant position in every important high-tech sector.[33] Moreover, as Japan has closed the scientific and technological gap with the West, its fundamental weaknesses in basic science and certain types of technological R&D have become of increasing significance. Already Japan is making major overtures for increased scientific and technological cooperation with Western industry and institutions of higher earning. Unless the United States and Western Europe are foolish enough to give away or weaken their own scientific and technological efforts, Japan will certainly be a very strong technological power, but it will not control all 'the commanding heights' of advanced technology. It is an exaggeration, therefore, to believe Japan could acquire such a commanding technological position that it would pose a threat to the rest of the world.

Of equal importance is the fact that Japan is changing. The idea promoted by some revisionists that the Japanese economy cannot change and is not responsive to market forces is not supported by the evidence. Over the course of the post-war period, changes in energy costs, in the value of the yen and the like have led to major changes in Japanese behaviour and economic policies. Japanese economic success is due precisely to the fact that Japanese firms are so very responsive to the market. Moreover, as Kester shows, while the structure and behaviour of Japanese businesses may be different, this fact does not mean they are contrary to economic rationality; on the contrary, Japanese economic structures and private economic practices do tend to be market-conforming and, in fact, are probably more efficient than most aspects of Western business. Moreover, while the Japanese market is restricted, as the revisionists point out, it is intensively competitive. This competition, however, tends to be Schumpeterian, that is, competition among a few oligopolistic firms based on product quality and technological innovation rather than being primarily price-competition. As Michael Porter argues, the super-competitive internal Japanese economy is a major reason for the global economic success of Japanese corporations.[34]

The neo-classical position is at least partially correct in contending that the convergence theory applies to Japanese economic development. As Japan has closed the economic and technological gap with the West, Japanese economic behaviour, Japanese economic performance, and Japanese economic policies have changed. In this chapter, it is impossible to record these important changes. However, three significant changes should be mentioned. First, as Japan has closed the economic and technology gap with the West, its rate of economic growth has slowed dramatically; whereas Japan was growing in double-digit figures in the past, the growth rate in recent years has slowed to less than 3 per cent.

Second, the ageing of the Japanese population has meant a substantial decline in the Japanese savings rate; from a high savings rate of 20 per cent in the 1970s, it had dropped to about 14 per cent in the 1990s and all indications are that it will continue to drop further. And, third, the Japanese labour force has declined and wages have risen, causing a severe shortage in certain occupations. The overall effect of these developments will eventually mean a decrease in Japanese competitiveness and decline in Japan's overall trade surplus.

At the time of writing, Japan is passing through one of the most dramatic periods since the end of the Second World War. As a consequence of public disgust with the corruption of the ruling Liberal Democratic Party, the collapse of the so-called 'bubble' economy of the 1980s and the resulting recession, and the substantial rise of the yen, Japan faces for the first time the prospect of substantial political and economic reforms. While this subject is of major importance and many years will necessarily pass before the outcome of these events unfolds, more and more Japanese leaders appreciate that Japan must change in fundamental ways. For example, in order to re-establish the profitability of its large corporations, Japan will of necessity need to eliminate many of the regulations that reduce the efficiency of the economy and have served to keep out foreign goods and investments. In addition, the domestic recession and the weakness of overseas demand are forcing Japan to shift away from the post-war emphasis on the strategy of export-led growth towards a much greater reliance on domestic-led economic growth, which in turn will redound to the advantage of foreign exporters. More speculatively, perhaps, Japan will have to do more to satisfy the growing desire of Japanese consumers for a better life. If Japan makes these reforms, which appear increasingly necessary, its political economy will have changed in significant ways; paradoxically, it should be pointed out, these reforms could very well make Japan an even more formidable economic challenge. If, on the other hand, Japan fails to make these changes, as the revisionist position would suggest, the result would be a much less formidable Japanese challenger.

Conclusion

Whether Japanese economic success constitutes merely a challenge to other countries, as the neo-classical exponents believe, or whether it poses a security threat to the West, as most revisionists believe, has become one of the central issues in the post-Cold War world. For many writers in the revisionist camp, Japan has displaced the Soviet Union as the foremost threat to the United States and Western Europe. The argument of this chapter is that the convergence theory is working sufficiently well inasmuch as Japanese economic and technological achievements are slowing and, as a result, Japan (whatever its intentions) could not become a security threat to the West. However, I should like to conclude with a cautionary anecdote. When I was a young boy growing up in rural and unsophisticated Vermont during the Second World War, my wiser seniors said that because of the Japanese people's slanted eyes they could never really learn to fly airplanes as well as Americans. This opinion was expressed, it should be noted, after the successful Japanese attack on Pearl Harbour. Many years later, when I was a junior member of the academic profession, a very distinguished Harvard neo-classical economist reassured a group of us over lunch at the American Academy of Arts and Sciences that Japan's rapid economic growth was nothing for Americans to be concerned about. This learned professor, expounding the convergence thesis, informed us that Japanese economic growth was due to their exploitation of American innovations. The Japanese themselves, he informed us, lacked creativity and were unable to invent technology of their own. Within a very few years, the American market would be flooded with a deluge of novel products and technologies invented in Japan. Some years later, this same distinguished Harvard professor at another such gathering in Boston told his listeners that the uniqueness and continuing remarkable success of the clever Japanese posed a serious threat to the American way of life. The moral of these tales from unsophisticated Vermonters and a sophisticated Harvard professor is that the Japanese should never be underestimated.

Notes

1. A discussion of earlier trade offensives can be found in W. Arthur Lewis, 'International Competition in Manufactures', *American Economic Review, Papers and Proceedings,* May 1957, XLVII, No. 2, pp. 578-87.
2. Samuel P. Huntington. 'America's Changing Strategic Interests', *Survival,* January-February 1991, Vol. XXXIII, No. 1, pp. 3-17.
3. Representatives of the neo-classical position include Hugh Patrick, Gary Saxonhouse and Charles Wolf.
4. The four most outspoken revisionists to whom the Japanese press refers to as the Gang of Four are Chalmers Johnson, Clyde Prestowitz, Karel van Wolferen and James Fallows. It should be pointed out that some critics of Japanese policies do use neo-classical techniques to explain the seemingly

unique aspects of Japanese economic behaviour. One example is W. Carl
Kester on Japanese corporations.

5. Edward Dension and William K. Chung, *How Japan's Economy Grew So Fast*, Washington, DC, The Brookings Institution, 1976.
6. Carl Kester, *Japanese Takeovers: The Global Contest for Corporate Control*, Cambridge, Harvard Business School Press, 1991.
7. *Ibid.*, pp. 51, 272.
8. Charles Wolf, 'Demystifying the Japanese Mystique', *The New York Times*, 26 May 1991, p. F11.
9. Convergence theory is discussed in William Baumol, Sue Anne Batey Blackman and Edward N. Wolff, *Productivity and American Leadership: The Long View*, Cambridge, The MIT Press, 1989.
10. Chalmers Johnson, 'The Japanese Political Economy: A Crisis in Theory', *Ethics and International Affairs*, 1988, Vol. 2, pp. 79-97.
11. Chalmers Johnson, *MITI and the Japanese Miracle: The Growth of Industrial Policy, 1925-1975*, Stanford, Stanford University Press, 1982.
12. Peter Drucker, *The Wall Street Journal*, 9 January 1990, p. A14.
13. Karel van Wolferen, *The Enigma of Japanese Power*, New York, Alfred A. Knopf, 1989.
14. *The Economist*, 11 January 1992, p. 61.
15. Gary A. Saxonhouse, 'Differentiated Products, Economies of Scale, and Access to the Japanese Market', in Robert C. Feenstra (ed.), *Trade Policies for International Competitiveness*, Chicago, University of Chicago Press, 1989.
16. Edward M. Graham and Paul R. Krugman, *Foreign Direct Investment in the United States*, Washington, DC, Institute for International Economics, 1989.
17. Quoted in *Newsweek*, 9 October 1989, p. 68.
18. Laura D'Andrea Tyson, 'Managed Trade: Making the Best of the Second Best', in Robert Z. Lawrence and Charles L. Schultze (eds), *An American Trade Strategy: Options for the Future*, Washington, DC, The Brookings Institution, 1990, pp. 142-94.
19. Chalmers Johnson, 'Their Behavior, Our Policy', *National Interest*, Fall 1989, No. 17 , p. 22.
20. Dennis J. Encarnation, *Rivals Beyond Trade: American Versus Japan in Global Competition*, Ithaca, Cornell University Press, 1992.
21. Clyde V. Prestowitz, Jr, *Trading Places: How We Allowed Japan to Take the Lead*, New York, Basic Books, 1988.
22. Huntington, *op. cit.*
23. Ryutaro Komiya, *The Japanese Economy: Trade, Industry, and Government*, Tokyo, University of Tokyo Press, 1990.
24. Mike M. Mochizuki, 'To Change or to Contain: Dilemmas of American Policy Toward Japan', in Kenneth A. Oye, Robert J. Lieber and Donald Rothchild (eds), *Eagle in a New World*, New York, Harper Collins, 1992, p. 339.

25. Kester, *op. cit.*, pp. 5, 7, 109.
26. *Ibid.*, pp. 54, 104, 110, 137.
27. Sylvia Ostry, *Governments and Corporations in a Shrinking World: Trade and Innovation in the United States, Europe, and Japan*, New York, Council on Foreign Relations, 1990.
28. Encarnation, *op. cit.*
29. Edward J. Lincoln, *Japan's Unequal Trade*, Washington, DC, The Brookings Institution, 1990.
30. *Ibid.*, p. 60.
31. *Ibid.*, p. 164.
32. Ronald Dore, *Flexible Rigidities: Industrial Policy and Structural Adjustment in the Japanese Economy, 1970-80*, London, Athlone Press, 1986.
33. Angus Maddison, *Phases of Capitalist Development*, New York, Oxford University Press, 1982, p. 42.
34. Michael Porter, *The Competitive Advantage of Nations*, New York, The Free Press, 1990.

Part II
Issues in Domestic Politics

4 The Need for Reform in Japanese Politics[1]

J.A.A. Stockwin

Introduction

At one time it was widely believed by Western observers of Japan that since Japanese culture was situationally relativist rather than individualistic and principled, the Japanese found little difficulty in changing direction fundamentally should the situation demand it.[2] It seemed to follow from this that Japan was prone to sudden changes of policy direction, and indeed that the most fundamental structures of politics, such as the current constitution or the political system itself, might be expected to change suddenly in response to new circumstances and pressures. Examples usually cited to support this case were the conversion of dissident *samurai* during the 1860s from rejection to emulation of advanced Western countries; the shift from semi-parliamentary politics in the 1920s to ultranationalism in the 1930s; and the rapid conversion from Emperor-centred military rule to a broadly liberal and democratic order after 1945.

Perhaps this attitude of Western observers is best summed up in General MacArthur's derogatory (and, as we would now say, racist) remark that the Japanese: 'are like all orientals; they have a tendency to adulate a winner'.[3] In other words, they were prone to 'get with the strength' and jump on to the latest bandwagon that seemed to promise success, being also in tune with their current interests, rather than stick with precepts of policy and organisation derived from universal principles, sincerely and consistently held.

Any comparison with the politics of major Western nations would show, of course, that consistency based on 'universal principles, sincerely and consistently held' was an ideal only patchily and imperfectly fulfilled in the politics of those nations. There is a whole history of venality, unprincipled adaptation to circumstances and free-for-all struggle between competing ideologies and interests for historians to document in virtually all of these countries.

More to the point, however, the political history of Japan since the immediate aftermath of the Second World War presents almost precisely the opposite picture to that identified by Herman Kahn and others, and derided by MacArthur. Rather than the unstable politics of a people chasing new trends and fashions with little regard for consistency or principle, politics and policy in Japan since the 1950s are now more commonly criticised for being excessively stable, in the sense that it is said to be lacking the capacity to adapt in the face of new situations and, in particular, lacking leadership sufficiently strong and able to effect needed change.

Interestingly enough, in some of the more extreme examples of Western criticism of Japanese politics for being excessively stable, there lurks the notion that somehow instability and lack of principle hides not far below the surface of excessive stability. Thus Brzezinski, writing in the early 1970s, argued that Japanese politics was 'metastable', that is on one plane it was extremely stable while on another it was brittle and potentially subject to radical destabilisation if subjected to certain kinds of shock.[4] Twenty years later, van Wolferen maintains the apparently paradoxical position that Japan has a 'system' but no leadership and that this creates what he terms the problem of 'no brakes and no pilot'.[5] In the van Wolferen view it is excessive stability (the 'system') that is dangerous because there is nobody capable of controlling what the system actually does.

The present writer is inclined to take a less alarmist view of Japanese politics than these views imply. The problem of perspective is a serious one confronting all observers of the Japanese political scene, whether those observers be Japanese or foreign, and it is important to avoid exaggeration. Too many foreign observers, brought face to face with a culture and body of political practice that seems unfamiliar, are prone to overstate its peculiarities. Meanwhile, some Japanese, whether concerned to insulate themselves from the outside world with notions of Japanese uniqueness, or conversely to attack their own system from an external perspective, also at times produce a distorted picture of how Japanese politics actually works.

In practice, though the politics of Japan has its own characteristic features, it is neither so peculiar nor so incapable of being subjected to comparison with other political systems as the kinds of criticism mentioned above appear to imply. While every political system is different, the Japanese system has many features in common with the political systems of other major nations with productive and sophisticated economies. It is from this fundamental standpoint that this chapter is written.

Having said this, we should not fall into the complacent and conservative view that Japanese politics lacks problems or has no need of reform. While from many perspectives, Japanese political stability has produced benefits for the nation over many years, the relative absence of change in the system over the same period has arguably led to a kind of political sclerosis that may need radical reform to recover. This is said in full realisation that in certain circumstances reform of a working system of government may not necessarily lead to improvement. The point is, however, that the absence of reform is not a panacea either.

It has become something of a cliché in Japan that the nation enjoys a first-class economy but a third-rate political system. Whether and to what extent this is correct is a matter for individual judgement, but the fact that it is said so widely suggests that dissatisfaction about the way politics is conducted may lead to serious attempts at reform in the foreseeable future.

The early 1990s are a period of massive international change brought about largely by the collapse of the Soviet Union. Increasingly it is becoming evident that the question of reforming the way Japan is governed cannot be divorced from a consideration of the ways in which the international system is evolving. One of the most striking features of the international scene since the collapse of Communism in Eastern Europe is the far slower pace of change in East Asia (including Japan) than in Europe. This means that, up to 1992 at least, Japan was still relatively free from the pressures affecting European nations as a result of the ending of the Cold War. All signs, however, were pointing to the emergence of increasingly pressing challenges to the governance of Japan, stemming from radical change in the international system.

In the rest of this chapter we shall attempt to place Japanese politics in an international comparative context, showing that it bears basic similarity to the British system, but with certain important differences. We shall examine aspects of the various central parts of the system in an attempt to demonstrate its essential dynamics. Finally, we shall argue that while in many ways the political system established in Japan during the Occupation period and during the 1950s has served the nation well, it now stands in urgent need of reform - a task to which the new international situation lends added urgency.

In arguing for reform we shall propose that of the approaches to reform that might be attempted, the one that is most likely to yield desirable results would be the creation of a system which in practice permitted alternation - or at least occasional change - in the party or parties forming the government. We do not argue that this is the only reform required, but that it might be considered as the centrepiece.

Japan's System of Politics in Comparative Perspective

Like the politics of almost any other country, the Japanese political system has emerged out of a long series of historical experiences. This is not to say that the process of development has been even and continuous, since it has been punctuated by episodes of discontinuity and new direction, such as the Meiji Restoration and the 1945 defeat and subsequent occupation. A favourite essay topic given by those who teach Japanese politics (at least in Britain) to their students is: 'Examine the Japanese political system under the 1889 and 1946 constitutions in terms of continuity and change.' The question is, of course, more difficult to answer than it appears to be at first sight, which is why it is such a good essay topic to set for students.

A shorthand way of describing the political system under the present constitution is to say that it is a type of 'Westminster system, with modifications'. That is to say, in formal terms, the legislative and executive branches of government are 'fused', in the sense that the electorate, in electing members of parliament, are also directly electing a government which both controls the legislative process and administers the executive branch through government ministries and agencies. In practice the link between electorate and government is strengthened by the existence of political parties. The voter, while voting for an individual candidate, is also, whether deliberately or not, giving a preference to the political party to which the candidate belongs (except in the case of candidates who are genuine Independents). In marked contrast to the system operating in the United States, there is no separate election for a chief executive, which means that Japanese political parties, just like their British counterparts but unlike parties in the United States, normally maintain, for the most part, strict voting discipline in parliament. Should they fail to do so, they risk losing office as the result of a no-confidence motion being passed against them.[6]

The current Japanese system in this respect contrasts with the system that operated under the Meiji Constitution, in the sense that the elites around the Emperor, the chiefs of staff of the armed forces, the Privy Council, the (non-elected) House of Peers, the *genro*, the *jushin*, etc., contested and eroded the effective power of the elected House of Representatives. When there were transcendental cabinets, there was in effect a separation of powers between the legislature and the executive, but in the period of Taisho democracy, when party cabinets existed, Japan had, though in incomplete form, something approaching the Westminster model. Continuity, therefore, between the pre-war and post-war systems could be discovered in this area by somebody who knew what to look for.

Indeed, the abolition by General MacArthur's Occupation forces of the various elites (including those associated with the Emperor and the armed forces) which contested the power of the House of Representatives before the war may be regarded as perfecting and enshrining the principles of the Westminster model. It was ironic that such a result should have been produced by Americans.

Having established that in its basic formal pattern the Japanese political system under the 1946 Constitution may be categorised as a 'Westminster model', we now need to focus on the significant differences that emerged in practice. Some of these have their origin in the pre-war system; others resulted from various political developments which have occurred since the 1950s.

The Emperor

The first point concerns the Emperor. The current status of the Emperor is often compared with that of the monarch in a constitutional monarchy attached to a British-type Westminster system. The basic principle of such a system is that the Crown is the theoretical source of all legislation, that acts of the executive branch are done in the name of the Crown, but that in practice the monarch has hardly any scope for independent political decision-making. It is sometimes said that the only conceivable circumstance in which the monarch might be able to exercise a decisive political role would be if a general election resulted in a distribution of seats in the House of Commons such that no party held a majority. In that situation the monarch might have scope for initiative (though, of course, after taking advice) by inviting one party leader rather than another to attempt to form a government.[7] It was widely expected (or feared) that such a situation might result from the general elections held on 9 April 1992, but in the event the Conservative Party won an absolute, though much reduced, majority.

It seems clear that even this degree of initiative is impossible on the part of the Emperor of Japan. Article 67 of the Constitution provides that, following a general election, the next prime minister is chosen by a vote in parliament. In most cases this is a formality, but where no party had a clear majority the vote in parliament would decide the issue, without any need for intervention by the Emperor.

What is remarkable is that for most of the period since the war the Emperor of Japan has had a strikingly lower profile than the British monarch (or indeed other European monarchs, such as the Dutch, Belgian,

Danish, Swedish or Norwegian), while the institution itself has remained controversial. This is a result of the uses to which the Emperor institution was put by the regime following the Meiji Restoration and its successors up to 1945. While the Emperor at no point had central decision-making power in practice, the Emperor institution was fashioned as the prime legitimising and mobilising instrument of power, in which potent religious symbols were used to great effect in order to foster loyalty and devotion. Degree of access to the Emperor (in practice, on most occasions, access to his immediate advisers) became the principal currency of power. The Emperor up to 1945 was thus a curious mixture of constitutional monarch ('organ of the state', according to Minobe Tatsukichi) and pontiff (though with more temporal power than any pope).

It was this legacy from the pre-war period, combined with the particular question of the Showa Emperor's war responsibility (which post-war governments were anxious to suppress), as well as the increasing problem of the Showa Emperor's age after about 1970, that has led to the extraordinarily low recent profile of the Emperor. Whether or not the funeral of the Showa Emperor in 1989 and the accession of his successor will have caused interest in the institution to increase enough to bring in changes in its nature remains to be seen.

Single-Party Dominance

The second characteristic of the current Japanese political system which may be regarded as a departure from the norms of the Westminster model is single-party dominance. This is such a fundamental feature of the system as it has developed since the 1950s that we need to examine it in some detail. The crucial year, as everyone knows, was 1955. In that year, following a decade of fragmented party politics on both left and right, Japan acquired what at the time was heralded as a two-party system. Although it was far from evident at the time that things would work out this way, one of the two parties was to prove more resilient over the long term than the other. The success of the Liberal Democratic Party (LDP) in winning every general election for the House of Representatives (in a few cases with the help of Independents) between 1955 and the present has shaped Japanese politics, which would have taken a much different form had elections turned out differently.

The reasons for this internationally unprecedented[8] length of stay in office by a single political party in a parliamentary democracy requires explanation. In broad terms, four types of analysis commend themselves to our attention, though it is important to realise that the explanations overlap to some extent. The first, and simplest, approach is to argue that the electorate, expressing its view regularly in free elections, has continued to prefer the LDP over any other party or combination of parties. Indeed, when we compare the percentage of voters voting for the LDP in successive elections with the percentage voting for the British Conservative Party over a comparable period, we see that the LDP has performed steadily and effectively by comparison, though votes cast for the British Conservative Party have remained at a constant level since 1979.

Table 4.1 *Percentage of electorate voting Conservative in Britain, and LDP in Japan, over successive elections*

Year	Voting Conservative (%)	Voting LDP (%)
1958		57.8 (won)
1959	49.4 (won)	
1960		57.6 (won)
1963		54.7 (won)
1964	43.4 (lost)	
1966	41.9 (lost)	
1967		48.8 (won)
1969		47.6 (won)
1970	46.4 (won)	
1972		46.8 (won)
1974 (Feb.)	37.9 (lost)	
1974 (Oct.)	35.8 (lost)	
1976		41.8 (won)
1979	43.9 (won)	44.6 (won)
1980		47.9 (won)
1983	42.4 (won)	45.8 (won)
1986		49.4 (won)
1987	42.3 (won)	
1990		46.1 (won)
1992	42.8 (won)	

Sources: Philip Norton, *The British Polity* second edition, New York and London, Longman, 1991, pp. 97-9. *Asahi Nenkan*, various issues.

A second explanation, overlapping the first, is that the LDP has been consistently successful at the polls because it has succeeded in delivering rising levels of economic prosperity and growth. It is impossible to be entirely sure about the truth or falsehood of this explanation because we cannot experimentally run through a hypothetical history of Japan from the 1950s assuming the economy did not grow, or grew only fitfully, and then test how people voted. There is, however, some considerable contrary evidence from the period 1958-72, during which the economy grew at historically unprecedented rates while the LDP vote fell steadily. In the more recent period of slower growth rates, the LDP has actually performed slightly better (See Table 4.1)

A third possible explanation relates to certain features of the electoral system for the House of Representatives. The failure of the electoral law to provide for any obligatory process requiring regular redrawing of constituency boundaries to reflect shifts of population has led to gross distortions in the value of a vote in different constituencies. About once per decade from the 1960s onwards the number of seats per constituency has been adjusted, though to a minimally acceptable extent, to reflect population shifts. The effect of these distortions has been to favour rural constituencies, which normally support the LDP, against urban ones, where the LDP is in general less strong. The LDP has consequently enjoyed an advantage of several percentage points (seats over votes) in successive elections. It is arguable that at least in the 1976, 1979 and 1983 elections this made the difference between victory and defeat.

There is another feature, however, of the Lower House electoral system which may well have given a considerable advantage to the LDP over the Opposition. The system based on a single non-transferable vote in a 'medium-sized' constituency (in most cases electing three, four or five members) has two particular effects. The first and most obvious is that, unlike the British system (first-past-the-post in single-member constituencies), the Japanese Lower House system is permissive towards fairly small parties. Where it is quite possible, as in a five-member constituency, for a candidate to be elected with 20 or even 15 per cent of the total number of votes cast in that constituency, a party which can muster about one-fifth of the constituency's votes has an excellent chance of having its candidate elected. Clearly the 'third party' in Britain, now known as the Liberal Democrats (previously the Liberal Party), who mustered 18.3 per cent of the total national vote in the general election of April 1992 but won a mere 3.07 per cent of the total seats, would greatly benefit from the introduction of the Japanese system into Britain.

The problem, however, created in practice for the Japanese Opposition by this system is that by being permissive to small parties it has been conducive to the fragmentation and proliferation of Opposition parties. The details of this are too well-known to need spelling out.

At this point the attentive reader will naturally ask the question: 'Why should the medium-sized constituency system have led to fragmentation of the Opposition, but not to fragmentation of the LDP?' I believe that in the answer to this question lies perhaps the most important clue to the extraordinarily long-term electoral success of the LDP. In my opinion there was absolutely nothing that was foreordained or easily predictable about the sustained electoral performance of the LDP, because essentially it was the result of intelligent advantage taken of opportunities presented to it by the electoral system, plus superior financial resources.

In a constituency where the Liberal Democrats are strong, the party may expect to capture, let us say, three out of five seats. This, however, is little comfort to a particular candidate who without his own independent effort could well lose, even though his party (in terms of votes going to other LDP candidates) might do very well. This has fostered a system where the *koenkai* and general support networks of individual candidates have come to play a crucial part in the electoral performance of individual candidates. These networks are extremely expensive to maintain and lie at the root of much of the notorious corruption and nepotism of Japanese party politics - especially the politics of the LDP. But in terms of optimising electoral performance, the competition between rival LDP candidates works remarkably well. The vigorous campaigns of energetic LDP Diet candidates facing fierce competition from colleagues in their own party contrast with the lethargic approach of many an older-style candidate of the Social Democratic Party of Japan (SDPJ) - formerly Japan Socialist Party (JSP) - who, as the sole candidate of his party in his constituency, is guaranteed enough votes from party stalwarts and some protesters against the government to have himself elected, and therefore scarcely needs to campaign.[9] That a substantial advantage accrues to the LDP from the inbuilt competitiveness of that party's candidates to the Lower House is attested by its much poorer showing in elections for the proportional representation constituency of the House of Councillors, where electors are voting for a party list and not for individual candidates.[10]

Thus the LDP has maintained its integrity as a single party (with the minor exception of the defection of the members who formed the New Liberal Club in 1976) essentially because it has created an effective political machine based on intensely competitive pork-barrel politics at the local level. The pork-barrel approach pervades LDP organisation at all levels; it is epitomised in the system of factions (*habatsu*) and policy tribes (*zoku*), and to be left out of it is extremely disadvantageous for the individual Diet member, as the New Liberal Club members found to their increasing disillusionment. The party stays together, in other words, because it has developed stable and sophisticated methods at various levels of materially satisfying its members while at the same time materially satisfying significant portions of the electorate.

The fourth, and in some ways most persuasive explanation for one-party dominance, is the partial political vacuum that has existed since the 1960s at the core of the Opposition: the SDPJ (or JSP). It is tautological that a governing party will continue to govern if the electorate judges that the Opposition is unfit to govern. What is now widely forgotten in Japan is that in the middle and late 1950s the Japan Socialist Party, for all its faults (which were evident enough at that time), was widely regarded as a potential party of government. Some time in the 1960s, however, the Socialists, instead of following the example of the 1959 Bad Godesberg conference of the West German Social Democratic Party, which moved away from Marxism towards social democracy, proceeded to turn in upon themselves, to reaffirm their Marxist roots inherited from the pre-war period, and to appeal to a shrinking interest group base, largely of *Sohyo*-type unionists. The result was that by the early 1970s the Socialists had lost much of their support in metropolitan areas to minor parties such as the *Komeito* and the Japan Communist Party (JCP), though they retained a certain amount of support in country and small-town areas where public sector workers were concentrated.

The twin evils of failure to maintain unity and failure to develop a broad-based appeal among opposition parties of the left and centre-left is not unique to Japan. One example that may be cited is that of Australia between 1949 and 1972, when the Australian Labour Party similarly turned in on itself and likewise suffered a split with the appearance during the 1950s of the Democratic Labour Party, a right-of-centre anti-Communist Party with Roman Catholic sponsorship and support.[11] Although differences in political circumstances, particularly between the Japanese and Australian electoral systems, mean that the parallel is not complete, the dynamics are extraordinarily similar and suggestive. In the Australian case a renewed Australian Labour Party under vigorous leadership regained power after a gap of 23 years in December 1972. In Japan the 'Doi Takako boom' between 1986 and 1990, even though it faded eventually without effecting a change in the party in power, was evidence of an unexpected receptivity on the part of the electorate to alternative ideas about politics and government.

Comparing these four possible explanations for long-term single-party dominance: conservatism of the electorate, economic growth, the electoral system and the weakness of the Opposition, we see there is some merit in all of them and that there can be no single-factor explanation. It is difficult, however, to escape the conclusion that the extraordinarily inept performance by the SDPJ (JSP) over many years, combined with the amazing success of the LDP in its performance of machine and pork-barrel politics on a grand scale, have led to the current outcome of one-party domination.

The Policymaking Environment and Structure of Power

A simple way of describing the system is to say that Japan has a strong state but a weak polity. We need, however, to qualify this generalisation to some extent. The Japanese state is indeed strong but tends towards immobilism.[12] It is entrenched and highly effective, but finds it difficult to move outside certain long-established policy parameters and is not good at managing fundamental changes of direction or handling unexpected crises. The Japanese polity, on the other hand, is relatively weak, but exercises considerable influence over certain political outcomes, largely, however, in the negative sense of wielding veto power over certain issues and providing a moderate degree of unpredictability in an otherwise highly-structured power system.

Let us take, in turn, six key aspects of the current system: Parliament; the LDP; leadership; the government bureaucracy; interest groups; and corruption.

The National Diet is not an insignificant part of the system, contrary to what some assume. Comparisons with the United States Congress are largely inappropriate, because of the quite different function of a legislature in a Westminster system from that in an American-style system based on the separation of powers. In Japan the House of Representatives rarely overturns (though it may modify) legislation presented to it by the Government, so long as one party maintains a majority of seats in that house. In exactly the same way the British House of Commons (the 'Mother of Parliaments') scarcely ever rejects government legislation on issues where the party in office has imposed a three-line whip (i.e. important legislation). In other words, a central principle of the Westminster model, as it has worked during the present century, is that the party in office at any one time has virtually total control over the legislative programme of Parliament until the next general election. An election may, of course, be precipitated if the government party loses its majority in parliament as the result of defections or by-election defeats, but this is rare.[13] The fact, therefore, that much legislation is actually drawn up within ministries and 'ratified' by the National Diet is also paralleled by a similar situation in the British House of Commons. There is no doubt some difference between Japanese and British government ministers in the extent of their influence over their ministries, and thus over the content of legislation, but that is another matter.

If the National Diet is regarded in isolation it may perhaps be regarded as weak, even irrelevant. When seen, however, in relation to the political system as whole, it may be categorised as an essential ratifier (and modifier, through Diet committees) of legislation, an arena of political competition and power-broking and, in a sense, the public face of party politics. Naturally, it becomes more important when the government's majority is narrow, and still more so when it disappears altogether, as happened in the House of Councillors in 1989. Arguably the National Diet is stronger and more important than the parliament (Assemblée Nationale) of France.

The LDP is a central and integral part of the current political power structure. We venture to suggest that this is true in a sense analogous more to the position of the Christian Democratic Party of Italy than to that of the Conservative or Labour parties of Great Britain. The two major British parties are competitors for power and temporary holders of it. Even the years of Conservative Party rule since 1979 have not removed the common belief that that party remains in office by kind permission of the electorate. In both Italy and Japan, however, there is a sense in which that belief has been lost. The ability to envisage the ruling party being voted out of office is an essential part of the construction of an alternative.

Even though LDP members of the House of Representatives have to fight regular elections in their constituencies, promotion to cabinet and party office is now determined by a *de facto* seniority system which mirrors that within government ministries. Hardly any LDP Diet members achieve cabinet office until they have been elected to the National Diet five times, and almost all have held at least one post by the time they have been elected seven times. Beyond that, promotion is essentially by 'merit', including ability in political manipulation, so that the careers of many Diet members are punctuated by the holding of cabinet office once, and once only.[14] The similarity to promotion patterns in major Japanese bureaucracies of the public and private sectors is striking.

A complex structure of LDP committees hammers out policy on political issues, links in with the committee structure of the National Diet, and coordinates with both government ministries and relevant interest groups. Extremely complex linkages exist between LDP Diet members, bureaucrats and interest group leaders in industry, commerce, agriculture and the professions. Some of them, involving members of so-called *zoku*, merit the description of 'iron triangles'. Few elements in this system are unique to Japan, but the element of one-party dominance in its Japanese context lends a characteristic structure of semi-permanence, turf-defence and inflexibility (though also a surprising amount of dynamism)[15] to it. To use a possibly far-fetched analogy, Japan's political system has more in common with rail-transport than with road-transport.

Thirdly, it is commonly alleged that Japan lacks political leadership, and that in particular the prime minister is too much hedged around with restrictions to be able to lead effectively.[16] By most Western comparisons cabinet reshuffles are frequent, and appear to be determined more by the logic of factional competition than by a desire to place the best person in the right post (though it would be naive to suppose that this was the only reason behind appointments to, say, British cabinets).[17]

When we analyse the position of prime minister, it is important to register the fact that a major structural change has occurred in the structure of the LDP since the 1980s, whereby a loose balance of power between five or six factions of comparable size has been replaced by a structure in which a single faction (the Takeshita faction) has become dominant. Successive prime ministers have been heavily dependent on the Takeshita faction, which has shown signs of seeking a new power balance that might incorporate some among the Opposition parties, notably the *Komeito*. The loss of its overall majority in the House of Councillors by the LDP in 1989 made some form of *de facto* alliance with Opposition parties a necessity, but the implications for the future are interesting to contemplate. We may hypothesise that these moves have much to do with a perceived problem of structurally caused leadership deficiency.

The fourth aspect of the system to be discussed are the ministries and agencies which constitute the government bureaucracy. Everyone agrees that Japan has a strong elite bureaucracy, and that the ministries (particularly the major ones) occupy extensive spheres of semi-autonomous policy influence, and behave virtually as 'empires' in their own right. The structure of Japan's government bureaucracy is in international terms extraordinarily stable, and it is certainly more influential by comparison with politicians than the British bureaucracy, though possibly not more influential than the equally elitist government bureaucracy of France. Its impact on policy is patent in many diverse fields, from the maintenance of high levels of inheritance tax to control of school-textbook selection. Much controversy exists about the extent and usefulness of government regulation of economic activity, but an atmosphere of regulatory activity persists despite the enormous increase in corporate resources and power that has occurred since the 1970s. The Nakasone period of the mid-1980s saw a number of privatisation initiatives, but some analysts have observed that 're-regulation', albeit in a different form, tends to follow deregulation.[18]

Fifthly, the activities of all manner of interests and interest groups, in Japan as elsewhere, form much of the stuff of day-to-day politics. The enormously strengthened corporate sector is, and always has been, close to government, and in general continues to support the LDP and its policies as the least unattractive political option. Like government ministries, *keiretsu* companies may be conceptualised as semi-autonomous 'empires', with their separate spheres of influence throughout Japan and indeed overseas as well. As is well known, they contribute a great deal of money to the LDP (and minor sums to other parties), and some of them make room on their boards for a certain number of retired government officials. Linkages throughout the system are cemented in this and many other ways.

Many other interest groups exert influence, some of them by force of numbers in strategic constituencies. Agriculture and small and medium industry have been extremely influential through their ability to command large numbers of votes which LDP Diet members cannot afford to ignore. While Calder's view that interest groups have grown powerful through a process of crisis-precipitation followed by government compensation is questionable as a synoptic explanation,[19] there is no doubt that government is involved in a variety of ways with many interest groups which it cannot afford to ignore. In this respect the Japanese situation is not wholly discrepant from that which may be found in a number of European countries.

Finally, corruption is frequently targeted as one of the main problems with the working of Japanese politics in practice, and indeed the sums of money which pass from hand to hand in Japanese politics are, by comparison with most European countries, astounding. From time to time (for instance during 1988-89 and in the early months of 1992), political corruption becomes the subject of a relentless campaign by the mass media. At other times it fades from the headlines. In Japan 'money politics' (political corruption under a polite name) flourishes for several reasons: legal sanctions are somewhat lax, and laxly enforced; the cost of being elected to the National Diet is extremely high, partly because of inadequate public provision for Diet members, and in part because of the personality basis of elections in multi-member constituencies; myriad commercial and industrial 'empires' compete with one another with constant ferocity (thus assuring economic dynamism across the economy), which means that in an environment where government regulation remains an important factor the temptation to buy advantage is considerable. Many parallels may be found in similarly regulated economies.

When we consider the various features of the Japanese political system outlined above, we find that it is highly complex and does not easily lend itself to quick generalisation. Broadly, however, we can say that the constitutional structure is of the Westminster type, but that political development within that structure has been rather narrowly channelled within the confines of single-party dominance and a strong elite bureaucracy. This in turn has resulted in a system which is extremely effective in certain ways but in others can be quite inflexible and prone to corruption. We should ask, therefore, how the system could be improved.

Problems and Prospects of Reform

Before addressing the question of possible reform, it is desirable to point out some of the advantages and achievements of the present Japanese political system. First of all, it has brought political stability to Japan, and in this respect has performed far better than the political system under the Meiji Restoration. However much we may be inclined to complain about immobilism, inflexibility, corruption and the like, the underlying stability that has prevailed has been an inestimable benefit, which the Japanese electorate is unlikely to relinquish lightly. Any proposal for reform, to be credible, must address this question of the maintenance of political stability and ensure that stability is not jeopardised.

Secondly, a key condition for stability in any political system is that forces of narrow extremism, whether of the far right or the far left, whether based on nationalistic or religious ideology or whatever, should be kept in check and so far as possible marginalised (not banned, however, which is usually counterproductive as well as objectionable in terms of democratic practice). Although the extreme right in Japan has a certain unhealthy capacity for intimidation of those who speak out on matters of principle, and infiltration of the conservative establishment, for the most part Japanese politics and government up to the present have probably not been unduly influenced by extremist elements.

A third, and related point is that since 1945 the people have been fortunate that no Japanese soldiers have had to fire shots in anger and that military influence on government and politics, so destructive of both internal stability and international responsibility in the previous period, has been kept to a minimum. Whatever the international criticism to which Japan has been subject in recent years for her constitution-based reluctance to participate in military operations beyond her boundaries, it seems difficult to escape the conclusion that the civilianisation of politics has been wholly beneficial to the political process.

A fourth point which may be taken as a significant benefit of the system as it has operated since the 1950s is that it has presided over a sustained rate of economic growth which has been difficult to match anywhere else in the world. This statement may seem to beg a number of questions relating to the role of politics in economic development, to allegations about international economic policies not being in the spirit of free trade, and to how far economic growth has led to genuine prosperity and a high quality of life for the people, yet a battery of economic and social indicators suggest that the Japanese performance has considerable - some would say spectacular - achievements to its credit.

Why then should we advocate the case for substantial reform of the Japanese political system or aspects of it?

Our first argument, though not in itself constituting a conclusive case for reform, is that the international situation, as mentioned much earlier in this chapter, has changed suddenly and fundamentally since 1989. The ending of the Cold War, which had formed the fundamental parameters of the international system since the late 1940s, has precipitated systemic change whose ultimate implications are still far from clear. What is clear is that any idea that the demise of Communism in the former Soviet Union and in Eastern Europe would bring about the 'end of history' and peace throughout the world is proving a chimera. As mentioned earlier, the pace of change is proving to be much slower in East Asia than in Europe. China and North Korea are still controlled by what may still be called Communist regimes, though the rate of economic growth based on essentially capitalist principles in much of coastal China is spectacular. Whereas it took less than a year from the opening of the Berlin Wall to the formal unification of the two Germanies, Japan and Russia have yet to solve a territorial dispute over some barren islands that is seriously inhibiting Japan from contributing to the desperately-needed rehabilitation of her northern neighbour's economy, which is perilously close to collapse. It is difficult to escape the conclusion here that the nature of decision-making in the Japanese system is contributing to a narrowness of vision that needs systemic change to remedy.

Japan-US relations encompass a range of difficult questions which it is beyond the scope of this chapter to address. It is not necessary, however, to adhere to one of the more pessimistic scenarios concerning the future of relations between the two countries to believe that serious difficulties may lie ahead both in the economic and the military-strategic areas. A dangerous tendency is evident in the US to identify Japan as a kind of substitute enemy now that Russia has become a friend, so that, without serious action to make life easier for American companies operating in Japan, relations could seriously deteriorate. At present, the Mutual Security Treaty between Japan and the US in effect gives the Americans bases on the cheap, but one wonders whether current Japanese decision-making processes are really adequate to the task of doing the strategic planning necessary to give Japan an effective and balancing role (not necessarily of a military nature) in the maintenance of international stability.

A second set of reasons for reform is that there is increasing evidence of electoral volatility which may eventually undermine some of the basic premises of the present system. As Nakamura Kenichi argues,[20] from about 1986 the electorate has been showing clear signs of unpredictability in its behaviour, a conclusion to which the extraordinarily low turnout in the July 1992 House of Councillors elections lends further credence. In the sophisticated Japan of the early 1990s there would seem likely to be limits to how far the electorate can be bought off in the time-honoured pork-barrel ways of factional politicians. If the LDP becomes unable to sustain a majority, however, one-party dominance, which has been the keystone of the existing political system, will become dislodged.

In order to prepare for such a scenario, what is urgently needed is the creation of a party (or political bloc) capable of mounting effective and principled opposition to the politics of the LDP. Exactly what form such a formation might take is hard to say. The Japan Socialist Party under Doi Takako for a while caught the imagination of the electorate, but then was unable to shake off its old ways, with which the electorate was profoundly disillusioned. The Rengo no kai appeared for a while to have momentum, but failed badly at the polls in July 1992. The New Japan Party won a handful of seats in the same elections, but not enough really to create a springboard for a challenge to the LDP. Various scenarios seem possible involving a split in the LDP, with various coalition possibilities emerging together with combinations of other parties. None, however, look particularly credible.

What is needed is the emergence of effective new leadership, both in the Opposition (principally SDPJ) and in the LDP itself. Such leadership would need to be capable of shaping a modernised political system, giving the electorate real policy choices, eliminating the pork-barrel element through serious electoral and other reform, and strengthening the capacity of decision-making, without, however, jeopardising stability.

All this may seem rather difficult to envisage at present, but it is becoming increasingly evident that without real systemic reform, Japanese politics can hardly be expected to perform as the electorate deserves and as the health and stability of the nation requires.

Epilogue

The collapse of LDP rule in summer of 1993 was preceded by a split in the pivotal Takeshita faction of the ruling party, and a consequent weakening of central control of the party. This in turn was accompanied by a series of corruption scandals, one of which led to the disgrace and effective withdrawal from politics of Kanemaru Shin, who had been the Takeshita faction's most dominant and canny leader. If erosion of central leadership in the LDP was the background element, the proximate cause of collapse was the decision by the Miyazawa Cabinet in the early summer of 1993 not to proceed with a plan to reform the Lower House electoral system.

In protest, two separate groups, the larger of which was the dissident half of the old Takeshita faction, broke away from the LDP and formed new parties. As a consequence, the LDP lost a motion of no-confidence in its government, the Miyazawa Cabinet dissolved Parliament and held new elections, which it lost.

To general surprise, a new government was formed under the prime ministership of a former prefectural governor, Hosokawa Morihiro. It consisted of no fewer than eight separate parties, the largest of which was the SDPJ (though that party had lost many seats in the elections). The Hosokawa Government embarked upon an ambitious programme of reform, including reform of the electoral system, an anti-corruption law, deregulation of industry and commerce, reform of the tax system and decentralisation of power to local authorities.

By the end of 1993 the new government found itself in difficulties, both because of divisions within its own ranks and because of pressure from the LDP, now in opposition. Early in 1994 the crucial electoral reform bills became law, but they had been substantially modified by comparison with the government's earlier proposals. The new electoral system for the House of Representatives was to be based on 300 single-member, first-past-the-post constituencies, and 200 seats contested in 11 regional constituencies by proportional representation. It was expected that the new system would reduce the impact of factionalism, which had been fostered by the multi-member constituencies, and also favour a more policy-oriented approach to political competition. Whether it would turn out like that, however, remained to be seen.

The early months of 1994 saw increasing strains emerging within the coalition government. Mr Hosokawa tendered his resignation in April, and was replaced by Hata Tsutomu, a former LDP politician with ministerial experience, who was closely backed by the most controversial leader within the former Hosokawa coalition, Ozawa Ichiro. Although the composition of the Hata Government was initially identical with that of its predecessor, the SDPJ pulled out almost immediately, alleging that it was being marginalised by the Hata-Ozawa leadership.

The Hata-Ozawa Government lacked a majority in Parliament and lasted a mere nine weeks. It in turn was replaced in June 1994 by a three-party coalition Government (SDPJ, LDP and a minor party), under a Socialist Prime Minister, Murayama Tomiichi. The Murayama Government seemed rather more stable than its predecessor, seeing that at least it enjoyed a Lower House majority, but in January 1996 Murayama was replaced as Prime Minister by Hashimoto Ryutaro, President of the LDP, which had thus regained the top political position after a gap of two and a half years.

The formation of the original coalition government in August 1993 was a surprise to most observers, but that reformist politics should be accompanied by political instability was virtually inevitable once the old LDP structure collapsed. Instability relates, however, to party politics, leaving much of the actual running of the country to government ministries, which continue to exercise a great deal of effective power whether there is a stable government in power or not.

Even so, political change is in the air, and the old structures are undergoing a process of significant review. Younger politicians are finding new opportunities opening up for them and there is some evidence of a new vigour entering the political arena. The pattern of party divisions existing in the middle of 1990s may well not last, since the new electoral system will impose new imperatives on politicians if they wish to remain in politics and close to the seats of power.

Japan has entered a vital period of political transition, which may, however, be expected to last for several years before the parameters of a new system are wholly apparent.

Notes

1. This chapter was completed in August 1992, approximately one year before the collapse of the single-party dominance that had characterised Japanese party politics for some 38 years. The Hosokawa coalition government, which took office in August 1993, put in place a programme of political reform, but the advent of coalition government also ushered in a period of political instability, as three differently composed governments were formed within the space of a year. Rather than rewriting this chapter to take account of the events of 1993 and 1994, the author prefers to have it as it was written in 1992, since the argument seems particularly relevant to the new political situation as it unfolds. An epilogue will briefly outline developments since 1993.
2. For instance, Herman Kahn, *The Emerging Japanese Superstate*, Harmondsworth, Penguin, 1970. Kahn's thinking about Japan was heavily influenced by Ruth Benedict, *The Chrysanthemum and the Sword*, Boston, Houghton Mifflin, 1946.
3. General Douglas MacArthur, US Senate, 82nd Congress, 1st session, Hearings before the Committee on Armed Services and the Committee on Foreign Relations, *Military Situation in the Far East*, Washington, 1951, pp. 310-13; quoted in Chalmers Johnson, *Conspiracy at Matsukawa*, Berkeley, University of California Press, 1972.
4. Zbigniew Brzezinski, *The Fragile Blossom: Crisis and Change in Japan*, New York, Harper and Row, 1972.
5. Karel van Wolferen, *The Enigma of Japanese Power*, London, Macmillan, 1989.
6. In May 1980 the Japanese Prime Minister, Ohira Masayoshi, was unexpectedly defeated in a no-confidence motion in which a number of Liberal Democratic Diet members abstained. The previous year in Britain the Labour Prime Minister, James Callaghan, was similarly defeated by a single vote. In both these cases the government resigned as a direct result of the loss of confidence in it by parliament.
7. There is a spectacular example of 'monarchical' initiative over the composition of government, from Australia. Under the Australian Constitution, the Governor-General, in theory at least, holds his position on behalf of the British Crown. On 11 November 1975, the Governor-General of the time, Sir John Kerr, dismissed the Australian Labour Party Government of Gough Whitlam, who had been attempting to govern despite the refusal of supply by the Senate, in which it lacked a majority. The Whitlam Government was defeated in the subsequent general election. The episode provoked much bitterness and controversy in Australia.
8. For a comparison of single-party-dominant political systems, see T. J. Pempel (ed.), *Uncommon Democracies: The One-Party Dominant Regimes*, Ithaca and London, Cornell University Press, 1990.

9. This point is made in Nakamura Kenichi, 'The Changing Quality of Japanese Politics', in J.A.A. Stockwin (ed.), *The Quality of Life in Japan*, London, Routledge, forthcoming.
10. The only elections where direct comparison is possible are the double elections of 1986. In the elections for the House of Councillors, the LDP won 49.4 per cent of the total vote, but in the proportional representation constituency of the House Councillors it won only 38.6 per cent. *Asahi Nenkan*, 1987, p. 101.
11. See L.F. Crisp, *Australian National Government*, Melbourne, Longman, Green and Co., 1965, Chapter 6.
12. J.A.A. Stockwin *et al.*, *Dynamic and Immobilist Politics in Japan*, London, Macmillan, 1988.
13. A British example may be found in the Labour Governments of Harold Wilson and subsequently James Callaghan between 1974 and 1979. Elected with a small majority in October 1974, the Labour Government eventually lost this majority through by-election defeats, but was able to continue to govern for a considerable period with the tacit support of some minor parties.
14. Stockwin *et al*, *Dynamic and Immobilist Politics in Japan*, p. 41.
15. *Ibid.*, passim, especially pp. 1-20.
16. The role of the Prime Minister, Kaifu Toshiki, during the Gulf Crisis and Gulf War of 1990-91 provides the best opportunity for a case study of this proposition.
17. The French Fourth Republic up to 1958 is a good example of frequent cabinet reshuffles. There may be a parallel also in Britain, though as the exception rather than the rule.
18. Stephen Wilks and Maurice Wright, *The Promotion and Regulation of Industry in Japan*, London, Macmillan, 1991.
19. Kent Calder, *Crisis and Compensation: Public Policy and Political Stability in Japan, 1949-1986*, Princeton, NJ, Princeton University Press, 1988.
20. Nakamura Kenichi, *op. cit.*

5 The Emptiness of Affluence: Vitality, Embolism and Symbiosis in the Japanese Body Politic

Gavan McCormack

The general outline of Japan's attainment of economic power over the past several decades is well known. Japan's GNP multiplied by 152 in the four decades from 1950, as compared with 39 times for the other post-war economic 'miracle', West Germany. Its proportion of the world's GNP rose from 1 per cent in 1950 (when the US share was 39 per cent) to 12.8 per cent in 1990 and is expected to reach 17 per cent by the end of the century.[1] Japan's regional predominance is such that its GNP came to make up 66 per cent of that of the whole of Asia (including China, India and Australia and New Zealand).[2] In the significant high-tech area of semi-conductors, long dominated by the US (with 83 per cent of world production coming from five US companies in 1965) Japanese output surpassed 50 per cent in 1988 (and held at 49.7 per cent in 1991), while the US share fell from 51.6 per cent in 1984 to 36.5 per cent in 1988.[3]

In the boom years of the late 1980s, Japan expanded by a 'Korea'-sized economy every year and by 'a France' over five years.[4] By the end of the century, if the US and Japan were to average 1 per cent and 4 per cent growth through the rest of the decade, a modest prediction given the record of the preceding decades, and assuming (conservatively) an end-of-century exchange rate of 109 yen to the dollar, Japan's GNP would then overtake the US as the biggest in the world.[5]

There may be questions about the stability and durability of the Japanese economy, but this essay is not a specialist economic analysis. Instead, some of the consequences and costs of three decades of high economic growth are considered, and the focus is on the relationship between social and political vitality and corporate dynamism. Does this record point to a surge in national vitality on the Japanese part, a rising of fresh sap in the veins of a people in the full flush of self-realising vigour? What has been the Japanese people's experience as their GNP multiplied and their corporations swept world markets? Has it liberated and energised them, releasing their vitality in a flow of joyful and exuberant creativity?

In 1991-92, while the Japanese 'system' attained unprecedented levels of collective 'affluence', the corruption of its inner fabric was exposed to an unprecedented degree. Its economy underwent an extraordinary period of contraction; its 'bubble' burst. Land prices fell by about 30 per cent and stocks on the Tokyo stock exchange 60 per cent from their December 1989 peak.[6] The deflation from 1990 of the 'bubble' of Japan's super-expansion of the 1980s exposed the inner workings of the Japanese system, revealing a web of corrupt and collusive links between the country's major political, bureaucratic, business and criminal worlds and eroding popular confidence in the nation's institutional infrastructure.

It was revealed that Japan's largest (and the world's largest) security houses, including Nomura, had been compensating major corporate clients against losses (thereby shifting the burden of such losses on to those without insider influence) and that Nomura and Nikko Securities had loaned vast sums to crime syndicate bosses; that Japan's major banks had advanced unsecured loans of about $3 billion to an Osaka restaurateur (who 'blew' much of it in speculative stock dealings); that major politicians had been involved in scams such as that of the Ibaraki Country Club which collapsed leaving about $1 billion debts, and Kyowa Steel, which collapsed with debts of $1.5 billion (a small proportion of which was recovered when politicians, including former Prime Minister Suzuki, 'returned' sums they had received from the company two years earlier and simply 'forgotten' to pay back),[7] and senior executives of the trucking firm Sagawa Kyubin were arrested for aggravated breach of trust involving $4 billion in payments and unsecured loans to major crime syndicates, other companies, and leading politicians - hundreds of them in this case, from both sides of the Diet and including the head of the ruling Liberal-Democratic Party and (apparently) several ex-prime ministers.

The government which presided over the series of revelations contained six 'veterans' of previous corruption scandals (Lockheed and Recruit). One of the largest gangster syndicates was revealed to have been involved in the 1987 process of selection of Mr Takeshita as Prime Minister.[8] By the end of 1992, officials including various heads of the security houses, the Treasurer (Hashimoto), the Governor of Niigata (Kaneko Kiyoshi) and the Deputy Prime Minister and leading power-broker in the country (Kanemaru Shin) had resigned, the former Hokkaido chief-executive and secretary-general of the Miyazawa faction (Abe Fumio) had been arrested and a former head of the Environment Agency (Inamura Toshiyuki) had been imprisoned. Various criminal and tax investigations continued, but the expectation was strong that the procuracy and the courts would not allow them to reach the point of destabilising the 'system'. Powerful figures, such as Kanemaru, who had been centrally involved in the selection of the past four prime ministers, first refused, with apparent impunity, to cooperate with investigations. Kanemaru then struck a deal whereby he issued a perfunctory apology for having accepted a US$4 million bribe, paid a fine of US$1666, and resigned from public office without answering questions.[9] The matter appeared to have been brought to rest with a statement from Prime Minister Miyazawa expressing pious regret over the connections between politicians and organised crime.[10]

The extent of embolism exposed in the Japanese body politic was such as to challenge the society with the need for fundamental reform. At the same time, the deterioration in Japan's human and environmental stock has become conspicuous. The test of Japan's vitality as it approaches the end of the century (and millennium) will be its capacity to respond creatively and radically to these challenges.

With the end of the Cold War, it might also have been thought that Japanese 'vitality' would be expressed in the projection of vision and policies for the creation of a more peaceful and equal world order, yet actually the major foci of Japanese diplomatic efforts in the early 1990s were quite opposite, concentrated with almost obsessive attention on two matters: territory (the restoration of sovereignty over islands disputed between Japan and the former Soviet Union, later Russia) and troops (the breach of the post-1945 legal and constitutional barriers to the overseas dispatch of Japanese troops). Here were unmistakable stirrings of a newly assertive Japanese state, but whether such campaigns could be described as evidence of Japanese 'vitality' is open to doubt.

The light into the inner workings of the Japanese state and economy shed by these scandals and crises suggested not so much exuberance and vitality as an entrenched and rigid system of privilege and irresponsibility, and an incapacity to transcend narrow sectoral or national interest. There were other indicators to suggest that the Japanese economy's success in productivity was being achieved at heavy social cost. The most intractable difference between Japanese and other advanced country industrial practice was in terms of hours worked, as the Japanese worker continued to spend about 300 hours a year more on the job than Americans and between 400 and 500 more than French or German workers.[11] While it is true that the 44-hour week became law in 1991 and civil servants work a five-day week since 1993, it is also the case that 'voluntary' and unpaid overtime in Japan may amount to several hundred hours in a year, and that two-thirds of Japan's workforce are employed in small and medium firms not covered by legislation and continuing to work a 55-hour week.[12] During the past decade the working hours of men aged about 30 have risen steadily, so that close to 60 per cent of them work an average of more than 50 hours, and another 20 per cent more than 60 hours per week.[13] Estimates of the annual death toll from overwork (*karoshi*) range up to 10 000 per year (although estimates in this area are necessarily very tentative).[14] Furthermore, the share of national income made up by employed people's salaries has steadily shrunk over the past decade,[15] and labour satisfaction, measured in comparative terms, shows Japanese workers nursing significantly higher levels of dissatisfaction with wages and conditions than workers in the US, Britain, Germany, Australia or Singapore.[16] According to the Japanese Labour Ministry, 61.7 per cent of Japanese want shorter working hours.[17] As for leisure, while over 80 per cent of people in Europe and North America expressed themselves satisfied with their leisure life, the equivalent figure for Japan was 37 per cent.[18] In the schools, where the society reproduces itself and its central values, competitive pressures remain at levels that many find intolerable, and the phenomenon of bullying, suicides and absenteeism (*toko kyohi*) lend further cause to doubt whether the system had particularly high levels of 'vitality'.

The *karoshi* may be the contemporary avatar of the wartime kamikaze - a statistically insignificant minority in the 1990s as in the 1940s - but what is striking is the prevalence through the intervening 50 years of an (officially promoted) ideology of subordination of the individual to the interests or needs of state and corporation (what was known in the 1940s as *messhi hoko*, or service to the state to the point of self-extinction, and survives in transmuted form in contemporary terms such as *kigyo senshi* or corporate warrior). The Japanese industrial system, now being reduplicated throughout East Asia, harnesses the feudal ethic of Japan's *messhi hoko* to modern enterprise capitalism. The alienation of the exploited white-collar workers whose energies are mobilised to achieve the corporate miracle is nicely caught in the words of a song, featured in a musical popular among white-collar workers in the early 1990s:

> Thanks to us salarymen,
> the Japanese economy is fine,
> our company is doing well;
> But the company will manage
> even without me;
> It will go on expanding
> even without you;
> What are we but faceless men?[19]

In the early 1990s, as the layers of corruption, arrogance and irresponsibility clotting and clogging the arteries of the Japanese system were revealed, dissatisfaction with their lot in the 'affluent society' became common among ordinary citizens. Pressure for change was multiplied by the effects of external pressures for Japan to play a much expanded and quite different international role. While regional integration proceeded elsewhere in the world, with NAFTA in America, Canada and Mexico and the Maastricht Treaty in Europe, observers noted that Japan was dangerously isolated.[20] The worst of the wave of 'bashing' associated with the economic expansion of the 1980s may have passed, but Japan continued through 1992 to build trade surpluses with the US at well over $100 billion per year; 70 per cent of people surveyed in the US saw Japan as an 'enemy',[21] most had only the vaguest of ideas of what sort of country it was,[22] and the notion that Japan was fundamentally different from other countries (*ishitsuron*) remained strong, having indeed been promoted for its own purposes from time to time by Japanese governments. Demands that it conform to the practice of the major Western powers could be expected to continue, and fears about the direction likely to be followed by the newly integrated economies of Europe and North America persisted. Growing difficulties in trade with the advanced industrial countries stirred a marked shift of interest in a Japanese future once again tied to Asia (although precedents for the achievement of equality and reconciling Japanese hegemony with 'vitality' were not good), and when senior officials in Tokyo scrambled to find formulae that would appease the Europeans and Americans, they could conceive of no more likely partner for an alliance than Australia.[23]

The depth of the crisis, however, stimulated trenchant, interesting, and unprecedented critiques and also some remarkable prescriptions for reform, some of the more radical of which came from the heart of the Japanese establishment. The test of Japan's vitality will be whether reform on the scale prescribed can be implemented.

1992 opened with a pungent exchange between two of Japan's leading commentators on economic and political matters: Takabatake Michitoshi of Rikkyo University and Sawa Takamitsu, head of the Institute for Economic Research of Kyoto University.[24] The system was described by Sawa as 'structurally collusive in everything', with a 'rotten structure of mutual reliance among the triumvirate - the political world, the bureaucracy and big business' - that constituted a 'Japan disease'. Politically, Takabatake observed that Japan could not be called either liberal or democratic, and the so-called Liberal Democratic Party was actually 'nothing but a business corporation'. Obsessive stress on efficiency and productivity, in an economic structure that was only nominally a free market economy but actually a 'market-simulating sham', was turning Japan into 'the world's orphan'.[25] The international competitiveness of Japan's corporations depended, in Sawa's view, on their running on dope, their vitality, he implied, being as 'natural' as Ben Johnson's.[26] Another well-known critic, Ohmae Kenichi, described the Japanese system as 'the embodiment of centralised bureaucratic power', neither liberal nor democratic, in need of complete reform.[27] Elsewhere, Takabatake, commenting on the power of the small group which dominates the Liberal-Democratic Party to run national affairs, described it as analagous to the control exercised by the Communist Party of the Soviet Union prior to the advent of Gorbachev.[28] A common criticism is that Japan is not so much a legal or constitutional order as a soft, mutually interpenetrating, amoeba-like growth, reinforced by the interpenetration of education, law, the bureaucracy and business, beyond the control, often even beyond the ken, of Japan's civil society.

Similarly harsh judgements became commonplace in 1992, and were expressed even by some of the country's most powerful and respected business leaders. Morita Akio, chairman of Sony Corp and vice-chairman of Keidanren (the Japan Federation of Economic Organisations), described Japan as being 'in desperate need of a new philosophy of management, a new paradigm for competitiveness, a new sense of self'.[29] His prescription was for substantially reduced working hours, increased wages, improved dividends, much greater corporate social and environmental sensitivity.[30] Until Japan proved ready to 'redefine' itself, he added, 'it cannot hope to be accepted on the same stage as Europe and North America'. What he implied was that the obsessive, even fetishistic, pursuit of market share had brought nothing but market share.

A similar call for transition to a softer, more conciliatory engagement with its own people and with the world, placing less weight on market share or profit, was enunciated by Hiraiwa Gaishi, chairman of Keidanren and head of Tokyo Electric Power Company.[31] Hiraiwa called for *kyosei*, a term which literally meant 'living together' but for which he offered the English equivalents of 'mutualism' or 'symbiosis'. The term had been used before, but in 1992 it became central to prescriptions for reform. The government-funded think-tank, the National Institute for Research Advancement (NIRA), was set the problem of how to realise *kyosei* in practice.[32] Keidanren chose as its 1992 orientation the quest for *kyosei* with foreign countries and the righting of 'the evils of a company-centred society'.[33] The Economic Planning Agency's 12th five-year plan, released in July 1992, projected a vision of Japan transformed 'from an aggressively competitive corporate culture into a consumer-oriented society where the quality of life takes precedence over the quantity of production'.[34] Unlike previous plans, this one adopted as mission the generation of a whole new 'philosophy' of life. The turning of Japan into a *seikatsu taikoku* (livelihood great power) became another common political slogan.

These concerns, and this new vision, were prompted not so much by any organised social movement for such change in Japan as by fear that the rising wave of hostility towards Japanese aggressive economic expansion in Europe and North America might otherwise prove impossible to contain. The programme was strategic and instrumental, its spokesmen themselves major architects or builders of the system in which they now found basic flaws. Only time would tell whether substantial changes would flow from the new business-bureaucratic consensus around *kyosei* or whether it would become rather an ideological instrument of obfuscation, a term of utopian fancy akin to the slogan 'co-prosperity' that was advanced in an earlier age to mask contradictions that actually could not be resolved within the system.

Within Japan, the combination of revelations of the 'rottenness' at the core of the system and worrying evidence about its weakness (drastic falls in share prices and land values) led to sombre suggestions that the characteristic Japanese 'network capitalism' that had achieved such strength might be quietly approaching a systemic crisis of proportions no less dramatic than those which led to the collapse of the Soviet Union on the one hand and the enfeeblement of the US (and corporations such as IBM) on the other.[35] Could it be that Japan was on the verge of moving from a generation which had been 'devoured by corporations' to one which would devour its corporations?[36]

The problem is whether the embolisms so dramatically exposed in Japan in the early 1990s are cancerous and already affect vital organs, or whether the public vitality has the potential to heal and regenerate the whole. Diseased organisms may possess formidable force and vigour, but such force is ultimately destructive. Public vitality may appear uncontainably vital and expressive, yet be susceptible of considerable manipulation and subjugation.

Disquieting questions about the health of the system are raised when the achievements of Japanese growth are set against human needs. The triumph, on a scale unprecedented in human history, in mastering the mysteries of sustained corporate growth, is indisputable. The capacity to produce and market lots of useful high-quality, attractively-designed consumer goods was the admiration of the world, and aspects of Japan's corporate culture - stable employment, long-term business perspective, quality control and intra-corporate egalitarianism (with pay differentials rarely more than 7:1) - had lessons to be studied, but the Japanese corporate world also retains much of the ethos of the Imperial Japanese Army, its expectation of total commitment from its members and its ruthlessness or unconcern with the fate of 'outsiders'. Morale has sunk low, satisfaction is conspicuously absent: there is a profound ambiguity at the heart of the Japanese achievement.

The goal of becoming a 'livelihood great power' is itself ambiguous: carrying an implication that the transformation that is required is material and quantitative, and that nothing less than 'great power' status will do for Japan (although in the balance between 'great power' and 'ordinary people' interests served by national policies to date it is clear that the circle is not easily squared). It appears to be easier for planners to conceive of 'remaking' the Japanese archipelago than of meeting simple and relatively modest demands for a better life. Grandiose and visionary schemes, frequently with disastrous consequences, have characterised the past several decades of Japanese planning and have become increasingly ambitious as bureaucrats seek solutions to the present crisis. From the mid-1980s under the Nakasone government, the various 'Maekawa Report' policies stressed slogans of *minkatsu* (revitalisation through reliance on the private sector) and *naiju kakudai* (expansion of domestic demand). Such terms meant simply pump-priming through large-scale infrastructural and public-works spending. The channels through which such projects are organised are deeply entrenched and a fundamental part of the process of reproduction of the Japanese political economy as a whole (often referred to by the term *doken kokka*, or 'public-works state').[37]

By the workings of the *doken kokka*, astronomical sums are appropriated for projects designed to maintain the engine of growth's momentum, enhance Japan's reputation as a 'great power', and ease trade frictions with the G7 member countries. Massive civil engineering projects are favoured: characteristically bridges, tunnels, highways, railways and airports. The circuits through which the 'construction state' functions ensure that sufficient largesse is thus spread locally to hold in place the ruling party's support network, with some funds in 'rebates' and kickbacks for the party's central apparatus. The expansionist drive and the determination of construction goals and priorities is done by the industry, stemming from its need to expand and replicate itself rather than in response to social forces expressing community needs. Enhancement of the quality of people's lives, when it occurs, is an incidental outcome; that quality is instead frequently diminished.

Characteristic 'big ticket' projects in the early 1990s included schemes to redevelop the national capital by bridging Tokyo Bay between Kisarazu City (in Chiba prefecture) and Kawasaki City (cost $10 billion, for completion by March 1996);[38] conducting extensive waterfront development and, if one prominent architect's plans were accepted, extending the capital by constructing a 30 000 hectare island within Tokyo Bay and cutting a swathe of canals and freeways in and around the city.[39] Five million people could be relocated on the island, and another million in a new city, Boso New Town, which would be built at the Chiba end of the bridge. Kurokawa, whose ideas have found strong political support in Japan since the Nakasone government years, also uses the term *kyosei* to describe his vision; in fact he may be the author of the term in its current sense.[40] The estimated cost of realising his vision amounts to $2450 billion (a sum twenty times greater than the cost of the Apollo space programme) over 35 years. For the trans-bay bridge presently under construction, the hills of Boso in Chiba prefecture are being levelled to produce 900 million cubic metres of earth (about twelve times that required to build the Suez canal).[41] The island construction projects would require a staggering 8400 million cubic metres of 'fill', 125 times the scale of Suez.[42] All told, there are 40 projects under way around Tokyo Bay, including the new Tokyo Airport (at Haneda, cost $11.5 billion, for completion in 1995), the 'Minato Mirai 21' or 21st Century Port City, the Makuhari 'New Capital', various projects for other new towns and islands, a 'Teleport' and a new 'Research and Development City' (at Kazuza).

Not to be outdone, the Kansai area around Osaka and the port city of Kobe has an even grander set of plans to create a vast, high-speed, network of 'intelligent city' 21st century megalopolis that would be known as Kansai.[43] Its 24-hour airport, being built on reclaimed land offshore, will cost about $14.3 billion and open in 1994; a new bridge, the longest suspension bridge in the world (at 3910 metres) is being built to link Kobe with Awajishima island (cost: $6.1 billion, for completion by 1997);[44] a high-speed 'Bay Area Expressway' is being constructed to link the main urban areas in the vicinity, and other schemes include a vast 'Theme Park', a site for a 21st century Olympic bid, and the 'Keihanna' science city,[45] where bureaucratic, business and academic functions can be combined with facilities for play and residence.

Transportation of goods within the vastly expanded Tokyo megalopolis could be facilitated by the construction of a network of 70 to 100 metre deep transport tunnels, and transport from Tokyo to Kansai by a 'maglev' linear motor, which would cut the present two-and-a-half-hour trip to about one hour. A second freeway link is now under construction (for completion by 2002 at a cost of about $80 billion), and new 'bullet train' lines are also being constructed in various parts of the country (with $14 billion to be spent on them by 2001). Other plans, so far only on drawing boards, envisage possibly sinking much of the Tokyo commuter rail network (Yamanote and part of Chuo lines) deep underground to free ground-level space for redevelopment,[46] and building other islands in various locations, such as one, imaginatively entitled 'Japan Sea Acropolis', in the sea between Japan and Russia and Korea.[47]

These grand tunnelling and nature-transforming construction projects will extend the perimeters of the already huge megalopolises of Tokyo and Osaka, shrinking what pockets of nature still remain in their vicinity. Tokyo now has no natural coastline left at all, while its adjacent prefectures of Kanagawa and Chiba have 6 and 2.9 kilometres respectively (in sum 1.2 per cent of the 753-kilometre coastline around Tokyo).[48] Tokyo Bay, once a rich trove of marine and aquatic life,[49] is 'threatened with extinction ... its waters will become a vast aquatic dump for the refuse of industrial civilisation'.[50] In the Osaka area, 2 per cent of the bay still remains but landfill continues with accelerated tempo and 'development' gradually integrates a 160-kilometre stretch of coastline adjacent to Osaka, Awajishima and Wakayama prefecture.

There are many similar projects, either on drawing boards or at various stages of execution. This predilection for gigantic, nature-remoulding projects has deep roots in Japan's 'construction state' political economy, but the contracted, accelerated and artificial world they would create would not necessarily do much to meet the popular desire for a just and humane social order and more rest and recreation; whether the energy manifest in such frenetic activity should be described as expressing 'vitality' seems problematic.

There could perhaps be no clearer example of the mismatch between the felt need for relaxation and communion with the natural order and the policies adopted in practice than the 1987 Resort Law.[51] By the end of the decade, 19.2 per cent of the land area of the entire country was designated for 'resort' development, 7.5 million hectares as against 5.5 million for agriculture.[52] This meant a proliferation of golf courses, ski facilities and luxury hotels, virtually all of which were, in the late 1980s, tied to the heart of the bubble of speculation and corruption. The construction of homogeneous, vulgar and *nouveau riche* resorts, drawn to identical Tokyo design, commonly entailed encroachment on either public or community assets, whether forest,[53] coastline, river, or catchment area, and (often) widespread damage to animal, bird, insect, marine and human life.[54] Apart from the loss of natural coastline, 40 per cent of all Japan's tidelands have now disappeared, owing to landfill, the construction of roads and other works.[55]

At the heart of the Japanese growth of the 1980s, which may be glimpsed in figures such as the above, was the dynamic, virtually irresistible process of appropriating, mobilising and focusing the vitality and energy of the Japanese people in a political economy of exploitation, both human and material, which ultimately exhausts rather than vitalises. Undoubtedly such visions express an extraordinary vigour and confidence and a Promethean energy, akin perhaps to that which marked the launching of crusades and the founding of empires in other times. The desire to lop off mountains, fill in the seas, and create a new and distinctive order out of the wealth that corporate Japan has accumulated in recent decades is not particularly surprising. One of the more philosophically minded of Japan's post-war corporate leaders, Matsushita Konosuke (of National-Panasonic), when advocating the construction of a new island (on such a scale that it would involve levelling 20 per cent, or 75 000 sq.km, of Japan's mountains and dumping them in the sea to create a fifth island, about the size of Shikoku, as a 200-year national project) argued that the containment and focusing of Japan's energies in some such gigantic project at home could create the sort of national unity and sense of purpose that formerly had come from wars.[56] Had Matsushita, writing in 1976, lived to see the depth of friction created internationally by Japan's untrammelled expansion in subsequent years, he would undoubtedly have seen in it further justification for his plan. The idea that the Japanese people should be mobilised (like the Duke of York's army that was marched up the hill and then down again) to level mountains and fill in the sea lest the force of their impact on the outside world provoke uncontainable anti-Japaneseness, or even lead to war, is a fundamentally impoverished, even deranged vision, redolent of despair in preferring to tie the Japanese people to the treadmill of endless (and meaningless) growth rather than face the possibility of constructive, imaginative engagement with the world.

Contrasting with the grand and supremely confident *kyosei* vision of men like Kurokawa and his big-business and bureaucratic backers, whose vision is predicated on the need to maintain growth and the equation of growth with large-scale application of concrete and steel and the marginalisation or conquest of nature, are the voices from non-mainstream elements of Japanese society - academics, philosophers, local activists, artists - who are scathing about the failures of three decades of planned regional development in Japan,[57] and urge more modest visions, of regional sufficiency and autonomy (including in food), a shrunken apparatus of central government, and preservation of existing rural, mountain and coastal communities rather than their displacement by gigantic development corridors of 'teletopias' and 'green cities'. They would turn villages into places in which people would want to live rather than expand the cities without limit. They have been fundamentally critical of the hubris of the nature-remaking schemes pursued in Japan over the past several decades. They are sceptical of the idea that Japan has become a 'prosperous' country as a result, and they warn of environmental catastrophe and social rootlessness and irrelevance to actual 'needs' implicit in the grand plans.[58] They too on occasion employ the word *kyosei* to encapsulate their prescription,[59] indicating the existence of a struggle to determine the content of the term, similar perhaps to the struggle in the 1930s to determine what would be the content of the closely related term *kyozon kyoei* (co-existence and co-prosperity). The attraction of the term, which, though translated as 'symbiosis', literally means 'living together', may be its association with an order of community and nature which is widely seen as past but which exercises a powerful pull on the imagination such that it continues to feed nostalgic longings or to be naively projected into utopian dreams of the future.

The Morita-Kurokawa-Hiraiwa notion of *kyosei* relies on elitist, 'from above', large-scale, bureaucratic and technical elite formulae designed to maintain growth and project grandeur, and on mobilising ordinary people so that their prescriptions will become wanted. The Miyamoto-Uzawa-Murota prescription relies rather on empowering local communities, subjecting the mega-power of corporations and bureaucracy to the constraints of citizen control, drastically curbing growth, and turning attention to the tasks of meeting social needs for housing, leisure, satisfying and meaningful work and the effort to heal the wounds inflicted on Japan's natural environment. The former are commonly seen as the epitome of Japan's vitality, yet the embolisms identified in the earlier part of this chapter are precisely the consequence of untrammelled pursuit of growth under the collusive and unchecked power of government and corporations. It is rather in this little-known, alternative view that may be seen the vitality of a long-suppressed Japanese tradition of *kyosei* in its sense of sharing, mutual respect, harmony with the surrounding natural order and understanding of its limitations.

Recent attempts to gauge the thinking of ordinary Japanese people suggest that their real spokesmen are not Morita, Kurokawa and their like, but the humble philosophers and critics of the citizens' movement. While the Diet was increasingly a preserve of entrenched, semi-feudal factional groups and of hereditary power (with over one-third of elected members being second or third generation), with a supine and ineffectual opposition that bore little relation to popular sentiment or aspiration, there were, nevertheless, indications that at a popular, grassroots level people were not only deeply dissatisfied but maintained a remarkably democratic, humane and internationalist outlook. Late in 1992, the Asahi's weekly journal, *Aera*, conducted a comprehensive survey of political and social thinking both among ordinary readers (1613 people) and among members of the Diet (securing responses from 116 out of 198 first- and second-term members contacted).[60] The most significant responses, reproduced here in slightly different order from the original, were as shown in Table 5.1.

Table 5.1 *Survey of support for political and social propositions*

Proposition supported	Politicians	Citizens
Substantial devolution of political power from Tokyo to regional authorities	92.8	83.7
Priority to Asia over US in determining Japanese foreign policy	69.8	70.6
Economic aid to Russia regardless of progress in settling territorial issues	75.0	58.6
Partial opening of domestic rice market	35.9	41.0
Easing of restrictions on foreign workers	69.6	66.3
Introduction of environmental taxes	60.2	66.7
Reduction of working hours (even at expense of economic growth)	68.6	62.7
Universal admission to university (even at substantial public cost)	64.8	65.4
Paternal child care leave	78.7	72.5
Dissolution of political factions		66.7
Direct popular election of Prime Minister		84.9

Such responses suggest a measure of health and vitality at the level of the public (and even parliamentary) Japanese body politic in sharp contrast to the spectacular embolisms discussed above. A single survey should not carry too heavy an interpretative weight, but this one has the ring of authenticity and corroborates the impression of an observer who has visited and studied Japan regularly over a thirty-year period: that there is a gap between Japan's 'civil society' and its bureaucratic-corporate and state structures which has narrowed little[61] and that a considerable structural transformation will still be required to establish a thoroughly democratic order in Japan.

Such a structural transformation is not impossible. Affluence, for all its emptiness, has largely eliminated poverty and unemployment. Japanese health provision is good and life expectancy among the longest in the world. For Japanese youth, in particular, life offers a wide range of choices and few material constraints. The quality and quantity of information available to the Japanese citizen is superior to that in any other country. Despite the pressures to conform, individualism, even eccentricity, remains strong and idealism persists. Japan's capitalist development has been almost classically 'uneven', leaving problems of centre and regions, people and work, people and nature, citizen and state. It is for the grassroots and community groups of Japan's civil society - union, environmental, women's, human rights, consumer, and the like - to find the strength to force open the system and generate the vitality to achieve a sort of cultural revolution.

New political movements which stood squarely for a devolution of power from Tokyo to the regions were launched in 1992. Citizens' movements continue to struggle on countless fronts to open and democratise the system. Alternative notions of a Japanese world identity were canvassed: of Japan as a 'global civilian power' of a new kind that would concentrate not on the trappings of conventional military power but on the provision to the world of 'international public goods, such as refugee resettlement, natural disaster relief, development of economic infrastructure, and human resources improvements', as well as on 'the exercise of leadership in guaranteeing human rights and clearing up the world's environment'.[62]

The search for a way to break the vicious circle of centralised power, mobilisation, alienating work, consumption and waste will be the true test of the vitality of the Japanese people in the years spanning the end of the century.

Notes

1. According to Japan Economic Research Centre figures, 'Ou, Bei, Ajia de san kyoku koso' (Triangular structure of Europe, America and Asia), *Nihon Keizai Shimbun*, 25 February 1992, pp. 27-8. According to this Institute, the relative weight of the US and Japanese economies would

gradually shift in Japan's favour, so that the US, with 23.6 per cent of world nominal GNP in 1990, would slowly decline, by .9 per cent, .8 per cent, and .6 per cent respectively over each of the following five-year periods to 2005, while Japan would expand its share by 3 per cent, .9 per cent and .6 per cent respectively, till, in 2005, the relative strengths would be 21.3 per cent for the US and 17.3 per cent for Japan. The confidence in the continuing dominance of the US and Japanese economies in world terms, and in the ability of Japan to strengthen its position *vis-à-vis* both the US and the world, is notable.

2. Okita Saburo, 'Japan-US Cooperation is Essential', *Japan Times*, 7 January 1992.
3. 1965 figures from Shigeto Tsuru, *Japan's Capitalism: Creative Defeat and Beyond*, Cambridge University Press, 1993, p. 199, and later details from Sakai Akio, '*Chiteki shoyuken no keizai-teki imi' o ika ni saguru ka*, Kyoto daigaku keizai kenkyusho, February 1992, tables 1 and 3, with 1991 figures from *Purejidento*, March 1992, p. 209.
4. Estimate by Kenneth Courtis, of Deutsche Bank, Tokyo, quoted in Christopher Wood, *The Bubble Economy: The Japanese Economic Collapse*, London, Sidgwick and Jackson, 1992, p.181.
5. Shindo Eiichi, 'Teki mo mikata mo nai jidai no gaiko' (The diplomacy of an age without allies or enemies), *Ekonomisuto*, 24 March 1992, pp. 19-20.
6. *Toyo keizai*, 12 September 1992, p. 44. (Values had, however, been inflated by 2.3 times in the period from 1986 in the case of both land and stocks.)
7. 'The reality of money-soaked politics', *Japan Times*, 28 February 1992.
8. Robert Delfs, 'Smoking Guns', *Far Eastern Economic Review*, 3 December 1992, pp. 19-20.
9. Various sources. See, for example, Robert Delfs, 'The Lost Throne', *Far Eastern Economic Review*, 22 October 1992, p. 12.
10. Richard McGregor, 'People power topples Japan's kingmaker', *The Australian*, 15 October 1992.
11. The Japanese Labour Ministry gives the figure of 2016 hours for 1991, down 2 per cent from 1990, as against 1957 hours for the US and 1638 for West Germany (though both of these were 1989 figures), *International Herald Tribune*, 1 February 1992. Figures produced by a German Economic Institute in 1992 were slightly different, but pointing to the same, or even slightly widening, discrepancy: Japan 2139; US 1817; Switzerland 1764; Germany 1499. Survey by IW Research, Cologne, reported in *Asahi Shimbun*, 1 May 1992.
12. Philippe Pons, 'Japanese ponder how to stop working', *Guardian Weekly*, 12 April 1992.
13. Shimada Haruo, 'The desperate need for new values in Japanese corporate behaviour', *Journal of Japanese Studies*, Vol. 17, No. 1, Winter 1991, pp.107-25, at p. 115.

14. Figures from International Educational Development (a US-based organisation), reported in *Japan Times*, 19 February 1992.
15. Consistently over 80 per cent in US and Western Europe, but in Japan consistently below 80 per cent since 1977. Ito Saburo, 'Ebareru? Nihon no rodo rinri' (Japanese labour ethics: something to be proud of?), *Asahi Shimbun*, 14 February 1992.
16. Survey conducted by International Survey Research Corporation (Chicago), findings presented in Riaz Hassan, 'Attitudes of Employees: 1991 International Norm Comparisons'. (My thanks to Professor Hassan, of Flinders University, Adelaide, for a copy of this unpublished paper.)
17. *Asahi Evening News*, 11 November 1991.
18. 'Yoka manzokudo kono rakusa' (Gap in leisure satisfaction), *Asahi Shimbun*, 30 May 1992.
19. From 'Yu ah! mai sun shain' (You there! My employee in Sun Co. Ltd), quoted in Sadaka Shin, 'Baburu hokai o yomu' (Reading about the bubble burst), *Asahi Shimbun*, 1 December 1991.
20. For a powerful expression of concern over Japan's isolation, see Helmut Schmidt, 'Nihon koritsuka susumu osore' (Deepening fears over Japan's isolation), *Nihon Keizai Shimbun*, 17 February 1992.
21. Funahashi Yoichi, 'Seiko monogatari, sore kara' (Success story, and then), *Sekai*, December 1991, pp. 10-33.
22. An October 1991 survey of US views of Japan's form of government found that 35 per cent thought of it as being freely elected, the rest believing either that it was 'run by the emperor' (20 per cent), a 'dictatorship' (20 per cent), under military rule (13 per cent), or else 'don't know' (17 per cent). William Watts, 'Domestic issues worry Americans', *Japan Times*, 7 January 1992.
23. Ogura Kazuo, Director-General of the Economic Affairs Bureau in the Ministry of Foreign Affairs, 'Chiiki togo to Nihon no sentaku (Regional integration and Japan's options), *Gaiko Forum*, December 1992, pp. 4-11.
24. Takabatake Michitoshi and Sawa Takamitsu, 'Japan acts as role model', *Japan Times*, 1 January 1992, p. 26.
25. Sawa Takamitsu, "Koritsu shijo' de wa jiyu shakai no koji ni' (Efficiency priority leads to Japan becoming the orphan of the free world), *Mainichi Shimbun*, 7 April 1992.
26. *Ibid.*
27. *Asahi Shimbun*, 30 October 1991.
28. Takabatake Michitoshi (with Kunihiro Masao), 'Dango fuhai seiji to ketsubetsu seyo' (Break with corrupt collusive politics), *Sekai*, December 1992, pp. 31-41, at p. 32.
29. 'Morita Shock: A new paradigm needed for Japanese management', *Japanese Business Today*, Vol. 60, No. 3, March 1992, pp. 41-2.
30. Morita Akio, '"Nihongata keiei" ga abunai' ('Japanese management' in danger), *Bungei Shunju*, February 1992, pp. 94-103.

31. Tsuji Yomei, 'Burokkuka suru sekai keizai' (World economy moving towards blocs), Part 16, *Asahi Shimbun*, 27 April 1992. (All three of these English terms were used by Hiraishi as he struggled to articulate what he meant.) See also Anthony Rowley, 'Ease up, Japan', *Far Eastern Economic Review*, 6 August 1992.

32. Tsuji, *op. cit.*

33. *Asahi Shimbun*, editorial, 7 February 1992.

34. Anthony Rowley, 'Kinder, gentler Japan', *Far Eastern Economic Review*, 9 July 1992.

35. Nagano Kenji, '"Kaishashugi" no shizuka no hokai' (Quiet collapse of 'company-ism'), *Sekai*, February 1992, pp. 44-51, at p. 47.

36. *Ibid.*

37. For a further analysis of this phenomenon, see my 'Pacific Dreamtime and Japan's New Millenialism', *Australian Outlook*, Vol. 43, No. 2, August 1989, pp. 64-73.

38. Sano Shin'ichi, 'Tokyo-wan ni nagekomareru yamayama' (Mountains dumped into Tokyo Bay), *Aera*, 15 December 1992, pp. 6-10.

39. Kurokawa Kisho (ed.), '21 seiki e no teigen: Tokyo to chiho no kyosei' (Proposal for the 21st century: Tokyo and the regions living together), *Lightup*, April 1992. This is a convenient resume of the more substantial text by Kurokawa and 'Gurupu 2025': *Tokyo kaizo keikaku no kinkyu teian: 2025 nen no kokudo to Tokyo* (Urgent proposal for a plan for reshaping Tokyo: Tokyo and the national lands in the year 2025).

40. See also Kurokawa's *The Architecture of Symbiosis*, New York, Rizzoli, 1988.

41. Sano, *op. cit.*

42. Kurokawa, *op. cit.*

43. 'Osaka-wan gururi daihenshin' (Total transformation of Osaka Bay), *Asahi Shimbun*, 5 May 1992.

44. This construction project will consume 200 000 tonnes of steel and 1.4 million cubic metres of concrete. Sano, *op. cit.*, p. 8.

45. Kansai bunka gakujutsu kenkyu toshi (Kansai Culture and Technology Research City), being built on lands adjacent to Kyoto, Osaka and Nara, from which it takes its name Keihanna.

46. A Kumagai plan, which it reckons could be done for about $80 billion. 'Chika 100 meteru ni JR sen', *Asahi Shimbun*, 15 June 1988.

47. A Tobishima corporation idea: a 3.14 sq. km island at estimated cost of about $250 billion (33 trillion yen), to be built over 15 years and accommodate between 50 000 and 100 000 people. 'Floating island proposed by Tokyo firm', *Japan Times*, 6 September 1991.

48. Sano, *op. cit.*, p. 7. The proportion of Japan's coastline as a whole that remains in a pristine state is probably around 40 per cent; for the inland sea area, it is much less.

49. Kevin Short, 'Tokyo Bay: Crabs and Concrete', *Japan Environment Monitor*, Vol. 2, No. 3, July 1989, pp. 1, 6-7, 16.

50. Yasuda Yasoi, 'Tokyo On and Under the Bay', *Japan Quarterly*, 35, 2, April-June 1988, p. 124.
51. For a detailed study, see my 'The Price of Affluence: The Political Economy of Japanese Leisure', *New Left Review*, No. 188, July-August 1991, pp. 121-34.
52. *Ibid.*, p. 123.
53. 1 per cent of Japan's forests was felled for golf construction by the end of the 1980s. Yamada Kunihiro, 'The triple evil of golf courses', *Japan Quarterly*, July-September 1990, p. 235.
54. For a summary account of Japan's 'pending biological disaster' as 'virtually one-quarter of all vertebrate populations in Japan can be regarded as at risk', with the otter and the crested ibis among recently vanished species and the brown and black bears evidently approaching extinction, see Mark Brazil, 'The wildlife of Japan: A 20th century naturalist's view', *Japan Quarterly*, July-September 1992, pp. 328-38.
55. 'Higata' (Tidelands), *Asahi Shimbun*, 6 September 1992.
56. Matsushita Konosuke, 'Watashi no kokudo baizoron', *Bungei Shunju*, May 1976, pp. 136-42, translated as 'Doubling Japan's Land Space', *Japan Interpreter*, Vol. 11, No. 3, Winter 1977, pp. 279-92.
57. Miyamoto Kenichi, 'Kokudo sono kaihatsu no 30 nen' (Thirty years of development of the national lands), *Sekai*, August 1992, pp. 169-76.
58. Perhaps the best known are Miyamoto Kenichi, Uzawa Hirofumi and Murota Takeshi of Osaka, Niigata and Hitotsubashi universities respectively. See, for example, Uzawa Hirofumi and Murota Takeshi, 'Jizokuteki kaihatsu to keizaigaku no yakuwari' (Sustainable development and the role of economics), *Ekonomisuto*, 10 March 1992, pp. 82-8; Miyamoto Kenichi, 'Shuchu hoka o abita Nihongata uotafuronto kaihatsu' (The concentrated fire of Japanese-style waterfront development), *Gekkan Asahi*, June 1991, and, also by Miyamoto, 'Kankyo hozon no wakuuchi de keizai o hatten saseyo' (Economic development within the framework of environmental preservation), *Ekonomisuto*, 17 March 1992, pp. 24-31.
59. See, for example, Osaki Masaharu, Murai Yoshinori and Murota Takeshi, 'Chiiki jiritsu to Ajia to no kyosei' (Regional self-sufficiency and co-existence with Asia), *Entoropi dokuhon 5* (The Entropy Reader, No. 5), The Bessatsu Keizai Seminar, Nippon Hyoronsha, August 1988.
60. 'Seiji kaikaku kinkyu anketo' (Urgent survey on political reform), *Aera*, 22 December 1992, pp. 6-24.
61. When the Peace Keeping Organisation bill was passed into law in June 1992 it had a mere 15 per cent level of popular support, according to the *Nihon Keizai Shimbun's* survey (although 40 per cent were in the curious category of seeing it as 'inevitable'). Among Japan's constitutional scholars, a mere 5 per cent thought the government's action constitutionally justifiable; 78 per cent still believe the very existence of the Self-Defence Forces is unconstitutional (*Asahi Shimbun*, 'Yonjugo sai o mukaeta heiwa kempo', *Asahi Shimbun*, 3 May 1992).

62. Yoichi Funabashi, 'Japan and America: Global Partners', *Foreign Policy*, Spring 1992, pp. 24-39, at p. 37.

6 Organised Dependence: Politicians and Bureaucrats in Japan[1]

E. B. Keehn

Introduction

By 1994 it had become anachronistic to think of Japan's system of ministries and elite bureaucrats as contributing to the political and economic vitality of the nation.[2] The bureaucracy is held responsible by some for increasingly rancorous trade conflicts with the United States.[3] With the LDP's loss of power in the summer of 1993, the intransigence of the bureaucracy on matters of policy, particularly on the issue of tax reform, has often left politicians looking inept and too willing to surrender the privileges and responsibilities of leadership to bureaucrats.[4]

This tendency of politicians to surrender leadership to bureaucrats is nothing new in Japan. Bureaucrats have traditionally enjoyed a highly privileged role in that nation's governmental system. The bureaucracy remains the major initiator of legislation and policy in the 1990s, as it has been throughout most of the post-war period. Moreover, the bureaucracy's control over the levers of national administration, and its management of a complex system of licensing and approval functions, gives it a degree of authority rarely found in other democratic settings.

Despite its excesses - indeed, perhaps because of them - a number of analysts cite the bureaucracy as a major source of public policy vitality for Japan.[5] This contribution occurred at two basic levels: strategic policies with regard to the economy; and helping the LDP to maintain conservative dominance in electoral politics between 1955 and 1993. Both of these contributions to Japan's vitality are controversial. On the issue of the economy, there is no doubt that the web of market and industrial regulations have helped to shape the behaviour and strategies of Japanese firms. The main question is whether its influence has done more harm than good.

For example, MITI's use of industrial policy is often cited as helping Japan to develop major industries, such as autos and electronics, into world-class competitors. MoF's regulation of the financial system, its management of the tax system, its ability to influence monetary policy and its grip on the annual budget-making process have all given it a particularly powerful voice in the shaping of Japan's economic and political life.

The economic contribution of bureaucrats to Japan's post-war vitality is only part of the story. At least as important has been the bureaucracy's contribution towards the maintenance of the LDP's conservative dominance between 1955 and 1993. The bureaucracy's willingness to work with the LDP in dispensing public goods to local constituencies was an important factor in helping the party maintain electoral control of the Diet for 38 years.

Of equal significance, the web of regulations controlled by the bureaucracy created fertile ground for LDP influence-peddling. The maintenance of regulations with questionable economic or social rationale provided numerous LDP Diet members with the opportunity to rent their influence to businesses in search of relief from bureaucratic over-regulation. By clinging to these regulations the bureaucracy was responsible for helping to create a highly energetic market-place for influence-peddling by the LDP.

Thus the bureaucracy contributed to two types of vitality and profit-making within the Japanese system: one based on general national benefit centred on economic expansion, and the other centred on the furthering of the particular interests of LDP Diet members and their clients.

What these different aspects of Japanese bureaucracy have in common is that the bureaucracy represents the power and policy high ground of political life in Japan. The inability of national politicians to exercise effective political and policy control over the bureaucracy remains an enduring criticism of political leadership in Japan. On the face of it, this is an odd criticism. Constitutional mechanisms for the formal coordination and political control of the bureaucracy exist in Japan. The American-written Japanese constitution is unambiguous on this point - unlike, interestingly, the US constitution. Yet none of these constitutional mechanisms, taken either separately or jointly, have proven adequate to the task.[6] This remains one of the basic problems in the issue of administrative reform in Japan.[7]

I shall approach this problem of control over the bureaucracy from several angles, beginning with the historical background and following up with a look at the bureaucracy's long-term electoral relationship with the LDP. The LDP's loss of power in the summer elections of 1993 brought the subject of bureaucratic reform to the forefront of political debate in Japan, but nothing has been done up until now to shift the institutional imbalance between politicians and bureaucrats in Japan's governmental system. If anything, this imbalance is more pronounced than it was under the LDP. Next I shall consider issues of information and policy dependence between the Diet and the bureaucracy. Finally, I shall examine the relationship between the policy interests of politicians and the manner in which this is superseded by the bureaucratic strategy of compartmentalising issues, a practice which complicates attempts at political leadership.

My purpose is to provide a short list of factors that help explain the distinctive organisational relationship that developed between the LDP, in power between 1955 and 1993, and Japan's system of elite bureaucrats. Some of these factors are controversial, but I nevertheless regard them as important in arriving at a fair understanding of the strengths and weaknesses of the bureaucracy's relationship with the Diet. In my view, modes of interaction between the bureaucracy and politicians represent the most important institutional relationship in Japanese government. It is here that political vision and leadership, to the extent it is articulated, must be translated into practical policy.

Historical Continuities in Japanese Bureaucracy

The problem of bureaucracy in a democracy is by no means recent. Woodrow Wilson placed this concern at the centre of American political science over a century ago with his dichotomy between politics and administration.[8] The debate has continued into this century - and will likely continue into the next - as reconciling the position of bureaucracy with the principles of democratic representation remains a fundamental problem in the study of government. The issue is particularly acute in Japan, though the historical reasons for this bear little resemblance to the historical concern for representative government expressed by Wilson.

The foundation of Japan's contemporary bureaucracy was established in the late 19th century in response to the forced opening of the country by Commodore Perry of the United States, ending approximately two-and-a-half centuries of enforced national isolation. In response to this opening, Japan's bureaucracy was established as a strategic arm of modernising elites to aid in mapping out and implementing Japan's response to the West. The fact that a highly strategic and task-oriented modern system of ministries antedated Japan's political parties, constitution and parliament is a defining characteristic of Japanese political and economic development. As Chalmers Johnson observes, 'Differing from the United States, [Japan's] ministries were not created to be civil servants, or to provide regulation of private concerns, or to supply jobs for party loyalists, but rather to guide Japan's forced development in order to forestall incipient colonisation by Western imperialists.'[9]

This has meant that the problem for bureaucracy in Japan has traditionally been how to integrate legislative institutions with the powerful, centralised bureaucratic structures of the modern state that preceded them.[10] From their inception political parties developed strategies that provided for their institutional inclusion within the interests of bureaucrats. As Bernard Silberman notes, by 1900 'political-party recruitment of ex-bureaucrats became characteristic of Japanese political life and an apparent consequence of the bureaucracy's dominant position.'[11]

The Diet did not begin to assert its independence until the era of Taisho Democracy, the years roughly corresponding to the reign of the Emperor Taisho between 1912 and 1926. Political parties first began to intrude into the governing of Japan in this period,[12] but it was a process complicated and curtailed by Japan's rapid expansion of its military and empire through the 1930s, and by its commitment to total war in 1941.

The Diet's struggle to assert itself was not automatically aided by the end of the Second World War and the US Occupation. While the US Occupation was predicated on the ideals of democratisation, in what was regarded as a matter of political practicality, Japan's system of ministries and the elite bureaucrats who managed them were retained as a major continuity with pre-war government. In fact, the civil bureaucracy was the sector least affected. T. J. Pempel writes in this regard that 'although the bureaucracy was indirectly affected by political changes in other areas, few direct attacks on the political powers of the Japanese national bureaucracy were attempted during the US Occupation.'[13] With the removal of the military as a rival power centre, the civil bureaucracy's position in government was further enhanced.[14]

This lack of reform, and the continuities with pre-war legal and elite attributes, leaves students of the Japanese state with the imposing task of seeking to understand how a complex developmental history has influenced the forms of bureaucratic authority. Akagi Tsuruki has pioneered this sort of scholarship. He points out that Japan's post-war ministries were allowed to continue operating under a form of institutional authority left largely unaltered by the US Occupation. Continuities in the pre-war legal structure of the bureaucracy were retained at least partially because Japan's bureaucrats successfully argued for a retention of their administrative power under the Occupation.[15] But it is not as if the US Occupation did not understand the implications of what it was doing. This arrangement was also in its interests. Its decision to rule through Japan's existing governmental institutions meant it could both rely on, and benefit from, an authoritative bureaucracy that could act on its behalf.

The US Occupation did initiate a major reorganisation of Japan's system of ministries and agencies at the level of formal organisation, but few elite bureaucrats were removed from office. Hans Baerwald points out that most of those purged were police officers within the Ministry of Home Affairs who were also members of the *Butokukai* (Military Virtue Society). They were not elite bureaucratic policymakers. In fact the ratio between purges of military and ex-military personnel and bureaucrats was approximately one hundred to one.[16] As a result elite bureaucrats successfully preserved elements of their pre-war status in the post-war system of ministries and agencies. However, as a group, they also vigorously adapted to the political realities of democratisation, learning both to cooperate with and penetrate the political party power structures of the post-war era.

Bureaucrats in Politics

The role of ex-bureaucrats in post-war Japanese politics is well documented. Ex-bureaucrats have accounted for 10 of Japan's post-war prime ministers. And until Tanaka Kakuei's rise to the prime ministership in 1972, all of the post-war period's most powerful prime ministers were ex-bureaucrats.

Historically, the LDP welcomed retiring bureaucrats as candidates to stand in the upper and lower house Diet elections, with the various LDP factions competing with one another to attract the most promising individuals. Ex-bureaucrats were prized because of the valuable policy networks they could call on within their old ministries. This continues to be the case in the 1990s, despite the LDP's loss of power, and despite arguments that politicians have become the independent and authoritative focus of policymaking in Japan.[17] If anything, competition to attract politically able ex-bureaucrats wanting to stand for election increased between LDP factions in that party's last few years in power. For example, of the 11 candidates fielded by the LDP's largest faction in the summer upper-house election of 1992, seven were former bureaucrats.[18] With the LDP's loss of power we can expect even more vigorous competition between the LDP and its breakaway factions for ex-bureaucrats willing to stand for elected office.

However, it is important to note that even at the height of its power, when its links with bureaucrats were at their strongest, the LDP was always careful to limit the number of ex-bureaucrats it brought into public office through an informal quota system. Even with the vagaries of a complex electoral system of multi-member constituencies and the uncertainties attached to any candidate's run for office, the number of ex-bureaucrats in the LDP remained fairly constant throughout the post-war period, generally accounting for one-third of the party's upper- and lower-house presence in the Diet. For example, in 1987, former bureaucrats held 75 of the 302 seats in the Diet's lower house, and 49 of 144 seats in the upper house.[19]

It is often argued that bureaucrats with political ambitions have been forced to leave their ministries earlier and earlier in their careers if they are to have any hope of gaining influence within the legislature. But Japan's most senior bureaucrats are still welcomed into politics as powerful players. For example, in the August 1989 upper house elections alone, the LDP supported the candidacies of four previous vice-ministers. Their respective bureaucratic careers had been in the Ministry of Finance, the Ministry of Construction, and the Ministry of Agriculture, Forests and Fisheries, and the Management of Coordination Agency.[20] And when Hosokawa Morihiro's reform party, the Nihon Shinto, ran candidates in the 1993 election, they also welcomed former vice-ministers into their party.

Until the summer of 1993 and the LDP's loss of power to the coalition led by Hosokawa, the Japanese bureaucrat-turned-politician was, almost without exception, affiliated with the conservative and dominant LDP. In rare cases these individuals opted for affiliation with one of the equally conservative minor parties such as the Komeito (Clean Government Party). If the LDP fails to regain power in the next lower house elections, it is likely that bureaucrats who turn politicians will begin to diversify their political affiliations. Not only is this to be expected on the grounds of self-interest, but there is also historical precedent for this. In the early post-war years ex-bureaucrats accounted for a minor percentage of those elected to the Diet on the Japan Socialist Party ticket (JSP).[21] It was only once the LDP cemented its electoral dominance in the late 1950s that bureaucrats with political ambitions began concentrating their electoral affiliations almost exclusively with the LDP.

In modern industrial democratic systems this sort of unidimensional political affiliation on the part of ex-bureaucrats has been uncommon in the extreme. The example of bureaucrats in France, often compared with their Japanese counterparts in terms of power and prestige, is instructive here. Ezra Suleiman notes that 'In the 1978 legislative elections, higher civil servants alone represented 10 per cent of the candidates in the

Republican Party, 7.2 per cent in the RPR (Rassemblement pour la République), 6.9 per cent in the MRG (Left Radicals), 5.2 per cent in the Socialist party, and 1 per cent in the Communist party.'[22]

The near exclusive LDP affiliation of the bureaucrat-turned-politician from the late 1950s to the early 1990s brought a wellspring of policy expertise into the LDP that could not be easily matched by opposition parties, with the ex-bureaucrat playing an important role in managing LDP relations with the ministries. In the realm of Japanese politics, an effective politician has always needed access to the ministerial dispensers of public goods to serve his or her constituency. Ex-bureaucrats enter politics with these connections already in place, and with an intimate knowledge of the political and bureaucratic processes that work to channel public goods in one direction or another. This contradicts the view that the role of the ex-bureaucrat in the LDP is declining in significance.[23]

The role of the ex-bureaucrat in the Diet can be overplayed, and there is a cadre of LDP politicians without a background in the bureaucracy who work effectively in the realm of policy, or at least have the ambitions to do so. But the general image of the bureaucrat-turned-politician dealing with policy is difficult to dispel, even among LDP politicians. Consider the comments of LDP Diet member Noda Takeshi. While serving as Minister of Construction in July 1989, Noda criticised Kanemaru Shin for his contention that the newly-introduced consumption tax be fully reviewed. As *The Japan Times* reported:

> Noda, a former member of the Finance Ministry and an expert on tax affairs, made his remarks at a news conference held after Friday's Cabinet meeting.
>
> Before launching his attack on farmers, he criticised former Deputy Prime Minister Kanemaru, who on Thursday called for a thorough review of the consumption tax and mentioned the possibility of freezing or abandoning it.
>
> 'If Mr Kanemaru were well versed in policy matters, his call would carry a lot of weight, Noda said. But he is a politician, aloof from policy matters.'[24]

It might seem unthinkable that a cabinet minister would publicly label a senior legislator and influential power broker in his own party incompetent in policy. But as an ex-Ministry of Finance bureaucrat, Noda felt qualified to do so.

Policy expertise is not the only thing ex-bureaucrats brought with them when they entered the LDP. Their concentration within that party also gave them the ability to build coalitions that could manipulate events from within the LDP, and so affect the course of national politics. Nakasone Yasuhiro, in significant part, owed his tenure as prime minister to the decision by ex-bureaucrats descended from the pre-war Ministry of Home Affairs and its offshoots - the Ministry of Health and Welfare, the Ministry of Labour, the Ministry of Construction, the Ministry of Autonomy, and the National Policy Agency - to cross party faction lines in support of his candidacy for the LDP presidency.[25] Since the LDP maintained a majority in the Diet in this period, the LDP presidency automatically conferred the prime ministership. It is generally acknowledged that Tanaka Kakuei was the kingmaker in Nakasone's rise to the prime ministership, but it was the support of this group of ex-bureaucrats who crossed faction lines that guaranteed the nation's highest political seat for Nakasone. It was this same support that maintained Nakasone in that post for three consecutive terms, even as Tanaka Kakuei's power waned. Their motivation? Nakasone was a young police inspector and a member of the minister's secretariat in the Ministry of Home Affairs in the years just before and after the Second World War.[26]

The political prominence of ex-bureaucrats in Japan is usually studied only at the national level, but it is a scenario repeated at the prefectural level. The numbers suggest that this is an area where research is needed. Ex-bureaucrats accounted for approximately one-third of all prefectural governors in 1989 (17 of 47), and nearly one-half by 1992. All were members of the LDP. They had served as elite bureaucrats either in the Ministry of Home Affairs, the Ministry of Finance, the Ministry of International Trade and Industry, the Ministry of Agriculture, Forests and Fisheries, or the Ministry of Foreign Affairs. In 1986 alone, ex-bureaucrats hailing from either the pre-war or post-war Ministry of Home Affairs accounted for one third of Japan's prefectural governors.[27] Also in 1989 the governors of the greater metropolitan areas of Tokyo and Osaka, Japan's two largest clusters of financial, industrial, and human resources, were also ex-bureaucrats - as were a number of mayors in such large industrial cities as Yokohama and Kawasaki.[28]

Bureaucracy, Information and the Diet

Ex-bureaucrats have also been welcomed into the Diet because of their sophisticated understanding of how ministries use information to create policy and, at least, of equal importance, slant that information to create the sort of policy analysis which supports their ministerial agendas. This has traditionally been a large area of concern in post-war Japanese politics because there are so few sources of independent analysis available to Diet members, regardless of party affiliation, outside of the realm of ministry interests. For the most part, information and analysis needed to make policy is almost exclusively controlled by the bureaucracy.[29] Even the LDP, with its nearly four-decade hold on the Diet, was always largely limited to information and analysis provided by the bureaucracy. Their numerous informal links with the bureaucracy, and their unbroken hold on ministerial cabinet posts between 1955 and 1993, ensured that the depth and breadth of the information available to them was far greater than that available for opposition parties. The opposition parties could receive rough data from the bureaucracy upon request, and the more astute opposition Diet members had well-established back-door links with ministries, but in principle the parties out of power received little information or analysis beyond that formally produced for the public.[30]

Information dependence on the bureaucracy has been further enhanced by the minimal research capabilities of the Diet. A junior Diet member usually has a staff of two - not even roughly comparable to the staffs of the most junior members of the US Congress. Of equal importance, Diet members, regardless of party affiliation, have no recourse to publicly funded information organisations to aid them in their policy deliberations. Japan's sole attempt to create an organisation that could achieve some form of independent policy analysis for input into government was the establishment of the National Institute for Research Advancement (NIRA) in 1974. But Namiki Nobuyoshi, an ex-MITI bureau chief, argues that NIRA's research is generally contracted out, they engage in little or no quality control, and the result is work of uneven quality that is often unusable in the creation of public policy.[31]

An added complication is that NIRA is predominantly staffed with retired bureaucrats, or bureaucrats on temporary leave from their ministries or agencies, and little is produced there that challenges the institutional interests of the ministries or the LDP. Finally, critics charge that the creation of NIRA actually represented a closing of the ranks between the powerful business organisations and elite bureaucrats that fund the organisation. Even if such criticism is discounted, it at least suggests the sort of doubts held about NIRA's ability to supply quasi-independent policy research for Diet members and the public.[32]

In the views of some critics, the systematic lack of independent sources of information has resulted in a strong political preference for narrow, sectorially defined policy issues. As Gotoda Masaharu, a prominent LDP Diet member and ex-bureaucrat, argues:

The data and information on which today's politicians base fundamental policy decisions are all held by the bureaucrats. They summarise it, collate it, put it into the party system, and something called policy pops out. The results are policies decided on the basis of ministerial and departmental interests. This makes it impossible [for politicians] to make fundamental, broad-based political decisions.[33]

The most frequently heard criticism of this system as described by Gotoda is that it results in public policy which protects and advances the policy preferences of bureaucrats and their closest clients. A bureaucratically structured public policy system that prefers practicality and the servicing of narrow interests still could work to Japan's advantage if it was obvious that political leadership capped the system and gave it direction. In fact, this is precisely the picture presented by the classic American foreign policy model of multiple advocacy.[34] But in Japan neither the cabinet, the Office of the Prime Minister, nor the Management and Coordination Agency - all charged with overseeing the bureaucracy and coordinating its activities - has the institutional or organisational means to direct the implementation of policy. Instead, implementation is left exclusively to each ministry.

Why has Japan's legislative branch shown such a lack of interest in creating institutions that can provide it with an independent research capability, and the means to force bureaucratic interests into a identifiably cohesive set of publicly and politically directed policies? This probably resulted from the LDP's multi-decade hold on political power, and the benefits it derived from its close links with the bureaucracy. The creation of an effective and independent research capability for the Diet would have benefited opposition parties as well as the LDP, and would potentially have allowed the opposition parties to begin a meaningful challenge to LDP hegemony in debates over public policy.

When the coalition headed by Hosokawa Morihiro pushed the LDP out of power in the summer of 1993, conditions were better than at any time since the US military occupation to create conditions that would allow for political control over the bureaucracy. The coalition could have taken a first step towards the creation of a diversification of sources of sophisticated policy research. In a policy speech to the Diet, Hosokawa made it clear that gaining control of the bureaucracy was one of his government's basic priorities. It was apparently not a priority shared by a majority of his coalition partners and no reforms were proposed to address the information imbalance between politicians and bureaucrats.

A politician's dependence on the bureaucracy for its information and analysis is replicated at the level of political appointees within the ministries. The parties in power can post a single minister *(daijin)* and one to two parliamentary vice-ministers *(seimu jikan)* into each ministry. These individuals are not powerless, and activist ministers can occasionally exert influence over their ministries. Nevertheless they are placed in a highly dependent relationship with their bureaucrats. As Campbell points out, political appointees lack the staff resources needed to develop policy on their own and so must defer to the career bureaucrats.[35] Without outside sources of staff, information, and analysis, even the activist minister is organisationally constrained to working within an arena determined by the processes and preferences of the surrounding career bureaucrats.

The prime minister has greater discretion in setting policy agendas than cabinet ministers, yet even Japan's highest political office is placed in a highly dependent relationship with the bureaucracy. Outside of political cabinet appointees, who are in any event chosen to provide a coalitionist balance between LDP factions, the prime minister is without an independently chosen staff. Instead, seconded bureaucrats compose the prime minister's personal staff, with the distribution of posts determined by the bureaucrats themselves. Moreover, the size of the Office of the Prime Minister was reduced in 1984 as a result of a campaign of administrative reform undertaken by then prime minister Nakasone.[36] Although Nakasone was widely regarded as a politician committed to presidential style leadership, his administrative reforms actually weakened the prime minister's ability to formulate ideas and policies separate from the interests of the bureaucracy.

Upper House Diet member Kakizawa Koji, a member of the LDP with experience in the cabinet, had this relationship of party dependence on the bureaucracy in mind when he explained that:

> The day before cabinet meetings, there is always a meeting of vice-ministers. It is not widely known by outsiders, but in reality, this meeting is the means by which the will of government is decided. Cabinet meetings (the next day) just confirm decisions made at the vice-ministers' meeting.[37]

This helps explain the observation that cabinet meetings are generally ceremonial affairs that exist to verify the decisions made the day before by vice-ministers. Issues that have not first been vetted by the bureaucrats are rarely discussed.[38] However, it should be pointed out that the vice-minister meetings are also generally formalities that exist to endorse positions already worked out in advance in all their details by the ministries.

Under these circumstances it is not surprising that a politician's sphere of policy influence is generally defined within the interests of whatever ministries oversee the policy area he or she is interested in. As the *Wall Street Journal* has suggested, 'In bureaucrat-run Japan, the politician plays the role of lobbyist.'[39] The attributes of dependence on the bureaucracy for policy expertise and information does not create a political environment that encourages the development of nationally minded politicians. As an editorial in the *Asahi* complains:

> What kind of politicians can be called pros? The pros are supposed to be people who chart the course for the nation to follow, provide for the life of the people, and discharge their legislative responsibilities. In practice, however, many politicians hardly attend to these tasks, leaving them to the bureaucrats.[40]

This sort of lament over the lack of political pros, that is politicians interested in leadership and in directing the bureaucracy, is by no means recent. In particular, it is a recurring concern of bureaucrats who have long worried that no amount of policy expertise can substitute for political vision.[41]

Conclusion

Earlier I suggested that the institutional relationship between the party in power and the bureaucracy is crucial because that is precisely where political vision and leadership must be translated into practical policy. In Japan's case, the dependencies in the relationship between the party in power and bureaucracy suggest that most of what gets translated into policy begins with practical bureaucratic concerns, not with political leadership. The factors underlying this include the following.

First, the LDP and the first three coalition governments which followed it in 1993-94 have shown a willingness to accept and maintain information asymmetries with the bureaucracy. A closely related factor is politicians' acceptance and maintenance of the bureaucracy's dominance in the creation of policy and legislation. During the years of LDP rule, the willingness to allow both information and policy dependence stemmed from the near-exclusive affiliation of the bureaucrat-turned-politician with the LDP. This contributes to high-level political reliability between the LDP and elite bureaucrats. It also gave the LDP exclusive access to ministerial venues of policymaking which they manipulated to service their electoral base. The coalition parties which have followed the LDP have not attempted to redress the asymmetries between bureaucrats and politicians.

The parties in power have also been largely content to allow ministries to define and divide policy spheres according to their own jurisdictional interests. This effectively surrenders political management of the bureaucracy. Japan's bureaucracy remains largely unresponsive to changes in political leadership. Or perhaps more seriously, politicians remain uninterested or unable to create the institutional requirements for leadership over the bureaucracy.[42]

In essence, the LDP-bureaucracy relationship evolved into an implicit political management system that was highly successful in delivering political stability and incremental policy change. Freed from policy responsibilities, the LDP concentrated on staying in power and securing its voter base by accessing public goods available within the bureaucracy, such as public works projects. At the same time, the relative lack of LDP intrusiveness into the bureaucracy meant the bureaucrats were free to maintain sources of institutional privilege and power.[43] What is disturbing is that the coalition governments which have followed the LDP, despite their rhetoric to the contrary, have shown little interest in creating a more neutral bureaucratic system.

It is worth speculating on what will happen to the bureaucracy without an LDP-controlled Diet. Of course, it is possible that new parties in power will not introduce reforms, and will instead attempt to gain the same bureaucratically derived benefits the LDP enjoyed before them. But even if post-LDP era parties want to reap LDP-style bureaucratic benefits, it is unlikely they will be able to do so. The benefits which resulted from asymmetries in the LDP-bureaucrat relationship relied on stable exchange networks which will be difficult to maintain in a system where parties continually re-coalesce to form new coalitions, or rotate in power. Moreover, it assumes that the bureaucracy will show no preference in who gains access to these networks, an assumption contradicted by the fact that political norms within the bureaucracy have shown themselves to consistently favour conservatism.

The ideal place for reform to start would be with the creation of independent sources of analysis and information for Diet members - something similar to the US Congressional Research Service. This would allow Diet members to more successfully design legislation and policy outside the interests of the system of ministries. More effective methods of exercising political control over ministries would also be needed. An increase in the number of political appointees within the ministries would help, particularly if it gave cabinet ministers the latitude to bring in trusted personal staff. Most Japanese specialists in public administration would also argue for a system of personnel management that rotates bureaucratic elites more thoroughly between ministries to break down career affiliations with a single ministry. All of this would then need to be brought under the control of the prime minister's office, which would need greatly strengthened mechanisms for forcing greater coordination of the bureaucracy.

None of these recommendations are new. All of them, and quite a few more, have been discussed in the Japanese press, in the Diet, and by political scientists and economists. A failure to reform the bureaucracy could carry serious consequences for Japan. One danger is that bureaucratic policymaking will become further insulated from political leadership. This potentially widens the already large gap between voter preferences and public policy in Japan. If there were doubts that Japan was a democracy under the 38 years of the LDP,[44] these doubts can only be given further credence by a party system that continues to occupy itself with forming new cabinets without bothering to form a basis for leadership on policy.[45] Any new party in power will find itself unable to direct policy without gaining political control of the bureaucracy. As of this writing, the institutional mechanisms to make this possible simply do not exist.

This returns us to the issue of vitality. If the bureaucracy has historically been a source of vitality for Japan, it has been an unfortunate source. The inability of politicians to systematically lead the bureaucracy on major issues like tax reform, deregulation and trade conflicts has done little to enhance Japan's vitality in the post-Cold War world. The resolution of these sorts of issues - issues that attack traditional areas of bureaucratic authority - will occur only with the creation of a political system capable of, and interested in, leading and creating a politically responsive bureaucratic system. Yet when it comes to this sort of reform, both politicians and bureaucrats seem to be following the advice Oliver Goldsmith gives in *The Vicar of Wakefield*: 'Let us be inflexible, and fortune will at last change in our favour.'[46]

Notes

1. A note on usage: this chapter is concerned with Japan's system of higher civil servants. The term bureaucrat is used to refer exclusively to this group. In addition the use of the term bureaucracy is limited to Japan's centralised system of ministries.

2. Ohmae Kenichi, *Heisei kanryo-ron* (Heisei era bureaucracy), Tokyo, Shogakkan, 1994.

3. Nancy Dunne and Michiyo Nakamoto, 'Ties with Tokyo in disrepair', *Financial Times*, 16 March 1994, p. 6.

4. 'Gyokaku ni "kan no teiko" shihageshii' (Fierce bureaucratic resistance to administrative reform), *Asahi Shimbun*, 10 June 1994, p. 11.

5. The two most frequently cited works in this regard have been: Chalmers Johnson, *MITI and the Japanese Miracle: The Growth of Industrial Policy, 1925-1975*, Stanford, Stanford University Press, 1982; Daniel I. Okimoto, *Between MITI and the Market: Japanese Industrial Policy for High Technology*, Stanford, Stanford University Press, 1989.

6. The cabinet, the Prime Minister's office, the Management and Coordination Agency, and the National Personnel Authority all provide the means to control the bureaucracy in Japan, at least on paper, but none of them functions to do so.

7. E. B. Keehn, 'Bureaucratic Demolition Techniques and Administrative Reform', conference paper for the Association of Asian Studies, Boston, March 1994.

8. Woodrow Wilson, 'The Study of Administration', *Political Science Quarterly*, Vol. 56, No. 4, December 1941, pp. 481-506. Reprinted from The Academy of Political Science, 1887.

9. Chalmers A. Johnson, 'MITI, MPT, and the Telecom Wars', in Johnson, Tyson and Zysman (eds), *Politics and Productivity*, Stanford, 1989, p. 187. MITI is the Ministry of International Trade and Industry and MPT is the Ministry of Posts and Telecommunications.

10. Hata Ikuhiko, *Kanryo no kenkyu: fumetsu no pawa, 1868-1983* (Research on bureaucracy: the immortality of power, 1868-1983), Tokyo, Kodansha, 1983.

11. Bernard S. Silberman, 'The Bureaucratic Role in Japan, 1900-1945: The Bureaucrat as Politician', in Silberman and Harootunian (eds), *Japan in Crisis: Essays on Taisho Democracy*, Princeton, Princeton University Press, 1974, p. 183.

12. Peter Duus, *Party Rivalry and Political Change in Taisho Japan*, Cambridge, Harvard University Press, 1968.

13. T.J. Pempel, 'The Tar Baby Target: "Reform" of the Japanese Bureaucracy', in Ward and Sakamoto (eds), *Democratising Japan: The Allied Occupation*, Honolulu, University of Hawaii Press, 1987, p. 179.

14. Chalmers Johnson, *op.cit.*, pp. 35-82.

15. Akagi Tsuruki, *Kansei no keisai* (The formation of bureaucratic structure), Tokyo, Nihon Hyoronsha, 1991.

16. Hans H. Baerwald, *The Purge of Japanese Leaders under the Occupation*, Berkeley, University of California Press, 1959.

17. There are many advocates of this view among both Japanese and American scholars, but perhaps the most prolific on the subject has been Muramatsu

Michio. For a good summary of his views, see 'Bringing Politics Back into Japan', *Daedalus*, Vol. 119, No. 3, Summer 1990, pp. 141-54.

18. 'Takeshita faction trying to consolidate power', *Mainichi Shimbun*, 8 July 1992.

19. Sogo Kenkyu Kaihatsu Kiko, *Jiten 1990 nendai Nihon no kadai* (An encyclopedia of issues for Japan in the 1990s), Tokyo, Sanseido, 1987, p. 581.

20. 'Kasumigaseki confidensharu' (Kasumigaseki confidential), *Bungei Shunju*, August 1989, p. 234.

21. The JSP now likes to be known as the Social Democratic Party (SDP). One of the most famous cases of an ex-bureaucrat in an opposition party is that of Wada Hiroo. Wada was known as a left-leaning bureaucrat in the Agriculture-Forestry Ministry during the war and went on to play a prominent role in the Japan Socialist Party from the time he joined in 1949. See Otake Hideo, 'Rearmament Controversies and Cultural Conflicts in Japan: The Case of the Conservatives and the Socialists', in Kataoka Tetsuya (ed.), *Creating Single-Party Democracy: Japan's Postwar Political System*, Stanford, Hoover Institution Press, 1992, pp. 68-78.

22. See Ezra N. Suleiman, 'Bureaucracy and Politics in France', in Suleiman (ed.), *Bureaucrats and Policy Making: A Comparative Overview*, New York, Holmes and Meier, 1984, pp. 123-4.

23. Gerald L. Curtis, *The Japanese Way of Politics*, New York, Columbia University Press, 1988, pp. 91-4.

24. 'Minister lashes out at farmers over taxes', *The Japan Times*, 29 July 1989, p. 2.

25. Kitakado Masashi, 'Naiyukai - OB batsu' (The Ministry of Home Affairs Friendship Association - the Old Boy Clique), *Seikai Orai*, July 1988, pp. 283-7.

26. Hata Ikuhiko, *Senzenki Nihon kanryosei no seido • soshiki • jiji* (Japan's Pre-war Bureaucracy: system, organisation, and personnel), Tokyo, Daigaku Shuppankai, 1981, p. 167.

27. Kobayashi Tokuichi, 'Kankai jimmyaku chiri: Jichisho no maki (Personnel geography in the bureaucratic world: Ministry of Autonomy), *Kankai*, December 1986.

28. These figures are drawn from the *Jichisho meikan - showa 63 nenkan* (Ministry of Home Affairs Registry - 1988 Annual), Tokyo, Jihosha, 1988, pp. 84-237.

29. Uchiyama Hideo, *Nihon no seiji kankyo* (Japan's Political Environment), Tokyo, Sanrei Shobo, 1988, p. 176.

30. Interview with Kawakami Tamio, member of the lower house, Socialist Party, 7 November 1989.

31. Namiki Nobuyoshi, *Tsusansho no shuen* (The demise of MITI), Tokyo, Daiyamondo Sha, 1989, pp. 234-5.

32. Watanabe Osamu, *Kindai Nihon no shihai kozo bunseki* (An analysis of the structure of control in contemporary Japan), Tokyo, Kadensha, 1988, pp. 198-9. Watanabe views the creation of NIRA as the model for Nakasone's approach to administration reform. That is, reform proposals based on the participation of powerful business and bureaucratic interests.

33. Gotoda Masaharu, 'Jiminto no itto eikyu shihai ni shushi o utsu. Sore ga Heisi Isshin no sutato da' (A blow to the LDP's eternal one-party control. That is the start of the Heisei Restoration), *Sapio*, 26 July 1990, p. 21.

34. Alexander L. George, 'The Case for Multiple Advocacy in Making Foreign Policy', *American Political Science Review*, Vol. 66, 1972, pp. 751-85.

35. John C. Campbell, 'Policy Conflict and Its Resolution within the Governmental System', in Krauss, Rholen and Steinhoff (eds), *Conflict in Japan*, Honolulu, University of Hawaii, 1984, p. 307.

36. Tahara Soichiro, *Shin • Nihon no kanryo*, Tokyo, Bunshun Bunko, 1988, pp.12-36. The Prime Minister's Office was reduced in size to create the Management and Coordination Agency. This was an attempt to give the prime ministership an organisational means to exert political control over the bureaucracy. By all accounts it created little more than a paper tiger and was a failed attempt. Whatever initial promise it showed was closely tied to the informal powers of its first director-general, Gotoda Masaharu. This will be taken up in a later chapter, as an example of weak attempts at institution building; bureaucratic politics can work to limit political leadership and change in Japan while also insuring the *status quo* distribution of power between ministries in Japan.

37. Quoted by Tahara Soichiro, *Nihon no kanryo 1980*, Tokyo, Bungei Shunju, 1980, p. 10.

38. Karel van Wolferen, *The Enigma of Japanese Power*, London, Macmillan, 1989, p. 32.

39. Masayoshi Kanabayashi and M.W. Brauchli, 'Rebuilding Japan: Prompted by the U.S., Tokyo Slates Trillions in Domestic Spending', *Wall Street Journal*, 3 January 1991, p.1.

40. *Asahi Evening News*, 17 February 1990, p. 6.

41. Sahashi Shigeru, 'Kanryo shokun ni chokugen' (Straight talk to the gentlemen of the bureaucracy), *Bungei Shunju*, July 1971, p. 112.

42. Ozawa Ichiro, viewed as a politician who very much wants to lead the nation and to tame the bureaucracy, is disappointing when it comes to concrete measures for reforming the bureaucracy. And where he does make concrete proposals, they are protective of bureaucratic interests. This is particularly true where the Ministry of Finance is concerned, since Ozawa rejects the idea that responsibility for budgeting should be removed from the ministry and placed under the prime minister's office. Ozawa Ichiro, *A Blueprint for Reform in Japan*, Tokyo, Kodansha, 1994.

43. The sources of bureaucratic privilege and power are varied and complex. The institutional side of the ledger would include lightly bounded systems

of authority, as expressed through practices such as administrative guidance, and the maintenance of an extensive system of licence and approval functions that gives them a prominent role in the economy. Japan's Fair Trade Commission estimates that nearly 40 per cent of the total value-added in the Japanese economy is subject to regulation by the bureaucracy. On the self-interest side of the ledger, though elite bureaucrats earn considerably less than their counterparts in finance and industry, the practice of *amakudari* (literally, descent from heaven), where these individuals retire from their ministries at the age of 60 or earlier to take lucrative advisory or executive posts in the private sector, is an important deferred incentive. Ministries also maintain an extensive network of public corporations that absorb large numbers of retiring bureaucratic elites into executive posts. Many of these posts are temporary, some running no more than one year, include large 'retirement' payments when these individuals move on to their next post-retirement position. See Chalmers Johnson, *Japan's Public Policy Companies*, Washington, DC, American Enterprise Institute, 1978; Murobushi Tetsuro, *Kokyu Kanryo: riken ni saita aku no hana* (Elite bureaucrats: the blossoming of an evil flower of vested rights), Tokyo, 1983; E.B. Keehn, 'Managing Interests in the Japanese Bureaucracy: Informality and Discretion', *Asian Survey*, Vol. 30, No. 11, November 1990, pp. 1021-37.

44. Van Wolferen, *Enigma*.
45. E.B. Keehn, 'Tokyo bureaucrats rule as leaders come and go', *The Times*, 5 July 1994.
46. Oliver Goldsmith, *The Vicar of Wakefield*, London and Glasgow, 1766.

Part III
International Political Issues

7 Japan's Contributions to International Society: The Limits Imposed by Domestic Political Structures

David Arase

Introduction

In the light of its new international responsibilities in a post-Cold War system there is no more pressing issue for Japan than its internationalisation. It is true that Japan can boast rapidly expanding economic and political ties with the rest of the world, but it would be naive to think that internationalisation merely means the increase of cross-border information or human exchanges. Although this is a necessary condition for true progress in Japan's understanding of, and responsiveness to, the expectations of the international community, it is not sufficient.

In general terms, the barriers to responsiveness and accommodation are primarily political and structural in the sense that densely organised networks of public-private sector interests impede the accommodation of unincorporated interests, whether foreign or domestic. Thus, the US has targeted Japan's *keiretsu* system of corporate relations as an impediment to liberal trade and investment, but as Chalmers Johnson points out: 'behind the cartels of production stand the cartels of the mind.'[1] Johnson was referring to state control over the writing of history textbooks, the virtual absence of tenured posts for foreign academics in Japanese universities, the inability of foreign firms to perform legal services in the Japanese legal system, and government control over the dissemination of information through the press-club system in Japan. Johnson concludes: 'Until Japan relaxes these cartels of the mind, its process of internationalisation is meaningless.'

Behind these cartels of the mind, however, are the structures of power and influence that have been institutionalised under the recently disestablished post-war regime of LDP rule. To study the problem these structures pose in its concrete aspects, one can examine Japan's efforts to address the Third World's aspirations for development. The case of Japan's official development assistance (ODA) reveals that the real impediment to more responsive and internationally viable policies is, in the final analysis, the bureaucratically dominated structure of political decision-making.

What is Japan's ODA Policy?

In 1991 the OECD's Development Assistance Committee, which has been reviewing Japan's aid policies for 27 years, had to ask the Japanese government bluntly: 'What is the basic rationale of Japan's aid programme and what are its objectives?'[2] The answer it got did not remove the confusion surrounding Japan's ODA policy. Foreign and domestic critics charge that Japanese official development assistance is wasteful, corrupt, and geared to Japanese business interests - and they have amassed an embarrassing amount of evidence to substantiate their claims.[3] The Ministry of Foreign Affairs (MFA) denies these charges and claims Japanese policy is now about saving the environment, upholding human rights, and preventing the spread of weapons.[4]

There is little doubt that in reality Japan's ODA is mercantilist, but this does not make Japan unique. For example, Australia's Minister for Development Cooperation is proud that Australia gets three dollars in private-sector revenue out of China for every one dollar of ODA given to China.[5] Unlike Australia, however, Japan has pledged increased ODA as an international public good to compensate for its shortcomings in trade and defence. In the current post-Cold War environment of sharpening geo-economic rivalry, Japan's continuing use of ODA to gain the competitive edge in developing country markets, especially in East Asia, has the potential to sharpen friction with the advanced Western economies. This issue has failed to gain salience, however, because the Japanese Foreign Ministry's vehement denials and the government's opaque decision-making procedures make it extremely difficult to discover what the actual policy is and how it is determined.

Confusion is rooted in the fact that there is still no Diet-passed legislation defining either the administrative objectives or procedures of ODA. This marks ODA as another area characterised by 'informality' in administrative procedure that has kept the actual procedures and objectives of decision-making very much within a black box.[6] As in the case of industrial policy, the original purpose of this informality was to create an effective public-private sector partnership in expanding Japan's trade and investment links with the developing world, but in recent years it has become clear that informal bureaucratic control has also shielded such corruption and waste in Japanese ODA that domestic outrage and calls for ODA reform are now a regular feature of Japanese media coverage.

Interestingly enough, even Japanese big business speaking through the Keidanren, the Third Provisional Administrative Reform Council, and the Keizai Doyukai now call for ODA reform.[7] These articulators of private sector strategic interests are mindful of the potential damage if current policies and practices continue. Moreover, Japan's successful penetration of developing country markets, especially in Asia, where Japan's trade surplus is greater than that with the US, reduces the need for covert tied-aid schemes and close public-private sector partnership. As a concession to demands for greater openness, the bureaucracy drafted an ODA Policy Outline (ODA Taiko) which was approved by the cabinet (*naikaku kettei*) in June 1992. This document, however, is a brief, disparate laundry list of idealistic policy goals that leaves the closed, bureaucratically dominated policymaking system intact. As a result within a year the *Nihon Keizai Shimbun* published an editorial supporting opposition calls for substantive ODA reform.[8]

The Peculiarity of ODA

Who directs whom in the Japanese political economy is a contentious issue. On the one hand, we have Chalmers Johnson's model of a powerful bureaucracy able to regulate market activity effectively to accelerate Japan's industrial growth and development. On the other hand, we have a number of qualified pluralist approaches arguing that interministerial conflict,[9] the proliferation of societal pressure groups,[10] and the growing role of LDP politicians in subgovernmental structures make the government increasingly responsive to particularistic concerns. The fissiparous and inclusive nature of policymaking thus makes the state merely a hypothetical construct which, if it did exist, would be unable to coordinate its many constituent compartmentalised policy domains to achieve strategic objectives.[11]

There is an intermediate model that centres on the notion of public-private sector linkages or networks that manage policy through what Richard Samuels has called 'reciprocal consent', in which 'the state often helps structure market choices, but public/private negotiations invariably structure state and market choices alike'.[12] Daniel Okimoto takes a similar position when he argues that the Japanese 'societal state' relies on: 'consensus, habits of compliance, and voluntary cooperation on the part of private actors to get things done'.[13] They argue that in industrial policy and energy policy MITI and its clients co-determine policy.

In this context the peculiarity of ODA must be noted. Japanese ODA policy does not fall under the purview of any one ministry or agency, and so it is not a typical case of 'iron-triangle' policymaking pivoting around the ministry regulating a discrete policy area.[14] ODA policy is jointly managed by 16 main ministries and agencies. Given the view that Japanese policymaking is vertically segmented, how is it possible for the 16 bureaux to preside over the world's largest ODA programme without conspicuous turmoil when in other areas fierce jurisdictional battles gain epic proportions? As for the private sector, the question is whether it has been able to transcend the compartmentalised structure of policymaking to articulate a collective interest in ODA policy.

As has been generally the case in Japanese policymaking, ODA policy rests on two structural premises: the system of *tatewari gyosei* (vertical administration) by which each main ministry and agency has been assigned exclusive regulatory authority over a certain range of societal activity; and the marriage of business and bureaucratic interests brokered by the LDP that nurtured intimate public-private sector collaboration in policymaking.

Under the system of *tatewari gyosei*, each ministry is assigned regulatory authority over a functionally defined sphere of societal activity, including any international cooperation conducted by actors within this sphere. ODA is a regulatory challenge to this system because it involves international cooperation activities that span the entire range of state-regulated activity from medicine to shrimp-farming. The response was to establish informal rules and mechanisms to balance as best as possible the need to respect the jurisdictional rights of each main ministry and agency with the desire to achieve a unified government position in dealing with domestic interests and other governments.

The challenge of organising economic cooperation with developing countries was met by the bureaucracy before it confronted the problem of ODA. State sponsorship of export-oriented high-speed growth after the Korean War spawned a policy area called *keizai kyoryoku* (economic cooperation). This aimed at subsidising the expansion of Japanese trade and investment in new developing-country markets. While many ministries and agencies had to be included in making economic cooperation policy, it was clear that the orientation towards industrial and trade policy goals would give MITI precedence in setting substantive policies, and this was reflected in the fact that it has published the government's annual White Paper on Economic Cooperation since 1958.

When Japan incurred the obligation to give ODA after it joined the OECD in 1964, the *keizai kyoryoku* system adapted itself to the task. The dilemma posed by this path of institutionalisation is that domestic policymaking structures and informal networks designed to strengthen Japan's overseas trade and investment activities were expected by the West to design and implement non-commercial, recipient needs-oriented assistance. Japanese ODA policymaking today still lives with this contradiction.

Defining *Keizai Kyoryoku*

Until the Japanese cabinet approved a statement of official ODA policy goals in June 1992, the only formal legal expression underlying Japan's ODA policymaking and implementation system was the Cabinet order (*kakugi kettei*) of December 1953 that established *keizai kyoryoku* as a policy area. It was entitled: 'Policy on Economic Cooperation With the Countries of Southeast Asia' (*Kakugi kettei - Ajia shokoku ni taisuru keizai kyoryoku ni kansuru ken*). The key passage in this brief statement was: 'in principle, economic cooperation is carried out through private sector initiative, and the government is to render the necessary assistance'.[15]

This policy statement, vague-sounding though it was, made explicit what had been only implicit in Japan's earliest post-Occupation overseas resource development and export promotion efforts. The basic objective or rationale was to help the private sector develop an export orientation, establish an international reputation, develop new products, expand markets, tap new sources of raw materials, and build new networks of business and political relations. This policy concept shaped specific *keizai kyoryoku* policies, routines, and organisational structures that first addressed the need to give reparations, and then to expand Japan's sources of imported energy and raw materials through a new programme of yen loans. The basic structure of this system is what Western pressure, applied through DAC, has began trying to change since Japan officially joined the OECD in 1964.

At the incipient stage of economic cooperation the private sector's views and policy recommendations were incorporated through officially sponsored advisory councils. As the Korean War came to an end the Ministry of Foreign Affairs (MFA) invited private-sector leaders to form an advisory council to discuss a coordinated public-private sector approach to expanding relations with Asia. This advisory body, the Asian

Economic Deliberation Council (*Ajia Keizai Kondankai*), was established in June 1953 under the chairmanship of Hara Yasusaburo, an eminent Asia-oriented business leader from the Mitsui group. One institutional innovation originating in this body's deliberations was the creation of the *Ajia Kyokai*, or Asia Association.[16] It was staffed by personnel from the old South Manchurian Railroad Research Department, and it evolved into the present-day *Ajia Keizai Kenkyujo*, or Institute for Developing Economies (IDE). But the most significant legacy of the Asian Economic Deliberation Council was the statement it drafted on *keizai kyoryoku* policy which gained cabinet approval in December 1953. At the incipient stage of economic cooperation, this deliberation council allowed the private sector to help define the terms of a largely informal public-private partnership in economic cooperation.

The first great test for economic cooperation was the need to give official war reparations to Japan's neighbours for damages inflicted during the Second World War. The *Baisho Jisshi Kondankai* (Reparations Implementation Deliberation Council) was created by the Foreign Ministry in 1954 to give private-sector leaders a hand in shaping policy. Through this vehicle certain basic policy principles emerged that remain central to ODA policy today.

Reparation funds were to be disbursed to Japanese private-sector firms - not to recipient governments. These firms would build capital-intensive projects in order not to displace normal commercial sales of Japanese goods and services. The Japanese government would require an official request for each reparations project. If approved, the recipient government could award the contract for project execution to the Japanese firm of its choice. This system gave the Japanese private sector guaranteed sales in unfamiliar developing-country markets for the heavy industrial goods they were then attempting to develop and export. It induced an influx of Japanese business development activity in the countries eligible for Japanese reparations.

A survey of the Showa period's economic history supervised by one of the chief architects of Japan's post-war economic strategy, Arisawa Hiromi, sums up reparations as follows: 'Reparations which began in 1955 and continued for the next 20 years gave post-war Japan its first foothold in advancing into South-East Asia.'[17] Ushiba Nobuhiko, a diplomatic councillor who helped negotiate the Burma reparations agreement (and who subsequently became a special cabinet minister for economic cooperation in the 1970s) stated, 'in reparations by no means did Japan suffer losses'.[18] In fact reparations activity was called 'business diplomacy' (*zaikai gaiko*) owing to the fact that Keidanren missions often conducted the actual reparations negotiations with foreign governments.[19]

Another key issue in institutionalising economic cooperation were coordinating the vertically segmented bureaucracy. In the case of reparations, which were part of broader diplomatic normalisation negotiations, the window through which the Japanese government and private sector had to manage cooperation was the MFA. This was reflected in the organisation of the Reparations Implementation Deliberation Council (*Baisho Jisshi Renraku Kyogikai*) chaired by the Foreign Minister and consisting of the administrative vice-ministers of the following ministries: EPA, MFA, MoF, MEd, MHW, MAFF, MITI, MoT, MPT, MoL and MoC. This council deliberated negotiating stances, broad policy, and screened reparations requests for Cabinet approval, and was supported by a working-level council with a similar structure.[20] This mechanism defined the detailed informal rules and procedures for case-by-case decision-making and formal cabinet approval.

By the end of the 1950s, this cumbersome system was streamlined until only the *yonshocho* (MFA, MITI, MoF, and EPA) met regularly for overall policy discussions. MITI and EPA worked with Japanese industry and commerce to target raw materials and export markets in ways that would raise Japan's position in the international division of labour. MoF controlled access to the budget and managed the international balance of payments, and so needed to be involved in policy deliberations. At this time MFA was focused on normalisation issues and defined its overall task in terms of supporting Japan's industrial recovery and growth. This left substantive budgetary, trade and investment promotion policy to MITI, EPA, and MoF.[21]

By the late 1950s it was clear to the private sector that an expanded programme of subsidised yen loans and equity financing was needed to secure stable access to developing country resources, yet the government was reluctant to fund a major new programme. The private sector appealed to the LDP, and in July 1959 it formed the Special Committee on Foreign Economic Cooperation (*Taigai Keizai Kyoryoku Tokubetsu Iinkai*) within the Policy Affairs Research Council. In August the committee issued a formal policy statement recommending creation of a ¥20 billion government fund to promote Japanese resource development projects in South-East Asia. This call was seconded by the Keidanren in November.

The result was that on 14 January 1960 the cabinet authorised a new economic cooperation agency, the *Taigai Keizai Kyoryoku Kikin*, otherwise known as the Overseas Economic Cooperation Fund (OECF), to be supervised by the *yonshocho*. This prompted a joint meeting of the Lower House Finance, Foreign Affairs, and Commerce and Industry committees, marking the first occasion where Diet discussions touched on Japan's basic posture toward economic cooperation. The Lower House Commerce and Industry Committee handled the authorising legislation for this new agency, which it passed by July 1960. Owing to the disrupted Diet term caused by Kishi's forced passage of the US-Japan Security Treaty, formal establishment of the OECF had to wait until March 1961.[22]

At its inception the OECF's terms of reference limited it to investments and yen loans to *Japanese* corporations building projects in the developing world. The basic intention was to advance Japanese ownership control over vital energy and raw materials production in the developing world. In the 1961-64 period, OECF scored 30 cases of equity participation or loans relating to overseas development projects, 15 of which were in mineral development or basic metal production. The OECF did not make a direct aid loan to a foreign government until 1965, a year after it had joined the OECD and became subject to DAC aid norms.

In June 1961 the Foreign Economic Cooperation Advisory Council (*Taigai Keizai Kyoryoku Shingikai*) was formed to review the emerging organisation of Japan's economic cooperation. It was chaired by the prime minister and contained prominent private-sector leaders. Although it met only three times, all within a 12-month period, it presided over intensive public-private sector deliberations that set the basic outlines of the system of economic cooperation that exists today.

In December 1961 the advisory council agreed that a number of discrete organisations conducting policy research and technical cooperation should be rationalised. The various technical cooperation programmes would be consolidated in a new official administrative agency (*tokushu hojin*) to be called the Overseas Technical Cooperation Agency (OTCA), the predecessor to JICA. Economic cooperation policy research functions of the Asia Association and other organisations would be consolidated in the Institute for Developing Economies (IDE) under MITI supervision, which would be raised from a semi-official non-profit organisation (*zaidan hojin*) to parity with OTCA, i.e. *tokushu hojin*. OTCA was put under the formal control of the MFA when it was established in June 1962, although by informal agreement key posts in OTCA were reserved for the nominees of other ministries and agencies.

Thus, what came out of the deliberations of the prime minister's advisory council was a system based on four first-tier implementing agencies: the Ex-im Bank, OECF, OTCA and IDE. The first two agencies would provide export loans, as well as loans and equity financing for overseas projects; OTCA would oversee technical cooperation; and IDE would analyse the economies of the developing countries. The *yonshocho* continued to coordinate the routine operations of this first tier. The prime minister's *Taigai Keizai Kyoryoku Shingikai* became the key mechanism for ratifying changes in *keizai kyoryoku*, and the LDP's Special Committee on Foreign Economic Cooperation was the system's window to the LDP.

Thus, a review of the basic structure and policy orientations of the *keizai kyoryoku* system as it crystallised in the early 1960s reveals that the private sector played a key role in its creation and design. Working around the constraints of *tatewari gyosei*, it was able to establish the *keizai kyoryoku* policy principle, substantially shape implementation in line with this principle, and create mechanisms such as the *Taigai Keizai Kyoryoku Shingikai* and the LDP *Taigai Keizai Kyoryoku Tokubetsu Iinkai* to help coordinate private sector and bureaucratic interests in policymaking.

Japanese ODA Today

Japan's bilateral ODA has five key traits that are direct carry-overs from the 1950s and 1960s.

1) Project Orientation

Roughly two-thirds of Japan's bilateral ODA is project-oriented, i.e. geared to the provision and operation of infrastructure, social welfare-related facilities, and productive enterprises. The rest is programme assistance, disaster relief, food aid, debt relief, etc.

2) Asia Orientation

Roughly two-thirds of Japanese ODA is directed to the Asian region stretching from the Indian subcontinent to China. Indonesia, China, Thailand, and the Philippines have been the largest recipients since the late 1980s.

3) Request-Based Procedures

The Japanese government acts officially only after another government requests Japanese aid through its local Japanese embassy.

4) Decentralised Authority

Sixteen ministries and agencies of the central bureaucracies share policymaking authority in bilateral ODA, and enter into decision-making over project requests. This unwieldy system is informally coordinated by MFA, MITI, MoF and EPA, who collectively are called the *yonshocho*. The management of project requests for loans is handled collectively by the *yonshocho*, while MFA coordinates grant and technical aid requests.

5) Case-by-Case Decision-making

Each aid request must be treated as an individual case owing to the decentralised distribution of decision-making authority. Informal bureaucratic rules have been established whereby the nature of the project request will determine which ministries and agencies must be consulted. These rules parallel those that apply to domestic policymaking. Thus, if a project request is for a dam to produce electricity, MITI will be consulted, while if it is a dam for water control, MoC will have authority. The informal rules governing interministerial consultation are enforced by the need for cabinet approval of each project request, a procedure that allows each ministry and agency to monitor and protect its own interests.

The implementation of Japan's bilateral ODA today is handled mainly by two agencies. The Overseas Economic Cooperation Fund (OECF) manages loan assistance, while the Japan International Cooperation Agency (JICA), the descendant of the Overseas Technical Cooperation Agency (OTCA) established in 1962, handles grant and technical assistance. The fact that OECF also takes equity positions in partnership with the Japanese private sector in overseas production projects, and that JICA supports such projects, reflects the broader *keizai kyoryoku* agenda of these agencies. Aside from these two implementing agencies, other research organisations such as the Institute of Developing Economies (IDE) and JETRO work on ways to strengthen the coordination of ODA with Japan's trade and investment activities to achieve Japan's industrial policy and economic security objectives.

Shingikai

The previously mentioned *Taigai Keizai Kyoryoku Shingikai*, whose chair traditionally has been the head of the Japan Chamber of Commerce and Industry (*Nihon Shoko Kaigisho*), plays a key role in ratifying new policy goals, and its membership represents the range of organisations linked by informal networks in ODA policymaking (see below). In addition, there are other advisory councils that sponsor significant public-private sector policy deliberations relevant to ODA. One key advisory council is the *Keizai Kondankai* (Economic Deliberation Council), which approves the EPA-drafted national social and economic plans. Since the 1980s these plans have registered the existing inter-ministerial and public-private sector consensus in ODA. Another advisory council is MITI's *Sangyo Kozo Shingikai* (Industrial Structure Council). It can be depended on to advocate the coordinated use of ODA, FDI, and trade policy measures to help Japanese industry build overseas production bases in the developing countries of East Asia. The generalisation that others have made about *shingikai* in policymaking applies to these councils.[23] They tend to ratify a consensus position worked out by staff and other less formal deliberation mechanisms such as ad hoc study groups.

Taikeishin Membership (August 1993)

Ishikawa Rokuro (Chair)	Japan Chamber of Commerce and Industry
Ito Tadashi	Japan Foreign Trade Council
Imai Keiko	Sophia University
Uchida Shigeo	Nihon Keizai Shimbun
Ohba Tomomitsu	International Finance Information Centre
Kakudo Ken'ichi	Central Agricultural Bank of Japan
Satomi Yasuo	Overseas Construction Association of Japan
Shimao Tadao	Association for Tubercular Prevention
Tagaki Tsuku	Bank of Tokyo
Tanaka Ryoichi	Japan Labour Union Federation
Nishigaki Akira	OECF
Fujiwara Ichiro	Electrical Power Development Corporation
Hoshino Masako	International Volunteer Centre of Japan
Maruyama Yasuo	International Labour Organisation
Monden Hideo	International Development Centre
Yanagiya Kensuke	JICA
Yamaguchi Mitsuhide	Export-Import Bank
Yoshino Bunroku	IDE
Yonekura Isao	Keidanren
Toyoshima Tooru	JETRO

LDP Interest Representation

LDP Diet members in ODA policymaking are oriented toward particularistic concerns. In the context of stable LDP rule, the Diet has been excluded from ODA policymaking by mutual agreement among the

LDP, the bureaucracy, and the private sector. This removed the need for LDP management of ODA legislation. The LDP's *Taigai Keizai Kyoryoku Tokubetsu Iinkai* within PARC has handled mostly routine matters pertaining to the adjustment of administrative procedures, and it otherwise serves as a forum for private sector and bureaucratic actors to keep the LDP informed about current policy debates between the bureaucracy and the private sector.[24] Because party policy blocks parliamentary initiative in ODA, LDP Diet members have had little incentive to debate ODA policy as such. Paralleling developments in other policy areas, they have turned their attention to serving the needs of particular private sector clients who needed assistance in negotiating the labyrinthine bureaucratic decision-making process to secure ODA project contracts.[25]

What is different about ODA, however, is no ODA *zoku* as such. Instead, those who have influence over bureaucratic decision-making earn this through membership in other groups. LDP politicians who have developed deep friendships with recipient country politicians through bilateral parliamentary leagues (*giin renmei*), or who have developed close relations with senior bureaucrats through conventional *zoku* and rotation through cabinet posts, are the ones able to influence the bureaucratically managed approval process. In at least some cases, a politician has been able to shepherd a project request through the entire process.[26] Thus, the LDP has had its own reasons to preserve the request-based, project-oriented, and informally regulated ODA system.

Implementing Agencies

Japan's aid-implementing agencies are public corporations or *tokushu hojin*. According to the MFA, in *keizai kyoryoku* there are eight main ones aside from JICA and OECF (see Table 7.1).

In reaction to Western pressure to meet ODA standards, the loan and grant activities that qualify as ODA have been put under OECF and JICA. Each *tokushu hojin* is established by Diet legislation or cabinet order, and it is supervised by the government through one or more main ministries and agencies.

The government is able to exert operational control through its financial support, and by its right to appoint officers, issue orders, collect reports, and make on-the-spot inspections.

Table 7.1 The eight main *tokushu hojin* in *keizai kyoryoku*

Name	Function	Supervising ministry	Year of establishment
Ex-im Bank (Nihon Yushutsunyu Ginko)	Trade and investment finance; structural adjustment lending	MoF	1950
Japan External Trade Organisation (Nihon Boeki Shinkokai)	Trade promotion	MITI	1958
Institute of Developing Economies (Ajia Keizai Kenkyujo)	Economic and political research to expand economic cooperation	MITI	1960
Employment Promotion Projects Corporation (Koyo Sokushin Jigyodan)	Technical training	MoL	1961
Metal Mining Agency of Japan (Kinzoku Kogyo Jigyodan)	Metal ore finding and development	MITI	1963
Japan National Oil Corporation (Sekiyu Kodan)	Oil and gas development	MITI	1967
The Japan Foundation (Kokusai Koryu Kikin)	Cultural exchange	MFA	1972
Agricultural Land Development Agency (Noyochi Kaihatsu Kodan)	Agriculture development	MAFF	1974

Source: MFA, *Kokusai kyoryoku handobukku* (International Cooperation Handbook), 1983.

Among the advantages of *tokushu hojin* are freedom in employing staff; flexibility in contracting with foreign and domestic entities; the ability to generate revenue, issue bonds, or accept private-sector equity participation; and legal 'distance' from the government. Because of their government backing via personnel, financing, and regulatory arrangements, *tokushu hojin* are able to operate in areas where the private sector cannot be freely induced to provide resources and services, or where a fair and impartial standpoint is required. These characteristics are useful in areas that cross the jurisdictional boundaries of government ministries, or in activities that have a quasi-public, quasi-private nature.[27] Some have noted the critical role they have played in promoting private-sector development in line with public-sector goals.[28] Okimoto argues that such formal intermediate organisations 'can be conceived of as the arms and legs of the state', or as a 'bridge between the public and private sectors',[29] but less attention has been paid to them as venues for interministerial coordination. Without these subsidiary organisations, the main ministries and agencies could not coordinate their policymaking input, nor could there be effective government coordination with private-sector firms in ODA. The actual situation is made confusing by the fact that formal authority over JICA and OECF is accorded to MFA and EPA respectively. In reality, the EPA and MFA do not exercise 'authority' over their subordinate agencies in the normal sense of the word, i.e. controlling the hiring and firing of personnel, and autonomously setting budget and policy guidelines for these organisations.

Instead, they preside over organisations whose chief function is to coordinate the input of 16 main ministries and agencies and their private-sector clients. Informal rules negotiated within the government distribute control over OECF and JICA staff and line operations to outside organisations. The other main ministries and agencies place their own personnel on JICA and OECF boards of directors through *amakudari*, and they and their private-sector clients also insert personnel into line operations through *shukko*. *Amakudari* and *shukko* staffing arrangements are the key to understanding how these agencies successfully coordinate policy implementation among such a wide range of actors.

Private-Sector Personnel in Official Aid Agencies

The official handling of aid requests could not work without heavy private-sector involvement through the exchange of personnel. The seconding of personnel by one organisation to serve on temporary assignment in another organisation (*shukko*) is well developed in the ODA system. *Shukko* is different from *amakudari* in that early or mid-career personnel are transferred to other organisations, usually for only a year or two. In the aid system the person imported by *shukko* is listed as an official member of the host organisation, though he or she continues to be paid by the real employer. The host organisation expects this person to bring skills and serve as a bridge to the home organisation. The home organisation wants this person to study the host organisation, and to promote home organisation interests.

When *shukko* occurs between public and private organisations, it gives the private sector a pipeline to inside information on policymaking processes and directions; and it gives government a better awareness of the problems and incentives affecting business decision-making, thus giving government a better ability to construct effective policy. When it occurs between organisations of different rank and prestige, *shukko* embodies an authority relationship. Staff sent from superior organisations can be expected to dominate key decision-making posts in lower-ranking ones, while staff sent up to superior organisations are largely restricted to staff positions.

A clear example of this in ODA is provided by the MFA's Economic Cooperation Bureau. This bureau has two main tasks in bilateral ODA. One is processing the official requests for grant and loan aid collected through its overseas embassies. Much of this work merely involves referring paperwork to the relevant ministries and agencies, but grant-aid paperwork is processed within the bureau. The other main task is explaining Japan's ODA to foreign and domestic audiences. The MFA's priority is on the latter as may be seen in the fact that the highest concentration of MFA officers is at the *shingikan* (minister) and *sanjikan* (councillor) level, which is above the *kacho* rank and which specialises in diplomatic representation in ODA issues. In contrast, the MFA makes only a minimal commitment of career officers to the processing of ODA requests.

To handle this paperwork the MFA relies heavily on personnel on *shukko* from other ministries, agencies and private-sector firms. The MFA may have two or three career officers in the loan, technical, and grant aid divisions (usually the director, deputy director and task coordinator), but the rest of the staff of each division are non-elite MFA employees or outsiders. In 1987 there were 117 full-time MFA staff of all descriptions working in the bureau, and 170 temporary staff from outside, of which 50 were officials from other ministries and agencies. Staff from private-sector financial institutions and project consultancy firms were actively being sought by MFA.

Posting of private-sector personnel to handle ODA as overseas embassy staff also occurs. There was a total of 134 full-time staff handling ODA in overseas embassies in 1987, but it seemed that on balance bureaucrats from other ministries and agencies dominated these positions.

The same reliance on private-sector personnel exists in the ODA staffing of other members of the *yonshocho*. MITI, MoF, and EPA each have one or more sections managing ODA and related activities, and their total full-time staff numbered 41, 37 and 19 respectively.

The significance of *shukko* in JICA and OECF is indicated by the fact that at any given time roughly a third of each agency's permanent staff is exported to other government or private-sector organisations, and they are replaced by imported personnel. The case of OECF is representative of what is found in the economic cooperation-related *tokushu hojin*. Unlike JICA, which is focused on supplying technical project expertise, OECF is focused on loan financing, but it does need expertise to appraise loan project proposals. *Shukko* alleviates this deficiency and creates functional interdependence with other public- and private-sector organisations. For example, in the three technical appraisal departments that were responsible for screening loan projects in 1987, 19 out of a total of 21 staff members were on secondment either from other government agencies or the private sector, and four out of the five *kacho* (department heads) were on secondment from MITI, MAFF, MoT, and EPA.

In the loan departments, which assess the financial feasibility of projects and administer loan disbursement and collection, more than half of the staff are from other public and private financial institutions. This is because private-sector loan officers have the skills to do financial analyses and to administer reliably the complicated financial procedures in disbursing and collecting OECF loans. The private sector financial institutions have an incentive to provide this personnel since they earn service fees for ODA-related financial services, and they also handle trade and investment financing associated with ODA projects. In addition, as Japan's financial industry internationalises, it is in great need of staff with experience in dealing with foreign project financing, official borrowing, and coordination with international financial institutions such as the World Bank.

The ability to borrow personnel and create intimate ties of functional interdependence explains how OECF's full-time ODA staff of 280 and JICA's staff of 951, the overwhelming majority of which are non-technical generalists, could administer $7.8 billion in aid commitments in 1989; or how, for example, OECF and JICA could oversee a programme disbursing $152 million dollars in 1986 in Pakistan with no locally-stationed personnel, while US AID had well over 200 officers in five different offices implementing a programme of roughly the same funding level. It also explains why there is little effective pressure to increase government personnel.

The implicit incorporation of the private sector through request-based aid procedures, and the heavy reliance on private-sector personnel through *shukko* explain why government personnel are so few relative to the size and scope of Japan's ODA activity, and it offers an interesting example of how *tokushu hojin* can be used to deal with the problem of *tatewari gyosei* and build public-private sector partnership in ODA.

The Private Sector's Interest in Reform

The single most important private-sector window to ODA policy is the Keidanren because of its role as the articulator of policy consensus within the Japanese corporate sectors, and its deep involvement in *keizai kyoryoku* through its Standing Committee on Economic Cooperation. By the 1990s, having helped to define the private-sector role in a new FDI-oriented economic cooperation policy,[30] Keidanren began to move cautiously on a different agenda of administrative reform that has direct implications for ODA administration. In 1990 Keidanren began to emphasise the following theme: 'minimum government intervention, even in industrial policy ... the business community must move away from overdependence on government and ... these efforts must coincide with further administrative reform and deregulation.'[31] With regard to ODA, Keidanren reiterated the importance of the private-sector role in ODA, but it stated that the government was too slow, inadequate at ensuring quality aid projects, and failed to meet domestic and international political expectations. It therefore recommended that the government draft an ODA charter to reduce secrecy and bureaucratic discretion in decision-making. But Keidanren stopped short of calling for Diet debate or legislation, nor did it call for a more centralised system of administrative or budgetary control.[32] This new agenda was a key impetus behind the drafting of the 1992 ODA Taiko.

Working within a narrower scope of relations, sectoral trade and business associations licensed by one or more of the 16 main ministries and agencies play key roles in ODA policymaking and implementation. They generally take the form of private non-profit-making foundations (*zaidan hojin*) or business associations (*shadan hojin*) officially licensed by one or more main ministries, and they serve as two-way pipelines of benefits and influence between the bureaucratic sponsor and private-sector clients. Not surprisingly, the largest and most influential family of ODA-related associations is clustered under MITI. In second place is MFA, but this family of associations tends not to be rooted in private enterprise and wields little political clout.[33] One key consequence of their organisational position and function is that unlike strategically oriented peak business associations such as the Keidanren, these sectoral associations still have a large stake in the *status quo*. They will press for the preservation of the *status quo* if reform means the loss of influence and bureaucratic patronage in the form of ODA-generated business referrals.

The Project Cycle

Project-oriented assistance is organised around the 'project cycle'. There are certain stages all aid projects must go through on their way to completion and successful operation. First, in the project formation stage, a project idea must be generated, and then technical experts are needed to propose a plan. The proposal is then evaluated by government agencies to assess its technical, economic and financial feasibility; social, political and environmental impact; harmony with current policy; merit relative to other proposals, and so on. If approval is given, project design and construction is contracted out and, after completion, evaluation is necessary to learn from the experience.

The problem at the start of the project cycle is that developing countries - by definition - suffer from shortages of the funds, skilled experts and administrators needed to identify and design projects such as telephone systems, bridges, hospitals or technical training centres. Moreover, the documentation required by the Japanese government for project proposals is complex, and recipient government agencies sometimes are unable to get past even the initial paperwork. Thus, there is a gap created between what Japan's request-based system requires and what developing countries are able to achieve in project formation. Recipients may request JICA financing for Japanese private-sector consultants to do a preliminary project design, but another official request for actual construction must then be made.

The official reason (*tatemae*) for request-based aid is respect for the recipient's sovereignty while the basic intent (*honne*) of request-based aid, going back to its inception in the 1950s, has always been to give Japanese business a boost in developing-country markets. The nature of this involvement is indicated by the following example:

> At the end of the 1960s Mitsubishi Corporation hit upon the idea of building an international airport at Mombasa, Kenya, to exploit promising tourist resources for regional development. A feasibility study begun in 1970 was enthusiastically received by the Kenyan Government which, however, was unable to finance the project. Mitsubishi then lobbied for a special yen loan from the Japanese Government. Though no such loan had ever been offered before to an African country, the Japanese Government, after some hesitation, was finally persuaded to extend it as economic assistance .... It took Mitsubishi over three years to secure the necessary funding and another five years to complete the airport. The company used its organiser/co-

ordinator capacity to arrange and supervise all the construction work; it hired builders and procured materials and equipment ...

Following the success of the Mombasa project, Mitsubishi Corporation was asked by Malawi, Kenya's southern neighbour, to construct a similar airport. The company again secured special loans from both the Japanese Government and the African Development Bank and began construction of an airport in 1978.[34]

Not only trading companies but also consulting firms and trade associations will often absorb the cost of preliminary design studies that will be given to the interested parties in the recipient government. Thus, it is not unusual for recipient government line agencies to have several ready-made proposals on hand at any given time. If a line agency decides to request a prepared proposal, it will have the backing of the injecting Japanese private-sector actor. This itself does not guarantee success for the requesting agency, but from a statistical viewpoint it generates enough success for the Japanese private sector for it to keep up this practice.[35]

A variation on this injection system is the so-called *puro-fai* (project-finding) mission that is financed by JICA or subsidised directly through other ministries and agencies. The project-finding mission is led by prestigious business leaders under the sponsorship of Keidanren or other trade associations. A high-level Japanese business delegation visits developing countries to discuss a number of large-scale preliminary project proposals with local officials and politicians. The objective is to reach informal agreement over which large aid projects to implement. When requested, these projects usually clear Japanese government evaluation procedures quickly.

Official aid requests are screened by the local embassy staff and sent to Tokyo with preliminary evaluations. In both grant and loan project requests, an appraisal mission is sent to evaluate the request and it drafts a recommendation after returning to Tokyo. Appraisal reports are deliberated by the relevant main ministries and agencies, and if approved, the MFA concludes an agreement with the recipient (exchange of notes) which is then passed through the cabinet approval process.

In approved grant-aid requests, project formation is dominated by the Japanese private sector financed by JICA, while in approved loan-aid projects, the origin of requests is less clear. According to official statistics, about one-third originate from JICA-financed feasibility studies, while in 40 per cent of the cases the borrower government produces the request, and 6 per cent are the result of project-finding missions.

The Private-Sector View on ODA Reform

There is now deep ambiguity in the business sector over the need for ODA reform. As mentioned previously, peak organisations have been calling for greater transparency in ODA decision-making. This reflects a new desire to limit bureaucratic discretion in policymaking. This change is due to the systemic corruption and abuse of bureaucratic regulatory powers revealed by recent Sagawa Kyubin, Nomura stock-price manipulation, and Recruit Scandals, as well as by the private sector's confidence that it now can meet the challenge of open competition with Western firms without government assistance. The new business perception is that, on balance, autonomous bureaucratic power no longer serves its strategic interests. The system operates at substantial cost to Japanese business and taxpayers and, even worse, it generates domestic and international ill-will that threatens to harm Japanese business interests overseas.

Through its peak strategic policy forums the private sector has been pushing the government to untie its aid, open up its decision-making procedures to public scrutiny, use ODA to improve Japan's international image, and widen the scope of ODA to include non-governmental groups (NGOs) in policymaking and implementation. At the same time, however, it believes that the basic *keizai kyoryoku* concept underlying contemporary ODA policy is correct because the Japanese private sector can increase the production of wealth in developing countries. For this reason, the Keidanren insisted that, as the government drafted the ODA Taiko in 1992, it recognise that:

> Toward the countries of Asia which Japan has emphasised in economic cooperation, following the provision of ODA for infrastructure and other facilities, private sector firms have carried out trade and investment, thus forming a three-into-one (*san-mi ittai to natte*) impetus to the economic vitalisation of aid recipient countries. Thus, as ODA and private sector activity have acted as the two wheels on a cart in the economic development of developing countries, government and private sector activities should more fully develop a system of effective relations.[36]

This view coincides with MITI's view of ODA, and together they put the need for three-into-one coordination into the ODA Taiko as a principle of ODA implementation. This private sector stake in the *status quo* explains why it joins the LDP and the bureaucracy in not wishing to see policy legislation introduced into the Diet. Although it would like more open and objective management of ODA, the private sector wishes to risk neither its influence in policymaking nor the basic orientation of ODA towards support of its trade and FDI activities.

Aid untying is now acceptable to the private sector in principle, but this *per se* does not preclude continuing ODA coordination with private-sector trade and investment activities. Aid tying is meant to help uncompetitive businesses penetrate new and unfamiliar markets. Japanese business today as a whole no longer needs tied-aid to win ODA project contracts because it is highly competitive, and thanks in part to past tied aid policy, it is a familiar presence in every corner of the developing world. Today, the challenge for Japanese industry is to upgrade its international competitiveness through the creation of globally integrated production networks. It can still use untied ODA as a lever to influence developing country policies to smooth the way for Japanese trade and FDI activity. And it still needs ODA to finance the development of physical infrastructure and manpower training to support private-sector FDI in developing countries.

The Issue of Bureaucratic Power

The case of ODA policymaking is consistent with the view that the Japanese bureaucracy has exceptional power and autonomy,[37] yet at the same time we have evidence of some kind of control or constraint being applied to bureaucratic decision-making through LDP politicians and private-sector actors through extensive informal networks of relations. The question is which of the three general views of Japanese policymaking outlined earlier best describes the pattern of ODA policymaking. We shall deal with this by discussing bureaucratic-private sector relations and bureaucratic-LDP relations in turn.

In any discussion of a generic bureaucratic role or interest, it might be legitimately objected that no bureaucracy is monolithic, and that the norm is interorganisational competition and diversity of viewpoints and agendas.[38] And as a practical matter there may be no instance in which all ministries will unify to face even an external opposition. Moreover, there is always a diversity of viewpoints within any one organisation. This is certainly true in the case of Japan.[39] But what distinguishes bureaucrats as a class of political actors and decision-makers is that, as tenured salaried government officials, they are preoccupied with issues of hierarchical authority, legally defined jurisdictions, administrative rules and routines, specialisation and technical efficiency - all of which are tied to organisational proficiency in carrying out assigned functions.[40] Unlike professional politicians, whose efforts focus on electoral activities and therefore must weigh policy decisions according to ideological and popularity considerations, bureaucrats are oriented towards the search for effective technical solutions to narrowly defined problems that must be managed in a complex organisational environment. The implications of such a class holding an extraordinary degree of power and discretion in decision-making raises the question of accountability and democratic responsiveness, which the case of Japanese ODA helps to illustrate.

The origins and institutional structure of Japan's ODA policy reflect the role of the post-war Japanese state in guiding the private sector towards national developmental goals. The circumstances that made this role natural were not only late development and the wartime destruction of Japanese trade and industry, but also Japan's high dependence on imports and exports for industrialisation. While the private sector was able to help shape state policy and to benefit substantially from it, in the final analysis, without denying that bureaucracy-private sector relations are marked by reciprocities and mutual influence, it was the state that retained superior leverage. The private sector has been accountable to the state; but the reverse has not been the case up to 1993. The lack of *accountability* - not the lack of *inclusion* - is at the root of the private sector's criticism of the ODA system today.

The problem of constitutionally and legally limiting bureaucratic discretion is not peculiar to Japan.[41] In the case of Japan, however, the problem is acute given the relative weakness of judicial remedies; lack of information disclosure statutes; and wide powers to license and regulate societal actors with very few objective procedural standards.[42] Accountability can be established through explicit, universally applied rules and standards by which administrative decisions can be measured and, if necessary, appealed against. In the case of ODA, however, we have the antithesis: secretive case-by-case decision-making performed outside a legally defined policy or procedural framework. The irony of the situation is that informal regulation is the means by which the bureaucracy escapes accountability, but it is also the means by which the private sector can be so flexibly included in policymaking and implementation.

The role of interest groups is a significant constraint on Japanese bureaucratic behaviour in ODA, and this point is consistent with what is observed in other advanced countries. The inclusion of interest groups in enduring subgovernmental structures is a general phenomenon because the increasingly technical and specialised nature of regulation in advanced societies requires the groups most directly affected to have access to bureaucratic policymaking. The role of the bureaucrat becomes that of a responsible balancer of bureaucratic, client and national interests who must define the use of public authority accordingly. But what distinguishes the Japanese bureaucrat is a high degree of discretionary power justified by the need to be effective in achieving policy goals. In the case of ODA the Japanese bureaucrat is an extraordinarily powerful political actor and is the focus of the decision-making process.

The goal that created the ODA administrative system was the speedy recovery and development of Japanese industry and trade. Discretionary power has been used to: (1) limit access to ODA networks; (2) create intimate and mutually inclusive policymaking and implementation settings; and (3) yield only marginal and largely symbolic concessions to peripheral domestic and international pressure groups.

On the one hand, this has avoided the problem of pluralistic paralysis or corporatist stagnation that societally oriented systems have experienced.[43] On the other hand, Japan's inability or unwillingness to reorient its policies has invited such criticism from domestic and foreign groups that, for reasons already mentioned, the Keidanren has begun to press for greater openness and accountability in official decision-making. While the exercise of bureaucratic discretion in defence of the ODA system was justified in the past by the need for rapid economic recovery and growth, after these goals have been achieved the only remaining issue of strategic importance to the bureaucracy is preserving its power and autonomy.

Relations between LDP Diet members and the bureaucracy in the area of ODA are organised in such a way as to facilitate rent-seeking by politicians. The absence of Diet action orients them away from broad policy thinking and towards representing the interests of private-sector contractors seeking favourable treatment by the bureaucracy. The predominance of bureaucratic informality managing opaque, case-by-case decision-making procedures in ODA makes it feasible to accommodate discrete interventions by powerful LDP politicians. In this sense, managing project-oriented ODA is similar to policymaking in domestic public works and construction where interlocked bureaucratic-politician-private sector interests manage the allocation of contracts.[44] The LDP's preoccupation with representing private-sector clients in a bureaucratically dominated decision-making system does not, however, mean that the LDP holds the bureaucracy accountable. The LDP has abdicated its Diet responsibility to define the principles and procedures needed to govern this policy area; this activity occurs elsewhere in officially sponsored *shingikai*, policy studies, and informal study groups. The LDP's informal interventions are more in the nature of rent-seeking than policymaking or the representation of the broad interests and values of voters and taxpayers. In this case the LDP role is hardly evidence that there is a broad range of interest groups free to compete for access to policymaking.

What is unusual about ODA is the routine coordination of 16 main ministries and agencies in policymaking and implementation. It appears unusual today because there is no issue in contemporary Japan that could overcome so many barriers to interministerial cooperation. But when it was designed and created in the 1950s, the felt need for reconstruction and development was so critical that these barriers *were* overcome, and rules and mechanisms for shared jurisdiction were successfully institutionalised. Today the system is anachronistic, if not dysfunctional, and there is no consensus within the government over what a reformed system might look like. But the entrenched organisational structures continue to shape policy outcomes, and these continue to benefit private-sector actors while advancing the agendas of various ministries, all in the name of Japan's contributions to global growth and welfare.

The system is not centrally coordinated, but it was not meant to be, nor could it be. It was designed in such as way that core structures in the government and private sector could jointly determine the means and ends of economic cooperation. In the private sector, the key interest aggregating structures have been Keidanren, Keizai Doyukai, and the Japan Chamber of Commerce and Industry. At the core of the government's organisational structure are MFA, MITI, MoF and EPA. The last three design Japan's strategic economic orientations in the international system, and both MITI and MoF can marshal powerful private-sector support in policymaking matters. Foreign observers unfamiliar with the evolution of Japan's economic cooperation and the details of ODA implementation have tended to overemphasise the role and importance of MFA.

This is understandable for a number of reasons. It is common for Western governments to put foreign aid in the hands of the foreign ministry. This preconception is superficially validated by the fact that in Japan only MFA is authorised to explain ODA policy to foreign and domestic audiences, and it is nominally in charge of JICA. To maximise Japan's reputation as an ODA giver, MFA is careful to minimise the significance of the three other members of the *yonshocho*. And it is true that the MFA is expanding its control over the types and distribution of ODA as criticism of the *status quo* rises. But the reality is that MFA's control over declaratory policy is used to overstate its importance as a substantive policymaker, and it is handicapped by the absence of a strong constituency of domestic clients comparable to MITI or MoF. Finally, as explained above, MFA is not free exclusively to control JICA policy or decision-making because in reality the ODA implementing organisations are coordinating mechanisms that allow other ministries to assume the management of functional areas under their respective legal jurisdictions.

In the case of ODA, policymaking does involve an extensive web of informal networks, intermediate organisations, and a structure of implementation that bridges the boundary between the government and the private sector. The relations are marked by mutual influence and reciprocal benefits, but the key distinction is that relations are asymmetrical, with the private sector being more dependent on, and more accountable to, the bureaucracy. It is a system that has not been responsive to a wide range of societal interests, and while ODA increases, aid untying and new emphasis on environmental aid are pledged to meet Western criticism, structural reform is not on the agenda for change because the bureaucracy is unwilling to make itself genuinely accountable to interest groups or the electorate.

Conclusion

The case of Japan's ODA illustrates that Japan's structure of autonomous bureaucratic power impedes its ability to make opportune and appropriate responses to the demands and expectations of the international community. The Japanese ODA system offers a remarkable example of extensive public-private collaboration, as well as interministerial coordination. The system can erase the barrier to information and personnel exchange between the public and private sectors, and it allows the bureaucracy to cede to the private sector a degree of inclusion that is needed to win private-sector cooperation. The interpenetration that intermediating structures allows does not, however, mean that the locus of authority shifts to the private sector. In the absence of any effective system of bureaucratic accountability, authority is retained by the bureaucracy and is used to achieve bureaucratically determined goals. Today the bureaucracy demonstrates its autonomous power by successfully resisting private sector demands for greater openness and accountability. This exercise of power maintains a *status quo* ODA system that can only be perceived as hostile to the interests of other donors and recipients who wish to maintain a liberal international political economy.

The loss of LDP control of the Diet in July 1993 creates a potential for reform because in theory the new ruling coalition can introduce and pass ODA policy legislation in the Diet. In light of its theoretical interest in economic deregulation, the Japanese private sector may even be persuaded to support such a measure. Thus the issue of ODA reform today has the potential to combine the issue of democratic supervision of the bureaucracy that concerns the new ruling coalition and the issue of economic deregulation the private sector wishes to address.

To counter this development the bureaucracy can promise informal pledges of reform and greater openness, threaten subtle retaliation against politicians and private-sector leaders who press for reform, and mobilise private-sector clients enmeshed in subgovernmental structures in support of the *status quo*. These are potent weapons, and they make the prospect for reform less likely than might have appeared to be the case after July 1993.

While it would be impossible to create the ODA system today if it did not already exist, the fact that it is heavily institutionalised gives it enormous inertia despite the pressures for fundamental change. It thus offers us an example of how past choices in institutional development foreclose or make more difficult certain avenues of change in the present. Even if there has been a breakdown in the post-war consensus and a diversification of the items of the national policy agenda, so long as the present structure of bureaucratic power remains unchanged, there will be no fundamental shift in ODA orientation.

Notes

1. Chalmers Johnson, 'Artificial Cartels of the Mind Justify Distrust of Japan', *International Herald Tribune*, 16 June 1993.
2. Organisation for Economic Cooperation and Development, Development Assistance Committee, 'Aid Review 1990/1991: Report by the Secretariat and Questions for the Review of Japan', Paris, OECD, 1991, p. 7.
3. Sumi Kazuo (ed.), *Noo moa ODA baramaki enjo* (No More Wasted ODA), Tokyo, JICC Shuppankyoku, 1992; Murai Yoshinori (ed.), *Kensho: Nippon no ODA* (Testimony: Japan's ODA), Tokyo, Gakuyo Shobo, 1992; Murai Yoshinori *et al*, *Musekinin enjo ODA taikoku Nippon* (Japan: The Irresponsible ODA Superpower), Tokyo, JICC Shuppankyoku, 1989; Mainichi Shimbun, Shakaibu, ODA Shuzaihan, *Kokusai enjo bijinesu - ODA was doo tsukawarete iru ka* (The International Aid Business - How is ODA being Used?), Tokyo Yaki Shobo, 1990; Asahi Shimbun 'Enjo' Shuzaihan, *Enjo Tojokoku Nippon* (Japan, the Developing Country in Aid), Tokyo: Asahi Shimbunsha, 1985. Doi Takako, Murai Yoshinori, and Yoshimura Keiichi, *ODA Kaikaku* (ODA Reform; English title: For Whose Benefit?), Tokyo, Shakai Shisosha, 1990; in English, see Margee Ensign, *Doing Good or Doing Well? Japan's Foreign Aid Programme*, New York, Columbia University Press, 1992; and the winner of the 1993 Loeb Award for Outstanding Business Journalism, Pete Cary and Lewis M. Simons,

'Profits and Power: Japan's Foreign Aid Machine', *The San Jose Mercury News*, 19-21 April 1992.
4. Kawakami Takaro, '21 seiki ni muketa Nihon no enjo seisaku' (Japan's Aid Policy Toward the 21st Century), *Gaiko Forum*, March 1993, pp. 4-15.
5. *Insight: Australian Foreign Affairs and Trade Issues*, Vol. 2, No. 13, 2 August 1993, p. 16.
6. Frank Upham, *Law and Social Change in Postwar Japan*, Cambridge, MA, Harvard University Press, 1987.
7. Keidanren, *Kokusai koken no tame no kongo no keizai kyoryoku no arikata - Seifu kaihatsu enjo taiko no sakutei in mukete* (Economic Cooperation for International Contribution), Tokyo, Keidanren, 24 March 1992; Keidanren, *Waga-kuni no enjo rinen to kongo no seifu kaihatsu enjo no arikata ni tsuite* (Japan's ODA: Its Philosophy and Future Development), Tokyo, Keidanren, 26 June 1990; Rinji Gyosei Kaikaku Suishin Shingikai, *Kokusaika tai'o - Kokumin seikatsu jushi no gyosei kaikaku ni kansuru dai-ichiji toshin* (Responding to Internationalisation - The First Report on Administrative Reform: Valuing the People's Life), Tokyo, Prime Minister's Office, 4 July 1991. Keizai Doyukai, *Kokusai kyoryoku no arata na tenkai o motomete* (Toward a New Direction in International Cooperation), Tokyo, Keizai Doyukai, 19 June 1987.
8. 'Nihon no enjo taisei wa jubun ka' (Is Japan's Aid System Adequate?), *Nihon Keizai Shimbun*, 17 June 1993, p. 2.
9. Sato Seizaburo and Matsuzaki Tetsuhisa, *Jiminto Seiken* (LDP Rule), Tokyo, Chuo Koronsha, 1986.
10. Muramatsu Michio, Ito Mitsutoshi and Tsujinaka Yutaka, *Sengo nihon no atsuryoku dantai* (Pressure Groups in Post-war Japan), Tokyo, Toko Keizai, 1986.
11. T.J. Pempel, 'The Unbundling of "Japan, Inc.": The Changing Dynamics of Japanese Policy Formation', *Journal of Japanese Studies*, Vol. 13, No. 2, Summer 1987, pp. 271-306.
12. Richard J. Samuels, *The Business of the Japanese State-Energy Markets in Comparative and Historical Perspective*, Ithaca, NY, 1987, p. 2.
13. Daniel I. Okimoto, *Between MITI and the Market: Japanese Industrial Policy for High Technology*, Stanford, Stanford University Press, 1989, pp. 226, 228.
14. Muramatsu Michio and Ellis Krauss, 'The Conservative Policy Line and the Development of Patterned Pluralism', in Kozo Yamamura and Yasukichi Yasuba (eds), *The Political Economy of Japan, Volume 1: The Domestic Transformation*, Stanford, Stanford University Press, 1987, pp. 516-54.
15. For the text see Ajia Kyokai, *Ajia kyokai - sono mokuteki to jigyo* (The Asia Association: Aims and Tasks), Tokyo, March 1959.
16. *Ibid.*
17. Arisawa Hiromi (ed.), *Showa keizai-shi* (A History of the Showa Economy), Tokyo, Nihon Keizai Shimbunsha, 1976, p. 357.

18. Ushiba Nobuhiko and Hara Yasushi, *Nihon keizai gaiko no keifu* (The Pedigree of Japan's Economic Diplomacy), Tokyo, Asahi Shimbusha, 1979, p. 252.
19. *Ibid.*, pp. 252-4.
20. Baisho mondai kenkyujo, *Nihon no Baisho* (Japan's War Reparations), Tokyo, Sekai, January 1963, pp. 87-105.
21. Kajima Heiwa Kenkyujo, *op. cit.*, pp. 38-40.
22. *Ibid.*, p. 40.
23. T.J. Pempel, 'Bureaucratization of Policymaking in Postwar Japan', *American Journal of Political Science*, Vol. 18, No. 4, November 1974, pp. 656-63; F. Upham, *Law and Social Change in Postwar Japan*, Cambridge, MA, Harvard University Press, 1987, p. 199.
24. Nathaniel B. Thayer, *How the Conservatives Rule Japan*, Princeton, Princeton University Press, 1969, p. 226.
25. J.A.A. Stockwin, 'Dynamic and Immobilist Aspects of Japanese Politics', in J.A.A. Stockwin *et al.*, *Dynamic and Immobilist Politics in Japan*, London, Macmillan, 1988, p.13.
26. Interviews of Japanese aid officials confirm this; for documentary evidence, see Mainichi Shimbun, *op. cit.*, and Pete Cary and Lewis M. Simons, *op. cit.* Also, see the 14 instalment series on ODA corruption run by the weekly magazine *Shukan Posto*, 1988-91.
27. Administrative Management Agency, 'Public Corporations', in Kiyoaki Tsuji (ed.), *Public Administration in Japan*, Tokyo, University of Tokyo Press, 1984, pp. 35-52.
28. Chalmers Johnson, *Japan's Public Policy Companies*, Washington, DC, American Enterprise Institute, 1978; M. Anchordoguy, 'The Public Corporation: A Potent Japanese Policy Weapon', *Political Science Quarterly*, Vol. 103, No. 4, 1988, pp. 707-24.
29. Okimoto, *op cit.*, p. 154.
30. KKC Brief, No. 43: 'A Blueprint for Upgrading Foreign Aid', Tokyo, Keizai Koho Center, August 1987.
31. 'Resolution of the 51st General Meeting - Our Resolve to Create a New Corporate Concept: Acting in Step with Communities', *Keidanren Review*, No. 123, June 1990, pp. 2-3.
32. Keidanren, *Waga-kuni no enjo rinen to kongo no seifu kaihatsu enjo no arikata ni tsuite* (Japan's ODA: Its Philosophy and Future Development), Tokyo, Keidanren, 26 June 1990.
33. For a fuller treatment, see David Arase, *The Political Economy of Japan's Foreign Aid*, Boulder, Lynne Rienner, 1994.
34. Kiyoshi Kojima and Terutomo Ozawa, *Japan's General Trading Companies: Merchants of Economic Development*, OECD, Paris, 1984, p. 8.
35. The operation of the 'injection' system was confirmed by various Thai, Filipino, Indonesian, American and Japanese officials interviewed by the author.

36. Keizai Dantai Rengokai, *Kokusai koken no tame no kongo no keizai kyoryoku no arikata - seifu kaihatsu enjo taiko no sakusei ni mukete* (Economic Cooperation for International Causes - A Proposal for Formulation of Basic Rules of Official Development Assistance), Tokyo, Keidanren, 24 March 1992, p. 4.
37. Chalmers Johnson, 'Japan: Who Governs? An Essay on Official Bureaucracy', *Journal of Japanese Studies*, 2, 1975, pp. 1-28.
38. Herbert A. Simon, *Administrative Behavior: A Study of Decisionmaking Processes in Administrative Organizations*, 3rd edn, New York, The Free Press, 1976.
39. Michio Muramatsu and Ellis Krauss, 'Bureaucrats and Politicians in Policymaking: The Case of Japan', *The American Political Science Review*, 78, 1984.
40. Max Weber, 'Bureaucracy', in H. H. Gerth and C.W. Mills (eds), *From Max Weber: Essays in Sociology*, New York, Oxford University Press, 1958, pp. 214-5.
41. Joel D. Aberbach, Robert D. Putnam and Bert A. Rockman, *Bureaucrats and Politicians in Western Democracies*, Cambridge, MA, Harvard University Press, 1981; also Joel D. Aberbach and Bert A. Rockman, *The Administrative State in Industrialized Societies*, Washington, DC, American Political Science Association, 1985.
42. Ogawa Ichiro, 'The Legal Framework of Public Administration', in Tsuji Kiyoaki (ed.), *Public Administration in Japan*, Tokyo, University of Tokyo Press, 1984, pp. 13-19.
43. Samuel H. Beer, 'Political Overload and Federalism', *Polity* 10, 1977 pp. 5-17. Gerhard Lehmbruch, 'Liberal Corporatism and Party Government', *Comparative Political Studies*, 10, 1977, pp. 91-126.
44. Ellis Krauss and Isobel Coles, 'Built-in Impediments: The Political Economy of the US-Japan Construction Dispute', in Kozo Yamamura (ed.), *Japan's Economic Structure: Should It Change?*, Seattle, Washington, Society for Japanese Studies, 1990, pp. 333-58.

8 Japan and America in East Asia in the Wake of the Cold War: Drift and Immobilism amidst International Upheaval

Donald C. Hellmann

International incidents should not govern foreign policy, but foreign policy incidents.

Napoleon I, *Maxims*

This admonition by Napoleon Bonaparte is today peculiarly relevant for the United States and Japan, great powers caught up in a world in transition. America and Japan emerged from the Cold War as the two most powerful nations on the international landscape. The United States was not only the hegemonic leader of the coalition that won the war, but was the only global military superpower and possessed the world's largest economy. Japan, although mired in recession for much of the period since the end of the Cold War, remains a global economic superpower as the world's largest creditor, at the forefront in a number of high-tech industries, and the dominant economic player in the fastest-growing region in the world, East Asia. Both, perforce, will be leaders in any future international order. However, the continuing failure of both nations to look beyond the now-anachronistic strategic policies and institutions of the Cold War, both military and economic, has itself become one of the features and problems of the international scene. A kind of strategic immobilism has afflicted both Tokyo and Washington regarding bilateral ties, the East Asian region and the global system. A number of reasons underlie this immobilism: both states are shackled by the success of previous policies; the domestic as well as the international institutions that were developed to manage foreign policy during the more than four decades of the Cold War are impediments to change as long as they remain in place in unchanged form; and political leaders in both countries (for differing reasons) are currently more concerned with domestic affairs than with international statesmanship. In view of the extreme changes that have beset and are besetting the international political economy, continued strategic immobilism will stand Napoleon on his head - that is, rather than shaping and managing a new world order, the foreign policies of the United States and Japan will be determined by the shifting tides of international events. Passivity will replace leadership, a historically unprecedented pattern of behaviour for great powers following victory in a great war.

The international system is in the midst of revolutionary upheaval of a scope and intensity seen only three other times in the past two hundred years: during and after the Napoleonic Wars of the early 19th century and the First and Second World Wars. In all of these previous ages of upheaval, which are junctures between one international age and another, the leading states and their statesmen moved decisively to shape the still-indeterminate future world order by creating new institutions to manage the radically different distribution of political, military and economic power resulting from the end of the conflict. Consequently, foreign policy was not left in the hands of those bureaucrats and diplomats responsible for the day-to-day conduct of international matters, people bound by the policies and institutions within which they operated, but instead foreign policy was set by statesmen with a sense of vision and history. Prince Klemens von Metternich, Woodrow Wilson, Winston Churchill, and George Marshall exemplify the statesmen, and their products are the Concert of Europe, the League of Nations, the United Nations (and Bretton Woods), and *Pax Americana*. No less is needed today. Accordingly, in addressing future security relations of Japan and the United States, there is an imperative for comprehensive overhaul, not incremental change, that is rooted in the systemic discontinuities in international affairs related to the end of the Cold War era and the dawn of a new era. It is prosaically inadequate for Washington and Tokyo to restructure their relationship through incremental modification of a bilateral hegemonic alliance negotiated at the outset of the Cold War when Japan was an occupied country with a GNP three per cent of the United States.

Perhaps the most remarkable feature of the current scene is the failure of the United States to respond with vision and verve to the challenge of creating a new world order. By reacting incrementally to specific issues, by not articulating a strategic concept to replace containment, by seeking to breathe life into old institutions devised in earlier times for circumstances not congruent with post-Cold War realities (e.g. the Japanese-American alliance, the antiquated security system of the United

Nations, the GATT), the United States has successfully managed specific issues, but has only superficially related them to the broader international context that is utterly transformed. Despite some notable short-term achievements, the Bush and Clinton Administrations have lost sight of the forest because of attention to the trees. This is especially true in the Pacific, where the residual power and legitimacy of the United States provides an opportunity to shape a new security order and recast in a constructive and comprehensive way the grotesquely unbalanced 'partnership' with Japan.

Discussions in both Tokyo and Washington of future security options in the Western Pacific focus on regional issues from a narrowly military perspective, even though it is inconceivable that any viable new long-term security policy in the Pacific can be devised that is not derivative from the global upheaval in both economic and political affairs. The strategic assumptions underlying the actions and statements of the Bush Administration (e.g. the 1990 Pentagon report, *A strategic Framework for Asia: Looking into the 21st Century*, a subsequent Pentagon report suggesting unilateral 'benevolent domination' as a replacement for containment) and the statements and actions by President Clinton and his State and Defence Departments are little more than updated projections of Cold War policies. What is explicitly stressed is bilateral relationships rather than a regional approach (ostensibly because the 'diversity of Asia' precludes such an endeavour), a phased withdrawal of American forces in the region at a timetable slower than planned for Europe (because the end of the Cold War has not quite yet made it to Asia) and reaffirmation of the Japanese-American alliance with enhanced 'burden-sharing' by Tokyo as the cornerstone of policy towards the region. The Clinton Administration, in contrast to its predecessor, has agreed to an initiative by members of ASEAN that Asian security matters be discussed at the semi-annual postministerial meeting, thereby assuring a multilateral venue for discussion of crises. Such passive incrementalism that leaves unmodified and unquestioned the massive ($45-$50 billion) American military commitment in the western Pacific held over from the Cold War is symptomatic of the shallowness of policy, not leadership. President Clinton did add a political summit to the annual APEC (Asia-Pacific Economic Cooperation forum) held in Seattle in November 1993 and explicitly gave added priority to the Asian dimension of American foreign policy. However, security matters were not included in a summit 'without an agenda' and astonishingly the 'Vision Statement' of the APEC Eminent Persons' Group (chaired by American C. Fred Bergsten) that elaborated a long-term programme to achieve free trade in the region *made no reference to military-security considerations.*

Despite the disintegration of the Soviet Union in 1991, there has been little alteration in the basic strategic assumptions of the United States towards Asia and the world. This approach, predicated on continuity with the past and management of bilateral relationships, has led to the substance and timing of a policy being dictated by three criteria: (1) the constraints of the defence budget and related deals in the corridors of power in Washington; (2) the shifting tides of American domestic politics, especially pressure from Congress, interest groups working through Congress and the presidential election considerations; and (3) international crises, such as the invasion of Kuwait and the incipient nuclearisation of North Korea.

The first two of these criteria are driven not by a comprehensive vision of the direction of international change in the Pacific and the way to maximise the role of the United States in this change but by domestic political events. The last represents passive incrementalisation in which the agenda is set by international events. Vision and leadership, the traditional hallmarks of statesmen in leading nations in an age of upheaval, are the most conspicuous casualties of the current approach.

> Gordius, the father of Midas, became the dominant political power in Phrygia (Asia). His authority and the political and economic welfare of the region were secured and symbolised by an intricate knot. It was said that whoever untied this Gordian knot would become the lord of Asia.
>
> Midas, the offspring of Gordius, was granted by the gods one wish for anything he wanted. Midas wished that whatever he touched would turn to gold. Dismayed that this power prevented him from leading his realm, or even eating, he quickly implored that the favour be taken back. Midas, whose name has become a synonym for a rich man, is also a symbol of folly, especially for those who would be leaders.
>
> Adapted from Edith Hamilton,
> *Mythology, Timeless Tales of Gods and Heroes*

The complex web of military alliances, international institutions, *ad hoc* economic transactions and political security actions that have defined the American presence in East Asia since the Second World War may be seen as a modern-day Gordian knot. Throughout turbulent decades of war, revolution and upheaval, the American knot provided a framework of security, stability and economic opportunity that facilitated the astonishing transformation of what was a war-ravaged, largely post-colonial international backwater into the most rapidly expanding economic region in the world. The benefits are unevenly distributed among the nations of

East Asia, but there is no doubt that the country that benefited most from *Pax Americana* in the Pacific is Japan.

If the United States can be seen as a contemporary Gordius, Japan is the modern-day Midas. During the seven-year occupation of Japan, the United States undertook comprehensive reforms to restructure and democratise all aspects of Japanese society, writing a new constitution and instituting radical and sweeping economic and social reforms. In the ensuing decades, Japan, Midas-like, matured as a kind of democratic-capitalist offspring of the United States - a close anti-Communist ally, a defence satellite in the Cold War and a salubriously interdependent economic partner. Sheltered within an American-made security greenhouse and nourished by the American-dominated free-trade oriented international economic order, Japan developed a golden touch. From being an impoverished international economic basket-case at the outset of the Cold War era (the consensus judgement of all observers in the early 1950s), by the end of the Cold War Japan had become the largest creditor nation in the world, with a per capita GNP 30 per cent greater than that of the United States and an aggregate GNP more than double that of any other nation. The Cold War era made Japan an economic superpower. Although the economic downturn in the early 1990s has moderated the more extreme projections of Japanese dominance, Tokyo has in hand the power for global leadership in technology as well as finance. If the basic structure of the world economy in the next decade remains essentially as it has been in the recent past, it is probable that Japan will continue to outperform the other major industrial powers. Moreover, in accelerating fashion the Japanese have come to dominate in trade, investment and aid in the most rapidly developing region in the world - East Asia.

Nevertheless, extrapolations of an impending Japanese economic order by both the critics and the defenders of Japan rarely take into account that Tokyo's golden touch has been dependent on an international political-security order created by *Pax Americana*. It was the willingness of the United States to maintain stability in the world that permitted Japan to develop in a unidimensional economic fashion during the decades following the Second World War, an era of global strategic confrontation and regional war and revolution. However brilliant the economic leadership by MITI and other technocrats, it was possible only because of the international greenhouse 'made in America'. Obviously, the preferred position for Tokyo is a continuation of this free ride on the back of the United States with regard to all matters of international conflict, be it 'containment' or 'global police actions'. There are numerous political and economic constraints making this highly unlikely. Unless you make the radical assumption that the United States will continue to act unilaterally as the world policeman or that international political conflicts will effectively retreat to the periphery of world affairs, some combination of nations reflecting the current distribution of economic and political power will have to work together to maintain order in the post-Cold War world. By any historically rooted criteria, Japan, currently the world's second largest economic power, must bear a huge part of the burden to maintain world order to facilitate prosperity. And here's the rub. Further corroborating the details of the myth, Japan's affluence is accompanied by a Midas-like incapacity for international leadership that is rooted in a reluctance and/or an inability to define in a credible way a national purpose beyond narrow economic self-interest .

In the latter part of the 1980s, the present-day Gordian knot, *Pax Americana* in the Pacific (and the world), began to unravel. First, the sudden collapse of East European and Soviet Communism led to a fundamental redefinition of global security. Second, a dramatic shift in international economic power, involving *inter alia* the substantial relative decline of the United States and the rise of Japan, severely inhibited the capacity of America to continue as a global political-economic hegemony in the pattern of the recent past. Because this unravelling was brought about not by a calculated policy choice by the new 'lord of Asia', but by basic changes in the structure of the global political economy, the international situation remains fluid and indeterminate. With the end of the prolonged post-war era finally at hand, Japan and the United States must now confront the emerging realities of a transformed world. Both the political-security and the economic relationship between Gordius and Midas must be reconstructed.

In the post-Cold War world a viable adjustment of Japanese-American relations requires the effective linkage of economic and strategic policy considerations. The hegemonic security alliance now operative was crafted in the early years of the Cold War when Japan was a devastated and poor society under American military occupation. The alliance is an anachronism. It is structured on assumptions about Japanese power and international behaviour appropriate to the years immediately after the Second World War and on the international role of the United States during the height of the Cold War in the 1950s and early 1960s. Perpetuation of the anachronistic asymmetry of this relationship has in recent years led to numerous astonishing and inherently non-viable results: for example, the world's largest debtor nation effectively underwrites the security of the world's largest creditor; Japan is the only nation to participate conditionally in the United Nations peace-keeping forces and it refuses to join any other multilateral overseas military activities despite the world's third largest defence force that is legalised by appeal to the United Nations charter.

These international anomalies, together with persistent and protracted bilateral friction over trade and investment, have provoked a strongly negative and increasingly populist political reaction in the United States. Hostile Congressional actions have grown in number and intensity; since the late 1980s, public opinion polls show Japan replacing the Soviet Union as the greatest threat to the United States; the American media has taken an increasingly adversarial position regarding Japan, and Japan has been central to hyperbolic presidential and congressional campaign rhetoric. These developments have introduced a volatile new variable into bilateral relations and make the policy challenge for the American president twofold: to bring the American-Japanese relationship into greater congruence with the new international realities of the post-Cold War world and at the same time to re-establish leadership on this issue in American domestic politics.

Any Japanese government that undertakes a fundamental restructuring of relations with the United States must respond to the changes in international conditions attendant upon the end of the Cold War and will also face a major challenge in domestic policy leadership. In the United States, this task involves a fundamental overhaul of strategic and policy priorities; for Japan, the challenge is even more daunting. On the one hand, it involves no less than defining a new national purpose that is more than the unidimensional, Midas-like aim of maximising national economic self-interest. This need is explicitly recognised by politicians (e.g. Ichiro Ozawa, the power-broker behind the split of the Liberal Democratic Party and the establishment of the Hosokawa government) as well as commentators on the Japanese scene. On the other hand, the implementation of policies appropriate to a new national purpose will require a kind of Japanese *perestroika* of the institutions of government that have been dominated by the bureaucratic-business-party elite for almost half a century. The end of almost four decades of rule by the Liberal-Democratic Party in 1993 was more than an electoral change. It marked the end of the so-called '1955 System' that involved a web of formal and informal relations among the political elite (i.e. the party politicians, the bureaucracy, and the business world) and also linked society and polity in organic fashion. The changes unfolding in Japan are rightly viewed as the beginning of a *perestroika* that will at the very least impede effective responses to the pressures for change imposed by an international system in upheaval. The comprehensive and revolutionary nature of this challenge domestically, and the burden of international distrust of Tokyo, the legacy of Japanese imperialism in the first half of the 20th century, make it extremely improbable that Japan will easily emerge as an independent international leader in East Asia (or the world) in the immediate future. Only by radically restructuring Japanese-American relations can Japan be smoothly and rapidly integrated into the post-war world as an 'ordinary nation'.

Does it make sense even to discuss a military role for Japan beyond that of defending its own territory? Domestically, the Japanese claim that its constitution permits only conditional participation in UN-sanctioned peace-keeping. Opinion polls indicate that over 80 per cent of the Japanese public oppose any major overseas military role for the country and the current jumble in party politics (currently a shaky six-party coalition government) impedes any bold policy move in this direction. Internationally, there is near-unanimity among Asian states opposing a significantly expanded overseas military role for Japan. Astonishingly, Pentagon reports, public statements by American military leaders and virtually all assessments of the future military role of Japan in the Pacific agree that 'the US security commitment to Japan links Tokyo to American goals and interests in the region while also reassuring states throughout the Pacific that they will not have to confront Japanese economic as well as military might'.[1] Japan is thus seen as much as part of the problem as its solution - as a 'militaryholic' nation, incapable of behaving in a responsible and orthodox way by militarily contributing to world peace. The US-Japan alliance is often viewed as the cap on the bottle restraining the genie of Japanese nationalism. To assume continuation of the enormous discontinuities between Japanese economic and political power, because of an implied flaw in Japan's national character manifested in behaviour during the Second World War and still latent, has an Alice-in-Wonderland quality that is singularly inappropriate for any effort to include Japan in a new world order with appropriate responsibilities .

Any new strategic order in East Asia must include the dominant regional economic power, Japan, but it is only under the leadership of the United States that change in the *status quo* is likely to come about. This was graphically illustrated in the Gilbert-and-Sullivan character of Tokyo's response to American pressure to join the coalition to confront Saddam Hussein. Prime Minister Kaifu refused to provide even symbolic military participation in an action President Bush called the prototype of a new world order, citing three reasons. First, the constitution, which clearly permits dispatch of military forces to UN-sponsored peace-keeping activities (Article 9 was rewritten by the Japanese in 1947 for that purpose, i.e. compliance with Article 43 of the United Nations Charter), was used as an excuse to avoid power politics. Secondly, Kaifu said public opinion was strongly pacifist and that this placed ineluctable limits on government policy - despite the fact that for four decades the government brilliantly designed and managed a foreign economic policy that involved protracted and excessive manipulation of the consumer by the government. If strategic leadership came from the top in economics, surely the government can similarly lead on security matters. Thirdly, the intra- and inter-party stalemate in the Diet was said to obviate any action involving the dispatch of troops. This was literally true, but reflected more on the personal leadership abilities of Kaifu and the severe limitations of the Japanese political system to display flexibility in the face of crisis. Eventually the Japanese reluctantly passed a bill permitting conditional participation in United Nations peace-keeping - but only in the context of overwhelming international pressure to do so. Throughout the post-war era, Japan has displayed similar immobilism when faced with major political issues in foreign policy (e.g. normalisation of relations with the Soviet Union and China, renewal of the United States security treaty in 1960). Accordingly, if the United States is to bring Japan into a new strategic order, sustained and sophisticated pressure (*gaiatsu*) on Tokyo is the most effective way to proceed.

Gaiatsu for what? The policy options for Washington will be constrained by the essential features of the post-Cold War world that will define the parameters of choice for both Japan and the United States in national security. In the past, the efforts to establish security relations appropriate to a new international era centred on ideas and institutions that prevented a recurrence of the spasm of violence that marked the end of the previous age. After 1945, peace was to be secured by replacing the political and economic nationalism that had given rise to the Second World War with a collective security arrangement (first the United Nations and the *Pax Americana*), the political and economic democratisation of the defeated nations (Germany and Japan) and the creation of a liberal world economic order.

The current global international situation is radically different:

(1) the end of the Cold War came not from a military victory on a field of battle but a cataclysmic collapse of European Communism - and this has muted the imperatives for building a new world order in the manner seen at the end of the First and Second World Wars;

(2) there is a more diffuse distribution of military and economic power (multipolarity) and an absence of a focused threat to peace, which together

complicate and inhibit efforts to institutionalise management of the global political economy;

(3) the United States lacks the resources and is burdened with massive problems of debt, deficits, and domestic social ills and has been reluctant boldly to take leadership in creating a new world order - and there are no other candidates;

(4) it is not the core industrial states but the Third World, with a surfeit of the ingredients fostering conflict (e.g. nationalism, ethnicity, poverty) and access to weapons of mass destruction that could be the primary sources of international conflict in the future; and

(5) the persistence of the nation-state system as the core of global affairs ensures that the enormously enhanced economic interdependence will magnify the economic component in national security calculations.

Any new Japanese-American security arrangement will be shaped by the three fundamental features of the post-Cold War world:

(1) the greatly increased level of economic interdependence, both globally and in the regions of Europe, East Asia and North America;

(2) the dissemination of affluence and/or technology necessary to conduct modern war to states on the periphery of the global international system (e.g. the poor states of the Third World and national groups in former socialist states); and

(3) the enormously enhanced recognition of economic interests as 'vital interests' on the national security agenda of all states. These developments mandate fundamental changes in the institutions that manage economic and military power, and mark a departure from the main approaches used in analysing the ties between economics and security seen during the Cold War era.

A policy that preserves an American-Japanese security entente, tangible Asian security needs, and the enhanced economic power of nations in the region is clearly within reach. Security in the Pacific is moving from hegemony and containment to what may be called complex strategic interdependence. There are three dimensions to the new strategic realities.

On one level, the strategic nuclear balance remains the preserve of the military superpowers. It will be addressed in the current ongoing arms control negotiations, as well as in traditional power-balancing manoeuvres. Political disarray within what was the Soviet Union and the potential of proliferation to North Korea make nuclear questions the highest priority. On this strategic level, a suitable venue is provided by the institutional framework inherited from the Cold War: the bilateral relations between the United States and the former Soviet Union, an extension of the Nuclear

Nonproliferation Treaty and an enhanced role for the International Atomic Energy Agency of the United Nations.

The second dimension relates to territorial defence. As long as there are nations and nationalism, every country in Asia will have a military force to maintain internal and external security. What is likely to change regarding conventional forces in East Asia in the post-Cold War era is the role of the United States (from hegemony to partnership) and the reshaping or abandonment of existing alliances as the imperative for 'containment' dissipates. National military forces will certainly be maintained, even with the establishment of a regional or global multilateral security arrangement. However, for Japan, a country that narrowly defined security as territorial defence throughout the Cold War, international pressure will mandate an expanded role of its military to address broader issues of security both in the region and globally.

The creation of multilateral 'constabulary security forces' is the third strategic dimension. There are compelling reasons for such a force:

(1) the need to respond to *ad hoc* crises in order to facilitate economic intercourse (a matter of increasing concern as the gap between rich and poor nations grows);

(2) the demand for force in addressing issues such as terrorism, the narcotics trade, or 'renegade' regimes (e.g. Saddam Hussein); and

(3) to address issues of conflict within multiethnic states. Other issues, such as regional nuclear or chemical wars or the protection of sea lanes could also demand the intervention of a multilateral police force. The global approach, through a reconstituted United Nations or new multilateral organisation is appealing, but would need an enormous diplomatic coup to succeed because of the dispersion of power in the world. A regionally focused effort, calibrated to the new economic realities of an Asia under the shadow of both Japan and the United States (and perhaps China), and the new military realities associated with the collapse of Communism and America's relative economic decline, remains another viable option. The United States perforce must be the midwife and leader in structuring any new regional or global security order.

To finance and staff either a global or a regional constabulary security force would require a multilateral alliance framework that would share political as well as economic risks and costs. Such an arrangement would facilitate an end to Japan's 'free ride' in the international system and could introduce Russia and other Communist and former Communist states into a redefined security arrangement with mutual benefits. It is absurd for Washington to continue to guarantee unilaterally the security of sea lanes to the Middle East from East Asia in which 98 per cent of the ships are not

American. If the deployment of American naval forces for this purpose continues, a "use tax" to cover the expenditures is appropriate. However, the multilateral solution, involving a redefinition of security and incorporating fully Japan and the other major East Asian powers, would provide one of the building blocks necessary to create the institutions needed for a new world order.

This initiative would nudge Japan into a more responsible and acceptable military role without igniting the flames of Japanese nationalism. It is a policy initiative open only to Washington, for despite an enormous expansion of economic power, Japan remains virtually a pariah state in matters of security, hobbled by history and its political culture.

The shadow Japan casts over much of East Asia in the decades ahead is an uncertain and threatening component of the new international era in this region. If the United States fails to provide a new strategic framework for solving this problem, the remarkable achievements of the past four decades will be at risk and the 10 trillion dollars and tens of thousands of American lives expended in winning the Cold War will be squandered.

The end of the Cold War and the persistence of widespread social and economic problems within the United States ensure that there will be substantial, perhaps massive reductions in defence expenditure in the near future, producing a 'peace dividend'. It appears that the Clinton Administration will not drastically cut the defence expenditure and pull back from Asia, but there is little evidence that the United States will leverage the achievements of victory in the Cold War and more than 40 years of military engagement in the region by seeking an 'alliance dividend'. For example, in early 1994, the United States moved to the diplomatic brink with Japan over trade without linking and leveraging the US security commitment. The realisation of such a dividend earned during the 40-year Cold War is internationally achievable and would have a profound impact on the massive costs involved in converting the American economy from a military to consumer economy.

Countries that have the highest growth rates in the world depend on the United States as their primary export market, and those that have lived under a conventional and nuclear security umbrella made in America have both the capacity and obligation to pay an alliance dividend to Washington. Whether this will be in the form of greatly enhanced funding of the American forces in the region or economic concessions related to our current trade deficit and capital needs, or assisting through multilateral channels the aid programme to the Soviet Union, are matters for negotiation.

However, the alliance dividend can be paid only if the United States understands its own long-term priorities. To compare the flair for leadership and the strategic imagination shown by the United States in the late 1940s with the current sporadic and incremental efforts to redefine America's role in Asia is to go from the sublime to the ridiculous. Despite a virtually unanimous desire for continued American leadership in Asia and a need for a broadened role for Japan, Tokyo and Washington have offered incremental passivity. All this after 'winning' the Cold War.

Note

1.   See, for example, Jonathan D. Pollack and James A. Winnefeld, *US Strategic Alternatives in a Changing Pacific,* Rand Corporation, June 1990, p. 14.

9 Domestic Constraints and Japan's Emerging International Role

Kent E. Calder

In view of global trade and current-account imbalances, unprecedented in post-war history, dramatic instability in world financial markets, and a surge of protectionist trade proposals across the industrialised West, pessimism has steadily risen regarding the long-run prospects for a liberal and open international economic order. Historically, liberal trade and monetary regimes have prevailed in the international economy only on two occasions, when there has been a clear hegemonic or dominant power - Britain from the Napoleonic Wars through the First World War and the United States since the Second World War. Yet with the United States heavily in debt to the rest of the world and carrying an annual fiscal deficit that has spiralled as high as $400 billion in the recent past,[1] American capacity to dictate and defend rules of the international system, to offer the dollar credibly as key currency, to open its market broadly to imports, and to discharge other functions of hegemony is coming increasingly into question.

Many ask whether it is not now Japan's turn to assume a more active role in ordering the global trade and financial systems. With persistent current account surpluses averaging well over $50 billion annually for most of the past decade, Japan has been experiencing capital outflows half again as large as those of all the OPEC nations combined at the height of their wealth. In the mid-1990s, with external assets around $300 billion, Japan is approaching a scale of international wealth, relative to its partners in the international system, rivalled only by the United States in the late 1940s or Victorian Britain in 1900.[2]

The United States has been actively pressing for an expanded Japanese international economic role for decades, being instrumental in securing Japan's admission to the IMF (1952), World Bank (1952), GATT (1955), and the OECD (1964). Over the quarter-century since its full admission to the community of industrialised nations, Japan has slowly built up credibility at the international economic institutions, as at the United Nations, through increasing financial support and consistent diplomatic backing for the principle of multilateralism. But there have been few independent Japanese initiatives forthcoming, either in the multilaterals or elsewhere. In the absence of foreign pressure Japan has rarely acted; Japan's international economic diplomacy has by and large been that of a 'reactive state'.[3]

Why should Japan move now to a more decisive global economic role? Most fundamentally, from the standpoint of Japanese economic interests, because there has been a sharp increase over the past eight years in Japan's external assets, coupled with rising instability in international exchange rates. This has been a dual shift unprecedented for Japan, both quantitatively and qualitatively. In 1980 new Japanese direct foreign investment flows overseas totalled $4.7 billion; this rose to $12.2 billion in 1985, but then by quantum magnitudes to $22.3 billion in 1986, and to over $67 billion in 1989. Following the collapse of the Japanese bubble economy, the pace of outward-bound direct foreign investment slackened, but remained strongly positive, increasing Japan's tangible physical stakes in the broader world by $56.9 billion in 1990 and a further $41.6 billion in 1991.[4]

Japan's portfolio investments flows assumed an even larger scale. Japanese offshore securities investment rose from a minimal level in the early 1980s to $87.8 billion in 1987, and to $113. 2 billion in 1989.[5] Even though the magnitude of new flows was reduced in 1990-91, the overall scale of Japan's portfolio position remained huge throughout the early 1990s.

With respect to trade, the surge of Japanese foreign direct investment, and the sharp yen revaluation which propelled it, signified that Japan was shifting rapidly from its internationally distinctive, but longstanding, dependence on exports to a new pattern of extensive overseas production, closer to that of major Western industrialised nations. Although in 1980 only 2 per cent of the production of Japanese corporations took place offshore, compared to 10 per cent for US firms, this ratio between US and Japanese offshore production was by the early 1990s moving rapidly toward equality. During 1992 Japan had $148.6 billion invested in the United States, but heavy commitments elsewhere as well - $12.7 billion invested in Indonesia, and $6.7 billion in Brazil, for example.[6] Overall, Japan had well over $200 billion in direct foreign investment outstanding - nearly double Germany's level, and next only to two traditional hegemonic powers, the United States ($422 billion) and Britain ($234 billion).[7] The movement from exports to investment gave Japanese firms - like their British and American predecessors in the investment game - broader stakes in political stability and patterns of economic management beyond Japan's borders than those prevailing when Japan's primary form of international economic association was exports.

With respect to finance, Japan's historic shift since 1981 from debtor to preeminent creditor, coupled with a deterioration in America's credit standing after 1985, also creates fundamentally new economic pressures on Japan for policy activism. These pressures have been made particularly acute by the rising turbulence in global currency and financial markets since October 1987. As long as the United States was a major international creditor, it had a vested interest in currency stability and activism in international financial affairs upon which Japan could rely, obviating the need for Japanese activism. But as Japan itself becomes overwhelmingly the largest global creditor, and the United States the direct beneficiary of persistent depreciation in Japan's huge US dollar holdings, US incentives begin to change, in ways not clearly congruent with Japanese interests. Heavy devaluation of Japan's dollar assets during 1985-87 not surprisingly stimulated Japan toward new activism in international monetary affairs, manifest in the Louvre Accords and the Miyazawa Plan for Third World debt-relief during the late 1980s. Similar pressures emerged with the sharp revaluation of the yen against the dollar during 1993.

Obstacles Confronting a Classical Japanese Hegemonic Role

Kindleberger has suggested that stability in the international economy requires a stabilising power.[8] Such a stabiliser makes and enforces rules of the economic system, provides a key currency, and also, in a liberal economic system, supplies a relatively open market of last resort - preeminently, in the current context, for the exports of developing nations. Despite Japan's rising economic wealth, the Japanese political economy appears structurally incapable in the foreseeable future of playing all these roles simultaneously, in the comprehensive way that the United States has assumed them since the Second World War. While Japan's defence spending is much higher in quantitative terms than often recognised (second largest in the world by NATO's definition at 1993 exchange rates), Japan lacks the vital ability to project its military strength internationally. Its air force, for example, is only a bit more than half as large as counterparts in Britain, France and Germany,[9] and Japan produces few of its own aircraft except under American licence. Autonomous defence capacity has been characteristic of all past hegemonic powers, and an implicit sanction behind their rule-making and enforcing authority. Japan is strongly impeded by both domestic and foreign opposition to rearmament from developing that sort of defence capacity, and even its tentative steps of the late 1980s toward expanded defence spending seem driven more by civilian technological rather than strategically oriented considerations.[10] Cultural factors, particularly lack of a transcendent sense of national mission, also complicate Japan's emergence as a dominant world power.

Most significantly, important domestic structural constraints persist, limiting Japan's emerging global role and rendering it almost invariably reactive. The fragmented character of state authority in Japan makes decisive action much more difficult than in nations with strong chief executives, such as the United States or Fifth Republic France. The problem of domestic coordination is compounded in Japan by the lack of either a functionally oriented administrative corps, like that of France, or authoritative codification of ministerial responsibilities to dampen bureaucratic disputes over jurisdiction. Japan has a hierarchy, or complex of overlapping hierarchies, in its administrative structure, but only weak central coordinating authority. In this respect there is some truth to the controversial revisionist analysis of Karel van Wolferen, overstated as it is in its general conclusion that the Japanese political economy is incapable of meaningful structural change.[11]

To be sure, Japan has powerful national ministries such as MITI and the Ministry of Finance, together with an experienced diplomatic corps. These lend an aspect of decisiveness to policy on narrow technical issues within their clear individual areas of technical expertise and established professional concern, such as technical standards for the consumer electronics industry or the establishment of research cartels in integrated circuits. Japan's elite bureaucracy will no doubt be the chief architects of their nation's expanding global role. But on broad, complex questions of global economic management, or on issues created by emerging technology or economic transformation where bureaucratic responsibilities have yet to be defined, ministerial jurisdiction is often unclear and internal conflict within Japan over how to proceed is often strong.[12] In such cases, of which many trade and some financial issues in the 1980s and early 1990s are clear manifestations, Japanese policies can hardly avoid being reactive.

Japan's complex, ongoing party-political transition, which saw the long-dominant Liberal Democratic Party replaced by a fragile coalition cabinet in mid-1993, also complicates the emergence of a decisive Japanese global role. Politicians are, as individuals, often more decisively pragmatic and more willing to take bold international steps than their bureaucratic counterparts, as the initiatives of former Prime Minister Nakasone Yasuhiro in summit diplomacy and US-Japan relations during the mid-1980s vividly showed. Hosokawa Morihiro, the first post-LDP coalition

Prime Minister, has also at times shown vision in international affairs, especially in redefining Japan's delicate relations with its neighbours in Northeast Asia. But the deep factional structure of the major Japanese political parties and the salience of grassroots pressures in their calculations - a salience enhanced by Japan's longstanding multi-member district electoral system - make the parties, including the LDP, slow to act on foreign-policy matters. The electoral reforms begun by Hosokawa will gradually reduce these domestic constraints on a more proactive international role by party politicians, but the transition could take several years.

The domestic constraints on a Japanese coordinating role in the global economy appear most clearly with respect to international trade. Japan has lent important diplomatic support to multilateralism over the years, through backing for institutions like GATT and the OECD, as well as support for new multilateral initiatives such as the Kennedy, Tokyo, and Uruguay rounds of trade negotiations. Japan's overall tariff levels on manufactured goods are lower than in either the European Community or the United States, and Japan uses quotas less extensively, outside agriculture, than most major industrialised nations.[13] Even in agriculture important liberalisation measures are under way, particularly on items of particular bilateral interest to the United States, such as processed food products. Phased liberalisation of rice imports into Japan is gradually being achieved through a transition from quotas to tariffication.

But the central test of Japan's ability to fill a global hegemonic role with respect to trade is not pragmatic, case-by-case concessions on a bilateral basis, but an acceptance on a non-discriminatory basis of products from the entire world, including the manufactured exports of developing nations. In 1985 the United States took around 64 per cent of LDC manufactured exports to the advanced industrial world. Japan took 8 per cent.[14] Despite accelerated offshore reduction of components from Japanese subsidiaries in South Korea, Taiwan and Southeast Asia during 1986-88, to partially neutralise the effects of yen revaluation on Japanese domestic production costs, Third World manufactured imports into Japan have otherwise just begun to grow. In 1992 Japanese manufactured imports from Southeast Asia, Korea, Taiwan, Latin America, and Africa were actually all down significantly from 1991 and indeed even 1989 levels, reversing promising earlier trends.[15]

Although imports into Japan of processed raw materials and captive industrial components from the Third World will probably increase steadily in the long run, labour-intensive manufactured imports present Japan with a much more complex structural adjustment problem, owing to the unusual dual structure of the Japanese economy. 74 per cent of Japanese manufacturing employment, and 52 per cent of Japanese industrial production, is undertaken in small firms with under 500 employees - ratios half again as high as in the United States, Britain, or West Germany.[16] The Japanese metal fabricating sector, with over 650 000 employees, has 50 per cent more workers than the entire steel industry.[17] Many of these labour-intensive sectors, such as metal fabrication and plywood, compete directly with prospective Third World imports. Most, with the potentially important exception of auto parts, do not compete too directly with products of the industrialised West. These labour-intensive sectors also have unusually strong ties with the Japanese political world; plywood, for example, is a prominent industry in the powerful former Prime Minister Takeshita Noboru's home prefecture of Shimane, and he has actively backed its interests in the past.

Rationalisation of Japan's highly inefficient distribution sector would also seem fundamental to Japan's emergence as an active mass importer. There, to be sure, encouraging developments in the 1991 US-Japan Structural Impediment Initiative (SII) agreement improved the prospect of some gradual liberalisation. Yet full-scale rationalisation is so seriously impeded by Japan's prevailing employment structure, and the natural support of vocal politicians for such a large constituency, that it can be changed only very slowly. Distribution in 1990 constituted 13 per cent of the entire Japanese labour force, compared with less than 3 per cent for agriculture; a large portion of those employees in distribution were redundant.[18] Japan has roughly twice as many retailers per capita as the United States, and 50 per cent more than any other major industrialised nation.[19] Yet the 1973 Large Scale Retail Store Act continues to complicate rationalisation, despite the SII accords. Modification of other existing obstacles will also be very difficult politically in Japan. Japanese political leadership will be under strong domestic pressure to avoid the hegemonic role of 'importer of last resort', especially with regard to labour-intensive Third World manufactures which compete with Japanese small business. For both political and strategic reasons Japan remains, after all, highly dependent on imported raw materials, including oil, whose prices are volatile. Japan would strongly prefer to reduce its trade surpluses through export restraint, accelerated foreign investment, and expanded Third World loans, coupled with *ad hoc* bilateral concessions to the United States and the European Community, rather than through the wrenching structural adjustment which large-scale imports of LDC-produced manufactures would involve.

The spectre of wrenching readjustment in Japan's unusual dual economic structure thus stands as a fundamental obstacle to Japan's assumption of a comprehensive American-style hegemonic role in a liberal world economy. Provided a few delicate issues like auto parts can be finessed, this reality need not seriously impede US-Japan economic relations, since their prospective trade is largely in agricultural products and capital-intensive manufactures. It need not, for that matter, seriously disrupt US-Japan bilateral political relations, or impair strategic Japanese support for ongoing multilateral negotiations on agricultural and service trade. But the political and economic realities of Japan's dual economic structure, which create major obstacles to Japan's becoming the flexible importer of last resort, do intensify the long-run complexities of maintaining multilateralism on a global basis and arresting the gradual *de facto* shift toward a world of discriminatory trading blocs. These assume particular significance against the backdrop of accelerating regional integration and challenges to multilateralism in Europe, as well as the emergence of the North American Free Trade Area (NAFTA) reconfirmed in late 1993 by the national legislatures of the United States, Mexico and Canada.

The Contours of Japan's Emerging Global Economic Role

The world economy, as it moves beyond the era of *Pax Americana*, clearly needs a stabiliser. Japanese corporations, as they become ever more multinational, increasingly share that functional need, which Japanese domestic political structure as currently constituted does not allow Japan to supply and which Japanese cultural values could not in any case easily sustain. Yet the likely outcome of this impasse is not inevitable chaos, despite the thorny issue of Third World manufactured imports considered above. Neither is a world of narrowly regional trading blocs likely; such blocs would serve neither the increasingly global interests of Japanese and Western multinationals nor the national interests of many trading states.

Given Japan's character as a 'reactive state' politically, but dominated by powerful multinationals with strong interests in a stable, relatively open international system,[20] the key to unleashing Japan's manifest economic strength for broader global purposes is the existence of a multilateral, pluralistic body external to Japanese politics, coordinating common regime-level interests of the major industrial powers. Such a body should possess three central characteristics:

(1) the ability to credibly exert *gaiatsu* (foreign pressure) in the direction of Japanese policy change; (2) the capacity to neutralise nationalist backlash within Japan from such outside pressure; and (3) a sensitivity to Japanese interests in the international system, particularly those of Japanese multinationals.

Although, in the short run, intensive US-Japan collaboration is clearly vital to global economic stability, a US-Japan 'G-2' condominium has long-range dangers as a mechanism for international economic management.[21] In addition to provoking European antipathy, such a framework could well intensify nationalist sentiments in both the US and Japan, owing to the intense, politically sensitive coordination it would constantly require. In the wake of the Gulf War and its complex aftermath, groups at many levels are clearly seeking alternatives to a narrow US-Japan 'global partnership'.[22] Bringing other nations into a pluralistic, multilateral co-ordinating unit organised on broader lines would defuse the nationalist impulses provoked with a US-Japan condominium while also maximising credibility within Japan and discouraging bilateral US-Japan scapegoating. Throughout the post-war period multilateral organisations, including the UN, have enjoyed substantial cross-party grassroots support within Japan; multilateral bodies of this sort, with membership restricted enough to be efficient and with sensitivity to Japan's unusual resource vulnerabilities and dual economic structure, could potentially gain Japanese support in addressing issues of financial and macroeconomic coordination.

In the wake of the November 1993 Seattle APEC Summit and the rising momentum of investment and trade within the Pacific Basin, the very real issues arise for Japan as to whether the optimal multilateral framework should be Pacific or global and, within the Pacific, whether the framework should be trans-Pacific or Asia-specific. Given Japan's underlying industrial competitiveness and role as a global capital exporter, it should rationally prefer the broadest possible framework. That is in fact what the big business community - more influential now than even under LDP rule - in fact does seem to prefer. But frustration with what is perceived in Japan as 'aggressive unilateralism' on the part of the US and Europe is clearly rising, just as Japan perceives its own regionalist options broadening with the explosive growth of Chinese and other Asian markets. The more the US or Europe aggressively promote regionalist schemes that exclude Japan, or discriminate systematically against Japanese firms, the more Japan will come to emphasise narrow Asian regional, as opposed to broader Pacific or global, frameworks as the locus for its activities and substantive commitments.

Within a multilateral framework, be it global, trans-Pacific, or Asian, any prospective Japanese leadership role in international economic affairs will be primarily technical and sector-specific, rather than broadly political, although in an Asian framework the political content would obviously be greatest. A technically oriented Japanese role will emerge most clearly in those areas such as energy and finance where bureaucratic jurisdiction is clear within Japan and where the national strategic need for activism is evident. To the extent that Japan moves toward an active leadership role in these sectors, however, the transition may be stormy and crisis-driven, as policy change in Japan frequently is. Japan will likely act in response to outside suggestion, only after others have proven unable or unwilling to do so.

In energy, Japan's continual concern must be neutralising the vulnerabilities which heavy reliance on imports generates. In 1990 Japan imported 84.1 per cent of its oil-equivalent energy, compared with 53 per cent for Germany and only 17.2 per cent for the United States.[23] Only Italy, among the industrialised nations, faced dependencies comparable to those of Japan.[24] Even following the oil price collapse of 1986, Japan had a trade deficit of around $20 billion in petroleum - 50 per cent greater than its iron and steel exports.[25]

Japan has played an active role in the International Energy Agency since its inception. It has also given substantial attention to alternate energy. Should the prospects of major energy shortages once again appear imminent and pressure increase for concerted action, Japan might well be willing to coordinate accelerated multilateral alternate energy development projects and to support them financially. Its incentives to do so have been strengthened by the volatility of Middle Eastern politics, including the Iraqi invasion of Kuwait in early August 1990, although structural fragmentation in the policy process complicated early efforts during the Kuwait crisis to respond to those incentives.[26] Soaring demand for energy in Asia, as the Chinese and Southeast Asian economies boom, also enhances Japanese interest in an active international role with respect to energy development.

Japan's capacity - and probably its incentives - to assume important stabilising functions for the world economy as a whole appear strongest in the area of international finance, principally owing to Japan's huge international portfolio investment position and the importance of its major banks.[27] Although the yen is clearly not a pre-eminent global 'key currency', its share of official international foreign exchange holdings has risen by more than half since 1983. In both international securities underwriting and international lending, yen-denominated transactions had surpassed by a considerable margin those in sterling and Swiss francs by the early 1980s; in 1986 yen-denominated bond issues in the Euromarkets surpassed those in Deutschmarks for the first time. The role of the yen in trade transactions is also expanding, with the share of Japanese exports denominated in yen having doubled since 1975. In official foreign exchange transactions, the financial authorities of the world, particularly in the United States and rapidly growing East Asia, have also significantly increased their use of the yen as an intervention currency .

Even more compelling than recent developments are prospective future trends, particularly if global exchange rates prove volatile. For years, a significant barrier to yen internationalisation was the weaknesses of Japanese financial markets, and the consequent illiquidity of yen-denominated assets. These obstacles are rapidly subsiding, as the range of financial instruments available in Tokyo steadily expands. Increased official and corporate holding of yen by non-Japanese is a likely result of Tokyo's emergence as a major financial centre. Japan's persistent creditor status, reinforced by rising portfolio investment income, should accelerate the process of yen internationalisation, provided stability in the political world and the securities markets can be attained. The climactic step toward a key currency role for Japan could be the widespread issue of yen-denominated US Treasury bonds, a step likely to be demanded at some point by Japanese institutional investors should global foreign exchange markets not prove stable and should faith in the US dollar decline.

Among the most notable Japanese initiatives in global finance thus far have been those strengthening multilateral mechanisms for encouraging the flow of private capital to developing nations, a trend which may well intensify. In June 1987 for example, Japan became the first industrialised nation to ratify the convention establishing the Multilateral Investment Guarantee Agency, which a long-time senior executive of Nomura Securities, Terasawa Yoshio, now a key adviser to Prime Minister Hosokawa, held until 1992. Japan has also become an increasingly prominent financial supporter of multilateral development banks, including the Inter-American Development Bank and the African Development Bank, as well as Japan's long-time concern, the Asian Development Bank, whose president is Japanese. Japan's capital subscriptions to IDA, the soft-loan window of the World Bank, have also been relatively large and rising. During the late 1980s, for example, these subscriptions consistently made up a quarter or more of the global total. In view of Japan's huge capital surpluses and domestic constraints on military contributions to international security, global pressure will continue to be strong for steady expansion in Japanese contributions to multilateral financial institutions.

Japan's other area of major future concern in the international financial area must inevitably be exchange rates. With total foreign trade still a surprisingly low 16.3 per cent of GNP in 1991, compared with 16.4 per cent for the US, but 49.0 per cent for Germany, 43.9 per cent for Canada, and 38.8 per cent for Britain, trade-related concern for exchange-rate stability *per se* is relatively low in Japan, compared with the major European nations.[28] But Japan, unlike the major Western European nations, is not insulated from global exchange-rate fluctuations by a regional stabilisation agreement like the EMS. Japan has a strong and rising stake in stable values for at least the yen-dollar exchange rate, particularly in view of Japan's large portfolio investments denominated in dollars. Japan's 24 major insurance companies suffered book value and revenue losses of ¥2.2 trillion (over $18.2 billion) in fiscal 1986 on their ¥10 billion in foreign-exchange holdings; losses by all Japanese financial institutions were considerably higher.[29] They also sustained major foreign-exchange losses in 1993. The larger Japan's external assets become, the larger the potential exchange losses for Japanese institutions will be - unless some means is found to consistently stabilise exchange rates.

Japan's dollar-related foreign-exchange stabilisation problems can be addressed initially through bilateral exchange rate and macroeconomic accommodations with the United States, such as the Baker-Miyazawa agreement of October 1986. But a 'G-7' arrangement with the United States, or a 'yen-dollar snake' analogous to the EMS, will be sufficient for Japan only in so far as Japanese trade and investment are concentrated within the Pacific Basin. Given the magnitude of Japanese assets, and the possible long-run political difficulties of concentrating huge investments exclusively in North America, both Japanese investments and Japanese financial policy concerns will need to be more global. Japanese activism in the initiation of multilateral stabilisation agreements and continual pressure for maintenance of *de facto* exchange-rate reference zones seems likely, as Japanese international monetary behaviour since the Louvre agreement of 1987 suggests.

The signs of greater Japanese activism in international affairs are slowly appearing, as evidenced in the assertiveness of Finance Minister Miyazawa Kiichi on global debt (1987), Prime Minister Kaifu Toshiki on China trade (1990-91), Prime Minister Miyazawa Kiichi on Cambodian peace-keeping (1992) and Prime Minister Hosokawa Morihiro on Japan-Korea relations (1993). The institutions to support a broader, more perceptive and enlightened global Japanese role are slowly being formed and the sentiment to create and sustain them is discernible more strongly within Japan in the wake of the 1991 Gulf War. But it would take an extended period of turbulence in the world economy with discernible, threatening contours to elicit strong movement away from the persistent tradition of the reactive Japanese state. However urgently and unanimously Japanese at many levels may desire a more proactive international role for their country, the tyranny of fragmented institutions and a political system beholden to parochial interest continues to inhibit that globally fateful development.

Notes

1.   The US budget deficit reached $399.7 billion in fiscal 1992, before receding to $349.9 billion in fiscal 1993. Figures are from the US Office of Management and Budget. See Keizai Koho Center, *Japan 1992: An International Comparison*, p. 80.
2.   At the end of 1991, according to Ministry of Finance data, Japan had net external assets of $383 billion. See Nihon Keizai Shimbun, *Japan Economic Almanac 1993*, p. 33.
3.   See Kent E. Calder, 'Japanese Foreign Economic Policy Formation: Explaining the Reactive State,' *World Politics*, July 1988, pp. 517-40.
4.   Figures are the accumulated value of approvals and notifications as calculated by the Ministry of Finance. See Keizai Koho Center, *Japan 1993: An International Comparison*, p. 55
5.   *Nomura Investment Review*, July 1991, p. 11.
6.   Keizai Koho Center, *Japan 1993: An International Comparison*, p. 55.
7.   Figures are again for the accumulated value of approvals and notifications. See *ibid.*, p. 57.
8.   See for example, Charles Kindleberger, *Power and Money: The Economics of International Politics and the Politics of International Economics*, New York, Basic Books, 1970; Charles P. Kindleberger, 'Dominance and Leadership in the International Economy: Exploitation, Public Goods, and Free Rides', *International Studies Quarterly* 27, 1981, pp. 5-10; and Charles P. Kindleberger, 'International Public Goods without International Government', *American Economic Review* 76, 1986, pp. 1-13.
9.   See International Institute for Strategic Studies, *The Military Balance, 1993-1994*, London, Brasseys, 1993, especially pp. 157-9.
10.   See T.J. Pempel, 'From Trade to Technology: Japan's Reassessment of Military Policies', *The Jerusalem Journal of International Relations*, Vol. 12, No. 4, 1990, pp. 1-28.
11.   See Karel van Wolferen, *The Enigma of Japanese Power*, New York, Alfred Knopf and Sons, 1989.
12.   On the processes at work in the high-technology sector, see Kent E. Calder, *International Pressure and Domestic Policy Response: Japanese*

Informatics Policy in the 1980s, Princeton, Center of International Studies Research Monograph No. 51, 1989.

13. See Keizai Koho Center, *Japan 1993: An International Comparison*, p. 43.

14. International Monetary Fund, *Direction of Trade Statistics*, 1986 edition.

15. In 1992 Japanese manufactured imports from Southeast Asia were down 0.6 per cent, from Korea 8.3 per cent, from Taiwan 0.5 per cent, and from Africa 6.1 per cent from 1991 levels. See Ministry of International Trade and Industry (Tsusho Sangyo Sho). *Tsusho Hakusho* (White Paper on International Trade), 1993 edition. Tokyo, Okurasho Insatsu Kyoku, 1993, especially pp. 271-354.

16. See Small and Medium Enterprise Agency (Chusho Kigyo Cho), (ed.), *Chusho Kigyo Hakusho* (White Paper on Small Business), 1989 edition, Tokyo, Okurasho Insatsu Kyoku, 1989, Appendix III.

17. Ministry of Labour (Rodo Sho) (ed.), *Rodo Hakusho* (Labour White Paper), 1985 edition, Tokyo, Nihon Rodo Kyokai, 1985, p. 138.

18. Keizai Koho Center, *Japan 1993: An International Comparison*, p. 20.

19. On the Japanese labour force in the distribution sector, see Kent E. Calder, *Crisis and Compensation*, pp. 326-7.

20. See Kent E. Calder, 'Japan's Public and Private Sector: Beyond the Revisionism Debate', *The JAMA Forum*, Vol. 9, No. 1, September 1990, pp. 3-7; and Kent E. Calder, *Strategic Capitalism: Private Business and Public Purpose in Japanese Industrial Finance*, Princeton, Princeton University Press, 1993.

21. On the G-2 framework, see C. Fred Bergsten, 'Economic Imbalances and World Politics,' *Foreign Affairs* 65, Spring 1987; and Yoichi Funabashi, *Nichibei Keizai Masatsu* (Japan-US Economic Conflict), Tokyo, Iwanami Shinsho, 1987, pp. 194-230.

22. On the post-Gulf War foreign-policy reassessment within Japan, see for example, Inoguchi Takashi, 'Japan's Response to the Gulf Crisis: An Analytic Overview', *The Journal of Japanese Studies*, Vol. 17, No. 2, Summer 1991, pp. 257-74; and Ito Kenichi, 'The Japanese State of Mind: Deliberations on the Gulf Crisis', *The Journal of Japanese Studies*, Vol. 17, No. 2, Summer 1991, pp. 275-90.

23. See OECD, *Energy Balances of OECD Countries* (various issues).

24. In 1990 Italy relied on imports for 83.9 per cent of total energy requirements - only a slightly lesser share than in Japan. See *ibid.*

25. OECD, *Statistics of Foreign Trade* (various issues).

26. See, for example, *New York Times*, 14 August 1990.

27. As is well-known, the eight largest banks in the world are Japanese. Although the ongoing wave of major mergers in the US financial world since mid-1991, coupled with the collapse of Japan's financial bubble, modifies this exaggerated picture somewhat, Japanese banks will continue to be extraordinarily important players on the international scene. For recent rankings, see *Fortune*, 24 August 1992.

28. Bank of Japan Research and Statistics Department, *Kokusai Hikaku Tokei* (International Comparative Statistics), 1992 edition, Tokyo, Nihon Ginko, 1989.
29. *Japan Times*, 5 January 1988.

10 Missions, Mechanisms and Modalities of Fledgling Cooperative Regimes in the Pacific

Takashi Inoguchi

Introduction

Cooperation often emerges when actors endeavour to mitigate or eliminate difficulties by acting together.[1] However, the way in which they act differs tremendously even when they intend to act together to resolve conflicts of interest. In the West European context, for instance, Flora Lewis contrasts the Anglo-Saxon tradition of establishing precedents with the Napoleonic codification.[2] Plunging out of the European Exchange-Rate Mechanism immediately after some tremor took place when many French and Danes showed hesitancy in ratifying the Maastricht Treaty were the British; those joining the move toward an eventual European Monetary Union included the French. The Group of Seven may be close to Anglo-Saxon practice while the Maastricht Treaty may be closer to the Napoleonic.

In the Asian-Pacific context, Ezra Vogel contrasts three ways of settling disputes in foreign direct investment.[3] The Americans usually rely heavily on lawyers, who resort to the exhaustive use of language to settle disputes as if the number of words and saturation of possibilities were conducive to a better settlement. The Chinese, diametrically opposite to the Americans, are normally excessively vague and often very pithy in wording when they form contracts and agreements. The spirit is *mama-huhu*, i.e. whether it is a horse or a tiger that is emerging on the faraway horizon does not matter. Baffled at these two extremes are the Japanese, making foreign direct investment in both the US and China. For the Japanese are comfortable when they have some written explanation registering basic understanding but have left the details of disputes to be settled by case-by-case pragmatic handling mixed with karaoke and golf.

In the US-Japan context, the Americans claim to be result-oriented, with various targets indicated to prod the Japanese into disentangling structural impediments. If the Japanese do not deliver, they pay the price of their failure to do so. As a Hong Kong businessman put it, the Americans are MacDonaldised in the sense that they yearn for results (hamburger) and that three minutes are their maximum limit for patience. The Japanese claim to be market-oriented, content with leaving most to market forces while, somewhat self-contradictorily, working assiduously to influence market forces. More recently, they have gone further to claim to be the guardian of free trade in the Pacific.

All caricatures and jokes aside, this chapter attempts to look at economic and security cooperation in Asia-Pacific afresh and is, I hope, free from a legalistically institutionalist perspective. Before examining economic and security cooperation, I shall first examine what I think are three major features of global change that have taken place over the last decade or so. Then I shall focus on three issues of cooperation, each associated with the three major features of global change. Lastly, I shall conclude that economic and security cooperation has been forged in a very primitive form, at least from an institutionalist perspective, in the Asian-Pacific region and that such format of cooperation has been more or less suited to the structural configuration of the Asia-Pacific.

Three Major Features of Global Change

In my view the following three major features should be noted.[4] I call them the end of the Cold War, the end of geography and the end of history and relate respectively to international security, the world economy and domestic societies. They are borrowed from George Bush, Richard O'Brien and Francis Fukuyama. But I attach to these phrases meanings different from those intended by their original authors. For George Bush the end of the Cold War was the victory of the US over Communism; for Richard O'Brien the end of geography heralded the victory of international financial market forces, and for Francis Fukuyama the end of history saw the victory of liberal democracy.

In my view the major features of global change should be captured more dialectically. By that I mean that, rather than depicting and examining the primary force working in one direction, forces working in mutually opposite directions should be examined in order to see the eventual outcomes of their competition. Excessive attention to a one-way dynamic of forces may mislead us to believe that the world is moving in one direction or another and that the eventual outcome is more or less predetermined. But in my view the world is in a pretty bewildering flux and attention should be paid to a number of forces that may try to overwhelm or undermine one another. It is impossible to suppress all other forces even when the primary and leading forces may have won because victory has itself been achieved by the existence of opposing forces. Even if the previously opposing force may have petered out, newly opposing forces usually start to manifest themselves, making life more complicated. Without trying to fathom these dialectics, it would be so easy to be misled by the simplistic and unidirectional perspectives.

The major feature of international security is the contradiction between short-term US military supremacy and longer-term inability to sustain military supremacy with a weakening technological, economic and financial basis. Similarly the major feature of the world economy is the contradiction between the deeper economic integrative forces pushing global liberalisation further and the sub-global forces of autonomy and protection. The major feature of domestic societies is the contradiction between forces of economic deregulation and political democratisation on the one hand and their destabilising consequences on the other.

International Security

The disappearance of the Soviet Union first as a military threat and then as an entity has propelled the US to enjoy absolute military supremacy in both strategic nuclear and conventional forces. Underlying the Soviet decision to discontinue the arms race with the US in the mid- and late 1980s was US technological progress. In particular, improvement in precision in the submarine-launched missile delivery system has given an advantage to the US. To keep competing with the US in the arms race meant a great sacrifice to the Soviet Union since it had been suffering from the decline of competitiveness in many economic sectors. The increasingly negative perception of its own capabilities, technological, economic and financial, to sustain its military supremacy in the longer term has made it far less willing to commit itself to war abroad. This tendency was recently commented on by Peter Tarnoff, now number two in the US State Department but formerly head of the Council on Foreign Relations which publishes the *Foreign Affairs* magazine, prompting some to call him the antithesis of George Kennan, who heralded the beginning of the Cold War with his 'X' article in the *Foreign Affairs* magazine.

In the Asia Pacific area as well, this tendency is evident. Though much slower and less drastic, the US military presence in the area is bound to go through a downsizing (or rightsizing) in the near future. The US seems to be determined to restructure regional security arrangements by introducing multilateral schemes, using whatever levers it currently retains over the region. This is a departure of some significance since it has long relied on bilateralism as a means of exercising influence over countries in the region, as is demonstrated by the absence of all-regional multilateral security arrangements and the predominance of bilateral schemes. Yet the long absence of institutional multilateralism as well as the historical diversity of the region seems to point to the prospect of a slow development of such multilateral security arrangements.

World Economy

Steady progress in information technology is globalising economic activities, disregarding national borders. Global market liberalisation has been promoted everywhere and global economic integration has been moving ahead year by year. At the same time a burgeoning opposing force has been equally ubiquitous. It may take the form of protectionism, erecting barriers and impediments to thwart competition from abroad. It may take the form of regionalism, liberalising the market on a regional scale while discriminating against extra-regional actors. Also it may take the form of subsidiarity, enabling the national government to abide by the principles of market liberalisation and economic integration and the sub-national government to skirt compliance with those principles. Since market liberalisation invites the intermittent alteration of comparative advantage and the concomitant need to make structural adjustments, the counteracting forces are bound to flourish. The crux of the matter is therefore to advance the former force while containing the latter if the common goal is to maintain free trade and facilitate deeper integration.

In Asia-Pacific, this contradiction is manifest in a number of forms. Most of Pacific Asian economies enjoy fairly high economic growth rates, enjoying market access to the US and accommodating Japan's foreign direct investment and importing capital goods from Japan. This structure tends to foster a perennial trade surplus *vis-à-vis* the US while producing a deficit *vis-à-vis* Japan. Japan itself is more extreme than most Pacific Asian economies since it does not import a large volume of capital and manufactured goods while enjoying market access to the US. The result is the perennial trade surplus - and a very large one at that - *vis-à-vis* the US. This provokes the US government's attempt to further liberalise the market. What is often seen as relentless pressure from the US government on the Japanese government towards further market liberalisation and more recently towards assured market access of US products is feared broadly in Pacific Asia, as US pressure might spread and permeate the rest of Pacific Asia as well as Japan, thus damaging the broad prosperity of the region. In the words of Tommy Koh, the question is 'whether the more muscular attitude toward Japan will also be the US approach to the rest of the region'.[5] Thus looked at very broadly, the liberalising and protectionist forces intertwine in a complex fashion in Pacific Asia. First, most of the Pacific Asian economies, like most of non-Anglo-American economies, are regarded by the US as relatively well regulated. Yet global liberalising forces are working steadily in Pacific Asia, its economy is one of the most rapidly developing and thus changing the fastest. In other words, Pacific Asia is fast liberalising. Naturally, to cope with fast liberalisation, various forces come up towards retaining what are considered to be the secrets of economic success, including the complex system of lifetime employment, inter-firm and bank-firm *keiretsu* relationship, and the inter-firm stock-sharing system and more broadly the complex business-bureaucratic-political triangle, which has been widely regarded as broadly protectionist and regulationist.[6] Second, US pressure means further market liberalisation of Pacific Asia and assured access of US products and services and further protection of US products from Pacific Asian intrusion. US pressure is not only economic in nature but also probably more importantly political as it pertains to its desire to keep its primacy and leadership role firmly grounded on fair and acceptable competitiveness.[7]

Domestic Societies

A vast number of developing countries started to deregulate their economies in a steady fashion in the 1980s. Excessive regulation has made the economy steadily obsolete in many cases when economic activities have been steadily globalising. Hence the conspicuous tide towards deregulation. In tandem with economic deregulation came the demand for political liberalisation and democratisation.[8] Bureaucratic regulation normally entails social and political clients and dismantling such bureaucratic regulation facilitates the realignment of social and political groups in the society. At the same time the tide of economic deregulation and political democratisation often becomes the major factor in social destabilisation. When the economy undergoes deregulation and structural adjustments, and when the political system faces increasingly strident popular demand for more participation and transparency, it is not surprising to see that many societies in transition and in the developing world are being destabilised to an alarming extent, especially when these changes are not accompanied by a certain combination of positive economic growth rate and positive evolution of political détente.

In the Asia-Pacific region as well, this contradiction is manifest. One noteworthy feature in the Asia-Pacific region has been the relatively high economic growth-rate registered and the relatively cautious political loosening implemented only step by step. Hence compared to many other regions this contradiction is not overtly and dramatically manifest in Asia-Pacific. Saying this does not mean that the contradiction does not exist. Rather, because of fast economic change, it has been latent in a potentially explosive form. Awareness of all this prevents many leaders in the region from attempting to liberalise and democratise politics quickly. Such examples include China and Indonesia, having dared suppress protesters in Tiananmen square and East Timor respectively and felt the tangible demand for political participation growing in tandem with the economic development the government itself has been assiduously pursuing.

Three Major Issues Awaiting Regional Cooperation

Having completed, if very briefly, my three-way description of global change and the change in the Asia-Pacific region in particular, I am now in a position to tackle some major issues which await regional cooperation. One issue is picked up in each of the areas featured above. They are nuclear proliferation, foreign direct investment and human rights. They are all regarded among the most pressing and most disturbing issues in the region and hence widely thought to require some regional cooperation.

Nuclear Proliferation

Nuclear proliferation has long been an issue in the world. But it has become one of the most pressing issues in the region in the 1990s for two major reasons. One is North Korea's threat of withdrawing from the Non-Proliferation Treaty and the other is the lax management of nuclear facilities in the former Soviet Union. North Korea and South Korea concluded an agreement in 1991 to remain militarily non-nuclear to facilitate a peaceful reunification of both Koreas.[9] Yet North Korea apparently wants to acquire nuclear weapons, as it considers itself 'besieged' by countries not sufficiently friendly and because its economy has been stagnating steadily. Although the reasoning of North Korean leaders is not entirely clear to outsiders, it looks as if those leaders have been thinking that nuclear weapons or the threat of producing them can be used as a bargaining chip to make a breakthrough in terms of somehow bringing the US to come to terms with North Korea and encouraging Japan to help North Korea reconstruct its economy. And to general astonishment, North Korea has been able to talk to the US directly and bilaterally. Furthermore, it has backed down from the withdrawal announcement on the Non-Proliferation Treaty and yet been able to continue refusing the International Atomic Energy Agency's inspection of the alleged nuclear production sites known as Yongbyon. And more as a by-product of its blackmail diplomacy, North Korea has been able to observe some vacillations in South Korea and in Japan as to what course they might choose once North Korea acquires nuclear weapons.[10]

Since North Korea has not been incorporated in any multilateral international institutional framework except for the Non-Proliferation Treaty, it is neither possible for the world community to utilise such institutions nor for any other countries to create *de novo* some multilateral framework to lead North Korea back into the fold of the Non-Proliferation Treaty. Given the perceived imminent danger of North Korea resorting to nuclear arms production, the US came to talk directly to North Korea, which it had been assiduously avoiding for so long. Talk of constructing a multilateral institutional framework involving the two Koreas, the US, China, Russia and Japan has been almost en route but whether it might be constructed in the near future is a moot question.[11]

The problem of laxity in nuclear facilities and nuclear wastes by the former Soviet republics, including Russia, the Ukraine and Kazakhstan, has been a real one needing immediate attention. Unlike North Korea, however, former Soviet republics have been seeking help in the management of nuclear facilities and nuclear wastes. Since there is an extensive array of agreements on nuclear management between the former Soviet Union and the US and since they constitute a multilateral institutional framework to extend assistance to the former Soviet republics, the construction of such a cooperative framework seems feasible and the process has involved not only the US but also the EU and Japan. The two major differences are the existing multilateral framework, no longer entirely relevant, and the lack of trust among the countries involved. Japan has been alarmed by what seems to their experts as the extremely poor management of nuclear facilities and wastes in the former Soviet republics. The Ukraine's toying with strategic nuclear weapons and aircraft carriers in addition with the memory of Chernobyl, Kazakhstan's nuclear facilities and environmental hazards created by testing of nuclear bombs, Russia's need to wind down nuclear facilities, its 'relaxed' manner of handling nuclear facilities and its 'broad-minded' approach to the disposal of nuclear wastes by throwing them into the Sea of Japan and the Arctic Ocean - because it lacks the financial resources to properly maintain such facilities and to dispose of such wastes - call for mutual cooperation without delay.

The former Soviet Union was a participant in agreements on nuclear weapons and energy along with, among others, the US, the International Atomic Agency and the European Bank for Reconstruction and Development. This basis seems to have been very conducive to the fairly constructive manner in which the world community started to tackle the issues. Especially the trust the US seems to place in Russia appears to be essential to get negotiations moving. Needless to say, the possibly imminent and present danger of a nuclear mishap encourages major countries to move in the direction of multilateral cooperation. The US, as the leading superpower, has good reason to keep Russia and other nuclear republics within easy reach while Europe and Japan have every reason to be apprehensive of nuclear developments in adjacent nuclear republics. Japan, which has not been able to develop a fully fledged and friendly relationship with Russia, started to move towards multilateral cooperation concerning the imminent danger of nuclear facilities and wastes and its need to get along with the Group of Seven. This is an interesting case in which the spirit of bilateral relationships has not been able to override that of multilateral schemes.[12] It can be argued that Japan's strong ideas on economic development, like its emphasis on social infrastructure, manufacturing and intervention, could well transform the course of multilateral assistance to Russia and other former Soviet republics, especially in Central Asia, where   Japan's financial contribution will be combined with political strength in the future.[13]

Foreign Direct Investment

Foreign direct investment increases as the globalisation of economic activities advances. Even if the end of geography has been permeating every part of the world economy, there is still ample room for national diversity. Hence the increasing disputes in tandem with the increase in foreign direct investment. Yet there has never been any international institution that codifies a general agreement on foreign direct investment. There is no counterpart in foreign direct investment to the GATT in foreign trade. The major reason seems to be the extent of national diversity and the almost intractable complexity when account is taken of the number of pairs of investor and recipient countries and their respective distance in terms of major criteria of diversity. Therefore most are left to bilateral and sometimes regional muddling-through.[14] Two bilateral relationships will be examined here: between Japan and the US, and Japan and China.

The US has been adopting a number of economic strategies simultaneously in pursuing its goal of economic renewal and competitiveness. One is naturally the GATT-focused recodification of economic rules, including some new agendas pertaining to their harmonisation, such as intellectual property rights. The second is the bilateral approach, such as the Japan-US Structural Impediments Initiatives talks, through which the US is attempting to eliminate or reduce Japan's impediments to imports and thereby achieve its twin goals of reducing its own trade deficits and enhancing its own competitiveness, with the ultimate objective of standardising and harmonising economic rules and practices. The US conducts its negotiations in the fashion which is widely interpreted in Pacific Asia as the US pounding and punishing not a surplus-rich but a jellyfish-like Japan without being able to produce any immediate tangible results.[15] Thirdly, the US has its regionalist approach. On its own territory it pursues the North American Free Trade Agreement policy, trying to accelerate market liberalisation in Mexico and Canada as well as in the US. The focus is to facilitate deeper integration, which would presumably enhance the competitiveness of the US and the Americas as a whole. In the US an increasing number of opinion-leaders seem to be of the persuasion that the GATT-type integration is too shallow to meet the challenges of global integration and liberalisation of economic activities and that, given the somewhat uncertain prospects for the GATT Uruguay Round, the US should get together with other countries to reach bilateral agreement concerning the codification of universal rules of economic conduct.[16] Here, on the part of other Pacific-Asian countries, the apprehension of and negative reaction to what seems to be the basic tone of the US, perceived to be similar to the US approach to Japan's further market liberalisation, namely, aggressive pounding and punishing, give rise to their negative reaction to President Bill Clinton's announcement in June 1993 on the enhanced Asian-Pacific Economic Cooperation Conference Scheme, whereby the current APEC scheme of foreign-minister-level meetings would be elevated to the prime-minister president level and whereby political and security issues would be included as formal agendas.

In Japan-US relations, foreign direct investment issues have been framed in the broader bilateral trade and economic talks in which the nature of the Japanese markets, whether it is trade or direct investment, is often alleged to be the primary cause of the US trade deficit. Quite apart from whether the alleged impenetrability of the markets is the major cause of the US trade deficit, the fact remains that the Japanese are not very comfortable in inviting foreign direct investment to an 'excessive' degree, whether it is in the financial market, the construction market or in the more ordinary machine-manufacturing market. One of the features of the Japanese economic developmental model is precisely the lower penetration of foreign capital in contrast to Latin American or African experiences in which the dependency model of economic development flourished.[17] This feature was enhanced especially during the second and third quarters of this century and it is only for the past decade or two that this feature has been watered down slowly and steadily by the globalisation of economic activities. It is not just a coincidence that the previously more radical dependency theory has been giving way to a more market-oriented 'development from within' strategy in much of Latin America and that the one-time radical Chinese strategy of 'self-reliance' has given way to the 'socialism-by-name-only' rudimentary capitalism.[18] All these have been caused basically by the globalisation of economic activities. But the Japanese are perhaps the most tenacious in clinging to their model of economic development, business strategy and political governance, if only because of their belief in their success being derived from their adherence to the model.

In contrast to the Japanese attitude to foreign direct investment is Chinese economic experience over the past 15 years. An amazing amount of foreign capital has gone to China for direct investment, largely from Hong Kong, Taiwan, ASEAN countries and the US. But most investors are ethnic Chinese. It can be argued that 70 per cent of foreign direct investment is from ethnic Chinese and that it should be called Chinese direct investment. And an astonishing amount of foreign loans make up central government revenue in China, which is arguably one of the world's lowest at controlling its GNP size. The most important loan extenders are the Japanese. After the Tiananmen massacre the Group of Seven countries, including Japan, resorted to economic sanctions against China for its brutal suppression of demonstrators. In 1989 the percentage of Japanese loans over the Chinese central government revenue was so large that Prime Minister Li Peng was said to have reminded a Japanese business delegation in the autumn of 1989 that the Japanese killed many Chinese in the 1930s and 1940s and to have told them that they should not kill more Chinese from starvation, this time by economic sanctions. At any rate

Chinese economic developmental strategy is quite accommodative of foreign capital.

Then how do the Japanese and the Chinese handle disputes deriving from direct investment? The answer is bilaterally.[19] Both governments concluded an agreement on this in order to encourage Japanese business firms to do so in China. The most important of the agreed incentives is to give Japanese business firms similar treatment to that accorded to Chinese business firms. However, two major problems have discouraged Japanese business firms from massively investing in China. First, the investment climate has not been good until recently. The state of Chinese transportation, communications, labour, management, energy, materials and parts and risk insurances are not particularly reassuring to normally very risk-averse Japanese firms. Second, more recently, although the economic climate has improved somewhat, the political and social climate may be deteriorating given increasing crime and the uncertain political succession; the central government is unable to gently steer the course of the already excessively heated economy. Since the bilateral agreement does not seem to go very far beyond the scope of conventional agreement on foreign direct investment, much remains to be resolved by business firms involved. As foreign direct investment in China has so far come largely from ethnic Chinese capitalists outside China and as most of these investors have not been involved in those sectors which require high commitments on the part of investors, i.e. those sectors which use a large amount of capital and very high-tech facilities and manufacture very high-value products, it may not matter much whether disputes are settled in an *ad hoc* manner. But once American and Japanese investors start to invest in those large capital and high-tech sectors on a much larger scale than they have been, their foreign direct investment is more likely to lead the Chinese economic system to change in a more drastic fashion by forcing the Chinese government to change laws meeting those demands from foreign investors. In other words, to meet the impact of steadily proceeding 'deeper integration' of the world economy, the Chinese separation of economics and politics (namely, the socialist market economy and the Chinese Communist Party dictatorship) might not be sustained and peaceful evolution might be precipitated.[20]

Seen in this way, it is clear that foreign direct investment is a force of change to be reckoned with in any society, that the resolution of disputes needs to be nationally and locally sustained, and that any universal package of rules pertaining to foreign direct investment is not easy to put forward if it is to be feasible.

Human Rights

The collapse of European Communism has boosted the morale of world liberals, especially in the US. To them it registered the victory of liberal democracy and its further spread is destined to be their mission. It is the imagined community of liberals that has led them to voice the cause of human rights and democratic values.[21] Rather disturbing to them is the situation of human rights in Pacific Asia, where, although the region has come to enjoy wealth, much remains to be done in terms of the spirit of human rights and liberal democracy. Furthermore, sometimes quite independently but sometimes in *de facto* concert with each other, both individual liberals and democrats and the government in the US are seen as acting to dictate their wishes and whims to Pacific Asia. It is widely believed in Pacific Asia that just as Zbigniew Brzezinski wanted to use the human rights issue *vis-à-vis* the Soviet Union, the number-one threat at the time, some like-minded opinion formers and policymakers want to use the issue to undermine and tame Pacific Asia's formidable challenge, the number-one threat today, whether it is led by Japan or China or more collectively conceived. A notable example is the US government's use of linkage between human rights and the continuation of the most-favoured-nation clause *vis-à-vis* China. Every year in the recent past has seen the US Congress raise the issue when the President hesitantly gives a qualified go-ahead to the continuation of the most-favoured-nation clause. The linkage is seen by the Chinese government as US interference in internal affairs and thus flatly rejected while it leaked the video-tape-recorded scene on TV in which Wei Jinsheng, a fifth modernisation fighter who has been jailed for years, was shopping in town seemingly in a relaxed fashion with his guard.[22] Another is the US government's suggestion that the Japanese government be more sensitive to the unacceptability of those governments known for their violation of human rights, suppression of democratic movements, large-scale purchase and sale of major weaponry, and rapid military build-ups as recipients of Japan's official development assistance. Partly in response to such criticism from the US government and non-governmental organisations, the Japanese government, following a cabinet decision in June 1992, issued the *Guideline for Official Development Assistance.* in which it explicitly mentioned the above four criteria warranting careful re-examination of Japan's official developmental assistance decision. But so far there has been no major cutback or termination of Japan's official development assistance, whether it is to China, Indonesia, Myanmar, Pakistan, Iran, Bangladesh or Peru.[23]

A number of major differences have been pointed out between Pacific Asians and Americans.[24] In the first place the former argue that US policy is an interference in internal affairs and an attempt to impose America's will on foreign governments and that local governments and peoples should decide how to attain human rights according to their local conditions while the latter claim they are a fundamental requirement for every individual and that the efforts to achieve them cannot be left to the state. Secondly, Pacific Asians point out that historical specificity tends to support the strategy of putting economic development first and then realising political liberalisation and democratisation step by step while Americans say political liberalisation and democratisation facilitate economic development as well. Thirdly, Pacific Asians, unlike Westerners, especially Americans, place more value on collectivist virtue rather than individual rights while Americans contend that the fully developed realisation of individual human rights must precede any consideration of collective benefits and virtues. It is evident that on both sides there are immense differences between the two schools of thought.

On the American side the liberals and democrats tend to diverge somewhat. The former place utmost emphasis on individual human rights whereas the latter stress minimum requirements for democracy such as civil and political freedom, including free and secret elections. On the Pacific Asian side, the non-governmental dissenters-individualists are more like American liberals and/or democrats while most governments and the majority of people place emphasis on national diversity, economic development and collectivist virtue and sometimes argue that the Americans have not been good teachers, citing, for example, the cases of Rodney King in Los Angeles and David Koresh in Waco, Texas, as well as (to an incredibly high number of Japanese, including more than one million donors to the Yoshihiro Fund) the Yoshihiro Hattori case in Baton Rouge, in which a Japanese high-school student was shot dead in a Halloween visit. Some, like Senior Minister Lee Kuan Yew, even argue that once Pacific Asians adopt an American kind of government, chaos would ensue and competitiveness drop. Or some others point out that the astonishingly rapid surge in Japanese mistrust in Americans within less than a year as registered in spring 1993, from 45 per cent to 65 per cent, is due largely to two events that took place at that time, the apparently 'tough and rude' manner of President Bill Clinton's meeting with Prime Minister Kiichi Miyazawa and the allegedly 'unabashedly racist' Baton Rouge judges and the people who clapped their hands when the verdict 'innocent' was announced in the court on the Hattori case.

How can there be reconciliation on this issue? A light at the end of the tunnel can be seen in the resolution of the Bangkok Conference on Human Rights along with the resolution of the Vienna conference on the same subject, both held in spring 1993. The former advances a strong counter-argument and demonstrates a sharp antipathy to the human rights arguments while the latter's resolution manages to reach a compromise between the two opposite arguments. In other words, the mainstream Pacific Asians and human-rights-conscious Americans are more likely to go their own way while in the formal global institutional settings a compromise may be reached on paper. But not more than that. Ideas on a conference on security and cooperation in Asia have not been received very enthusiastically in Pacific Asia, in part because of the difficulty of reconciling differences on the human rights issue along with the more fundamental difficulty of accommodating the US in a predominant position in such a regional organisation.[25]

Conclusion

I have first portrayed the basic nature of global change, especially as manifest in Pacific Asia, and then examined the three salient issues of nuclear non-proliferation, foreign direct investment and human rights to observe how conflicts of interest are handled. In all three issue areas, a number of common factors are easily identified. First of all the immense diversity of views of possible participants from the various regimes, a diversity which strongly argues for a loose, open, pragmatic and minimalist format of meeting challenges. You cannot get majority support in many cases, let alone consensus. Secondly, the predominance of the US in terms of its ability to shape whatever might emerge as an institutionalised regime. This factor also strongly argues for the loose, open, pragmatic and minimalist format of negotiating agendas on the basis of overall trust. Once firmly established, institutions function long after their supporting structure weakens. Thirdly, the strong consciousness of state sovereignty in Pacific Asia on the part of governing elites tends to argue for a loose, open, pragmatic and minimalist format for the creation of a regional regime. The general reluctance to make concessions on issues perceived to be highly related to state sovereignty is hardly conducive to community-building of a deeper nature, such as a security community. Fourthly, the prospects for Pacific Asia's clout and for intra-regional fluidity into the 21st century have become increasingly clear. This factor also strongly argues for the loose, open, pragmatic and minimalist format for the future development of Pacific Asia. When reality is perceived as transitory, time and effort is not normally invested in the construction of a regime of any kind other than that of a fairly flexible nature. Fifthly, the widely shared perception that time is on the side of Pacific Asia's rapidly increasing economic competitiveness and economic clout strongly encourages governing elites to take the view of letting market forces shape the future rather than striving for a political solution. Given these five factors encouraging the open, loose and flexible nature of administration in many policy areas, it is perfectly understandable that Pacific Asia has so far been able to construct only fledgling cooperative regimes, which will possibly remain so for some time to come. Only when these five factors start to change in some concerted fashion might less open, less loose and less laissez-faire regime construction efforts be observed in Pacific Asia. How soon that prospect becomes reality is a moot question.

Notes

1. See, *inter alia*, Robert Keohane, *After Hegemony*, Princeton, Princeton University Press, 1984; Kenneth Oye (ed.), *Cooperation in Anarchy*, Princeton, Princeton University Press, 1986.
2. Flora Lewis, 'The G-7$^2/_1$ Directorate', *Foreign Policy*, No. 85, pp. 25-40.
3. Ezra Vogel in my conversation with him on 29 March 1993. Further elaboration in the chapter is my own.
4. Takashi Inoguchi, 'Dialectics of World Order: A View from Pacific Asia', in *Whose World Order? Uneven Globalisation and the End of the Cold War*, edited by Georg Sorensen and Hans-Henrik Holm, Boulder, Westview Press, 1995. The titles of Richard O'Brien and Francis Fukuyama are *Global Financial Integration: The End of Geography*, London, Pinter, 1992, and *The End of History and the Last Man*, New York, Basic Books, 1991, respectively.
5. *Newsweek*, 12 July 1993, p. 13.
6. Ronald Dore in Fukada Yusuke and Ronald Dore, *Nihon gata shihonshugi nakushite nanno Nihon ka* (What Kind of Japan Would It Be if There Were No Japanese-Style Capitalism?), Tokyo, Kobunsha, 1993.
7. Samuel Huntington, 'Why International Primacy Matters', *International Security*, Vol. 17, No. 4, Spring 1993, pp. 68-83; Laura d'Andrea Tyson, *Who's Bashing Whom?*, Washington, DC, Institute for International Economics, 1993 .
8. Samuel Huntington, *The Third Wave*, Oklahoma, University of Oklahoma Press, 1992.

9. Takashi Inoguchi, 'Developments in the Korean Peninsula and Japan's Korea Policy', *Korean Journal of Defense Analysis*, Vol. 5, No. 1, Summer 1993, pp. 27-39.

10. *Yomiuri Shimbun*, 17 July 1993.

11. See Takashi Inoguchi and Grant Stillman (eds), *Northeast Asian Regional Security and the Role of International Institutions*, Tokyo, United Nations University Press, forthcoming.

12. *Asahi Shimbun*, some time in spring 1993. Also see James Clay Moltz, 'Divergent Learning and the Failed Politics of Soviet Economic Reform', *World Politics*, Vol. 45, No. 2, January 1993, pp. 301-25.

13. Takashi Inoguchi, 'Nihon-teki hatten moderu no shin tenkai ka?' (Are We Seeing the New Development of the Japanese Economic Development Model?), *Ekonomisuto*, 24 August 1993, pp. 95-8.

14. Debora L. Spar, 'Foreign Direct Investment in Eastern Europe', in Robert O. Keohane, Joseph S. Nye and Stanley Hoffmann (eds), *After the Cold War*, Cambridge, Harvard University Press, 1993, pp. 286-309.

15. When Winston Churchill, then Chancellor of the Exchequer, was observing the Britsh bombing of anti-foreign riots in the Yangtze valley cities in 1927, he noted wryly: 'Our navy bombarding Chinese riots would not bring any long-term benefits to us. Punishing China is like beating a jellyfish.'

16. Peter Cowhey and Jonathan Aronson, *The Management of the World Economy*, New York, Council on Foreign Relations, 1993.

17. See, *inter alia*, *Koza Nihon keizaishi* (Series Japanese Economic History), multi-volumes, Tokyo, Iwanami shoten, 1991-92.

18. For instance, Oswald Sunkel (ed.), *Development from Within: Toward a Neostructurist Approach for Latin America*, Boulder, Colorado, Lynne Rienner, 1993.

19. Ogura Kazuo, 'How the "Inscrutables" Negotiate with the "Inscrutables": Chinese Negotiating Tactics *vis-à-vis* the Japanese', *The China Quarterly*, No.79, September 1979, pp. 529-52.

20. Susan Shirk, 'The Chinese attitude and policy toward deeper integration of the world economy', presented at a conference on the integration of the world economy, The Brookings Institution, Washington, DC, 17-18 March 1993.

21. Benedict O. Anderson, *Imagined Communities*, London, NLB, 1983. Edes Hanson, President of Amnesty International Japan, notes in the *AIJ Newsletter* that the imagined community does exist and it functions when members send letters of protest/petition to leaders of governments to grant amnesty to those unjustifiably jailed.

22. On 29 March - 1 April, I had the opportunity to give three lectures in Chinese at Peking University on the subject of Japanese politics. During my stay in Beijing I saw the news in Beijing at the time US President Bill Clinton was considering the continuation of the extension to China of the most-favoured nation clause.

23. See Takashi Inoguchi, 'Comments on Robert Orr's paper on Japan's ODA', paper at a conference on Japan-US cooperation in Official Development Assistance, Tokyo, 12-13 October 1992.

24. See Takashi Inoguchi, 'Children of Traditions', *Far Eastern Economic Review*, 25 July 1991, p. 15.

25. See Takashi Inoguchi, 'Zen chikyu ampo kyoryoku kaigi o teisho suru' (A Proposal for a Conference on Security and Cooperation on the Earth), *Chuo koron*, March 1991, pp. 124-37.

Part IV
Social Issues

11 Creativity without Diversity? The Anomalous Case of the Japanese University

Ivan P. Hall

Is it possible to have cultural creativity - in the realm of the intellect, in the arts, in matters of the spirit, in technological innovation and the like - without cultural diversity, in particular without human diversity, that is to say, without a direct personal interaction and openness between creative minds from differing cultural, racial and national backgrounds?

In the United States it has become a matter of national faith that you cannot; that human diversity within academic, artistic, religious, and corporate structures is necessarily more creatively productive than a narrow exclusionist insularism. Most of the world would be inclined to agree, if perhaps not quite so dogmatically, and would be puzzled by the very posing of the question since so many of the great historical civilisations have been enriched by their receptivity to outsiders and by their human multiformity within. The *Civis Romanus*, the borderless polyglot origins of modern European science and the trans-national and trans-racial strengths of the great universalistic religions of Buddhism, Christianity and Islam spring at once to mind.

The Japanese give a rather different answer to this question about the causal relationship between diversity and creativity. When pressed, they are likely to demur, or even to affirm an opposite conclusion - namely, that it is the presence of strong social and cultural homogeneity (and the absence of too much distracting human diversity) that truly nurtures creativity - at least their own creativity. It will be my purpose in the following pages to explore this Japanese view through the particular case of the university - perhaps the most central, typical, and revelatory of all cultural institutions. For the Japanese - proceeding both from their past experience and from their future anxieties - have applied with particular rigour to the realms of teaching and scholarship their assumptions that creativity *is* possible without human diversity; that it is even *more* likely to occur without too much of it; and that the direct participation of non-Japanese in their own social and cultural institutions, including the university, will *undermine* Japan's own cultural integrity, identity, and creative dynamism.

Japan's geographical and cultural isolation - not only during the official 250-year 'Seclusion' of the Tokugawa period, but from its very historical beginnings right up to the mid-19th century - has been unique among the greater cultures or civilisations of mankind. It is not surprising, therefore, that a strong residue of insular attitudes should persist even today. After all, when measured in generational terms it has been a mere four or five families back since the advent of Commodore Perry.

This powerful sense of difference and detachment from the rest of the world - including nearby Asia - also derives from the manner in which Japan's appropriations of foreign civilisation (first from China, then from the West) were achieved through sharply defined, intermittent, and deliberately controlled spurts. The door was opened a crack to take in new things, then closed again for a process of cultural integration and refinement. This occurred in the 17th century (following a heady era of foreign trade and Catholic missionising) and again in the ultranationalist 1930s (after a half-century's forced march towards Westernisation). It was also partially true of the post-Second World War period, when Japan's inward-looking obsession with economic growth was made possible by the cocoon of American political and military sponsorship and protection against outside threats. And it may be happening again even now in the 1990s, on a more subtle psychological and ideological plane, as an economically successful Japan concludes that it has little more to learn from the West and starts to turn its attention once again to the leadership - as yet largely unsolicited - of Asia .

What is relevant here to our conundrum of diversity-and-creativity is the fact that Japan's ingestions of foreign civilisation have taken place with very little of that constant interflow and direct human encounter (be it in war or peace) with 'the Other' - that has characterised the development of the European, Islamic, Indian, Southeast Asian, or even Chinese, civilisations. Except for a minuscule number of foreign advisers who were invited in as short-term guests during the Meiji Period, and the relatively minor impact of resident foreign missionaries and traders, cultural contacts during the pre-war decades were primarily a matter of the Japanese themselves voyaging out to bring home, stash away and very carefully adapt certain elements of outside culture. Even the American Occupation, with its new rules and slogans and institutional tinkerings, rested very lightly on the traditional social and cultural structures of the Japanese people. And post-war Japan has experienced relatively little of that massive, two-way, and above all personal, flow of students, scholars, artists and intellectuals across national borders that has taken place since 1950 within Europe, between Europe and America, and between the West and its former colonies. For decades the flow with the West was unilaterally outward and, until very recently, personal interchanges with the nearby continent were severely restricted for political reasons (as with China), or by the emotional legacy of the immediate past (as with Korea and Southeast Asia).

Most of man's history suggests that the creation of civilisation benefits from diverse inputs - both through external stimulation and internal variegation. The point, indeed, has been made that the rich and dynamically developing culture of Japan's own seclusionist Edo Period was made possible, in the absence of strong foreign stimuli, by its often underrated regional, socio-economic, and intellectual diversity. On the other hand, what the Edo example primarily indicates is that creativity *can* at times take place within a closed and homogeneous cultural centrifuge, and there are instances in the West which suggest that periods of relative isolation and internal focus may be helpful, if not mandatory, for the creative incubation of new and distinctive *national* cultures - England in the 16th century; America in the 19th; and the inward turning of Germany after the Napoleonic conquest.

The reply to our original query, therefore, is bound to be elusive, and it is not my intention here to provide a definitive answer. The following three sections will simply seek to lay out the fact that the Japanese tend towards a somewhat atypical view of the matter; to illustrate the consequences of that belief in a particular institutional setting - specifically in the reluctance, from Meiji up to now, to hire foreign professorial staff permanently at Japan's elite national universities; and to suggest that, at the present stage of Japan's relation to the outside world, these fossilised attitudes, and the 'intellectual-access' barriers they have spawned, can only be judged unproductive and 'counter-creative'.

An 'Internationalisation' of Things, Not of People

'Internationalisation' - the English rendition of the Japanese neologism *kokusaika* - is one of the most mutually misunderstood concepts in the recent dialogue between Japan and its partners about the further opening of the Japanese economy and society to foreign participation, and the greater participation of Japan in the world outside. This newly-contrived Japanese term (to which the old English term was subsequently attached) came into fashion during the 1970s and especially after 1980, as Japan achieved economic superpower status and suddenly found itself the object of unprecedented foreign expectations, criticisms and demands. The expression is used by the Japanese to convey the idea of 'becoming more international' in the sense of achieving a greater congruence with widely accepted social and economic standards or practices - both to lubricate concrete transactions with the outside world, and to avoid being seen as too divergent or stand-offish. (The English translation, of course, originally had the much narrower connotation of multinational access to certain facilities or terrain under international law, e.g. as in the 'internationalisation' of the Dardanelles.)

Upon hearing this expression, enthusiastically touted by their Japanese friends, many foreign observers (and by no means Westerners alone) have assumed that becoming more 'international' means becoming more cosmopolitan, and that being more cosmopolitan (as fuller 'citizens of the world') implies a greater co-mingling of peoples in direct personal and intellectual contact - that is to say, a greater number of non-Japanese persons actually present and genuinely functioning within Japanese society itself. This is not at all how the Japanese interpret this term. For them, *kokusaika* refers to smoother adjustments on, or beyond, Japan's tangential surface with the outside world - things like greater financial and personnel contributions to international organisations, lower tariffs, synchronised school years, or short-term cultural exchanges - rather than to any fundamental opening of their society to non-Japanese.

The term *kokusaika*, indeed, has been cobbled together from the two Chinese ideographs for 'country' and 'furthermost edge', and is used in clear distinction to a much older and better-established expression which really does mean 'opening of the country', namely *kaikoku* (which most foreign observers erroneously suppose to be the purpose of *kokusaika*, or 'internationalisation'). *Kaikoku*, or 'opening the country', has generally been used of only two periods in the modern era - the early Meiji and the immediate post-war years, the one brought on by the intrusion of Perry, the other by the landing of MacArthur. *Kaikoku*, accordingly, is not without a certain nuance or stigma of capitulation to foreign *force majeure*, and the Japanese from the mid-1980s have been asking themselves - with the 'nays' still outnumbering the 'ayes' - whether or not their country should now undertake a third *kaikoku*, this time on its own initiative .

Both sides clearly have been talking past each other, and there has been mounting impatience abroad with Japan's reluctance to accord to foreign journalists, lawyers, scholars and students the same professional opportunities that Japanese nationals have long enjoyed in other countries, particularly in the US and Western Europe. To place the Japanese university in the context of this broader debate, it may be helpful at first to spell out more fully these divergent expectations regarding the greater 'internationalisation' of Japan. There is nothing wrong with the Japanese definition as far as it goes, and many fine things have been accomplished in its name, but the tenacity with which Japan clings to it may be the greatest initial barrier to a genuine opening of the country.

The difference, in a word, is between an 'internationalisation' of *people* (what the outside world increasingly expects) and an 'internationalisation' of *things* (what the Japanese continue to cling to). It is the difference between a greater openness to foreign participation within Japan (both in the market, and in professional and intellectual activities), and a continuing but impersonal receptivity to foreign artefacts, culture, and ideas - that which the Japanese have always seen as the central and sufficient task of 'internationalisation'.

What I mean by a *kokusaika* of 'things' in Japan has included over the past century not only the entire panoply of Western material civilisation from railroads to hamburgers, but also all of those importations and activities that are abstract and impersonal in nature - the adaptation of entire legal and educational systems, the appropriation of foreign arts and technologies from playing Beethoven to flying planes, the mastery of foreign languages, the translating into Japanese texts of everything under the sun, and the earnest study and appreciation of other civilisations and cultures. In a matter of only decades the Japanese managed to digest enormous chunks of alien civilisation, they continue to do so now, and they are justly proud of their achievement. They insist (quite rightly) that it is now the turn of others to reciprocate this process of learning from and about other countries, and continue to define that process as the touchstone of 'internationalisation'. The essential point here, of course, is that none of the foregoing required any great amount of human contact, save perhaps at the very outset - when the Meiji government dispatched carefully-selected groups of officials and students to study abroad, and invited foreign experts to teach and advise in Japan. Both processes were drastically reduced in scope as the requisite new skills and knowledge came to hand. In other words, 'internationalisation' at arm's length.

This is not the sort of *kokusaika* most of the outside world is clamouring for today. For the ordinary foreign student or teacher seeking courteous and non-prejudicial treatment, or for foreign corporations whose effectiveness in the Japanese market will ultimately require a larger and more penetrating human presence here, 'internationalisation' means no more, really, than a willingness to accept as fellow human beings and co-

workers people who have different faces or who come from different
cultures from one's own. It also means for the Japanese, I think, learning
to associate more easily with foreigners on a one-to-one basis as
individuals rather than through the more comfortable collectivity of the
Japanese group .

Yet it is striking how many of Japan's cultural spokesmen still cling
implicitly to the old emphasis on 'things', and to two other notions which
work against an 'internationalisation' of 'people'. One is the assumption
that the social and professional barriers to foreigners today are the
product of an ancient and slowly evolving cultural tradition resistant to
rapid change rather than the result of concrete laws and regulations,
politically motivated and deliberately imposed *during* the process of
modernisation. The other is the supposition - when one really digs to the
bottom of Japanese anxieties - that opening Japan to fuller participation
by foreign people would debilitate and eventually destroy Japanese culture
and identity itself, something to be avoided at all costs. Indeed, in a
confidential in-house study conducted by a leading national daily in 1987
of possible responses to rising foreign pressures for an open market, there
was a powerful minority opinion arguing that, in order to preserve
cultural autonomy, Japan should continue to restrict access to its markets
and society, even at the price of foreign economic retaliation and a
lowered standard of living.

The argument for an essentially restricted form of 'internationalisation',
together with some of its defensive premises, has been lucidly presented
by the Tokyo University political scientist Seizaburo Sato in *Shin
Nihonjinron* (A New View of the Japanese). Professor Sato notes that
'internationalisation' has often been a code-word for the cultural
adaptation of weaker nations to the stronger - as the 'developing'
countries still tend to ape the industrially developed or as the transnational
empires of China, Rome, Britain, or the recent *Pax Americana* drew
others into the orbit of their own 'imperial' language and civilisation. The
point is well taken, and, for his fellow Japanese, Professor Sato prescribes
a 'third' type of 'internationalisation' which he defines as the
'achievement of self-relativity ... of mixing well in international society by
understanding common and different aspects with others without losing
one's identity'. Specifically, he proposes three tasks: the retention of
Japan's own cultural 'subjectivity' or identity; the understanding and
appreciation of cultures and values of other peoples; and the training of
Japanese who can deal 'flexibly' with the problems arising from 'cultural
frictions'.[1]

Unfortunately, these three tasks do not explore the increasing influx of non-Japanese as a creative opportunity for 'internationalisation', nor does the formula directly address the central barrier of Japan's closed society. The reaching out to others proposed here remains essentially impersonal - the old, strictly intellectual, grasp of foreign cultures. Ignoring differences, of course, would be unwise, but I think that what the Japanese need to ponder most today are those things that can (and already do) bind them to others - lest they become like the proverbial gentleman who fails to cross a street for agonising over all its possible dangers.

Finally I should mention a popular aspect to this emphasis on 'things' which likewise overlooks the human and personal dimension. This is the flaunting of what might be called 'international chic' - the conspicuous display of expensive imported automobiles and *haute couture*, the jetting off to overseas scholarly conferences, the Christian-style wedding ceremonies, the showy use of foreign languages in front of one's monolingual countrymen. Japan has no monopoly on this sort of faddism or affectation, of course, but it does contribute to the assumption that this is true 'internationalisation' - while giving the entire concept a bad name among everyday Japanese.

The Meiji University - Origins of the Closed Shop

This defensive attitude towards foreign participation in the internal intellectual and cultural life of the nation has nowhere been better illustrated than in the continuing *gaikokujin kyoshi* or 'foreign pedagogue' system that for exactly a century has fixed the Deshima-like status of foreign professors at national universities - outside of the Japanese academic mainstream, as short-term contractual employees. (Deshima was the island in Nagasaki harbour where the Dutch during the Tokugawa seclusion were permitted to maintain the sole Western trading post in Japan.)

I limit my discussion here to Japan's state-run national universities for three reasons. They are vastly more prestigious than the private schools and monopolise access to the higher bureaucracy that has largely run the country for a hundred years. Unlike private institutions, their restrictions on the foreign professoriate have been made explicit in statutory regulations and official justifications. And their governmental tie makes them more indicative of the true attitudes and intentions of Japan's national leadership.

The faculty appointment system for Japanese scholars was systematised in 1893 when the Minister of Education, Kowashi Inoue, introduced the *koza* (*Lehrstuhl* or 'chair') system whereby one full professor and one associate professor were assigned (with immediate lifetime tenure) to chairs in each major academic field. From that time to this day the regular (i.e. full-time) academic staff at all Japanese universities - private as well as national - have been 'tenured', in the American sense of the term, from the moment they receive a full-time appointment. Once permanently hired, promotion within the university depends on a variable mix of performance, power politics, and seniority, not all that different from the actual practice in many other countries. It is also neither unusual nor frowned upon - as it would be in Japan's corporate world - to move on to another institution of higher academic standing and social prestige. Nevertheless, wherever a Japanese scholar finds himself - and there are still very few female professors at national universities - he is there on a non-term-limited appointment and cannot be fired short of criminal conduct or serious ethical lapses involving the honour of the school. In the case of the latter the miscreant, covered with shame, normally initiates his own speedy resignation.

Japanese universities do not have a sorting system based on a strenuous period of apprenticeship followed by a peer review leading to tenure. Permanent appointments are made, generally around the age of 30, based on scholarly record and promise and, quite often, on some previous connection with the employing institution. Indeed, in the older national and private universities such as Tokyo or Keio, most of the new appointees are protégés of senior professors who have groomed them from graduate or even undergraduate days as their eventual colleagues and putative successors. As one administrator confided to me, even if the junior scholar does not marry his senior's daughter - as some do - and inherit the ancestral tablets, he is there to provide a reverential worship and a reassuring sense of continuity after death and in the bleak years of post-retirement and old age.

For two decades foreign scholars had played a vital role in the development of Tokyo University (until 1898 Japan's sole officially recognised 'university') when the Ministry of Education, in its new regulations of 1893, relegated them not only to strictly subordinate positions but - what was far more significant - to a special status entirely outside the regular professorial system. To start with, there was the nomenclature: whatever their rank and qualification in their own countries (and these ranged from full professors down to mere university or college graduates), the foreigners were now all designated as *kyoshi* - a rather low-level, generic term for 'teacher' or 'instructor', bereft of academic or scholarly flavour, burdened with the pejorative nuances of 'pedagogue' or 'schoolmaster', and applied most often to primary school teachers, flower-arranging or judo masters, and language instructors - which is what most of Japan's foreign academic staff in actual function soon became, whatever their nominal eminence. (The regular, permanently tenured Japanese faculty were categorised as *kyoin*, meaning 'teaching staff'; to distinguish *kyoshi* from *kyoin* in English, I shall simply refer to 'pedagogues' versus 'staffers'.)

The essential difference was between temporary as opposed to permanent status. A contract with a time limit is not 'tenure', and a post without the most fundamental consideration of job security can hardly be considered equivalent to one that provides it. Under the *kyoshi* ('pedagogue') system there was no rising up through the ranks for foreign scholars at national universities and other schools under the Education Ministry's control, because they were not even in the ranks. Denied admission to faculty councils and other academic meetings, they were barred from positions of administrative leadership and had no voice at all in matters of personnel or curriculum - a major motive behind the new rules. They taught longer hours of presumably easier material - indeed, their duty was seen in the classroom rather than in original research - the only advantage they enjoyed over their Japanese counterparts being their salary. This was adjusted well upward to meet home-country standards, or even to exceed them as an inducement to come, in a day when Japan's standard of living lagged well behind that of the West.

The *kyoshi* appointments were all based on fixed-term contracts, each of which had to be requested on an extraordinary basis by the institution's president and approved by the Ministry. These procedures were totally outside the regular academic recruiting process, and so they remain to this day. In a phrase that said it all, the ordinance stated that such contracts might be issued only for positions that were 'extremely difficult or impossible' to have filled by qualified Japanese nationals. That was intended to cover both subjects for which the Japanese were still in training, and those such as language-teaching in which non-Japanese might enjoy a permanent edge. In either case, foreign appointments were the device of last resort.

Another professionally debilitating exclusion was imposed through the rule against foreign participation in any of the regular meetings of the Japanese staff, and by the ban on foreign supervision of bachelors' or graduate dissertations. To suggest the intractability of the old 1893 system, I might mention that just before my arrival in 1984 at the new 'model' and 'internationalising' National University of Tsukuba there had been some tentative experiments to relax these two rules. These were gradually but firmly rescinded under bureaucratic pressure to conform to the original stipulations. Foreign 'pedagogues' were asked to stop attending departmental business meetings and were relegated once again to the second readerships of graduation theses. In the hypothetical case that a foreign scholar might be entrusted with *de facto* primary supervision, it was explained that this still would have to take place under the nominal head readership of a Japanese national.

Why did Japan take this inward turning in 1893?

During the two opening decades of Meiji, roughly up to the mid-1880s, Japan had been awash in extravagantly paid, elegantly fussed-over foreign advisers, many of them American. The Ministry of Education in the early 1870s was virtually being run by the Rutgers mathematician David Murray, while General Horace Capron, the US Commissioner of Agriculture, came over to plan development for the entire island of Hokkaido - awesome, heady responsibilities. Responding to the insatiable appetite of Early Meiji for Western learning, the smaller American fry - young college graduates, sometime missionaries, schoolmarmly spinsters and others who could roust up the trans-Pacific passage - were having a field day as English-language teachers, not all that different from the 1970s and 1980s; and at Tokyo University during its opening years the top professorial positions were held by Americans and Europeans, many of eminent standing, whose classroom lectures and assigned texts were exclusively in their own languages.

During the 1870s Japanese higher education was conducted almost entirely in English, French and German, a situation which placed the senior foreign scholar on an Olympian pedestal and even the humblest of the language drill-masters in remunerative clover. Judging from the munificence of their salaries, the eagerness of their students, and the flattery from their employers, many foreign academics misread the extent of their actual welcome in Japan. Their presence was in fact viewed as a nasty hardship to be borne temporarily for the sake of the country, a form of 'forced internationalisation' (in the words of the educational historian and critic Kazuyuki Kitamura) or (as the official history of Tokyo University's first half-century puts it) as 'something we were driven by sheer necessity to do'.[2]

The underlying attitude and rationale at the time were best captured by Tetsujiro Inoue, the first holder of the professorial chair in philosophy at

Tokyo University from 1890 and for some years Dean of the Faculty of Letters. This Inoue was the introducer to Japan of Hegelian idealism and a zealous propagator of the new Emperor-centred ideology promulgated with the Imperial Rescript on Education in 1890. He has best been remembered in the intellectual-history books for his running polemic with Japanese Christians as to whether their faith was compatible with the new political orthodoxy. As Inoue reminisced in later years on the role of foreign scholars:

> We had many foreigners as teachers at Tokyo University in the early years of Meiji, in order to make up the deficiency in Japanese professors. In principle, however, professors at Japanese universities should all be Japanese. Accordingly, we managed to dismiss the foreign instructors relatively quickly from the Faculties of Medicine, Law, and Science so that there was not one of them left. That was the policy throughout the university. In the Faculty of Letters, too, we were guided by the belief that every field should be taught exclusively by Japanese staff, and that the number of foreigners should gradually be reduced and ultimately eliminated altogether. That meant that Japanese would hold the leading professorial posts in English Literature or French Literature or whatever and teach and guide the students, although there would be no problem in having foreign instructors or lecturers assisting them in those duties. The Japanese university is a place where Japanese should perform the professorial tasks - it is very different from a colonial university. [3]

By the early 1890s the party was over for the once-fêted foreign academics. Young Japanese scholars who had been sent to study abroad (precisely for the purpose of replacing the foreigners) were now finding their way back into the system, bumping out their former mentors and rapidly translating the entire corpus of Western learning into the Japanese language, where it most surely belonged. This was no more than a normal and healthy process of indigenously directed, non-colonial modernisation. But the 1880s also happened to be a period marred by reactionary nationalism and emotional antiforeignism, and when the door shut it was slammed perhaps too firmly and, some thought, without sufficient grace. The *gaikokujin kyoshi* system of 1893 permanently marked the foreign scholar in Japan as a technical adviser, to use today's terminology - that is to say, as a short-term serviceable tool in the drive for modernisation - rather than as a member of the community of scholars.

This system has continued now almost without alteration for a full century. It is a relic of the mid-Meiji period with its forced marches towards modernisation, its paranoia towards the Western powers, its wounded national pride under the Unequal Treaties they had imposed, its desire to absorb the maximum of Western technological expertise with a minimum of outside cultural contamination. The *gaikokujin kyoshi* even today are best seen as the functional equivalent of the foreign technical or economic-aid advisers in Third World developing countries - as transitory, disposable, transmitters of knowledge or technique - rather than as fellow labourers in the ongoing quest for human knowledge. So even today the foreign 'pedagogues' at national universities have yet to become the genuine scholarly reciprocal of those Japanese academics employed by universities in other advanced industrialised countries.

Historically it may be useful to recall that the earliest buddings of the modern university at Bologna and Paris were 'international' to a fault, with their foreign teachers and students often outnumbering the natives. The same cosmopolitan spirit infused the great Islamic institutions that had guarded the flame of classical scholarship during Europe's Dark Ages. And, for all its occasional nationalistic perversions at the hands of its Treitschkes and Heideggers, and for all its philandering in the alleyways of Anglo-American social snobbery, the Western university as an intellectual institution has never strayed too far from the 'universe-alism' of purpose and membership implicit in its very name. The pursuit of truth and knowledge knows no national boundaries. It is an endeavour that is mutually supportive and sustaining, and one that is particularly dependent (more so, I think it could be argued, than in artistic innovation) on openness, variety, and objectively vetted standards of excellence for its creative vitality. Alas, that is a conceptual threshold which the Japanese national university has yet to cross with respect to the potential contribution of its foreign personnel. It is a leap of the imagination that has been delayed not only by a too stark, outmoded, zero-sum concept of the national interest as against the outside world, but also by that utilitarianism in which the institution was originally conceived and which still largely governs its sense of purpose. Originally the incubator of Meiji's bureaucratic leadership, it continues today as the moulder of an economic superpower's 'Organisation Man'.

It would have been unnatural had there not been some jealousy and resentment on the campuses of Meiji Japan of high-stepping foreign 'pedagogues', as well as an instinctive urge to channel and tame the seeming tidal wave of inflowing Western cultural and intellectual influences by gaining exclusive control over the sluice-gates. Tokyo Imperial was hardly in danger, however, of becoming another Calcutta University, churning out a secretarial class for a colonial overlord. Much as the Meiji Japanese chafed under the presence of extraterritorial Western enclaves and limitations on their tariff autonomy, they were full masters of the direction, style, pace and content of their internal modernisation processes. Their political and economic systems were entirely of their own choosing, and there was no attempt by the foreign powers to meddle in the lively internal debates or power struggles of the era. The Japanese were in full strategic command of their own territory and with growing military forces which were sufficient, and sufficiently unimpeded, to project gunboat diplomacy towards Korea as early as 1876 and to overwhelm first China and then Russia in 1895 and 1905 - during those very years when their schools were nervously banging their doors shut against outsiders.

The control by the Meiji Japanese of their own educational and intellectual development was particularly well assured. There was, to be sure, considerable bafflement and anxiety over the new influences which they themselves had chosen to usher in, but the borrowing from the West had been undertaken very consciously in the national interest, and the foreign advisers had all been invited in on Japan's terms, and hardly ferried in at gunpoint - although that is the way some Japanese at the time apparently viewed them. Unlike some of the real barbarian nuisances - such as the boozing, whoring foreign traders in the extraterritorial enclaves, or some of the more narrow-minded and holier-than-thou missionaries - the higher academics who graced Japan's university and college-level foreign staffs during the earliest years were for the most part sensitive and sophisticated men, solicitous of Japanese needs and of the complexity of the country's transition pains, entranced by the traditional culture, in love with the people, and profoundly dedicated to their work. From 1893 to the onset of the era of militarism and ultranationalism in 1934, the number of *gaikokujin kyoshi* at Japanese national universities in any given year was usually well under 30, peaking at 41 in 1926 - hardly an invading colonial army.[4]

When Japanese academe turned closed-shop in the middle of Meiji, it was less the fact than the spirit of the closure which contemporary foreign observers found disturbing, and which is most suggestive of the true nature of the problem today. For this, we may best give voice to two of the earliest and most prominent of the *gaikokujin kyoshi*, Erwin von Baelz and Lafcadio Hearn, whose personal trials and tribulations with that closed shop have been largely buried under their more general reputations as sympathetic interpreters of the new Japan.

Japan took its modern medicine from Germany, and much of its higher medical education through the Leipzig-trained physician Baelz, who was instrumental in developing the medical school at Tokyo University from 1876 to 1902 in addition to his duties as an official court doctor. Baelz's diary for the first year brims with the newcomer's enthusiasm for the diligence of Japanese students and the country's eagerness for Westernisation (25 October 1876), but by 1879 he remarks sourly that at the ceremonies opening the new medical facilities not a word of thanks was expressed to the Germans to whom the Japanese were entirely indebted for them. 'Rather discourteous to us German teachers', he notes, interpreting the snub as a deliberate signal to the European powers of Japan's displeasure with their foot-dragging on proposals for revising the Unequal Treaties (22 April 1879).

Welcome to Japan, Erwin.

The following year, 1880, he notes that a campaign is already under way to dismiss the foreign instructors as rapidly as possible. 'It seems to be certain that few of the professors at our medical school will be asked to sign new contracts' (29 November 1880). As the seniormost and still indispensable figure, Baelz was to remain for another two decades, but by the turn of the century he sensed the eagerness of his Japanese colleagues - quite rightly, he thought - to take over entirely. Complaining that, 'the way in which the foreign professors are being treated has gradually become intolerable to me' (18 April 1900), he had suggested several times that it was time for him to resign but was repeatedly urged to stay on.

What particularly annoyed Baelz was the way in which he was finding himself increasingly 'cold-shouldered in all important questions' despite the fact that he had been begged to remain. 'The Japanese have continually seized opportunities of slighting us foreigners', he complained in his diary on 18 April 1900, and on learning that plans for the new hospital had been launched without consulting him, Baelz finally submitted his formal resignation to the president. Once again, he was roped into staying with promises that his advice would be sought on 'all important matters', but by 1902 Baelz had had enough and made the final break, noting bitterly that at his farewell banquet neither the president's speech in Japanese nor his own in German had been translated into the other language: 'Considering it all in all, I must say that the university does not treat its foreign professors fittingly' (3 July 1902).

At his own 25th anniversary festivities in 1901, Baelz touched on what he saw as the root cause of Japan's shabby treatment of foreign scholars. The Japanese, Baelz suggested, often seemed not to understand the true source and nature of Western science, mistaking it for a sort of machine which could be easily carted off to new places and made to perform the same work, rather than seeing it as an organism requiring a carefully nurtured atmosphere. Foreign scholars from many countries had worked hard to implant the spirit of modern science in Japan, but although they had come to nurture the tree itself, their mission had largely been misunderstood. The Japanese had treated them as no more than peddlers of the final fruits, and had been content to get the latest plums from them, without seeking to appropriate the spirit that had nourished the tree.

'Soon there will be very few foreign teachers left in the country', Baelz concluded. 'Let me advise you to give those that still remain more freedom than you have done in the past, more opportunity for independent work; and let me urge you to keep in close touch with them in fields besides that of their strictly educational work.... In that way you will learn more of the spirit of science, the spirit with which you cannot become intimately acquainted in lecture theatres ... but only in daily association with those engaged in research' (22 November 1901)[5].

Lafcadio Hearn's experience is far better known, and was more poignant in that he had done so much to 'equalise' himself to the indigenous situation - assuming Japanese citizenship, marrying into a Japanese family and taking his wife's surname. Of all the early interpreters of Japan, Hearn was arguably the most perceptive, sensitive and supportive. Nevertheless, after seven years of teaching English literature at Tokyo University, Hearn resigned his post in high dudgeon in 1903 when he found a third of his teaching hours summarily transferred to the young Soseki Natsume, the budding novelist who had just returned from London and was being groomed for the departmental chair. According to the dean at the time, Tetsujiro Inoue, the Professor of English Literature had to be Japanese. But Hearn *was* a Japanese citizen. Apparently being 'Japanese' was less a matter of naturalisation papers than the look of one's face - although it would only be fair to add that Hearn had balked at taking the huge salary cut that would have made him the economic equal of the Japanese 'staffers'.[6]

Universities Today - The Never-Mending Story

The New Law

As late as 1981, there were still only 940 full-time foreign teachers at Japanese national, public and private universities, less than one per cent of the regular (full-time) academic staff of over 102 000 nationwide. 70

per cent of Japan's universities employed no foreigners at all, and among those that did there was a strong preponderance of institutions stressing or specialising in foreign-language, artistic, or Christian religious instruction. Only a quarter of the foreigners were *gaikokujin kyoshi* at national universities, the remaining three-quarters teaching at private schools.[7] Although private institutions were far more generous with long-term or even permanent positions, and with rights to participation in faculty meetings, they were - below Keio, Waseda and perhaps two or three others - perceived by the Japanese public as being radically inferior to the national universities in quality of students and instruction.

Kazuyuki Kitamura has been quite right, I think, in insisting that the central challenge in the 'internationalisation of university education' - the title of his book - lies in opening up Japan's professoriate: in 'welcoming foreigners with a different cultural background and way of thinking as our comrades and professional colleagues', and in admitting them to the 'common quest for general learning' and to a 'shared community life'; and that, although the deeper stumbling points are attitudinal rather than legal, the central practical question on which it all turns is that of tenured appointments. The matter will not be fundamentally tackled by 'the warm reception of foreigners as occasional guests' or by 'sprucing up the physical plant for cultural exchange', Kitamura avers. Nor, would I add, by synchronising school-year calendars, by working out equivalencies for academic degrees, by getting the Japanese to speak better English, or by introducing more foreign area studies into the university curriculum. These are important blocks in the 'internationalisation' edifice, but not the capstone.[8]

By the 1970s, university appointments had been thrown open to all qualified comers in all of the advanced industrial nations of Western Europe, North America, and the British Commonwealth. Only in Japan, despite its rise to globe-girdling economic activity and power, did the ivory tower remain bolted. France had often conveniently been cited by the Japanese as an example of a similar state-run university system where all staff, as civil servants, were required to be citizens of that country. But even French universities, as one of the more benign results of the great campus upheavals of the late 1960s, were now admitting foreign scholars into all but the top administrative posts - posts so onerously administrative, given the French bureaucracy, that very few would want them anyway. Everywhere else, even in West Germany, where professors were public officials of the individual states (Länder), there was no longer any restriction on the employment or advancement of foreign scholars into any teaching or administrative position on the economic ladder.

As with other sectors on Japan's 'liberalisation' front, the first criticisms and complaints about the academic closed shop came from outside the country - yet another example of *gaiatsu* ('foreign pressure') having to provide the initial jolt. These pressures were met in the first instance, again so typically, not by the sector to which they were addressed but by the political arm, which took action less on the intrinsic merits of the issue (such as the possible benefits to Japanese education) than to stave off a potentially negative impact on Japan's external relations. Finally, the affected sector itself - in this case the universities and the academic community in general - did what it could to postpone, water down, or hamstring the measures about to be foisted upon it.

In November 1971 an OECD survey team turned in a rather severe report on its recent visit to Japan, noting the closed nature of Japanese university life and the 'need for new attitudes', calling on the country to reorient its higher education for 'world participation' and 'for world needs, not only for Japan's domestic needs', and recommending that the system for employing foreign scholars be entirely revamped to engage them for permanent positions on the same terms as the Japanese. In response to this exhortation, the ensuing decade witnessed a stream of recommendations, from the government's deliberative councils and from private industry, for greater educational and cultural 'internationalisation' and exchange. These left little to be desired - as blueprints on paper. Young Japanese would have to be trained to greater skills in self-expression, debating, sociability and English; there would have to be a greater emphasis on basic research, on joint international projects, on foreign area and comparative studies, on the expansion of Japanese studies and Japanese language training abroad, on bringing many more students from the developing countries to Japan, on opening up the teaching profession to foreign scholars. The 1970s also saw a strengthening of the mechanics for international exchange: the Ministry of Education added a new international bureau, each national university received a special officer in charge of exchanges, and the Japan Foundation appeared on the scene with new funding.

The underlying tone of much of this discussion as summed up by Professor Kitamura, however, remained reactive and tactical. Japan's one-sided, piecemeal absorption of Western knowledge, together with its rapid economic expansion overseas, had made the Japanese look insular and self-complacent to other countries and had given rise to mischievous misconceptions and a lack of trust towards Japan. As a small island nation with few natural resources, Japan had no alternative but to learn to associate with the rest of the world - so went the thinking, in essence a lament. Once again, things had to be done because Japan had its back to the wall. And, as Kitamura astutely observes, an increase in cultural exchange - what I would call the limbering up of the flow *between* Japan and other countries - by no means ensures that the university itself, as an *internal* institution, will open up.

Political pressure for access to tenured teaching positions first came in 1972 from the resident Korean academics in Japan, those with North Korean ties joining the ROK-affiliated in the same organisation in the wake of the OECD report. The foreign-tenure question, beyond its international ramifications, was part of a wider struggle by Japan's 600 000-strong Korean community to overcome second-class status in the land they had chosen permanently to live in. Indeed, there were a number of occasions when I was told by Japanese educational authorities that it would be difficult to consider certain academic programmes that American cultural diplomats in Japan were requesting, because it would mean opening the door wider to the resident Koreans as well. At the time I was representing the US Government's Japan-US Friendship Commission in Tokyo (1977-84), and the argument reminded me of something I had experienced years ago as a young assistant cultural attaché at the American Embassy in Kabul (1958-59). The Afghan government, in turning down an American request to build a cultural facility in downtown Kabul, had given as its rationale the fact that they would then have to let the Russians do the same thing and, of course, neither we nor they wanted that. (In the event, the US Information Service placed its library and auditorium inside the embassy compound, but provided access from the street for subversives intent on viewing films on the life of Lincoln or boning up on the poetry of Edgar Lee Masters.)

The push for the 1982 Diet act permitting the integration of foreigners into the regular Japanese university staff as *gaikokujin kyoin* (i.e. as 'foreign staffers', no longer mere *kyoshi* or 'pedagogues'), came neither from Japan's academic circles nor from the bureaucracy which initiates and drafts the lion's share of the Diet's legislation, but from a group of politicians in the progressive wing of the ruling Liberal Democratic party who, impatient with the merry-go-round the issue had been getting in a variety of government ministries and in the national media, presented their own parliamentary bill in 1980. The general alignment of forces saw the Foreign Ministry and the more liberal-minded elements in the Diet and the Education Ministry - all concerned for the foreign-policy implications of the issue - pitted against educational nationalists, political conservatives, the Justice Ministry and the Cabinet Legislation Bureau, which stuck by its old legalistic interpretation - a pure expression of the old Meiji statism, many progressively-minded Japanese complained - to the effect that Japanese citizenship was required of national university professors, 'since they are civil servants, and as such participate in the formation of the national will and in the exercise of public power'.[9]

That was the hoary old rubric that had been used to deny foreign professors the right to attend and vote at faculty councils, but without that right no meaningful 'integration' with Japanese staff would be possible. It was a dizzily high view of the political impact of routine academic duties, and one that had probably occurred to very few of the Japanese themselves. Precisely because of its obvious obscurantism and the well-publicised debate over it, the restriction on attendance and voting at faculty meetings was swept away in the new bill, along with all other points of discrimination except two.

Foreigners were not to be made deans or presidents, posts to which some had risen at Japan's private universities. Since such officials at national universities spent most of their time and energy on budgetary battlegrounds, this arguably was not the most important test of full collegiality in scholarship and teaching. But the matter of tenure most surely was. The new 'Kyoin Law' (as we may call it) settled this issue, after much heated debate, by allowing the universities to set term limits to foreign appointments as they saw fit. That did leave the possibility of not specifying any particular term of years at all, thereby placing foreign hires on the same open-ended, implicit-tenure footing as the Japanese. Permanent appointments to the new *kyoin* category had simply been taken for granted by the bill's original drafters, but that goal was now made dependent on the hypothetical magnanimity of each university in opting *not* to establish any time limits. Even more disturbing were some of the arguments advanced in favour of stipulated terms of service, exposing as they did the powerful political and academic forces that wanted to keep the shop closed simply by replacing the bolted portal with a revolving door.

At the eleventh hour in the Diet's deliberations, Takeo Nishioka and other members of the ruling party's nationalistic right-wing insisted on term restrictions for foreign staff, reasoning that this would conveniently pave the way for similar limitations on the Japanese professoriate - a long-sought-for handle on the legion of bothersome left-wing academics. Given their opportunity by this loophole in the original tenuring ideal, Japan's university leaders then thought up additional arguments in favour of restricting foreign competition in the academic marketplace.

The conservative politicians for their part argued, somewhat irrelevantly, that international academic exchanges were built around specific, short-term projects and that term limitations and a 'rotation system' would 'facilitate' the foreign hiring process for the universities. When the parliamentary committee visited Kyoto University for an academic reaction, President Toshio Sawada (an irrigation engineer) was said to have supported the fixed-term system on the grounds that foreigners preferred specificity in contracts, that the option to 'reappoint' gave the system a desirable 'flexibility', and that there was considerable anxiety over the qualifications and 'compatibility' of scholars hired from other countries (no need to inundate *his* ricefields with the foreign tide!). But there were already numerous devices at hand for short-term appointments, so why even bother with new legislation at all?

The Reluctance to Implement

The new 'Kyoin Law' of 1982 had been difficult enough in the making. A half-decade later, there had been a gradual increase in the number of foreign scholars filling the new *gaikokujin kyoin* positions at the national universities. Nation-wide figures from the Ministry of Education in 1987 showed 20 national universities employing 50 foreign professors, associate professors, and lecturers in the new 'foreign staff' category. Only four, however, were without term limits - two at Tokyo University, the nation's premier institution, and two at Kyushu National, the leading university in southern Japan. The other scholars were all on term appointments - most generously at Tsukuba National University with its five-year contracts, the rest mostly for three years and some for only one or two. And the chief increments in number of foreign appointments were to be found at relatively minor or less prestigious institutions.[10]

The following five years witnessed a modest growth in the number of schools and teachers involved. As of 1992, there were 2685 regular foreign staff (at all levels) among the 129 029 full time staff at all Japanese universities. Of these, 1780 were to be found in the private sector, 819 at national universities, and 86 at municipal and other 'public' universities. At the rank of professor and associate professor there were 134 foreigners among a total of 32 230 at national universities, and 1002 among a total of 41 004 at the private schools.[11] However, there has been no relaxing of the term-appointment rule, and no change since 1987 in the number of non-term, genuinely tenured, appointments - still, as of 1994, only four. This is a mind-boggling shortfall, considering that we are dealing with the second largest university system in the First World. It is as if the elite universities of the United States had chosen to place on permanent tenure only 41 non-American scholars - less than one scholar in each of the 50 states! If the intention of the new 'Kyoin Law' was to integrate the foreign staff - bearing in mind the key point of tenure - then it must be judged to have failed thus far in the implementation. Japan's academe seems to have missed the whole point of the exercise.

The first two appointments under the new law, given much media attention, were for two-year contracts - a German lecturer at Tokyo University's Productivity Centre and an Englishman as assistant professor of Japanese Literature attached to Kyoto University's Centre for Humanistic Research. Neither of these were genuine, long-term, departmental teaching posts - indeed, they looked suspiciously like the old short-term visiting researcher positions in a new guise. Later on in 1983 Kyoto hired on a three-year contract as full professor a Cambridge-trained molecular engineer from Nottingham University who was 58, exactly three years short of Kyoto's mandatory retirement age. One picture magazine fêted the 'epoch-making' event, showing the kindly looking scholar - Japan's 'first true foreign professor' - comfortably ensconced in the university's new hostel for foreign staff; standing in the city tram, sandwich-bag in hand, like any common Japanese commuter; thoughtfully slowing down his English-language lectures so that his students could understand .

By decreeing a three-year term for foreign 'staffers' Kyoto University set a mischievous precedent. Reappointments were possible, but that still left job security and a settled professional lifestyle as problematical as they had been for the old foreign 'pedagogues'. The first permanently tenured position at Kyushu University went to a German associate professor who had already been there a number of years as a *kyoshi* and had been transferred to the new category on the strength of a special waiver - 'strictly and exceptionally applied' - to Kyushu's three-year rule. Only Tokyo University, under heavy lobbying by its forward-looking President, Ryuichi Hirano, made a straightforward effort to implement the option for non-term appointments. The two Americans there were genuinely integrated, the associate professor of geophysics and the professor of Chinese Law having both received letters of appointment without any reference to term of service - the standard procedure for Japanese staff. They were also fluent in Japanese, which meant that they lectured in the language of their students and were fully functional in departmental conclaves and other professional activities.

There was another important, if unpublicised, issue at stake in the Tokyo University appointments. The two Americans were at home in the language of Japan, as well as in its social grammar, and there was a group at the university which believed that precisely such facility should be made a prerequisite for permanent posts. If that was too much to ask at the time of hiring, then at least it should be understood as a long-term goal. That is what Japanese scholars do as a matter of course when they choose to work in the West, and its feasibility in the reverse direction has been demonstrated time and again by the foreign missionary staffs at church-affiliated universities in East Asia, whether Catholic or Protestant. That this is true 'integration' would hardly seem to need argument, but there was a sizeable group at Tokyo University which still preferred to define 'internationalisation' as having a pure and unacclimatised alien presence on campus - the two-dimensional presence of the linguistically incapacitated, culture-shocked foreign newcomer as exotic ambience.[12] Just another twist to the old habit of merely importing 'things'.

The depth of resistance to the spirit of the new law was most dramatically revealed at Tsukuba National, which had been created during the 1970s with massive political and financial support from the ruling party, the business establishment, and the national treasury, to serve as Japan's new model, bell-wether university for the 'age of internationalisation'. Tsukuba was quick to enrol the largest number of foreign students among the state schools, and today it has a modest complement of three or four foreign scholars in the new 'staffer' category, on five-year renewable-term contracts - the lengthiest term for any national university. In 1985, however, with its initial effort to introduce the new system, Tsukuba stumbled badly when the university suddenly fired four foreign scholars (Korean, German, American and Taiwanese) at the *start* of the new academic year in April. The incident created a minor international scandal (covered, for instance, in an irate editorial and news columns in the 10 October and 21 November 1985 issues of *Nature*, perhaps the world's most widely read science magazine).

All four scholars had been serving in the old-fashioned 'pedagogue' positions - the first two, both professors, for nearly a decade. In 1984 they had been persuaded to relinquish those posts from 1985, since Tsukuba had recently decreed a four-year cut-off for that category. All four, however, had been officially graded and approved for transfer to the new *kyoin* status, promised fresh 'staffer' posts from the new academic year, and had been asked not to seek employment elsewhere while their prospective reappointments were being steered through the shoals of academic politics and the brewing storm of a bitterly contested presidential election. In the end, after waiting out an anxious half-year, they saw their promised appointments shot down in the intra-Japanese brouhaha and found themselves suddenly out on the street at a point much too late for seeking positions at another university. The Korean historian (a native Korean citizen, not a Japan-born resident) had been the first foreigner to receive a doctoral degree from Tokyo University, and decided to take the university (in effect the Japanese state) to court.[13] He died, a broken man, just days before the scheduled hearing at which he and other witnesses were to make their major depositions.

In short, the implementation of the 'Kyoin Law' a decade after its promulgation suggests that it has really produced no more than a slight adjustment to the old *gaikokujin kyoshi* system, leaving much of the letter and nearly all of the spirit of the old regime intact. The three-year rule (on the average) has spread throughout the system, which means that foreign scholars still stand on the outside. For the loss of perhaps a quarter of their old 'pedagogue' salary, the new 'staffers' now have genuine academic titles and the privilege of attending interminable faculty meetings. They do not, however, enjoy any of that clout in academic management and campus politics that comes only with a permanent position - since, even as *kyoin*, the new foreign 'staffers' remain dependent on the goodwill of their Japanese colleagues for their reappointments. And especially for those *kyoin* newly-hired offshore who do not have the language or experience of Japan to make good use of their attendance at faculty meetings, the new deal looks more and more like a poor man's *gaikokujin kyoshi* post.

Apologists for the term-limitation system have stressed the possibility, usually, of onward renewals. But the corrosive effect of repeated renewals on a serious scholarly career - and the basic disingenuousness of equating the possibility of serial reappointments with genuine tenure - were poignantly illustrated in the case of a non-Japanese acquaintance of mine who survived two rounds of renewals only to be thrown out at the third. This happened after nine years of service to a well-known national university that had been employing him on annual contracts, but with a triennial review of his status. His Japanese was functional, and he had done his employers a singular service by launching a record number of seniors into leading graduate schools abroad. Every third year this scholar waited anxiously as his name was thrust back into the hopper with those of all the other new prospects both foreign and Japanese. After each reappointment he could look forward to about two years of stabilised work, but from the third he was compelled to start negotiating all over again with his Japanese colleagues about the next court of assize, wondering where a negative verdict might leave him a year later. In the end, he was ousted to make room for a young protégé of one of his Japanese colleagues. His supporters, originally a majority, took the face-saving route of abstaining during the vote. 'A decade is long enough to have taken care of a foreigner', one of the expellers is reported to have exclaimed, as if the expellee had been permitted to work with them all that time as a special favour.

Japan's private universities, finally, differ from the national schools less in basic attitudes towards foreign scholars than in the absence of any system-wide rules for handling them. Most of the non-Japanese staff at Japan's private universities, although enjoying the traditional academic titles and often participating at faculty meetings, are there on renewable annual contracts, often strung out indefinitely but never proof against a sudden capsising. Highly qualified scholars have been abruptly dropped after lengthy years of service or shunted about from one private campus to another at the end of each contractual period for the simple reason that the private universities have been slow to develop a rationale and system - acceptable to their Japanese staff - for long-term foreign appointments. Some foreign teachers have anchored their futures by taking on foreign-liaison chores which make them more valuable to their employers, but only two institutions, both in Tokyo, have placed significant numbers of foreigners in permanent and genuinely integrated positions. One is the Jesuit-operated Sophia University with its naturally 'tenured' foreign scholar-priests, the other being the Protestant-affiliated International Christian University, which is formally structured around a dual-language curriculum and a combined Japanese and foreign faculty.

It bears emphasising that despite the larger numerical presence of foreign staff at the private schools, many of them are part-time hires. Also, a large number of the full-time regulars are specialists in language and/or literature, teaching and working entirely in the medium of their own native tongue, with only a tangential social and intellectual contact with their Japanese colleagues. A psychologically comfortable arrangement for enough persons on both sides, this ghetto phenomenon runs through the private system like an archipelago. It is a pity that so few attempts have been made to integrate the rarer foreign academic capable of teaching a substantive disciplinary (non-language) subject and with a command of Japanese sufficient for full participation in the administrative business of the university. For that would seem the minimal premise for a genuinely 'creative' intellectual connection

This brings us, in conclusion, back to my original point about the 'internationalisation' of people as opposed to things, and to that personal interaction which can contribute so much to creativity. Japanese have often complained that outsiders do not make a sufficient effort to understand their language and culture. When non-Japanese do try however, and particularly when they do so on location in Japan and become quite good at it, there inevitably comes the time when they desire to participate and be accepted more fully. But it is precisely at this point, alas, that the professional doors start to close. The desire for participation, however, is only human. After all, what is the point of making that cultural and linguistic investment in the first place? Surely not just to have the outsider take a more appreciative or indulgent attitude towards Japan's trade or other foreign policies. For any person anywhere in the world undertaking to cross a major cultural barrier, the quest inevitably develops a personal dimension. And that holds even if someone's original fascination, say with Japan, stemmed from something as recondite as the ancient Jomon Period pottery shards. Ultimately, one's relationship to a foreign culture has to be grounded in human contact and empathy.

The marginalising of the foreign professoriate clearly has a 'devitalising' impact on the personal and intellectual lives of the individual scholars concerned. Wings have been clipped. The energising fascination of simply being in Japan wears off after a while, and mundane but fundamental debilitations begin to take their toll - the limits to professional advancement and recognition; the psychological drain of insecure employment; the absence of challenge through full participation and responsibility for the ongoing business of the university; and above all the withholding of a truly interactive collegiality (as Dr Baelz remarked) of the mind and spirit. 'In this society, differences are not allowed', is the conclusion of Professor Yasunori Fukuoka, a Japanese sociologist who has analysed the plight of Korean residents in Japan.[14] Foreign scholars in Japan are a mere drop in the bucket compared with the Korean community, but the basis of exclusion - simply that of being different, that is to say non-Japanese - remains the same.

And what of the impact in the other direction - on the Japanese university itself - of this eschewal of human variety, based not on professional qualification but on nationality and ethnicity? There are few Japanese today who would claim the university as one of the more animated of their national institutions, brimming with vitality as a general teaching-and-research ambience - as opposed to the creativity of certain individual scholars who manage to surmount their frequently unsupportive *milieux*. On the contrary, we have been hearing a litany ever since the mid-1960s about the lack of a stimulating and challenging academic environment in Japan, be it for students or for teaching staff. This lack of institutional verve has been attributed variously (but by no means exclusively) to the demographic explosion of the post-war student population; the levelling-down to mass-education standards; the obsolescence of the 'general education' curriculum introduced during the US Occupation; the intellectually stultifying cram schools and rote-memory examinations endured by nearly all entering collegians; the opposition to curricular and other reforms among faculty cliques quite comfortable with the old ways; and the lack of open doors to the outside world.[15]

Only the last of these numerous explanations need concern us here. After a quarter-century of contact with Japanese universities (not only as one of their professors but also as a US cultural diplomat and as Harvard's representative in Japan) I may state that the reason mentioned time and again by those Japanese calling for a greater foreign professorial presence on Japanese campuses has been that it would bring a fresh stimulus and challenge to the Japanese staff. Making the same point from a different angle, others have confessed that the real resistance derives from the fear most of the Japanese staff have of foreign scholarly competition. They worry (rightly or wrongly) that the foreigners would prove to be more energetic, productive, and goal-oriented. They would publish more voluminously, cancel fewer classroom lectures, and might even stir up too much argumentative intellectual controversy.

The nub of the matter was perhaps best touched on by the 1987 Nobel Prize winner in Medicine, Dr Susumu Tonegawa of the Massachusetts Institute of Technology, when he told a *Fortune* magazine interviewer that, 'much in Japanese culture is hostile to the individualism needed to do creative science'.[16] Tonegawa was making a distinction between basic theoretical scientific thinking as a product of Western individualism, and applied science at which the Japanese have excelled because of the teamwork required for its success. Except for the applied sciences, however, the vast majority of disciplines taught at modern universities - spanning the liberal arts and social sciences as well as the basic natural sciences - depend for their creativity and 'vitality' on the independent rather than the communal mode. Professor Fukuoka's comment on the overriding drive towards conformity in Japanese society is no news, but the impact of such conformity on individual intellectual innovation at Japan's institutions of higher education has been given relatively little attention to date. It is bound to come under far greater scrutiny, however, as the world - for the first time, really - starts to look to Japan for innovation and leadership in the realm of ideas.

The Deshima-like treatment of foreign teaching staff at Japanese universities probably stems both from that lack of tolerance for social and ethnic 'differences' alluded to by Professor Fukuoka and from a certain anxiety about that cutting, intrusive Western intellectual individualism recommended by Dr Tonegawa. The enormous attitudinal gap on the issue of foreign staff - as between American and Japanese universities, at least - may best be illustrated by a concluding example contrasting two institutions with which I have been intimately affiliated.

For three years I had the privilege of teaching at the Gakushuin University, one of the smaller but respected private universities in Tokyo, most famous for having served for over a century as the school for Japan's emperors and other members of the imperial family. As of 1993, there were no foreign faces at all in its law and economics faculties, where some 65 exclusively Japanese scholars taught international law, world politics, foreign trade, diplomatic history and other subjects relating to the outside world to nearly 4000 exclusively Japanese students.

At my own *alma mater*, Princeton University (with about 5000 students in all), there were in the same year 900 foreign students, both graduate and undergraduate, and 300 foreign faculty members and researchers.[17] Equally significant and typical was the rationale given by President Robert Bowen in 1986 for bringing one of the foreign scholars, a Japanese national with valuable knowledge of research in his own country, to serve as the dean of the School of Engineering:

> We wanted someone with a lot of energy and enthusiasm, with a sense of what can be built here, with breadth and outstanding scientific credentials .... We think his different perspectives and different experiences will be very valuable here .... The university continues to be a genuinely international place.[18]

The reader may decide which of these two approaches, the closed or the open, promises the greater creativity and 'vitality.' The important thing to bear in mind, however, is that the vast majority of Japanese academics still tend to associate social and intellectual homogeneity with energy rather than with its opposite and to fear too much foreign diversity in their midst as a threat, vaguely adumbrated yet real, to their own Japanese *élan vital.*

Notes

1. Seizaburo Sato, symposium comment in Yomiuri Shimbunsha, editors and publishers, *Shin Nihonjinron* (A New View of the Japanese), Tokyo, 1986, pp. 12-13.
2. Kitamura Kazuyuki, *Daigaku Kyoiku no Kokusaika* (The Internationalisation of University Education), Tokyo, Tamagawa Daigaku Shuppanbu, 1984, pp. 30-1. I am indebted to Professor Kitamura, both personally and through his book, for many of the insights and information on the tenure question. For the tenure system in the Meiji period, see Kitamura, *op.cit.*, chapter 4. For a general background on the Meiji university, the reader is referred to two of my previous writings: Ivan P. Hall, *Mori Arinori*, Cambridge, Harvard University Press, 1973, and 'Organisational Paralysis: the Case of Todai', in Ezra F. Vogel (ed.), *Modern Japanese Organisation and Decision-Making*, Berkeley, University of California Press, 1975.
3. From Inoue Tetsujiro, *Kaikyuroku* (Reminiscences), 1943, as quoted by Kitamura, *op.cit.*, p. 40.
4. Kitamura, *op.cit.*, pp. 46-7.
5. Quotations from Erwin Baelz, Toku Baelz (ed.), *Awakening Japan: the Diary of a German Doctor*, Bloomington, Indiana University Press, 1974; translated from the German, *Das Leben eines deutschen Arztes im erwachenden Japan*, Stuttgart, J. Engelhorns Nachfolger, 1931.
6. Kitamura, *op.cit.*, p. 39, and Elizabeth Stevenson, *Lafcadio Hearn*, New York, Macmillan, 1961 p. 311.
7. Kitamura, *op.cit.*, pp. 110-12, and Monbusho (Ministry of Education), Monbu Tokei Yoran (Ministry of Education Statistical Handbook), Okurasho Insatsu Kyoku (Ministry of Finance Printing Bureau), Tokyo, 1993. The Ministry's statistics for five-year intervals show a total of 102 989 regular academic staff for 1980.
8. See Kitamura, *op.cit.*, pp. iv-vii. I am entirely indebted to this work, particularly chapters 5 and 6, for the following details on the origin and progress of the new law on tenuring foreigners. Professor Kitamura, formerly head of the Research Institute on Higher Education at Hiroshima University (Japan's premier research centre on the tertiary school sector), is not only the nation's pre-eminent expert on this and related issues of university 'internationalisation', but has been one of the most outspoken and effective advocates of creative changes towards that goal.
9. Quoted in *Asahi Shimbun*, 19 July 1980, p. 3.
10. Kitamura, *op.cit.*, from the revised edition, 1989, pp. 244-5.
11. Monbusho (Ministry of Education), *Gakko Kihon Chosa Hokokusho (Heisei 5-Nen): Koto Kyoiku Hen* (Report on the Basic Survey of Schools (1992): Higher Educational Institutions), Tokyo, 1992, p. 176.
12. Personal communication from a Japanese professor on the Tokyo University faculty, 1988.

13. Japanese coverage of the Tsukuba incident was carried in the *Tsukuba Gakusei Shimbun* (Tsukuba Student Newspaper), 10 June 1985; *Asahi Jaanaru* (Asahi Journal), 27 September 1985, pp. 6-15; and Margarete Sawada, 'Taiho Shita Kokusaisei' (A Step Backward in International Character), in *Chuo Koron*, August 1985.

14. Professor Yasunori Fukuoka of Saitama University, quoted in the *Japan Times*, 24 March 1994.

15. The oft-bemoaned lack of vitality in Japanese universities, and its multiple causes, would require another essay in its own right. I have explored some of its aspects in my previously referenced article: Ivan Hall, 'Organisational Paralysis: the case of Todai'.

16. In the words of the author, Joel Dreyfuss, 'How Japan Picks America's Brains', *Fortune*, 21 December 1987, p. 51.

17. *Princeton Alumni Weekly*, 7 April 1993, p. 8.

18. President Robert Bowen commenting on the appointment of Dr Hisashi Kobayashi, *Princeton Alumni Weekly*, 29 January 1986, p. 10.

12 Socialisation and Social Vitality: A Psychocultural Perspective

Takeyuki Tsuda and George A. De Vos

Indices of Social Cohesion Related to Social Vitality

Economic and Material Indices of Social Vitality: An Incomplete Assessment

Most observers of Japan would agree that Japanese society is characterised by a high level of social vitality. Since such assessments are usually based on economic considerations, they are dominated by images of a country with a highly efficient industrial system that exports vast quantities of quality goods abroad and accumulates tremendous wealth at home. Social vitality in Japan is thus most frequently measured by economic indicators such as GNP, industrial productivity, trade surplus, stock market performance, unemployment, economic growth, etc. Despite the 'objectivity' of these criteria, such narrow economic accounts of Japanese social vitality seem inadequate, especially for holistically minded anthropologists who traditionally address social issues from a comprehensive multi-dimensional perspective which examines not only economic factors but also cultural, institutional, educational, interactional and psychological indices of social interaction and social continuity.

An approach that focuses almost exclusively on particular explanations of why a specific sector of Japanese society (economics and business in this instance) maintains its vitality will not reveal the more fundamental reasons for Japanese social vitality as a whole. What must be considered are not only economic measures but also various processes of social cohesion and alienation on a broader level in both individual and group behaviour.

Indices of Ecological Vitality

Many of these direct economic assessments do not sufficiently consider how continuity in ecological balance is being maintained in Japan. Ecological considerations may sometimes be opposed to the immediate economic benefits of industrial development. The record of Japan in this respect has been improving notably in the past 20 years. There have been serious social movements within Japan to safeguard the environment (Nishimura 1984, Reich 1984, Upham 1987). Some of these sociopolitical protests have tested democratic processes within the courts and in the legislature (Gresser, Fujikura and Morishima 1981, Krauss 1984c). In numerous incidents, these protest movements have alerted the populace to the dangers of environmental deterioration that were becoming evident since the late 1960s.

Protest Movements as an Index of Vitality in Political and Legal Processes

The Japanese attempt to make representative democracy more effective in the face of serious problems in their political and legal system. This is fully covered in other contributions to this volume. We would simply like to add, from a comparative standpoint, that voluntary group activity seeking political improvement retains its vitality. These continuing organised protest movements have become part of Japanese contemporary political and social life and involve the direct participation of many citizens. Such movements, whether in respect to the environment or for other causes, effectively influence the courts and the legislature and have become one source of ameliorative social change (Taniguchi 1984, White 1984).

Indices of Social Control and Deviance

Interpersonal and group violence is another measure of social cohesion. When internal violence or discord is spontaneously avoided, or heavily sanctioned within social units, cultural continuity is better assured. Social regulation in Japan, by and large, is not a matter of coercive police regulation or force since social conformity is remarkably 'self'-regulated, that is, 'internalised'. Moreover, violence and other forms of individual crime remain relatively low when compared with other modern states. Statistics demonstrate that overall rates of individual crime and delinquency are the lowest of any modern national nation (Shain 1984). Violent crime, particularly, is very low especially when compared with an anomic American society (Enomoto 1984).

Since the Japanese police force is relatively professional, effectively organised, and well-trained, it is respected, if not loved, by the general public (Ames 1981, Hoshino 1984). Nationally organised but neighbourhood based, it interacts relatively well with other institutions such as the schools and the courts (Bailey 1984).

Even criminal behaviour among the Japanese is highly organised. The Japanese underworld consists of perhaps 50 000 professional criminals called Yakuza with many members drawn from Korean and Burakumin minorities. This professionalised underworld is probably the best organised group operating in any society, if military organisations in some countries are not considered as criminal.

Problems Related to Minority Status

A continuing internal problem generally hidden from the outside world is the relative social plight of the Japanese minorities (Wetherall and De Vos 1975). Relatively small in number, the Ainu are not too significant a problem. Although there are over a million Okinawans, they are doing relatively well economically and socially. However, Ryukyuan youth are experiencing an increasing identity crisis and the Okinawans feel a sense of resentment towards mainland Japanese, who either ignore past cultural differences, of which Okinawans are proud, or treat them as vaguely inferior Japanese.

Serious problems are more apparent in the two large minorities comprising between 3 per cent and 4 per cent of the Japanese population. The Korean minority includes about 750 000 openly acknowledged 'foreigners' and 200 000 who are 'passing' more or less successfully disguised as ordinary Japanese, except when it comes to marriage (Lee and De Vos 1981). The close to 3 million Japanese who are the descendants of a pariah caste (De Vos and Wagatsuma 1966) are particularly hidden from foreigners as well as ordinary Japanese themselves by the suppression of newspaper coverage. Called non-pejoratively 'burakumin' until recently, they still intermarry for the most part with majority Japanese. They are subject to various forms of informal discrimination that result in the same anomic signs of social disintegration noted among the more visible Koreans. Discrimination directed towards these groups remains racist in tone. Alienated behaviour erupts at times in various forms of social and personal disruption among members of these minorities (Tsurushima 1984). Childhood in these groups is marked by poor school performance and widespread patterns of delinquency. Adults are more prone to various forms of deviancy, including severe alcoholism and instability in family life.

Indices of Personal and Family Malaise

The usual indices of personal malaise and family disruption provides us with a continuing picture of relative social cohesion in Japan. For the most part, indicators of personal and family disruption remain relatively low when compared with other modern industrial states. Nevertheless, there are signs of discontent appearing in the public media.

Although divorce or desertion are infrequent, family life does show some strains over an inability to realise more modern ideals of a companionate relationship between men and women. Fathers and husbands generally are too totally absorbed and preoccupied with vocational-social activities to make significant domestic contributions. There has been criticism that mothers at times are either overly solicitous about their children, or have recently become too involved with working outside the home and thus neglect their children (e.g. Eto 1979). Japanese mothers also place tremendous pressures on their sons to succeed academically. In fact, many Japanese mothers tend to make a full-time career out of supervising their children's education to the extent that they have become a popular cultural category - the *kyoiku mama* (education mother) (see Lebra 1984b: passim, Rohlen 1983:82, Simons 1991 for descriptions).[1] By assisting and pushing her child through an ultra-competitive educational system focused on college entrance exam preparation, the *kyoiku mama* derives vicarious psychological satisfaction from the child's educational attainments (Hendry 1989:94). Possible changes in such fundamental patterns of maternal dedication to children because of a rise in more career-minded professional women would seem socially disruptive to most Japanese.

Since parental pressures from within the family are compounded with pressures towards conformist behaviour experienced in the schools, some children find it difficult to comply with expectations. There has been a growing public awareness of school phobias and student violence inflicted on 'different' children. Other forms of adolescent dissent appear in delinquent-prone behaviour (see Lock 1991, Kawai 1986, Sato 1991). These are seen as serious and threatening social issues because child-rearing and educational problems strike at the very core of Japanese social vitality. They are negative portents for the future.

Present-day affluence of parents is encouraging patterns of conspicuous consumption in youth not previously possible. For example, the unlimited use of credit cards is causing a rash of bankruptcies due to overspending. The continuing indulgence of children into adulthood combined with more general affluence now allows for types of social behaviour not previously visible in the past, except in extraordinarily rich families.

In the context of signs of malaise appearing throughout the life cycle, suicide among youth and the older generation remains relatively high. However, compared internationally, Japan's overall rate of suicide has fallen during the post-war period. As we shall discuss further below, Japanese youth of all social classes show some restlessness in late adolescence and early adulthood. Working-class youth (who number about 60 per cent of the youth population) are absorbed directly into the work force. They do not experience unemployment or give as much evidence of the liminal anomic patterns noted in American and some European youth. Psychological strains are greater among Japanese college youth than among youth of the working class. Although these strains are released in rebellious behaviour during the period of liminal transition at university, such expressions of personal conflict remain transient in nature (Tsuda 1993a).

Social discontent is appearing in Japan related to retirement practices and the care necessary for an increasingly ageing population. Forced retirement at age 55 is practised to lower the cost of tenured employees with seniority, although these individuals are not psychologically or socially ready for retirement. There is also a potentially disruptive welfare problem arising from the ballooning costs of caring for the old and incapacitated.

Community Cohesion

The neighbourhood community as a social unit remains relatively stable with Japan's low geographic mobility. Nevertheless, some parts of the countryside show the anomic effects of depopulation which threatens the continuity of agricultural patterns. But by and large, throughout the modern century, Japanese migration into growing cities has been integrative rather than disintegrative (Wagatsuma and De Vos 1984, Chapter 1). Also, labour activities have not been characterised by the frequent disruptions and slow-downs of other industrial states.

Measures of Vitality in a Multilevel Approach

In brief, social vitality is undoubtedly a very complex issue, involving many social measurements. But more than that, various levels of analysis are necessary in order to adequately explain and understand the human patterns of behaviour which promote social cohesion and continuity. This involves issues that must be examined on a psychological level as well as on a directly social or institutional level. In other words, such a multi-dimensional 'etic'[2] analysis considers not only social structural perspectives such as economic, political, and institutional processes, but also underlying 'personality' variables as they influence overt social behaviour. These etic levels of analysis are conducted by outside observers who examine the structural features of society or personality that influence social behaviour. Structural considerations are usually outside the conscious awareness of social participants themselves. At the same time, however, we must also examine the personal subjective experiences occurring within a society. Such 'emic'[3] experiential perspectives on an individual and group level include psychological motivation, subjective consciousness, childhood experiences, and the development of a self within the context of culture and social roles. Only through such a multilevel approach that is inclusive (not exclusive) can we comprehensively understand the fundamental basis for the proper operation and functioning of Japanese society and its various institutions in general.

All human social systems and institutions, whether they be economic, industrial, educational, or political, are ultimately composed of individuals who occupy specific social positions or roles. These individual social roles are in systematic, structural relationships with one another and are the basic units of the social system. Therefore, to understand social vitality in any society, we must first examine what subjectively motivates individuals properly and more or less willingly to execute their assigned social expectations. This requires an analysis not only of the institutional *structure* of social roles, but also the culturally conditioned, psychological *experience* of internalised motivation. In other words, at the psychological level of personality, why do Japanese individuals willingly conform to the cultural norms and collective standards of behaviour associated with each designated social role?

In essence, the issue of social vitality in Japan addresses a fundamental concern of psychological anthropology. Every society needs a certain level of *functional congruence* between 'culture' and 'personality' in order to survive (see, for example, Spiro 1961a, 1961b, Inkeles and Levinson 1969). That is, only when personality needs and dispositions expressed in behaviour sufficiently conform to what is culturally shared and accepted - the requirements of social roles - will social interaction retain the manageable predictability and mutual intelligibility necessary for coordinated social activity and the relatively smooth operation of society.

For this to occur, the inner dispositions of the personality must resonate sufficiently with collectively accepted cultural norms and expectations so that what is socially and culturally prescribed is also personally satisfying.

If we assume that Japan has high social vitality, this logically indicates sufficiently high congruence between sociocultural patterns and personality structure. Because their personalities are highly internalised and correspond well with cultural standards and regularities, the Japanese diligently fulfil their socially assigned roles by consciously complying with collective standards of behaviour. As a result, the continual maintenance of the social structure and the relative vitality of their society is ensured. However, such a functional 'fit' or compatibility between psychologically motivated behaviour and the impersonal cultural requirements of the social order is never automatic, but must be actively maintained for each subsequent generation. Therefore, in order to understand this fundamental source of Japanese social vitality, we must examine indigenous patterns of personality socialisation - the learning and internalisation of culture - as well as other cultural mechanisms which induce a continuing high functional congruence between Japanese culture and the personalities of its people.

Such an analysis may be dismissed as merely another argument promoting the group model of Japanese society, which is based on an image of Japan consisting of conformist individuals who are willing to sacrifice personal desires and needs for group goals and collective social harmony.[4] The group model has been questioned, if not rejected, by scholars who stress the importance of disruptive conflict in Japanese society.[5] However, although a simple group consensus conception does not cover all facets of Japanese society,[6] it cannot be ignored or dismissed as a mere ideology, especially when addressing a topic such as social vitality. The chaotic diversity of individual personalities must be confined and limited to some extent to the collective cultural regularities of group consensus and conformity for any society to operate in an efficient and orderly manner. Indeed, the group harmony versus conflict issue should not be a mutually exclusive either/or question (see also Lebra 1984a: 56) because both alternatives co-exist in Japan and are necessary for a full comprehension of Japanese social dynamics. Accordingly, our analysis of social vitality also incorporates conflict processes and how they are resolved in Japanese society, both on a social as well as an individual level.

Hence, instead of advocating one model of Japanese society over another, we are conducting a multilevel psychosocial functionalist analysis of the underlying factors behind Japan's remarkable social vitality. This type of analysis is crucial for understanding social vitality in any society. At the same time, though, we wish to avoid the shortcomings of traditional functional analysis which seems to assume *a priori* the existence of a harmonious social order and then proceeds to demonstrate how various institutions and rituals functionally correspond with each other in structure or process. This type of analysis seems to *describe* societies in a condition of smooth operation with functionally interlocking parts and systems, but does not *explain* how such beneficial and stable functional equilibriums are created or actively maintained in the first place. Thus, instead of simply demonstrating a correspondence between personality structure and sociocultural structure and then arguing that they functionally reinforce each other to maintain social cohesion and vitality, we are problematising the relationship between the two variables by examining the complex processes through which psychological motivation becomes sufficiently synchronised and compatible with cultural norms and regularities. Social vitality and cohesion is not a foregone functionalist conclusion but must be actively sustained and preserved by a continuing dynamic interaction of social and psychological systems.

Socialisation Practices: Internalisation in Japanese Society

Socialisation ultimately is a set of interactional sequences (e.g. between mother and child) which consists of various practices, mechanisms, and pedagogic strategies that somehow instil fundamental personality dispositions. Since individual personalities are always constructed and developed within specific cultural constraints, socialisation is the fundamental process through which cultural standards and meanings are internalised to some degree by individuals and then externally expressed in more or less socially conforming role behaviour. As emphasised earlier, this ensures that a sufficient number of individuals continue to resonate with the requirements of designated social roles.

Psychological Mechanisms Underlying Behavioural Control: Shame, Guilt Induced through Self-Sacrifice, Dependency, Paternal Distance and Indulgence

During socialisation, individual personalities are developed through structured social interaction with parents and superiors, who reinforce and reward culturally approved behaviour, while discouraging or even punishing culturally inappropriate behaviour. As certain types of behaviour are consistently reinforced by the repetition of this fundamental interactional pattern in different situations and with various significant others, the cultural meanings, values, and norms associated with these approved behaviour patterns are more or less effectively internalised as part of the personality of the individual.[7] Once the personality internalises these cultural dispositions, the individual can be expected to engage in these types of appropriate behaviour even without the active presence of an immediate sanctioning socialisation agent. In this manner, behaviour that is psychologically motivated on a voluntary basis is no longer an idiosyncratic impulse or gratification of selfish primordial desires, but has become sufficiently congruent with collectively accepted cultural standards. The individual has 'matured' as a culturally conforming member and can be entrusted to execute properly the various social roles necessary for social vitality.

Although such a fundamental socialisation process occurs in all societies, the specific methods of reward and punishment vary cross-culturally, some being more effective than others. As with most societies, the Japanese have no dearth of mechanisms and strategies which are quite successful for keeping children, and later adults, under control, thus ensuring obedience and cultural conformity. Even though Japan is notable for its relative lack of direct physical and verbal punishment, other effective types of negative sanctions are used to discourage and reduce misbehaviour. These mechanisms will be mainly discussed in the context of early socialisation within the family, but some form of social sanctioning is operative throughout the individual's life.

Shame and Guilt: Internal and External Control

Shame is one *external* social sanction that parents apply to the child to ensure that its behaviour roughly conforms to cultural regularities. In this manner, the developing individual quickly realises that failure to execute properly ascribed social roles and their cultural requirements results in social rejection, ostracism, ridicule and, ultimately, a loss of reputation, status and self-esteem. Traditionally, Japanese parents create an intense sensitivity and fear of shame, ridicule and ostracism by constantly warning the child that misbehaviour will embarrass the parents, tarnish the family name, and that others will laugh at the child (Benedict 1974: 286-8, Lanham 1966:325, Vogel and Vogel 1961). Direct teasing and ridiculing of the child by the parents was also used. As Lebra (1983:193) notes, the

Japanese have been especially sensitive to shame arising from improper role behaviour because individuals' actions are more exposed to significant audiences and cultural norms are well recognised (so that violations are easily detected).

Parents, emphasising family values, also instil a deep sense of guilt as a powerful *internal* constraint against disobedient behaviour that violates parental and cultural expectations. A failure to conform to proper role behaviour has been associated with hurting the parents, especially the mother, who takes responsibility and blames herself for the child's misbehaviour (De Vos 1973: Chapter 5). Self-sacrificial behaviour on the part of a parent generates a sense of potential guilt in a child. Because the mother is seen as devoting herself so completely to raising the children by enduring suffering and self-sacrifice, the child experiences intense guilt if such benevolence is not properly reciprocated by conforming role behaviour. Therefore, the fundamental basis for the emotion is a sensitivity towards the potentially negative consequences for the family that is tied to one's 'selfish behaviour'. This pattern of maternal self-sacrifice is what may be weakening in present affluent circumstances. Endurance as a family response to hardship is not always experienced by growing children nowadays. Being personally *indulged* is no longer counterbalanced in the child by a guilt-induced personal *responsibility* for the welfare of the family and the preservation of social status through adversity.

Lebra (1971) explains that guilt arises when a person in a reciprocal relationship with another is unable to sufficiently pay back the other for his/her benevolence and thus injures the benefactor. This inability to live up to mutual reciprocal obligations is especially strong for the parent-child relationship, since it is commonly acknowledged that not even a fraction of the benevolence that the child receives from the parents can be repaid. The child's sensitivity to guilt is thus magnified and becomes a strong motivation towards behaviour conforming to parental wishes. This holds true not only for parents, but also for other benevolent superiors and for social groups to which one is deeply indebted.[8] The child realises from an early stage that misbehaviour has negative consequences not only for the specific individual involved but also for those to whom he/she is affiliated and dependent because they take responsibility for the individual's failure to comply with collective cultural norms.

Guilt is an especially powerful means of cultural control in socialisation because sensitivity to a potential for guilt is *generated within the individual* in adapting to one's social role.[9] Therefore, guilt operates as an inner constraint even in social isolation because (unlike most types of shame) it is not dependent on the constant social presence of evaluating others, such as the parents and superiors who are sources of the emotion. Although initiated through interaction with parents, the mechanism evolves into an internal form of self-punishment against one's own deviant behaviour.

Maternal Closeness as Cultural Control: Dependency

Dependency is another psychological emotion that parents utilise to monitor the child's behaviour in accordance with cultural expectations. Feelings of dependency are most intensely focused upon the mother, the primary figure involved in socialisation. Whereas there are universal aspects which characterise mother-child relationships in all societies (perhaps derived from biological/mammalian requirements and needs as well as universal cultural constraints), such a fundamental relationship is again elaborated in locally specific ways depending on the particular sociocultural milieu, thus generating a multitude of cross-culturally distinctive patterns.

Japan is perhaps unusual in the relatively great emphasis placed on dependent closeness in the mother-child relationship, which continues into adulthood. There are various reasons for this remarkable attachment of the mother to the child, such as the general absence of the husband from the family and the mother's psychological need for an intimate, gratifying relationship, which she is frequently unable to fulfil with her husband. Japanese mothers foster close interdependency with the child by avoiding the exercise of authoritarian control and by constantly staying close to the child with a protective, permissive, and caressing attitude, which often involves prolonged physical contact (see Lebra 1976:138 for three ways in which interdependency is created and reinforced). Accordingly, Japanese mothers do not approve of leaving children alone in a room or with baby sitters and day-care centres, preferring instead to strap the child on their backs when busy and to even stay with the child during sleep (Azuma 1982, Hendry 1986:21, Caudill and Weinstein 1986). In fact, the mother does not seem to view the baby as a separate, autonomous individual who should think independently for itself and express its desire and needs, but instead views the baby as an extension of herself. As a result, there is less development of sharp ego boundaries between mother and child (Caudill and Schooler 1973:325-6, Caudill and Weinstein 1986: 205).[10] Such a close attachment is fostered and reinforced by an indulgent attitude on the part of the mother who encourages the child's needs for passive dependency (*amae*) to an extent not allowable in other more distant social relationships (Doi 1973:38-9).

This indulgent dependency relationship with the child places the mother in a very advantageous position when it comes to regulating the child's behaviour. Since the child has become so deeply dependent on the mother's protection, comfort, closeness and love, the mother can prevent misbehaviour in the child and maintain discipline by threatening to withdraw her willingness to *amae* and passively indulge the child. In this manner, Japanese mothers (and parents in general) frequently threaten to expel and exclude the misbehaving child from the family, either by locking the child out or having someone take the child away (Befu 1971: 153-5, Kondo 1990:149, Hendry 1986:106-17, Lanham 1962:220-32, Smith and Wiswell 1982:227). Because the child comes to fear the potential loss and withdrawal of the close maternal dependency relationship and *amae* gratification, this separation anxiety becomes a powerful motivation for children to conform to the parents' wishes.

Despite the particular nature of this mode of behavioural control, the process does not end when the individual finally leaves the mother's circle of influence. Since the hierarchical mother-child dependency relationship becomes a fundamental interpersonal model that is then generalised to other hierarchical social relationships later in the individual's life, the social superior's ability to deny the dependency needs of the individual remains a successful means of eliciting obedience and compliance from subordinates. The threat of social isolation in general is effective as a tactic to enforce cultural discipline.

Paternal Distance in Child-Rearing

If the mother-child relationship is characterised by an unusual level of closeness and dependency, the father-child relationship is remarkable for its relative amount of distance and detachment. Although there is wide variation in the Japanese father's level of participation in child-rearing, he is usually quite uninvolved. Of course, this is not because of the inherent aloofness or indifference of Japanese fathers to children. In most cases, the father is simply not home.[11] Among the various reasons for the father's absence, the most salient is usually his intense commitment to work.[12] The father also participates in much after-work socialising related both to his work duties and the maintenance of social prestige (fathers of higher corporate rank are expected to spend less time at home). Overall, there is a resultant lack of intimacy or closeness between husbands and wives. In addition, the home is not always a satisfactory place of relaxation for the father because of the general lack of space and psychological satisfaction in domestic activities. According to Hendry (1986:53-4), many fathers are indeed interested in child-rearing and some actually are closely involved. However, as Lebra notes (1984:179), even if the father is around often he can distance himself from the mother-child relationship. Indeed, there seems to be a culturally prevalent gender belief that fathers should not be active participants in child-rearing or other domestic duties.

The absent-father syndrome has been blamed recently for various developmental problems ranging from violence in the home to refusal to attend school (Boocock 1989:59-60). Yet the absent father should not simply be regarded as an abnormality which can only have negative effects on child development. In Japan the missing father is frequently used in a constructive manner in socialisation as yet another means to ensure the child's compliance with ideal cultural standards. This does not simply mean that the children learn that they should work just as hard as their father when they grow up. As various scholars have noted (Benedict 1974:55-6, De Vos 1973:23-4, 45, Hendry 1986:99-101, Lebra 1976:118, 148), parents are careful to be exemplary role models in the family for the children to observe and emulate because it is believed that children tend to mirror parental behaviour. However, since the father is frequently missing from the family, the Japanese mother tends to create and project an idealised image of the father for the children, regardless of the actual shortcomings and personal inadequacies of the father himself (see De Vos 1973).

Ideally, the father is treated as a distant and respected figure whose masculine role is used by the mother as a standard to evaluate the child's behaviour. Since the child thus eventually learns to emulate the ideal father-image constructed by the mother, the absent father can actually enhance the teaching of proper role behaviour in family socialisation. Perhaps it is better for the father to be away since he will have fewer opportunities to ruin the idealised masculine role-image the mother has constructed for her children.

The absent father's authority, status and respect are also used by the mother to discipline the children. The mother frequently keeps the children in line by threatening to tell the father of the children's misbehaviour (Benedict 1974:264, Befu 1986:15). Thus, although the direct disciplining is still being performed by the mother, the father can facilitate her efforts by playing the role of disciplinarian even in his absence.

Cultural Internalisation through Indulgence

What is most remarkable about Japanese socialisation practices is the relative lack of direct punitive measures and authoritarian control. Even in the face of overt misbehaviour, the Japanese mother responds not by punishment, but by indulgence and nurture, even to the extent of begging the child to behave properly.[13] Since misbehaviour is frequently interpreted as some sort of *amae* deprivation or the child's refusal to acknowledge its dependency needs, the mother's response is to increase the level of indulgence. In general, the Japanese mother prefers to yield to the child rather than injure their close, dependent relationship (Hess *et al.* 1986:156). This persuasive, indulgent approach to behavioural regulation is also reflected in the Japanese mother's preference for reasoning with the child rather than directly enforcing compliance through her power and authority. In other words the Japanese mother attempts to persuade the child not to engage in certain types of behaviour by explaining why the behaviour is inappropriate instead of categorically outlawing and punishing it.[14] Such socialisation practices are directly related to the Japanese concept of human nature as inherently good (Hendry 1986:17, Lewis 1989, 1991, Yamamura 1986:34-7), unlike Western religious beliefs in which man is innately sinful and must constantly struggle against evil temptations. Because the child is thus seen as basically good, misbehaviour is not attributed to malicious intent or conscious wrongdoing but to a lack of understanding or to forgetfulness of what is correct and proper. The mother's response in such a context is not to punish the bad and evil child, but to appeal to its inherent goodness by giving the child an explanation and reminder of appropriate behaviour. The mother, in effect, herself takes responsibility for any errant behaviour on the part of her child.

The result of such non-coercive and permissive socialisation is a greater internalisation within the child of parental expectations and cultural values (Hess *et al.* 1986:156-7, 163, Lewis 1989, 1991). Thus, indulgence is another socialisation practice that effectively maintains the close culture and personality congruence characteristic of Japanese society. It may seem strange that a more indulgent, permissive and less authoritarian approach based on reasoning and explanation would develop greater cultural internalisation than a more strict punitive approach based on firm parental control. However, the reasons behind this are rather clear.[15] If proper behaviour and obedience are enforced only through external controls by a seemingly arbitrary and authoritarian system of rewards and punishments, when this external parental coercion is removed later in life the incentive to conform and obey will likewise disappear. However, when the reasons for proper behaviour and compliance are explained instead of imposed simply by external force and parental pressure, the child will come to internally regulate its own behaviour through a personal understanding of the reasons behind parental expectations (i.e. why certain behaviour is considered good or bad). In such a situation, even when the external parental controls are removed, the child will have sufficiently internalised the proper cultural values and will continue to obey properly. In such a situation, even when the external parental controls are removed, the child will have sufficiently internalised the proper cultural values and will continue to obey properly. Therefore, instead of regulating behaviour merely by outward constraints, the Japanese mother (consciously or not) is also attempting to develop internal voluntary controls within the child.

There are other reasons why early indulgent socialisation practices later develop highly internalised personalities that are in sync with cultural processes and demands. As many have stressed, the Japanese self is constructed and defined in relationships and interactions with others (Bachnik 1986, Kondo 1987, Ohnuki-Tierney 1990).[16] Of course, this is true for all societies including the West, for nowhere are selves developed in abstract vacuums hermetically sealed from social influences. In Japan, this interconnectedness of the self with others is especially salient, tracing back from a premodern Confucian emphasis on a strong 'self' (Tu 1986) defined by social relationships rather than individualistic endeavours (De Vos 1992).

Many of the social relationships within which Japanese selves are developed are hierarchical, involving power inequalities. As Kondo (1987, 1990) observes, selves are 'relationally defined' and 'rafted' in 'shifting discursive fields of power' and cultural meanings.[17] However, because the negative connotations of forced submission and raw exploitation are missing from such hierarchical power relationships in Japan, they actually facilitate cultural internalisation. In fact, these relationships are in a sense psychologically gratifying for subordinates not only because the superior is perceived as benevolent and indulgent but because they expect to eventually attain the respected position of the superior by properly incorporating and internalising his skills, power and cultural attributes.[18] Present endurance is associated with future reward.[19]

Of course the formation of a self within such power relationships begins in the family during childhood. Within the context of the hierarchical parent-child dyad, the dependent child internalises various cultural expectations and other social material from the mother. The various socialisation mechanisms through which this is done have been outlined in the previous section. This process of incorporating the power and qualities of the superior into the self continues throughout life as the individual is embedded in a multitude of changing hierarchical relationships with various superiors, especially at school and later in the work place. A general example is the traditional master-apprentice relationship in small Japanese shops and factories, in which the apprentice attempts to incorporate material (skills, discipline, cultural expectations) from the master in an effort to eventually become the master himself.[20]

Similarly, the Japanese collective self (national identity) has also been constructed within contexts of power: in this case, the hierarchical international relationships between countries, also called the World System. Much of modern Japanese history has been a constant process of national identity formation and redefinition by incorporating and mastering (through emulation, imitation and importation) the sources of Western superiority - technology with its positive cultural meanings and values of superiority, civilisation and power. After years of diligent learning and endurance of subordinate status, the Japanese have attained, and perhaps surpassed, the technologically superior position of the West. In other words, the apprentice has become the master in the international work place.

Since socialisation and cultural learning, by definition, consist mainly of relationships and interactions between those with unequal power and status, the general attitude of the superior (whether mother or company boss) becomes a critical determinant of the level of internalisation in the subordinate. If the learning of restrictive cultural expectations and values is associated with yielding to the powerful coercion of a ruthless superior, the subordinate may comply temporarily, but the eventual reaction will be resistance and disobedience. When cultural prescriptions and dictates come to take on such negative personal significance, they will not be properly internalised. Of course, the situation is reversed if the relationship with the superior is not based on coercive power but on permissive and indulgent benevolence, as is idealised in Japan. In this instance, since the hierarchical relationship is imbued with future-oriented positive feeling, the cultural values and norms expressed in the interaction with the superior will be internalised with the willing consent of the subordinate.

This is true not only in the Japanese family but also in Japanese companies, where relationships between superiors and subordinates - *oyabun/kobun* (parent role-child role) or *senpai/kohai* (senior-junior) - are characterised by a close age-graded emotional attachment and benevolent sense of paternalism, again facilitating the learning and eventual mastery of proper cultural attitudes and behaviour as well as necessary skills from the superior. Like the Japanese mother, the 'older' superior nurtures and indulges the subordinate by advising, guiding, encouraging and defending and helping him during times of trouble.[21] Because such positive personal feeling is attached to the subordinate's relationship with the superior, he anticipates and takes to heart the expectations of the superior with gratitude and approval by diligently fulfilling the duties of his assigned social role. In this manner, external and impersonal cultural requirements become associated with the arousal of positive internal psychological emotions, thus facilitating their incorporation into the personality.

In the context of hierarchical relationships, the connection between greater indulgence in socialisation and a higher level of internalisation of culture can also be understood within De Vos' guilt model. In other words, it is precisely because the Japanese mother insists on maintaining an image of a benevolent and forgiving superior authority who patiently relies on appeals rather than autocratic coercion that the child will feel obliged to gratefully repay, by proper behaviour, the mother's *on* (benevolence) and the suffering she endures as a result. Such an internal, guilt-motivated desire to conform would not arise if the child was confronted only with a punitive authority to whom little gratitude can be felt. In fact the more benevolent and indulgent the mother is towards the child, the more guilty the child will feel for misbehaviour and the stronger the *internal* motivation to obey her wishes and expectations.

Internalisation and Independence

Although none of these Japanese socialisation techniques (shame, guilt, dependency, role training and indulgence) require external force or the direct exercise of authority, they are extremely successful nonetheless, precisely because of their implicit nature. Therefore, given the effectiveness of these various mechanisms used in Japanese socialisation to develop personalities which properly resonate and comply with cultural demands, we can conclude that, normatively, the Japanese are indeed highly internalised. Much of normative Japanese culture has been effectively incorporated into individual personalities, so that self-motivated behaviour becomes compatible with the proper enactment of social duties and role requirements necessary for social health and vitality. This high level of cultural internalisation is confirmed by psychological studies which show that the Japanese are *cognitively* field-*independent* while remaining *socially* field-*dependent* (see De Vos 1980, Vaughn 1988). The classical assumption in psychology is that individuals who are cognitively field-independent (i.e. greater internal locus of control and ability to judge for oneself) must also be socially field-independent (i.e. more self-reliant, autonomous, and less dependent and susceptible to group norms and pressures). However, while many Japanese possess the capacity to make *independent* cognitive evaluations and judgements within themselves, they have simultaneously internalised cultural norms to such a degree that these personal and independent inner thoughts are not expressed or verbalised in external social behaviour. Thus, they can also remain social conformists highly sensitive to cultural norms and group pressures (socially field-*dependent*). Again, this is evidence that cultural obedience is internally generated within the personality.

Socialisation in Later Life: Corporate Training and Ethics Programmes

As we all know, socialisation does not end with childhood and youth, but continues throughout life as individuals constantly redefine their identities in response to various experiences relevant to personality formation. Although not systematically treated in this chapter, the Japanese educational system continues many of the socialisation processes and mechanisms for cultural discipline and control practised in the family. In an equally rigorous and effective manner, the educational experience further reinforces the culture and personality congruence initiated early in the family.

Another interesting aspect of post-family socialisation are corporate training programmes (see Rohlen 1974) and ethics retreats (Kondo 1987, 1990), which are independent programmes that companies frequently use for their employees. Both of these again utilise traditional Japanese socialisation methods to accomplish the goal of social conformity. Indeed, they serve to reinforce the culture and personality congruence established in earlier socialisation and also act as corrective if these earlier efforts were inadequate or inefficient or if their effects have since worn out.

As Rohlen describes, company training programmes provide employees not only with the necessary techniques, skills, and business training for their new jobs but also with 'spiritual education' that attempts to build proper moral character and company loyalty and are thus 'designed to foster self-reliant people harnessed to the work of the organisation' (Rohlen 1974:211). According to Rohlen, many older company men felt that the training programmes were crucial because the new young employees lacked a sense of responsibility, sustained commitment and motivation to work, as well as proper manners. In other words, the new recruits needed additional on-the-job mentoring before they would fit the cultural standards of the company. It is also interesting to note that the corporate training programme that Rohlen studied was not only for new recruits but also retrained current workers who were unhappy, lethargic, and had problems on the job. Therefore, the programmes were designed to make up for earlier inadequate socialisation, both at home and at the company.

Some of the methods these company and ethics retreat programmes use to socialise individuals include: (1) Group activities in which individuals collectively engage in identical behaviour and shared hardships in order to reinforce a sense of mutual belonging, loyalty, group dedication, cooperation and encouragement. Activities include cleaning, marathons, exercises, lectures, baths, songs, and collective shouts of encouragement. (2) The creation of guilt feelings by sensitising individuals to the suffering endured by their parents and also by holding the group responsible for the infractions of one of its members. In turn the group comes to monitor and evaluate its members, generating a sense of shame and loss of face and reputation for members who fail to comply with social duties and rules. (3) Enforced tests of physical hardship and endurance which teach that any social task, however difficult and painful, can be accomplished by relentless perseverance, effort and focused determination.

When such intense socialisation experiences are translated to the work place, the implications are clear: these programmes act as one conservative force that allow individual proclivities to be readapted to the constraints of the corporate system. As Rohlen observes at the bank he studied, any initial personal resistance towards ideology and social constraints is eventually reduced for most company men. In other words, company men 'must achieve some sense of themselves that is reasonably consistent with the requirements of their jobs and their participation in the organisation' (1974:209). When such effective vocational socialisation processes are generalised for the society as a whole, we have the fundamental basis for social vitality in Japan.

Conflict and Social Vitality

Some readers may have reservations about the socialisation processes described so far, which seem to portray the Japanese as perfectly internalised and obedient individuals whose inner personality desires and needs have somehow become completely identical to external cultural and group pressures. Such images of relative social harmony are only part of the picture, and must be tempered by opposing considerations of inner conflict as well as observable social dissension.

Although we have emphasised the importance of effective Japanese socialisation for the maintenance of social cohesion and vitality, even the most sensitive generalisations are always subject to many exceptions, local variations, historical disruptions, and different individual experiences.[22] Obviously, Japanese individuals are not merely automatons ground out by an all-powerful socialisation machine and we are not intending to promote such a simplistic image. Indeed, no matter how effective socialisation mechanisms are in any society, an *absolute* functional congruence is never attained since the variability in individual personality dispositions is always much broader than the range of variability that can be permitted at the cultural level. This discrepancy between cultural restrictions and the wide range of individual personality needs is never fully extinguished or obliterated. Since there is substantial conflict against cultural norms, both within the personality and in the wider society, a comprehensive account of social vitality in Japan must take the implications of recurring conflict into its framework of analysis. As a result, we must re-examine those aspects of the Japanese self and inner motivation that are incompatible with cultural regularities in order to assess what influence this conflict has on Japanese social vitality.

Omote and Ura: Social Behaviour and Self-Revelation in the Japanese Self

The recent debate and tension over the group and conflict models of Japanese society are relevant to a consideration of inner self-experience because each of these approaches is based on completely different assumptions about the nature of the Japanese self. The traditional group-harmony model presumes a Japanese 'personality' that properly conforms to cultural norms and whose inner individual needs and desires closely resemble collective goals and standards. The conflict model argues against the image of such a socially subservient self, claiming that Japanese individuals act according to self-interest and instrumental advantage and are frequently in conflict and competition with one another instead of always upholding group consensus (see especially Befu 1977, 1980, 1986). According to this view, the Japanese person pursues his or her own goals and maximises personal opportunities through the exchange of scarce resources.

Which is the true version of the Japanese self? As mentioned before, this consensus versus conflict question is misplaced because the two opposing alternatives are not mutually exclusive. In fact, *both* an experiential self subserviently dedicated to group consensus and a potentially conflictful, socially nonconforming self interested in furthering individual interests are necessary for a more complete, complex understanding of the inner tensions underlying Japanese behaviour. These two opposing tendencies coexist and are both part of a dynamic portrait of the Japanese self, but are confined to different regions of self-experience - the *omote* (public, outside, formal) and the *ura* (private, inside, informal) (see Doi 1986). The issue is to understand the resultant social behaviour of a continuous *omote-ura* tension and the accommodative relationship between these two supposedly incompatible components of inner experience.

The public *omote* self strictly conforms to the group cultural norms which are necessary for the proper execution of one's social role and thus represents the 'mask' or 'social face' (the *tatemae*) that the Japanese present in public social interaction and behaviour. It seems to receive primary concern and emphasis as the core of self-identity and understanding (De Vos 1985, Lebra 1976: Chapter 5). This is the aspect of the self that we have closely examined thus far. As analysed earlier, conformist cultural dispositions for outer behaviour are internalised in the *omote* self through various socialisation processes and create social sensitivity to the feelings of others in various spheres of social activity. Therefore, the *omote* self is not just superficial play-acting; it is governed by normative cultural dispositions that are internalised.

Simultaneously, however, the Japanese do develop an independent, 'individualised' self-awareness somehow distinct from these normative social requirements. Indeed, in the deeper recesses of the Japanese experience underneath the dominating *omote* social self lurks an inner *ura* self of true individual feelings, intentions, beliefs, proclivities and desires (the *honne*), which is distinct and often contradicts the external cultural standards and pressures of the *omote* self (De Vos 1985, Lebra 1976: Chapter 9). This private, subjective and intensely personal *ura* self that is incompatible with, if not antagonistic to cultural norms and formal social role requirements usually remains carefully hidden within the personality. Idiosyncratic *ura* inclinations and dispositions are seldom, if ever, overtly expressed in formal social behaviour. As we shall discuss, there is little social space available in Japanese society for their expression. These individual proclivities can be more or less conscious, depending on the individual.

The existence of this hidden *ura* self is shown by certain types of tests and surveys done on the Japanese. For instance, an early seventies study (cited in Cummings 1980:235, Shimahara 1979:160) indicated, contrary to expectations, that Japanese youth had by far the highest dissatisfaction rate (among 11 countries) with their society in general, including its political, occupational and educational aspects. Likewise, Caudill and Scarr's study of dominant value orientations in Japan surprisingly revealed that the 'individualistic' orientation was generally dominant over the 'collateral' and 'lineal' value orientations. Also as mentioned above (De Vos 1980, 1992, Vaughn 1988), psychological studies demonstrate that the Japanese are cognitively field-*independent* (which should mean, on a social level, that they are psychologically differentiated, self-reliant, autonomous and less dependent on group norms) rather than cognitively field-*dependent* as would be expected. Such results have perplexed a wide variety of Japanese scholars who always viewed the Japanese person as non-autonomous and non-individual - harmoniously conforming to social expectations and institutions and completely dependent and subservient to the group and its collective goals. However, the confusion disappears as soon as we realise that such studies are measuring the hidden *ura* self of independent, individual feelings, not the external *omote* self that appears in regular social interaction (which social scientists are used to observing). Surveys, especially questionnaires, and certain psychological tests on which these studies were based are conducted mainly in isolation and anonymously in the absence of normal Japanese group pressures and social constraints. Thus, in contrast to ordinary social situations, the individual can express his/her true individual *ura* feelings and *honne* desires, which are distinct from and opposed to social standards, values and institutions.

This is where Befu's emphasis on an 'individual' self becomes relevant. However, to characterise this *ura* self as motivated by pure 'self-interest', personal gain and economic rationality is problematic. Such a rational choice/exchange theory model presents a simplistic picture of society based on scheming individuals who are always motivated by their calculating assessments of gains and losses in any situation. The conflict approach in general tends to be built on such problematic assumptions about the individual: 'Conflict theories assume that each person wants to advance or protect his own interest and, moreover, that this self-interest inevitably produces conflict when the interests are mutually exclusive or the goals are incompatible' (Krauss, Rohlen, Steinhoff 1984:5). This type of *homo economicus* social theory assumes that action is always geared towards rational economic ends, implying that supposedly universal and abstract economic rules of social resource exchange[23] motivate behaviour, not the intricacies of local cultural systems, personality dispositions and situational circumstances (for an extended critique of utilitarian praxis theory, see Sahlins 1976).

Since we have extensively examined the formation of the *omote* aspect of the personality by the effective socialisation of self in culture, it is also necessary to understand why an *ura* self opposed to such cultural pressures emerges. Our previous analysis has stressed how self and personality formation is ultimately a process of accommodation to the immediate social and cultural environment. However, although Japanese people tend to be dependent and sensitive to cultural contexts for identity and content, they are never simply passive entities which merely incorporate cultural patterns and pressures through a process of indiscriminate osmosis.[24] Japanese socialisation does instigate a type of cognitive development that not only permits but also fosters forms of independent judgement and perception in many Japanese.[25]

Therefore, instead of meekly internalising culturally defined expectations during socialisation, the cultural meanings on which selves are built are multiple and diverse and are actively contested by individuals who resist, reinterpret and selectively appropriate these meanings in their own idiosyncratic ways. In other words these cultural/role expectations which serve as a basis for personality formation are not absolute, unchallenged and uniform meanings which are categorically imposed upon the self but are frequently vaguely defined and understood, leaving much to the discretion of the individuals involved. This leeway allows for the development of a distinct and independent inner sense of identity (the *ura* self) that can be incompatible and incongruous with normative cultural patterns.

Another factor that contributes to the formation of an *ura* self is the Japanese tendency to stress outward behavioural compliance in socialising and teaching. As many Japan scholars (starting with Benedict 1974 and most recently Kondo 1990) have noted, Japanese socialisation and training imposes a variety of outward behavioural forms upon the individual without clarifying the content or principles behind the external behaviour. This type of content instruction is used in the Zen arts, tea ceremonies, dance, martial arts, Suzuki musical training, high school education (see Rohlen 1983: Chapter 8), as well as in the teaching of proper manners and body comportment by Japanese mothers (see De Vos 1992: Chapter 1).

This method of self-construction is also relevant to the formation of Japanese national identity in relationship with a 'superior' West. Sometimes Western technology (the outward form) was indiscriminately adopted, even when it was clear that the citizens and workers lacked the technical knowledge, understanding and expertise to operate the material.

Even today, Western symbolic forms and images continue to be incorporated without an understanding of the meaning behind them. Examples include gestures such as the peace/victory hand sign which the Japanese use merely as a stylish photo pose, and T-shirts with grammatically senseless English phrases. As long as the thing looks Western, the content is not really important.

Such an action-before-understanding type of training assumes that after the rigorous repetition and perfect execution of the external behavioural form, proper understanding will naturally and eventually result. However, when these role behaviours are mechanically imposed on the individual without explicitly defining the cultural meanings and expectations accompanying them, individuals are given much freedom to construct and develop their own feelings, opinions and attitudes towards these external behavioural forms. This type of socialisation creates a situation in which individuals conform externally to proper *omote* social behaviour, but hold idiosyncratic inner beliefs and feelings within the *ura* self which may conflict with the cultural principles underlying these *omote* actions.

The Ura Personality and Social Vitality

Let us return to the fundamental question that led us to consider the potentially antagonistic aspects of the *ura* part of the personality. What significance does its existence have for the remarkably efficient operation of Japanese society? A traditional assumption has been that the conflictful *ura* aspects of the self are not ordinarily expressed in normal social behaviour and interactions, but are kept mostly hidden within the personality.[26] As Befu observes, 'Inasmuch as behaviour is required to be formalised, one's inner thoughts, feelings, and convictions - in short, one's *honne* - tend not to be directly expressed' (1980:176). Thus, one continues to behave, self-protectively, in socially (culturally) expected ways - whatever is hidden within (De Vos 1985:180) so that the *ura* self is basically maintained only in social isolation and introspection (Lebra 1976:158-9). Likewise, Doi observes that although the *ura* self is 'actually very much within reach ... (it) does not seem to emerge on the surface (of social interaction)' (1986:56). It is not socially shared with others, except in rare instances of intimate revelation. Sometimes one's intimate thoughts are written in a diary. Of course, the *ura* is never completely suppressed in social behaviour, as will be discussed later, but its successful confinement in most types of formal social interaction is quite notable, especially when compared with other societies. Because the Japanese are always acutely aware of their *ura* self, it is more appropriate to consider it as *suppressed* rather than *repressed* (De Vos and Wagatsuma 1970:347-8).

Therefore, although the *entire* content of the self (which includes both the *omote* and *ura*) does not correspond with cultural prescriptions, the influence of the culturally nonconforming aspects of the self on formal public behaviour seems negligible. As long as there is this sufficient congruence at least on the overt behavioural level between culture and self (regardless of inner psychological conflicts), social roles will continue to be properly executed and social vitality maintained. The delicate balance of psychologically motivated cultural behaviour is not threatened in most cases.

The Controlled Containment of Disruptive Tensions at the Social Level

This concealment of conflict within the *ura* domain is reflected in various types of social activity. Two examples worth brief examination are political legislation processes and litigation.

Conflict in the Japanese Diet is usually well managed and contained so that an effective style of compromise and partisan accommodation has emerged (Krauss 1984b). According to Krauss, 'Increasingly, government (the bureaucracy and the Liberal Democratic Party) and opposition parties seemed to be resolving their differences through bargaining within normal parliamentary channels' (1984b:244). Bitter political clashes in the Diet have virtually disappeared and 'debate has gone out of style in the Diet' (Pharr 1982:35). This is not because there are no controversial issues, but because disagreements and potential conflicts are resolved privately or covertly in *ura* situations. Indeed, there is 'A cultural predisposition to settle major issues of policy in private (*ura*) through intermediaries, and in public (*omote*) only to ratify ... policy questions' (Calder 1982:5). A considerable amount of legislation is created in informal, private, and closed-door (i.e. *ura*) policy committees in which potential conflict among the relevant parties is implicitly resolved. According to Krauss, the *ura* atmosphere of these House Management Committee meetings conducted by the chairman and directors facilitates the quiet resolution and mediation of conflicts between opposing groups: 'Since these *rijikai* (directors' meetings) are closed and the interaction that takes place there is informal, all the directors I interviewed reported that real negotiating takes place .... The secrecy and informality provided by closed meetings of a small group of directors obviously facilitate the working out of interparty disagreements' (1984:273b). In fact these meetings are characterised by 'secret bargaining, trust, and friendship relations transcending partisan differences' (Krauss 1984b:277). After conflicting differences are implicitly accommodated in these *ura* committees, the resulting legislation is then publicly presented to the Diet (the *omote*) where it is almost always approved.[27]

Because the House Management Committees are able to negotiate most of the issues between the government and opposition through such informal and private consultation, conflict is contained within this *ura* arena and does not escalate into open (*omote*) confrontations in the Diet.[28] An ideology of collective harmony and political consensus can thus be sustained at the *omote*, public level.

The legal process is another example of how conflict tends to be confined to the *ura* areas of Japanese society. As many have noted, Japan is characterised by a relatively low rate of litigation. The number of civil suits per capita brought before the courts in Japan is roughly between one-twentieth and one-tenth of the figures for the United States and Great Britain (Tanaka 1988:194). Many conflicts that Westerners would simply bring to court are resolved outside this legal machinery in Japan.

Although there are perhaps many reasons for this reluctance to litigate,[29] this is another example of the Japanese preference to resolve disputes and conflicts informally and privately with the intervention of a third-party mediator (see Hendry 1989:192). As Henderson (1965) observes, informal conciliation procedures have been widely used historically as an alternative to formal litigation in Japan. Again, there is a strong sense that conflict must be controlled and contained privately within the group if at all possible and kept away from the public *omote*, where consensus is supposed to prevail. Resorting to a public and formal court trial would be disruptive to the *omote* social order (see Kawashima and Noda 1988:191).[30]

Ura Conflicts and Harmony Ideology

In general, personal resistance and antagonism against culturally enforced regimentation and harmonious group processes in Japan is thus kept muzzled in private, both at the level of individual behaviour and in group processes. As a result, conflict can usually be managed and accommodated backstage without disrupting and destabilising the front-stage performance of the social order. Such suppression and control of inner conflict, so essential to the efficient operation of Japanese society, seem to be actively motivated by internalised desires to maintain harmony and consensus on the *omote* level of public behaviour, despite the personal costs.

In explaining this accommodation of conflict for the purposes of social cohesion and vitality in Japan, we cannot ignore the role of the Confucian-inspired ideology of social harmony in the development of socialised inner attitudes. Although the notion of group harmony and consensus is indeed an ideology as Befu notes (1980:177), this does not mean that it is a false illusion with no continuing effect on social behaviour. Instead, ideologies, whether implicit or explicit, have a powerful influence on people's social perceptions and actions. Since social consensus and harmony ideologies obscure and mask the true processes of potential conflict in Japanese society, people come to believe the ideology as an accurate representation of their society. This is especially true for individuals who have not attained a certain level of detached social consciousness to realise how power elites (Mills 1956) can use ideologies as a means of conceptual as well as behavioural control. Because individuals immersed within a group do not possess independent means to assess the actual state of society, the ideology becomes reality for them. Convinced by the ideology that their society is indeed harmonious and cohesive, they will attempt to actively restrain potential conflicts and disputes. In other words, individuals begin to structure their behaviour in accordance with the ideology since they do not wish to disrupt the social order. Therefore, when ideologies of harmony and social consensus are effectively imposed, they become internalised as guidelines for thought and behaviour, thus frequently forcing conflict to recede into the background. As we all know, ideologies to a certain extent are self-fulfilling.

Social vitality is undoubtedly a complex issue that involves both processes of consensus as well as conflict. Indeed, social vitality in Japan depends not only on the internalisation of cultural norms through effective socialisation in family and work place, but also on the continual internal control of *ura* conflicts and anti-social impulses which inevitably arise in the personality. In this regard the importance of both early and later ideological socialisation becomes clear.

The Release of Conflict: Liminality and Social Vitality

Of course, a complete confinement of personal and social conflict for the promotion of social vitality is impossible. Even in the most regulated societies, considerable conflict, opposition, and protest against restrictive sociocultural demands are openly released and expressed, whether in everyday resistance or in more widespread and dramatic ways. In Japan, as already mentioned, there has been a notable amount of sustained and overt public resistance and social protest, both on a daily basis and in organised collective demonstrations.

In accordance with our psychocultural framework, we must return to the origins of conflict behaviour - the Japanese personality - in order to assess the impact of such overt disruptions on the vitality of the social order. As emphasised thus far, the efficient operation and functioning of the Japanese social system requires the Japanese person to impose self-constraint upon individualised, *ura* desires and dispositions, preventing them from being released into social behaviour. Yet, despite the effective subordination and suppression of the anti-social, idiosyncratic *ura* self under such cultural mechanisms, it is never completely extinguished or destroyed. The Japanese personality is never simply reduced to social roles and cultural norms. Despite dominating and relentless social and internal pressures which create cultural conformity on the surface of personality, the individual is always acutely (if not painfully) aware of autonomous and distinct inner desires and proclivities that contradict and oppose the normative sociocultural demands of the external *omote* self. Yet, it is difficult to maintain this sense of an autonomous unique self intact if it is restricted only to the inner world of thought without being reinforced and reaffirmed through tangible and overt self-expression in the individuals' actual behaviour. Thus, the suppressed *ura* component of individuals' desires within the personality constantly seeks release in actual social behaviour and exerts unrelenting psychological pressure against the external *omote* self.

It thus seems that the previously discussed mechanisms of socialisation are not completely adequate. As noted, the external compliance of the personality with cultural standards of behaviour and roles is certainly achieved through socialisation, but at the expense of suppressing and denying gratification to important *ura* aspects of the personality. Since the dispositions and desires that run counter to cultural role expectations are not extinguished but constantly demand release through behavioural expression, considerable psychic energy and effort is undoubtedly required for suppressing and preventing such disruptive internal desires from breaking through and being released into public behaviour and interaction. For some, a psychological conflict or antagonism constantly exists between cultural norms and inner personal desires, which undoubtedly generates considerable psychological tension and stress. This greatly complicates the individual's efforts to establish a coherent, unified self-identity, thus threatening the personal integration essential for psychological health. A more or less painful discrepancy and chasm is created between inner thought and external behaviour because the *omote* personality dispositions displayed in overt behaviour remain fundamentally incongruous with a deeper sense of who one truly is or what one wants at the level of subjective self. Although such a personality conflict between the public outer self and the private inner self is undoubtedly universal, it is especially acute in societies like Japan where demands for social conformity and normative group pressures are intense and the expression of centrifugal individual tendencies are strictly discouraged. This is in contrast to 'Western' societies where the assertion of individual uniqueness and autonomy is ideally cherished, although sometimes implicitly discouraged, and slavish conformity is actively scorned.

Indeed, the forced submersion of imperious *ura* personality impulses and desires under the exterior façade of the social *omote* self not only generates considerable psychological strain, conflict and fragmentation, but can also in some instances cause an intense build-up of frustration and pent-up aggression. Contrary to some common conceptions of the Japanese, we believe there is a substantial potential for violence and aggression based on such psychic tension and dissatisfaction which is hidden in the subjective experience of the self.[31] Aggression consistently prevented from being outwardly released can be turned inward, ultimately leading to a type of 'egocentric suicide' (De Vos 1973:451-4).[32] In turn, other psychological disorders such as *shinkeishitsu* and 'role narcissism' can also result.

Shinkeishitsu is a personality rigidity and nervousness arising from excessive self-constraint and an 'over-socialised' fear that the inadequate and imperfect inner self will break through the social mask to become publicly exposed. The individual suffers from an extreme and neurotic sensitivity to the thoughts, opinions, and evaluations of others and believes that he/she is giving off the wrong or improper social cues. However, because it is difficult to perceive what others are truly thinking about oneself (especially in a culture where the *tatemae* dominates and *honne* feelings are rarely expressed), the result is a nervous fear of human relationships in general that can leave the individual socially incapacitated. What is often going on unconsciously is a rebellious desire to reject social roles and tasks.[33] On the other hand, continual denial of the gratification of inner needs by excessive control and suppression can create a situation where the *ura* self virtually disappears. De Vos has called this 'role narcissism' - an excessively rigid devotion and over- preoccupation with one's social role as the only source of meaning for life so that even a slight disruption in proper role execution, either by inner failure or outer circumstance, creates a psychological malaise that can even result in suicide (this concept is elaborated in De Vos 1973:468-9).

Undoubtedly, because of the imperious nature of these subjective needs and desires, their intentional confinement under restrictive cultural role expectations simply generates inner psychological stress, conflict, frustration, and aggression and threatens psychological health. Given the inadequacy of these traditional Japanese cultural mechanisms employed to maintain social vitality by simply suppressing culturally nonconforming *ura* aspects of the personality, it becomes obvious that the only means to truly maintain the harmonious operation of Japanese society while simultaneously ensuring psychological stability is through some form of overt behavioural expression and satisfaction of these persistent anti-social *ura* impulses and pressures without disrupting the social order.

In this regard, Japanese society provides individuals with various Turnerian *liminal* experiences (Turner 1969) which allows the overt behavioural expression and release of these normally forbidden anti-social pressures, desires and impulses within the personality in a controlled and socially safe environment. The Japanese university is a classic example of a transitional period during which social requirements and normal social responsibilities are suspended (see Tsuda 1993a for a detailed analysis of the university liminal experience). Working-class youth are more quickly directed into the labour force, wherein they usually are integrated by some mentoring concern on their behalf by older workers. They do not experience alienated peer group isolation as frequently occurs in American lower-class minorities.

In contrast, Japanese university students are more isolated from the traditional social structure of hierarchical relationships with all their attendant cultural obligations, especially the exigencies of the guilt-driven work ethic. This is an abrupt change from the strictly regulated and psychologically restrictive student life during high school, which is governed by an expected preoccupation with academic achievement and dedicated studying. When these students reach the university, however, they are suddenly spared from these usual social constraints and obligations. This temporary, liminal social detachment and freedom provides them with an opportunity to critically examine their society, and finally discharge and express some pent-up unrelenting dispositions and socially incompatible desires which have been building up inside. Student liminality was most evident in the protests starting in the late sixties. In these movements, students were allowed to 'ritually' rebel and attack social authorities, thus expressing their inner psychological resentments and hostility towards the oppressive social order they would be constrained to enter. The present-day university continues to serve this function as a temporary pressure valve, but in less dramatic ways. Students engage in more modest forms of defiance against the social order by refusing to comply with academic standards and expected student role behaviour. In the liminal freedom of the university period, the students are able to indulge and gratify their personal desire for prolonged fun, relaxation, and enjoyment strictly proscribed in non-liminal periods of restrictive social responsibility.

Release of anti-social psychological material in liminality does not fundamentally disturb or threaten the social order because liminal beings are separated and isolated from society itself. Since individuals in liminality are marginal figures who do not occupy integral positions which are crucial to the operation of the social system, the rebellious violation of social norms in such positions does not threaten overall social functioning or cohesion. Indeed, if such psychological outbursts of social disobedience occurred during non-liminal periods when individuals occupy socially important roles (as in business or industry), the catastrophe would be overwhelming.

The university protests thus became regular occurrences analogous to Gluckman's 'rituals of rebellion' (1963) - an open expression of resentment towards social authorities through an institutionalised protest which ultimately does not have any enduring disruptive effect on the social structure. Such ritualised conflict can gratify psychological needs, but ultimately remains 'safe' for society. In this sense, the students' violent clashes with the police were preplanned and were not the result of peaceful protests getting out of hand and losing control. The 'violent' battles were scheduled, staged, and became expected engagements between police and students, replete with masses of expectant spectators.[34] Since there can be no ritual of rebellion against society unless the social authorities agree to show up and participate, the students always issued plenty of advance warnings (De Vos 1973:435) for a coming ritual showdown with the police, thus providing ample time for police to prepare and engage the students at the designated time and place. Otherwise, the students constantly kept track of where police would be concentrated in order to ensure themselves that a violent conflict would in fact occur (Bakke and Bakke 1971:55). Because of this routinising, or ritualising of protest, the conflict could be localised and contained within the confines of the university. The outside society could be protected from its disruptive effects by encircling the students with armies of well-trained and armed police. University protests could thus remain effective outlets for expressive psychological outbursts without becoming socially threatening.

Institutionalised liminality, through its progressive psychological functioning, also serves to defuse or, if you will, 'burn out' rebellious tendencies of the youthful activist in Japan, instead of producing permanent dedication to social causes. Despite their rebellious behaviour at the university, these young students upon graduation are suddenly willing to occupy the lower rungs of corporate positions characterised by routine, mechanical work. Having behaviourally expressed and gratified such socially prohibited psychological drives in the freedom and safety of liminality, they then seem to be more willing to obediently comply with restrictive requirements of social roles after graduation. Because of the reduction of internal psychological turmoil through the brief sublimated release of socially prohibited inner drives during liminality, they can now suppress such *ura* desires with less psychological pressure and conflict and, as a result, they can more effectively conform to the rigid standards of the social system. Such students seem to feel psychologically refreshed and are able to return to society with a renewed sense of vigour and dedication to normative social role performance. Again, these condoned liminal experiences, by channelling inner *ura* conflicts and defusing psychological tensions in socially non-disruptive and beneficial ways, promote social vitality by ensuring that the wide diversity of personality dispositions is kept within the socially manageable confines of cultural regularities.

In fact, Japanese society abounds with such liminal experiences. Some youth seeking more dramatic and socially rebellious forms of aggressive expression than offered at the current university can, for example, participate in *bosozoku* motorcycle groups, which again allow youth to explore anti-social behavioural possibilities strictly prohibited in later, non-liminal periods (see Sato 1991, Tsuda 1993b). These activities do not reach the levels of social disruption seen in American gang behaviour.

For psychologically restricted business and 'salary men', there is after-work socialising at bars and periodic company parties and outings. During these engagements, salary men can become irresponsibly and safely drunk and therefore express their dissatisfaction with company work conditions and engage in raucous or even infantile behaviour. Likewise, the year end *bonenkai*, or 'forget the old year party', is a massive Japanese ritual cleaning-out of resentment under the safety of total drunkenness. One can even tell the boss off with impunity.

Such liminal situations are located in the flourishing *mizushobai* (water business) liminal zones of every Japanese city. The well-exploited sex industry provides safe outlets for the sexual frustrations that many men experience in their socially restrained and confined domestic lives. In general, the liminal entertainment industry, symbolically and geographically located between work and home, provides daily periods of free relaxation and escape from socially demanding responsibilities. The individual can 'let off steam' and have his ego temporarily titillated by the flattery of accommodating bar hostesses (for various descriptions of these liminal experiences, see Buruma 1984, Clark 1979:207, Lebra 1976: Chapter 7, Plath 1964).

All of these experiences share a similar liminal atmosphere in which individuals are allowed to briefly detach themselves from ordinary social constraints and are given the opportunity to release various types of usually suppressed psychological pressures and impulses before they re-enter commercial or industrial organisations as conforming members. Indeed, these collective liminal experiences provide the necessary psychological lubrication that keeps the Japanese social machine running with the smooth efficiency that sometimes astounds Western observers.

Conclusion: The Future of Social Vitality in Japan

In accounting for the remarkable level of social vitality in Japan from a multilevel analysis, we have focused on the most fundamental aspect of all human social processes - the psychodynamics of individual motivation. For without a sufficient number of individuals properly socialised to maintain cultural continuity, there can be no stable social order and institutional cohesiveness. After assessing some of the peculiar emphases in Japanese family and vocational socialisation that ensure sufficient congruence between 'culture and personality' in each succeeding generation, we have examined the inevitable social conflict which can arise from errant inner proclivities and have suggested some mechanisms, both ideological and liminal, through which disruptive inner pressures are either suppressed or carefully channelled without fundamentally disturbing the basic structure of society.

There are undoubtedly other aspects to social vitality than those to which we have referred. However, regardless of the perspective taken, most social scientists, whether from a psychological or sociological perspective, would probably point to Japan as an example of a relatively 'successful' society. In contrast, the self-reflective assessments by Japanese themselves may not be so positively optimistic. While many outside observers marvel over Japan's past accomplishments and current strength, the Japanese themselves are feeling a deep sense of unease and apprehension about their future. Many feel that the social vitality Japan has so far enjoyed may not last.[35]

Indeed, various issues and problems confront Japan today which could lead to progressively disruptive effects on the social order in the near future. Trade conflicts and general problems with US-Japan relations, based on the tremendous past growth of Japan's economy, may deteriorate before they improve. At the same time, the speculative bubble economy of the eighties has collapsed, resulting in what the Japanese consider to be a serious economic recession. The current Japanese recession is a deep concern especially because the Japanese economic system is so highly dependent on global conditions. Such problems are compounded by a severe labour shortage, fears over a possible decline in the Japanese work ethic,[36] and the need for corporations to further adapt to the shift in economic focus from heavy industry to high technology. Yet, a single-minded orientation that equates social vitality with economic prowess will no longer suffice in a new post-Cold War era where other countries are expecting Japan to assume global political responsibility commensurate with its economic stature. A serious reconsideration of Japanese military defence policies as well as international political behaviour is necessary. Japan will also need to become increasingly involved in environmental issues.

In addition to such global concerns, there are increasing demographic problems at home. Japan now has the highest life expectancy in the world, which is quite an accomplishment considering the hazards of urban congestion, pollution, and the high incidence of smoking and drinking. Yet, such good news is dampened by the problems of an ageing population. Japan's over-65 population is now at about 14 million and is projected to grow to 26 million (18.8 per cent of the population) by 2020 (Ikeuchi 1988:232). This puts additional pressures on corporations, which must deal with an ageing work force, as well as on youth who must support their elders in the future. Even with slower economic growth, Japan is struggling with an extremely severe shortage of unskilled labourers in small and medium-sized manufacturing firms. Japan has come to realise that large amounts of foreign migrant workers may be permanently necessary to maintain economic vitality. According to 1988 estimates, there were 600 000 foreign workers in Japan. Currently, there are well over 260 000 illegal workers in Japan,[37] mainly from Southeast Asian and Middle Eastern countries.[38] This sudden, massive influx of racially and culturally different foreigners, although economically necessary, is a source of great unease for the Japanese, who have cherished their ethnic homogeneity in the past. Reports of discrimination, mistreatment and human rights violations are not infrequent. There have also been some early signs of public intolerance. A racially-based revision of the

Immigration Control and Refugee Recognition Act in June of 1990,[39] allowing foreigners of Japanese descent to be legally accepted as unskilled workers while applying tougher penalties against illegal workers, is perhaps an implicit effort at ethnic 'purification'. This has resulted in a tremendous influx of Japanese-Brazilians, now estimated at 120 000.[40] Treated as strange 'foreigners' by the Japanese because of their alien cultural characteristics, these Japanese-Brazilians are becoming an isolated ethnic minority. When considering the foreign workers issue, the Japanese are currently concerned about social and ethnic conflict, rise in crime, disease and cultural contamination. Although the Japanese, at least at the national and municipal levels, are preparing to cope with such mass immigration and its problems, the full implications will not become clear for several years.

Under such pressures, Japanese attitudes towards foreigners, as well as exclusive conceptions of Japanese-ness, must gradually change in ways that are more congenial to multiethnic accommodation. Other ingrained and traditional cultural orientations will also be transformed as Japan faces new economic, political, and ethnic conditions. For instance, a change in gender attitudes and expectations is possible as women adapt to new social circumstances (such as the labour shortage) and begin to challenge traditional patterns of behaviour involving marriage and the household.[41]

Many of these required social changes are being instituted at the legal level. Examples include the 1985 Equal Employment Opportunity Act for women as well as the recent PKO decision which allows Japan's Self-Defence Forces to participate in United Nations peace-keeping missions. Despite these surface legal changes, however, a corresponding transformation of fundamental attitudes towards women and Japan's international responsibilities has not occurred. Real change in such deeply ingrained cultural beliefs is a much slower and cumbersome process (this might be called a 'cultural lag').

As argued in this chapter, social vitality in the past has required the preservation and maintenance of a well-run sociocultural system ultimately based on conservative socialisation processes. In contrast, social vitality in the future will depend on whether Japan can make some necessary fundamental changes to this traditional system. Given the current situation, a stubborn maintenance of the *status quo* will mean stagnation, not stability, for Japan. Undoubtedly, Japan's remarkable ability to adapt to rapidly shifting circumstances both at home and abroad will continue to be tested.

Notes

1. Such 'normative' Japanese cultural patterns are most characteristic of the urban middle class and do not directly reflect behaviour among those in the working class. Many of the generalisations made about 'Japanese culture' by Japanese scholars are restricted to the middle class, which tends to be the most accessible and familiar to the researcher.
2. As currently used in anthropology, an etic analysis refers to a form of analysis conducted by an outside observer who is guided by an analytic theory alerting one to determinants of behaviour that may not be in the awareness of those participating in the society itself. For example, in Marxian theory, workers may not be aware of patterns of instrumental exploitation governing their employment.
3. An emic approach is one that works out from the conscious views or motivations of the social participants of a society.
4. As Befu remarks in his critique of the group model, 'Those who contributed towards the psychological processes of the group model, too, were bent on demonstrating the functional fit between psychological and social processes and the psycho-social basis of societal structure.' (1980:177).
5. See Befu 1977, 1980, 1989, Krauss, Rohlen and Steinhoff 1984, Eisenstadt and Ben-Ari 1990.
6. This will receive further elaboration later.
7. However, when a certain type of behaviour is inconsistently reinforced - rewarded in one situation by one person and punished in another situation by the same or a different person - the individual will receive conflicting signals. This results in a lower level of cultural internalisation.
8. Doi notes that although guilt has many sources, 'What is characteristic about the Japanese sense of guilt, though, is that it shows itself most sharply when the individual suspects that his action will result in betraying the group to which he belongs.' (1973:49).
9. Indeed, many mothers never directly verbalise the amount of evident suffering they endure in raising the children.
10. Although a passive dependency *amae* relationship creates less ego boundary differentiation between mother and child, this does not mean that the Japanese child has not properly understood or developed a self-other distinction or that this boundary can ever collapse. As Doi remarks (1973:94-5), although a close attachment with the mother is present, the child must first develop a sense that it is an independent entity separate from the mother before it can begin to ask for *amae*. If the child feels no distinction between it and the mother, there would be no need to ask the mother to indulge its passive dependency needs since they would be the same being.
11. This absence of the father may be less prominent for self-employed family business where he can work more closely at home (Befu 1986: 17-18).

12. Among the many possible reasons why Japanese work so hard and long are guilt-driven achievement motivation based on a sense of hierarchical reciprocity (repayment of superior's benevolence), intense peer pressure (shame), competition for promotion, high cost of living, strong sense of company loyalty, etc.

13. Even before formal research on Japan began, foreigners always described Japanese child-rearing practices as remarkably indulgent (Azuma 1986:8-9, Hendry 1986:1).

14. The Japanese preschool continues many of these family child-rearing practices and methods. Like the Japanese mother, preschool teachers again use minimal control, coercive authority, or punishment, preferring instead to create a permissive atmosphere in which understanding of proper behaviour by children is stressed. This socialisation tendency is also reflected in Japanese texts of ethics and morality which are more open-ended, less concerned with rewards/punishments than equivalent American texts (Lanham 1986). See also Befu 1971:156-7, Conroy *et al.* 1980, Hendry 1986: Chapter 4, Lanham 1966:324.

15. The explanations Lewis (1989) offers to explain why greater indulgence produces greater internalisation are unclear and not satisfactory.

16. Plath (1989) uses the word 'circle' to refer to the group of close associates that shapes a person's life course and self.

17. Such 'postmodernist' language confuses far more than it clarifies.

18. Kondo does not sufficiently consider this aspect of Japanese power in her discussion of the work place. Western models of power do not apply here.

19. In this regard, Japanese age-graded hierarchies are an important way to avoid overt social conflict between those of unequal power and status. This contrasts with the West, where *egalitarian* ideologies are used to reduce conflict and social tensions.

20. Although the traditional master-apprentice relationship is rapidly changing, especially with the rise of large corporations, the hierarchical structural relationship is still relevant to the Japanese work place.

21. Of course there are many different experiences and not all hierarchical relationships in Japanese companies conform to this ideal. Yet highly personal relationships are still the norm.

22. Although we have tried to be careful, any essay that deals with such a grand topic as 'social vitality' probably has some generalisations that do not apply to all cases and are thus not completely valid on an empirical level. However, it is hard to say anything theoretically significant in social science without making broad generalisations.

23. As Befu (1986) states, however, such 'resources' may be instrumental or expressive in content.

24. According to Ohnuki-Tierney: 'A Japanese individual, although defined in terms of a kinship network and deeply involved in interpersonal relationships, does not necessarily lack an independent mind or personality. The expectations and rules governing interpersonal

relationships (that is culture) should not be translated directly into individual psychology.' (1984:216-17).

25. Japanese literature demonstrates well the complexities of introspection, and the delving into complex inner motivation of which many Japanese are capable. Neurotic patients also reveal the convoluted inner tensions that can result in particular instances. Japanese acutely experience modern forms of alienation and personal malaise (De Vos 1968, Wagatsuma and De Vos 1978).

26. Again, we are not merely advocating the simplistic generalisation that the Japanese always subordinate their self-interests and inner proclivities for the sake of group consensus.

27. In fact when the decision of the budget committee was rejected by the Diet in 1979, it marked 'the first time in 31 years that a committee decision had been reversed on the floor' (Curtis 1988:38).

28. Of course there are other ways to manage conflict in the legislative process, but this is probably the dominant method.

29. These may include a cultural and psychological unwillingness to engage in open and direct dispute, the financial costs, the lack of easy access to competent legal service, elite control and discouragement of litigation, or social ostracism and pressure against litigation (see Taniguchi 1984, De Vos 1984:7, Upham 1987:22, Hendry 1989: 190-1).

30. Indeed, the Japanese bureaucratic elite actively discourages formal litigation and promotes alternative, informal types of dispute resolution. If the elite allows conflict and protest to erupt into the *omote* through the active use of formal litigation process and courts, this would destroy their control over policymaking and social change and threaten the sociopolitical *status quo* (Upham 1987:16-22).

31. During the Pacific war, instances of Japanese brutality were indeed visited on peoples under the control of the Japanese army. Such usually suppressed psychological aggression and violence are also revealed in TATs (Thematic Apperception Test), which measures collective patterns of subjective experience relevant to interpersonal concerns. As De Vos and Murakami have shown (1974:156-7), Japanese lower-class youth show a higher rate of concern with discord, disharmony and violence (including active and passive forms, verbal aggression, and physical violence) than would be intuitively expected from the restrained, conforming, and well-mannered Japanese.

32. Of course much more can be said about the self-destructive aspects of the *ura*. This is, however, beyond the scope of this paper (see De Vos 1973, Chapter XVII).

33. Such Japanese forms of psychotherapy such as Morita therapy treat the socially incapacitated by restoring sufficient positive motivation to apply oneself to required tasks rather than exploring the origin of the symptoms (see Reynolds 1980).

34. Although the analogy can be taken too far, the student protests perhaps resembled a football game. The participants are 'serious' (as shown by the expected injuries), but the entire activity remains a ritual with no really socially threatening consequences.

35. In a recent *Asahi Shimbun* poll (1/1/91, p. 12), only 50 per cent of those surveyed believed that Japan would remain a superpower in the 21st century. A surprising 37 per cent felt that Japan's prosperity is in danger, with the older generation expressing more pessimism than youth.

36. This seems unlikely (for instance, see Vaughn 1988).

37. This is a conservative estimate based on recent Ministry of Labour figures.

38. Immigration authorities have not been strict. Although many foreign workers have been denied entry and a number of deportations have occurred, the government in general has (perhaps purposely) been lax towards illegal workers.

39. According to this revision, other legal foreign workers include 'trainees' and students and those involved in research, education, and company transfers, and some professional services.

40. The total number of Latin American *nikkejin* (Japanese descendants living abroad) who are currently in Japan is estimated at about 150 000, according to the Ministry of Labour.

41. A possible rise in more career-oriented women in turn would mean a decline in maternal dedication to children and their proper education and upbringing. The Japanese would view this as a grave threat to their future.

References

Ames, Walter. 1981. *Police and Community in Japan*. Berkeley: University of California Press.

Azuma, Hiroshi. 1982. Current Trends in Studies of Behavioral Development in Japan. *International Journal of Behavioral Development* 5:153-69.

1986. 'Why Study Child Development in Japan?' In Harold Stevenson, Hiroshi Azuma and Kenji Hakuta (eds), *Child Development and Education in Japan*. New York: W. H. Freeman and Company, pp. 3-12.

Bachnik, Jane M. 1986. 'Time, Space and Person in Japanese Relationships'. In Joy Hendry and Jonathan Webber (eds), *Interpreting Japanese Society: Anthropological Approaches*. JASO Occasional Papers 5. Oxford: Anthropological Society of Oxford, pp. 49-75.

Bayley, David. 1984. 'Police, Crime and the Community in Japan'. In George A. De Vos (ed.), *Institutions for Change in Japanese Society*. Berkeley: Institute of East Asian Studies, University of California, pp. 177-99.

Befu, Harumi. 1971. *Japan: An Anthropological Introduction*. San Francisco: Chandler Publishing Company.

1977. 'Power in The Great White Tower: Contribution to Social Exchange Theory'. In Raymond D. Fogelson and Richard N. Adams (eds), *The Anthropology of Power*. New York: Academic Press, pp. 77-87.

1980. 'The Group Model of Japanese Society and an Alternative'. *Rice University Studies* 66(1):169-87.

1986. 'The Social and Cultural Background of Child Development in Japan and the United States'. In Harold Stevenson, Hiroshi Azuma and Kenji Hakuta (eds), *Child Development and Education in Japan*. New York: W. H. Freeman and Company, pp.13-27.

1989. 'A Theory of Social Exchange as Applied to Japan'. In Yoshio Sugimoto and Ross E. Moore (eds), *Constructs for Understanding Japan*. London: Kegan Paul International, pp. 39-66.

Benedict, Ruth. 1974. *The Chrysanthemum and the Sword*. New York: Meridian.

Boocock, Sarane Spence. 1989. Controlled Diversity: An Overview of the Japanese Preschool System. *The Journal of Japanese Studies* 15(1): 41-66.

Buruma, Ian. 1984. *Behind the Mask: On Sexual Demons, Sacred Mothers, Transvestites, Gangsters, and other Japanese Cultural Heroes*. New York: Meridian.

Calder, Kent E. 1982. '*Kanryo* vs. *Shomin*: Contrasting Leadership in Postwar Japan'. In Terry Edward MacDougall (ed.), *Political Leadership in Contemporary Japan*. Ann Arbor: University of Michigan Press, pp. 1-28.

Campbell, John Creighton. 1984. 'Policy Conflict and Its Resolution within the Governmental System'. In Ellis S. Krauss, Thomas P. Rohlen and Patricia G. Steinhoff (eds), *Conflict in Japan*. Honolulu: University of Hawaii Press, pp. 294-334.

Caudill, William A. and Carmi Schooler. 1973. 'Child Behavior and Child Rearing in Japan and the United States: An Interim Report'. *Journal of Nervous and Mental Disease* 157:323-38.

Caudill, William and Helen Weinstein. 1986. 'Maternal Care and Infant Behavior in Japan and America'. In Takie Sugiyama Lebra and William P. Lebra (eds), *Japanese Culture and Behavior. Selected Readings*. Honolulu: University of Hawaii Press, pp. 201-46.

Clark, Rodney. 1979. *The Japanese Company*. New Haven: Yale University Press.

Conroy, Mary, Robert D. Hess, Hiroshi Azuma and Keiko Kashiwagi. 1980. 'Maternal Strategies for Regulating Children's Behavior: Japanese and American Families'. *Journal of Cross-Cultural Psychology* 11(2):153-72.

Curtis, Gerald L. 1988. *The Japanese Way of Politics*. New York: Columbia University Press.

De Vos, George A. 1968. 'Suicide in Cross-Cultural Perspective'. In H. L. P. Resnick (ed.), *Suicidal Behaviors: Diagnosis and Management*. Boston: Little, Brown and Co., pp. 105-34.

1973. *Socialization for Achievement: Essays on the Cultural Psychology of the Japanese*. Berkeley: University of California Press.

1980. 'Ethnic Adaptation and Minority Status'. *Journal of Cross-Cultural Psychology* 11(1): 101-24.

1984. 'The Police as an Institution for Change'. In George A. De Vos (ed.), *Institutions for Change in Japanese Society*. Berkeley: Institute of East Asian Studies, University of California, pp.174-6.

1984. 'Introduction: Trends toward Social Democracy in Japan'. In George A. De Vos (ed.), *Institutions for Change in Japanese Society*. Berkeley: Institute of East Asian Studies, University of California, pp. 3-19.

1985. 'Dimensions of the Self in Japanese Culture'. In George A. De Vos, Francis L. K. Hsu and Anthony J. Marsella (eds), *Culture and Self: Asian and Western Perspectives*. New York: Tavistock Publications, pp. 141-84.

1992. *Social Cohesion and Alienation: Minorities in the United States and Japan*. Boulder, CO: Westview Press

De Vos, George A. and Eiji Murakami. 1974. 'Violence and Aggression in Fantasy: A Comparison of American and Japanese Lower-Class Youth'. In William P. Lebra (ed.), *Youth, Socialization, and Mental Health*. Honolulu: University of Hawaii Press, pp. 153-77.

De Vos, George A. and Marcelo M. Suarez-Orozco. 1986. 'Child Development in Japan and the United States: Prospectives of Cross-Cultural Comparisons'. In Harold Stevenson, Hiroshi Azuma and Kenji Hakuta (eds), *Child Development and Education in Japan*. New York: W. H Freeman and Company, pp. 289-98.

De Vos, George A. and Hiroshi Wagatsuma. 1966. *Japan's Invisible Race: Caste in Culture and Personality*. Berkeley: University of California Press.

1970. 'Status and Role in Changing Japan'. In Georgene H. Seward and Robert C. Williamson (eds), *Sex Roles in Changing Society*. New York: Random House, pp. 334-70.

Doi, Takeo L. 1973. *The Anatomy of Dependence*. Tokyo: Kodansha International.

1986. *The Anatomy of Self: The Individual Versus Society*. Tokyo: Kodansha International.

Eisenstadt, Shmuel, N. and Eyal Ben-Ari (eds). 1990. *Japanese Models of Conflict Resolution*. London: Kegan Paul International.

Enomoto, Jerry. 1984. 'The Police: Structural and Cultural Considerations in Comparing Japan and the United States'. In George A. De Vos (ed.), *Institutions for Change in Japanese Society*. Berkeley: Institute of East Asian Studies, University of California, pp. 230-5.

Eto, Jun. 1979. 'The Breakdown of Motherhood is Wrecking our Children'. *Japan Echo* 6:102-9.

Gresser, Juhan, Koichiro Fujikura and Akio Morishima. 1981. *Environmental Law in Japan*. Cambridge: MIT Press.

Gluckman, Max. 1963. *Order and Rebellion in Tribal Africa*. London: Cohen & West.

Henderson, Dan Fenno. *Conciliation and Japanese Law*, 2 vols. Seattle: University of Washington Press.

Hendry, Joy. 1986. *Becoming Japanese: The World of the Pre-School Child*. Manchester, UK: Manchester University Press.

1989. *Understanding Japanese Society*. London: Routledge.

Hess, Robert D. *et al.* 1986. 'Family Influences on School Readiness and Achievement in Japan and the United States: An Overview of a Longitudinal Study'. In Harold Stevenson, Hiroshi Azuma and Kenji Hakuta (eds), *Child Development and Education In Japan*. New York: W. H. Freeman and Company, pp. 147-66.

Hoshino, Kanehiro. 1980. 'Organized Criminal Gangs and Recidivism'. *Japanese Journal of Sociological Criminology* 5:42-63.

1984. 'Post-war Law Enforcement: Its Social Impact'. In George De Vos (ed.), *Institutions for Change in Japanese Society*. Berkeley: Institute of East Asian Studies, University of California, pp. 199-223.

Ikeuchi, Masato. 1988. 'The Impact of Aging'. In Daniel I. Okimoto and Thomas P. Rohlen (eds), *Inside the Japanese System: Readings on Contemporary Society and Political Economy*. Stanford: Stanford University Press, pp. 231-3

Inkeles, Alex and Daniel J. Levinson. 1969. 'National Character: the Study of Modal Personality and Sociocultural Systems'. In Gardner Lindzey and Elliot Aronson (eds), *The Handbook of Social Psychology*, second edition, vol. 4. Reading MA: Addison-Wesley Publishing Company, pp. 418-506.

Ishida, Takeshi. 1984. 'Conflict and Its Accommodation: *Omote-Ura* and *Uchi-Soto* Relations'. In Ellis S. Krauss, Thomas P. Rohlen and Patricia G.

Steinhoff (eds), *Conflict in Japan*. Honolulu: University of Hawaii Press, pp. 16-38.

Kawai, Hayao. 1986. 'Violence in the Home: Conflict between Two Principles - Maternal and Paternal'. In Takie Sugiyama Lebra and William P. Lebra (eds), *Japanese Culture and Behavior: Selected Readings*. Honolulu: University of Hawaii Press, pp. 297-306.

Kawashima, Takeyoshi and Yosiyuki Noda. 1988, 'Dispute Resolution in Contemporary Japan'. In Daniel I. Okimoto and Thomas P. Rohlen (eds), *Inside the Japanese System: Readings on Contemporary Society and Political Economy*. Stanford: Stanford University Press, pp. 191-3.

Kondo, Dorinne K. 1987. 'Creating an Ideal Self: Theories of Selfhood and Pedagogy at a Japanese Ethics Retreat'. *Ethos* 15(3):241-72.

1990. *Crafting Selves: Power, Gender, and Discourses of Identity in a Japanese Workplace*. Chicago: University of Chicago Press.

Krauss, Ellis S. 1984a. 'Conflict and Its Resolution in Postwar Japan'. In Ellis S Krauss, Thomas P. Rohlen and Patricia G. Steinhoff (eds), *Conflict in Japan*. Honolulu: University of Hawaii Press, pp. 377-97 .

1984b. 'Conflict in the Diet: Towards Conflict Management in Parliamentary Politics'. In Ellis S. Krauss, Thomas P. Rohlen and Patricia G. Steinhoff (eds), *Conflict in Japan*. Honolulu: University of Hawaii Press, pp. 243-93.

1984c. 'Protest and Social Change: A Commentary'. In George A. De Vos (ed.), *Institutions for Change in Japanese Society*. Berkeley: Institute of East Asian Studies, University of California, pp. 166-72.

Krauss, Ellis S., Thomas P. Rohlen and Patricia G. Steinhoff. 1984. 'Conflict: An Approach to the Study of Japan'. In Ellis S. Krauss, Thomas P. Rohlen and Patricia G. Steinhoff (eds), *Conflict in Japan*. Honolulu: University of Hawaii Press, pp. 3-15.

Lanham, Betty B. 1962. 'Aspects of Child Care in Japan'. In Bernard S. Silberman (ed.), *Japanese Character and Culture: A Book of Selected Readings*. Tucson, AZ: The University of Arizona Press, pp. 220-236.

1966. 'The Psychological Orientation of the Mother-Child Relationship in Japan'. *Monumenta Nipponica* 21:322-3.

1986. 'Ethics and Moral Precepts Taught in Schools of Japan and the United States'. In Takie Sugiyama Lebra and William P. Lebra (eds), *Japanese Culture and Behavior: Selected Readings*. Honolulu: University of Hawaii Press, pp. 280-96.

Lebra, Takie Sugiyama. 1971. 'The Social Mechanism of Guilt and Shame: The Japanese Case'. *Anthropological Quarterly* 44:241-55.

1976. *Japanese Patterns of Behavior*. Honolulu: University of Hawaii Press.

1983. 'Shame and Guilt: A Psychocultural View of the Japanese Self'. *Ethos* 11:192-209.

1984a. 'Nonconfrontational Strategies for Management of Interpersonal Conflicts'. In Ellis S. Krauss, Thomas P. Rohlen and Patricia G. Steinhoff (eds), *Conflict in Japan*. Honolulu: University of Hawaii Press, pp. 41-60.

1984b. *Japanese Women: Constraint and Fulfillment*. Honolulu: University of Hawaii Press.

Lee, Changsoo and George A. De Vos. 1981. *Koreans in Japan*. Berkeley: University of California Press

Lewis, Catherine. 1989. 'From Indulgence to Internalization: Social Control in the Early School Years'. *Journal of Japanese Studies* 15(1): 139-57.

Lock, Margaret. 1991. 'Flawed Jewels and National Dis/Order: Narrative on National Dissent in Japan'. *The Journal of Psychohistory* 18(4):507-31.

Mills, C. Wright. 1956. *The Power Elite*. New York: Oxford University Press.

National Police Agency. 1979. *The Cost Benefit of the Methods for Controlling Organized Crime*. Tokyo.

Nishimura, Hiromi. 1984. 'Environmental Pollution Cases: Recent Trends and Their Implications'. In George A. De Vos (ed.), *Institutions for Change in Japanese Society*. Berkeley: Institute of East Asian Studies, University of California, pp. 41-52.

Ohnuki-Tierney, Emiko. 1984 *Illness and Culture in Contemporary Japan: An Anthropological View*. Cambridge: Cambridge University Press.

1990. 'The Ambivalent Self of the Contemporary Japanese'. *Cultural Anthropology* 5(2):197-216.

Okimoto, Daniel I. 1988. 'Liberal-Democratic Party Dominance in the Diet'. In Daniel I. Okimoto and Thomas P. Rohlen (eds), *Inside the Japanese System: Readings on Contemporary Society and Political Economy*. Stanford: Stanford University Press, pp. 175-8.

Pharr, Susan J. 1982. 'Liberal Democrats in Disarray: Intergenerational Conflict in the Conservative Camp'. In Terry Edward MacDougall (ed.), *Political Leadership in Contemporary Japan*. Ann Arbor: University of Michigan Press, pp. 29-50.

Plath, David W. 1964 *The After Hours: Modern Japan and the Search for Enjoyment*. Berkeley: University of California Press.

1989. 'Arc, Circle, and Sphere: Schedules for Selfhood'. In *Constructs for Understanding Japan*. Yoshio Sugimoto and Ross E. Mouer (eds), London: Kegan Paul International, pp. 67-93.

Reich, Michael. 1984, 'Crisis and Routine: Pollution Reporting by the Japanese Press'. In George A. De Vos (ed.), *Institutions for Change in Japanese Society*. Berkeley: Institute of East Asian Studies, University of California, pp. 148-65.

Reynolds, David K. 1980. *The Quiet Therapies: Japanese Pathways to Personal Growth*. Honolulu: University of Hawaii Press.

Rohlen, Thomas P. 1974. *For Harmony and Strength: Japanese White-Collar Organization in Anthropological Perspective*. Berkeley: University of California Press.

1983. *Japan's High Schools*. Berkeley. University of California Press.

Sahlins, Marshall D. 1976. *Culture and Practical Reason*. Chicago: The University of Chicago Press.

Sato, Ikuya. 1991. *Kamikaze Biker: Parody and Anomy in Affluent Japan*. Chicago: The University of Chicago Press.

Shain, I. J. 'Cy.' 1984. 'Recent Trends in Japanese Criminality: Some Comparative Perspectives'. In George A. De Vos (ed.), *Institutions for Change in Japanese Society*. Berkeley: Institute of East Asian Studies, University of California, pp. 224-30.

Simons, Carol. 1991. 'The Education Mother *(Kyoiku Mama)*'. In Barbara Finkelstein, Anne E. Imamura and Joseph J. Tobin (eds), *Transcending Stereotypes: Discovering Japanese Culture and Education*. Yarmouth, MA: Intercultural Press, Inc., pp. 58-65.

Slote, Walter. 1986. *The Psycho-Cultural Dynamics of the Confucian Family: Past and Present*. Seoul: The International Cultural Society of Korea.

Smith, Robert J. and Ella Lury Wiswell. 1982. *The Women of Suye Mura*. Chicago: The University of Chicago Press.

Spiro, Melford E. 1961a. 'An Overview and Suggested Reorientation'. In Francis L. K. Hsu (ed.), *Psychological Anthropology: Approaches to Culture and Personality*. Homewood, IL: Dorsey Press, pp. 573-607.

1961b. 'Social Systems, Personality, and Functional Analysis'. In Bert Kaplan (ed.), *Studying Personality Cross-Culturally*. New York: Harper & Row, pp. 93-127.

Suzuki, Shigenobu. 1983. 'What's Wrong with the Education System'. *JapanEcho* 10:17-23.

Tanaka, Hideo. 1988. 'The Role of Law and Lawyers in Japanese Society'. In Daniel I. Okimoto and Thomas P. Rohlen (eds), *Inside the Japanese System: Readings on Contemporary Society and Political Economy*. Stanford: Stanford University Press, pp. 194-6.

Taniguchi, Yasuhei. 1984. 'The Post-War Court System as an Instrument for Social Change'. In George A. De Vos (ed.), *Institutions for Change in Japanese Society*. Berkeley: Institute of East Asian Studies, University of California, pp. 20-40.

Turner, Victor. 1969. 'The Ritual Process: Structure and Anti-Structure'. Ithaca, New York: Cornell University Press.

Tsuda, Takeyuki. 1993a. 'The Psychosocial Functions of Liminality. The Japanese University Experience'. *Journal of Psychohistory* 20(3):305-30.

1993b. Book Review of *Kamikaze Biker: Parody and Anomy in Affluent Japan*, by Ikuya Sato. *Anthropological Quarterly* 66(2): 101-3.

Tsurushima, Setsure. 1984. 'Human Rights Issues and the Status of the Burakumin and Koreans in Japan'. In George A. De Vos (ed.), *Institutions for Change in Japanese Society*. Berkeley: Institute of East Asian Studies, University of California, pp. 83-113.

Tu, Wei Ming. 1986. 'An Inquiry on the Five Relationships in Confucian Humanism'. In Walter Slote (ed.), *The Psycho-Cultural Dynamics of the Confucian Family: Past and Present*. Seoul: The International Cultural Society of Korea.

Upham, Frank K. 1987. *Law and Social Change in Postwar Japan*. Cambridge: Harvard University Press.

Vaughn, Curtis. 1988. *Cognitive Independence, Social Independence, and Achievement Orientation: A Comparison of Japanese and U.S. Students*. PhD Dissertation, University of California at Berkeley.

Vogel, Ezra and Suzanne H. Vogel. 1961. 'Family Security, Personal Immaturity and Emotional Health in a Japanese Sample'. *Marriage and Family Living* 23(2):161-6.

Wagatsuma, Hiroshi and George A. De Vos. 1978. 'A Koan of Sincerity: Osama Dazai'. *Hartford Studies in Literature* 10(1-3):121-4.

   1984. *Heritage of Endurance: Family Patterns and Delinquency Formation in Urban Japan*. Berkeley: University of California Press.

Wetherall, William and George A. De Vos. 1975. 'Ethnic Minorities in Japan'. In William Veenhoven (ed.), *Case Studies on Human Rights and Fundamental Freedoms, A World Survey*, Vol. 1. The Hague, Martinus Nijhoff.

White, James W. 1984. 'Protest and Change in Contemporary Japan: An Overview'. In George A. De Vos (ed.), *Institutions for Change in Japanese Society*. Berkeley: Institute of East Asian Studies, University of California, pp. 53-82.

Yamamura, Yoshiaki. 1986. 'The Child in Japanese Society'. In Harold Stevenson, Hiroshi Azuma and Kenji Hakuta (eds), *Child Development and Education in Japan*. New York: W. H. Freeman and Company, pp. 28-38.

Annex
Excerpts from the Discussions at the Conference

Introductory Remarks

A. Clesse: Good morning, ladies and gentlemen. In the name of the Institute for European and International Studies of Luxembourg and of the Japan Institute of International Affairs, I would like to welcome you to this meeting on 'the *vitality* of Japan in a comparative perspective'. Since the appropriate management of time will be our most severe challenge, I will give the floor, without losing any time, at once to Ambassador Matsunaga, who will say a few introductory words in the name of the Japan Institute of International Affairs, of which he is the President.

N. Matsunaga: Thank you, Mr Chairman. I would like to introduce myself a little bit: I was born in 1923 in Tokyo. At the end of the last World War, I was drafted into the Navy during the last moments of the war. When I entered the Navy, there were no ships or planes, so I stayed, fortunately, on land. Immediately after the war, I entered the Ministry of Foreign Affairs and served until two years ago. During 44 years in the foreign service, I served in several countries abroad, including France, the Soviet Union, Switzerland, and Mexico before becoming Vice Minister of Foreign Affairs in 1983. In 1985, I was appointed Ambassador to Washington, where I served for five years, and returned back to Japan at the end of 1989. As I said, I retired from the service two years ago and became the President of the Japan Institute of International Affairs.

It is a great pleasure and honour to welcome you all here to Tokyo for this third meeting of the *vitality* of nations. On behalf of the Japan Institute of International Affairs, I would like to thank Dr Clesse and the Institute for European and International Studies for making such an important and timely meeting possible. And I look forward with great anticipation to the discussions, conclusions, and questions to be raised over the next two days. The timing of this conference and the importance of the subject is, by now, all too apparent in the period of profound change and restructuring in the international community. The notion of *vitality*, whose meaning needs continual reassessment and defining as we make our historical examination and comparison, must be viewed with an entirely new perspective in this post-Cold War, post-Gulf War world. With the decline of the Soviet Union and the democratisation of Eastern and Central Europe, bipolar superpower rivalry is being superseded by an ambiguous, but nevertheless apparent, new world order promoting multilateral linkages among interdependent nations.

Already, we can see the emergence of three main peers in this new order: the United States, Europe, and Asia, which, to a large degree, are driven by the dictates of economic principles, economic priorities. The question with which we should concern ourselves within this forum is what this fundamental restructuring means for the process of evolution among nations under the measuring index of *vitality*.

A few years ago, Paul Kennedy's important examination of the Rise and Fall of Great Powers helped initiate this debate and raised many of the questions which were addressed in the previous two meetings of this project, and which we must address in the context of Japan and the Asian Pacific region. Recently, Francis Fukuyama has published a controversial book updating his 1989 essay on the End of History. Despite the implausibility of such a conclusion, it nevertheless raises interesting questions regarding the historical evolution, which we should consider in our discussions and application of the vitality concept to our designated regions of the world.

In recognition of the unprecedented changes gripping the international stage over the past few years, we are eager to explore the untapped potential and fruitful possibilities that a Japan-EC relationship can hold for the future. In line with this, we are particularly delighted to assist Luxembourg's Institute for European and International Studies in holding this conference. With Luxembourg at the heart of Europe, there is no better way, in our view, to endorse and further promote the foundations laid by the Japan-EC Joint Declaration of last July, which was promoted under the auspices of Luxembourg's chairmanship.

F. Scott Fitzgerald once said that *vitality* shows not only in the ability to persist, but in the ability to start over. In this post-Cold War, post-Gulf War world, some of the nations in our re-aligning international community will be attempting to start over, and others will face the equally challenging prospect of merely persisting. What we might find is that, for countries like Japan and many of the other advanced nations in the West, there may be not only a desire to persist, but also a more profound need to start over in a certain sense. In its very essence, *vitality* supports the ability to adapt and survive and the unexpected and inevitable changes in the world. In this sense, the victors of the Cold War will be those who have the courage and the foresight to embrace their *vitality* and test it in uncharted waters.

Now, before closing, I would like to submit for your consideration during our discussions of today and tomorrow two or three points which I consider extremely important when we look at the actual situation of the world community. First of all, what has brought about the ending of the Cold War and subsequent collapse of the Soviet Union? It is quite apparent that the ending of the Cold War demonstrated and proved the failure and defeat of the so-called 'Soviet Communism' in confrontation against the so-called 'Western world'. However, whether this proves the final success and victory of capitalism and free democracies is a different question, and it seems that this question remains to be answered in the future. In other words, we democracies of today are facing an enormous challenge in the world, whether the basic principles of freedom, democracy, and market economy will ensure the stability and prosperity of the entire world. In that sense, Japan, together with Europe and the United States, is met with an urgent responsibility to put forth our best effort to demonstrate to the world community that these basic principles will be the basis of the new order of the world community.

The second point I would like to put forward is that the future we have before us is covered by a thick cloud of uncertainty, instability, and unpredictability. Nobody knows or can predict what will happen within one year, or even within six months, in Asia, Russia, and other parts of the world. And this makes it even more important that we concentrate our efforts and attention into what we are going to do today and tomorrow.

The third point concerns the world economy. It is quite apparent, in my view, that the world economy has become a global economy of inter-dependency. In one sense, the world economy has become very small, but with tremendous varieties and differences of each component. Every nation has its own history, culture, tradition, etc. But it is my strong belief that differences, varieties, or complexities do not and should not create any obstacle for international cooperation. At the same time, we are seeing a general recession of the entire world economy which, together with the points I mentioned above, leads me to strongly believe that we are facing a very challenging task in determining a common objective and way of cooperation by which we will be able to look at the possibility of ensuring the stability and the prosperity of the entire world community.

I want to thank once again all participants to this meeting for coming here this morning and would like to assure particularly all the foreign participants that we at the Japan Institute of International Affairs will do everything possible to make your stay enjoyable. And, therefore, I would like to beg all participants not to hesitate to let us know if you need any help or assistance. Thank you very much, Mr Chairman.

A. Clesse: Thank you very much, Ambassador Matsunaga. You also provided us with some interesting conceptual clues, to which we will come back in a moment. First, I would like to introduce the President of the Executive Committee of the Institute for European and International Studies of Luxembourg, Monsieur Fernand Braun.

F. Braun: Ladies and Gentlemen, I wish on the behalf of the Institute for European and International Studies of Luxembourg, on behalf of Dr Clesse particularly, to welcome you also on this occasion. And I would like to stress how grateful we are for the help our Institute was given by the Japan Institute of International Affairs, without which this event would not have happened. I wish to say a few words to those of you who are new to debates organised by the Luxembourg Institute. Who are we? First, I would say that we are a very young Institute indeed, less than two years old. The Institute was created by Dr Clesse and some of his associates. I must also acknowledge the financial help of the Luxembourg government; otherwise, we would not have been able to launch this venture. The activities were built upon an exemplary relationship which had been established by the Luxembourg-Harvard Association, which was also guided for a number of years by Dr Clesse. We have over the last two years organised important symposia on subjects related to the one which was suggested by the Ambassador a few moments ago, on an issue which is most important and changing at every moment, largely of course in Europe; as we are all Europeans, our attention was very much addressed to the changes in Eastern and Central Europe. And I think we have been able to bring about exchanges of views which were put also into policymaking of our member states and the European community.

We consider the *vitality* of nations a most important project, a very ambitious one, a research project which will extend over several years, with important works realised and published, in different forms and at different moments. Discussions, by the way, with Eastern European countries showed that *vitality* for them meant first identity and viability, rather than *vitality* as we, in the Western, industrial part of the world might consider it, as an issue of people well-established in their identities and having showed their viability. So, *vitality* was a way of enhancing their viability and their identity. In the case of Central and Eastern Europe, the problem is not yet this. Relating to this, we need to face the new pattern and determine how to enhance our *vitality*, or in economic terms, our competitiveness. It is quite evident that competitiveness is not necessarily *vitality*. Without copying systems that are not always appropriate, how can we learn from each other? For many of us, it is also an examination of elements we have not always been conscious enough of, perhaps not so much by researchers, but by those more intensively preoccupied with guiding policies. As I said, competitiveness is not the only measuring device for *vitality*; it is only one.

The professors and academics who have been coming to this meeting and for whose presence we are so grateful come from many different sectors. It is a multidisciplinary event; it is not just economics. It is politics, sociology, and history at the same time. So, I hope we will benefit from the insights of each of you and that you all will benefit at the same time. I would like to close my remarks here so that you can commence at once with the important discussions, following the procedure which Dr Clesse will now suggest.

A. Clesse: Thank you, Monsieur Braun. It is now half past nine. I will just make a few remarks regarding the structure of the subsequent sessions, and also some administrative arrangements. This meeting will consist of mainly two parts. One will be the description of the *vitality* of Japan in recent years up until the present. The more empirical part, the manifestations of *vitality*, will focus largely on social sciences, concern dependent variables, such as economic growth. The second major part will focus on the explanation of the *vitality* of Japan. Looking at the sources of *vitality*, it will focus more strongly on independent variables. There will be a third part evaluating the *vitality* of Japan looking at the limits of *vitality* and, of course, an outlook for the future *vitality* of this country.

This should be a brainstorming meeting with the purpose of looking at the basic elements and at the sources of *vitality*. We should also try to see how we may best approach the phenomenon and what we should mainly focus on, where there is a need for more investigation, which questions require more clarification, on which issues possible future research should focus. In other words, we should consider what has been done and what has not been done so far. We should certainly not try to come up with definite answers to questions that are extremely complex. Identifying the significant questions, stating the major need for further clarification will contribute to creating a sound basis for future research efforts. This could be in the form of studies to be commissioned to individual scholars, or teams of scholars, for those present here today and tomorrow who have an interest in the project. I think that the sheer composition of our group, with participants from so many different backgrounds and from so many different countries, should also be an important prerequisite for the issues under discussion. This project should take a more operational form, on the basis of the studies I have just mentioned; but we will come to this later. Let me remind you that the contributions here should be either short or very short. As the moderator of the discussions, my major task will be to enforce a certain discipline.

Perhaps we should start this morning with a session of conceptual brainstorming. Professor Matsunaga has already mentioned a few interesting points, as I said. For example, he commented on the capability not only to persist, but the ability to start over. Resilience, or resiliency as the word is in English, I think is an important factor in speaking about *vitality*. He mentioned also the ability to adapt and survive in the face of the unexpected, inevitable changes. Adaptability, for example, is also a very important element; we have in previous meetings discussed such notions. Competitiveness as a measure of *vitality* was also mentioned.

I have discussed conceptual elements with some of you in the past weeks and months, so perhaps some participants would like to make a few reflections in this context. I thought, for example, since I have discussed these arguments with them, Professor Inoguchi, Ivan Hall, David Arase, and whoever else, would like to make at this point some remarks of a conceptual character. Before then, we would come to one of the major aspects describing the economic *vitality* of Japan. Kenneth Courtis cannot be with us today and I know that he has some interesting ideas in this regard, but he will be here tomorrow and will certainly comment on the sources of *vitality*. But if you agree, Professor Inoguchi, would you be prepared to make a few remarks?

General Considerations

T. Inoguchi: Thank you, Mr Chairman. I would like to discuss two issues: Firstly, our nations and nation states will be made to be of primary importance in organising mankind in the future. This can be disputed, but I will discuss this aspect. Second, *vitality* can be defined easily and succinctly as the ability to meet challenges from within and from without. But that is not enough. We have to go even deeper than that. And especially at a time of great change and upheaval, I think the perspective one has to adopt to discuss the *vitality* of nations must be broad in the simple sense. Being political scientists, we are quite interested in these kinds of things.

One way has been suggested by Professor Samuel Huntington. In one of the previous meetings he has depicted artistic activities and technological innovation, economic growth and prosperity, military power and the capacity for leadership and status; that is fine, wonderful. But I would like simpler ones, a little more vivid ones, and I would like to propose two key variables whereby we can look at the *vitality* of Japan in a comparative perspective. Somewhat more illustratively, one variable would be the *ability to learn*, however, not only to learn, but *also to forget*. I think the latter aspect is very important because, as you said, generals tend to fight the last war endlessly. You have to forget in order to meet the challenges, the nature of which is very different from previous ones. So I would like to stress the ability to learn and to forget, depending on the situation, and depending on the resources you have.

The second variable is about the *ability to cooperate and to compete*. This looks contradictory, but sometimes you have to cooperate among yourselves as well as externally. Also, you have to compete among yourselves. I will explain very briefly.

First, the learning: this is important. If you look at the Japanese history, 16th century or the mid-19th century, this is an era of great upheaval. If you look at the 16th century, great inventions came. This was the military technology called the guns. It was by chance imported to the small island in the southernmost island, Kyushu, in 1534. It came by chance, but the Lord of Tanegashima, Mr Tokitaka, learned to shoot by himself a week after the guns arrived. A few months later, the local gunsmiths started to produce guns, though imperfect in many ways. And ten years later, the Portuguese gunsmiths were invited to refine the local smiths' technology. And they started to produce guns. And the Lord of Tanegashima, Mr Tokitaka, conquered the adjacent island with these guns.

And in 1575, the great unifier of Japan of the warring period, Mr Oda Nobunaga, conquered Japan by the most advanced military technology ever invented by humankind in the Battle of Nagashino, 1575. You must have seen this battle through Akira Kurosawa's movie. The musketry volleys, the brand new strategy was guns, enormous guns, assembled and utilised very flexibly, in a very dynamic manner. It was only in 1631 when these musketry volleys were practised in Europe by Gustavus Adolphus at the Battle of Breitenfeld near Leipzig.

So this kind of very speedy and effective learning is one of the aspects which is necessary to keep *vital* the fate of nations, I think. Of course, no less important is forgetting. The Japanese started to forget all of these advanced military technologies one century later. Because the challenge came from within, not from without. How to keep internal unity, peace and stability through non-military means became the primary preoccupation. By mid-17th century, our ideas and the institutions of military technology were kept very dormant. So by the time Westerners arrived in the mid-19th century again, we were quite out of date in terms of military technology, but another kind of learning started at that time. At any rate, this just is to stress how important it is to learn and to forget because the nature of challenges differs tremendously.

The second key variable is called 'compete and cooperate'. If you meet challenges from within and without, you have to cooperate. One great statement is not enough. Collective action is necessary. Therefore, you have to cooperate somehow. But cooperation is not enough, the intensity of national identity is not enough. You can hate other people, you can unite, you can enjoy solidarity among yourselves in facing a foreign enemy. But that is not enough. You have to compete among yourselves within your society as well as with other societies, for the simple reason that you have to enhance and enrich yourself. You have to compete among yourselves.

And these kinds of variables did play very important roles in mid-16th century to mid-17th century periods of great upheaval, as well as during the 19th and 20th centuries. I will not give you more historical examples; I think I will stop here, again, just to underline two key variables: the ability to learn and to forget, and the ability to cooperate and compete. And the latter key variable is no less important than the former, which is often given more stress. The latter one must be stressed as well.

A. Clesse: Thank you. Ivan Hall, would you be prepared to continue with a few remarks?

I. Hall: Yes. I am rather embarrassed to start out with what are basically footnotes, ideas that just popped right out of my head, very basic questions I thought at some point would have to be addressed and would certainly, perhaps, be interesting to think about. My first point is about definition. I think we have had a very good set of definitions from Professor Huntington. At some point, I think we will probably need an overall definition of *vitality* for purposes of aggregate comparison. I would suggest we also need sub-definitions, definitions in very specific areas, such as cultural and economic areas and so on. In other words, we are really talking about *vitalities*. Also, the possibility of a paradox, if you like, of the *coexistence of vitality in one sector and non-vitality, sloth and decadence*, if you will, in *another*.

Or even a paradox when we take an example from recent American intellectual, cultural history, the 1920s, which were considered to be a rather dry period for American writers and intellectuals who felt alienated in the strong business culture of the day, many of them expatriated themselves to England and France. Actually, what is perhaps the greatest wave of literary creativity in American literary history: O'Neill, Sinclair Lewis, Hemingway, and so on. So perhaps there is a certain type of *vitality that requires a certain amount of unhappiness, misery, and alienation*; I just throw that out as a possibility.

And then, really just a footnote, what about the great historical definitions of *vitality* by the great cultural historians such as Spengler and Gibbon, or Hegel? Now there are five additional questions that relate to the matter of definition, or perspectives and angles on a broader question. And I just throw these out at random.

The first relates to economic efficiency and productivity, and/or a high degree of social mobilisation and social energy. I simply ask whether these necessarily add up to *vitality* and, if so, with what disclaimers? Obviously, I am thinking of the case of Nazi Germany, which released a great deal of energy, a certain kind of animal *vitality*, on both economic and social scores. But do we really want to call that *vitality*? I think there will have to be a consideration, perhaps, of what I see emerging as two very different sets of *vitalities*. The Japanese model, the East Asian model, where I think the emphasis is on economic productivity and output and a high degree of social organisation. And the Western model, particularly the American model of *vitality*, which emphasises political liberties and individual and cultural creativity. I just throw these out, without a value judgement; I think there are probably pluses and minuses on both sides.

Then a couple of questions which relate more specifically to the Japanese case. What about *homogeneity versus diversity*? We Americans, certainly, take as a matter of faith that diversity is automatically creative somehow. And I believe the Japanese have a great faith in the power of homogeneity, the contribution of homogeneity to *vitality*. I think they tend to see this as a key to the *vitality* of their own society and nation; it certainly has be stressed by people as high up on the ladder as Prime Minister Nakasone recently. And I think there has been some feeling that the period of Tokugawa isolation actually is sort of a seedbed in which a really rich native culture was able to emerge without disturbance from outside influences. Although I think you could also argue that it was the very considerable internal scale and diversity of Tokugawa Japan which created for a lot of that *vitality* in Japan even before Perry. My own personal feeling about the homogeneity argument today is that it tends to cover up, at times, a certain inertia and therefore a non-*vital* sort of insularism that tends to prevent Japan from making perhaps its greatest possible *vital* contribution to the global system today, a contribution commensurate with its economic and financial power.

A second sort of pair of questions or alternatives would be *isolation versus connectedness*; I was talking about homogeneity versus diversity. These would be on the domestic scene, the complexity or the diversity of the internal culture or the nation. And then again on the outside its degree of connectedness to other cultures. Here again I think of the United States, particularly, quintessentially, for the West believes that the maximum degree of connectedness is automatically a good thing. Whereas I think, even today, there is a certain feeling in Japan that there have to be certain limitations with connectedness. I think you see this not only in some of the trade issues but in some of the other problems of access to professions and the extent to which foreign workers or participation should be permitted within the Japanese culture itself. I am simply raising these questions. I think you can sense, perhaps, my own prejudice or views on them, but I think that there is great latitude for discussion and healthy argument here.

The next point is simply the question of the *borrowing of cultures*. We do have a great deal of borrowing, an increasing amount of intermeshing of cultures, a transfer of systems and ideas. Some of these have been imposed either through colonial legacies or through occupation, the American occupation of Japan, for instance, the Japanese colonialism in Korea. Systems have been voluntarily adopted, and I think of Petrovian Russia and the great adopting and adapting efforts of Asia/Japan. I simply want to suggest that perhaps the imposed legacies are not necessarily all negative. I have just come from Korea and it is possible, I think, to argue that there were aspects of industry, education, and so forth where there were contributions. Again, every self-chosen borrowing does not necessarily work and I think the attempt to impose a Western European Marxist vision on the backward peasant society of Russia demonstrates this whole question of cultural borrowing, whether it is voluntary or imposed.

Finally, I think there are inevitably in the discussion of the issue of *vitality* itself aspects or potentials of an ideological propagandistic or political nature. Again, the example of Nazi Germany comes up, which is almost so extreme as to hardly merit attention. I think a better example is the political uses within the United States that are being made now, rhetorically, in political argument over some of the implications of Paul Kennedy's book - questions of the balance of the military versus social spending and American economic policy and so on. I think the question, the argument itself, of the *vitality* of a certain social or economic system has a political, certainly, and potentially propagandistic aspect. My own hope is that in this conference we can talk, particularly, about the question of *vitality* being defined in terms of economic and social health, efficiency, productivity, and so on.

Then, also, the question of *vitality* that comes inevitably from the individual level of free expression and creativity.

G. De Vos: When we approach this topic I think one of the problems is that we are dealing with a metaphor that is broken down in certain directions. Yet it is helpful to use this metaphor, a biological metaphor actually, in talking about *vitality*. But one comment about the economic aspects: I think the economic aspects should not be seen out of the context of the ecological and demographic ones. When you are comparing entities, you have to think of alternatives that are going on in the world as far as models one can point to.

I consider the question of *scale* as another problem; that is, in considering political entities or units what scale of political or social integration are we considering? We have seen the Soviet Union collapse as a political entity. It was, perhaps, the last of the imperial units that still existed. We have given up on political imperialism as a possible model, however, there are still forms of economic imperialism extant. We can consider other type models besides the Japanese: we have the USA, which is a multi-ethnic model as a contrast to Japan which pretends to be an ethnically homogeneous state, with no minorities. There are other possible large scale political and social entities we are not considering, such as Indonesia, China or Brazil, with their different demographic and ecological settings of a complex nature. Therefore, when looking at various functioning models, Japan is to be considered comparatively.

I suggest that there is another conceptual question that gets buried a bit by using a *'vitality'* model. That is, in considering specific forms of political continuity, whether of nation states or other units, one has to consider relative questions of cost in human malaise, and relative amounts of continuing internal conflict or accommodation. There are differing models of internal segmentation or integration, each with attendant problems. In each instance, Marxists look for and emphasise 'class' conflict and economic maldistribution. But, there are other forms of internal conflict or stress that are usually not considered. For example, 'caste' is another form of conflict or accommodation which contemporary India and Japan still share to some degree. Relative social status of men and women, or 'gender' has become of social, political and economic concern in different ways in many of today's nation states. We also have generation conflict as a consideration in rapidly changing societies, some with aging population

Of course, my special area of interest has been 'ethnic' conflict. One other political (and possibly cultural, territorial, religious, linguistic or occupational) entity which we haven't considered is the 'ethnic' community as a sub-unit. Everywhere there are repeated attempts at political integration or disintegration which involve highly complex issues of ethnicity, territoriality. Briefly, some necessary consideration of any political entity involves possible internal ethnic conflict. In Eastern Europe and the territories of ex-Soviet Union, we witness unresolved territorial-ethnic conflict.

There are also 'biological' concepts of ethnicity. The Japanese maintain a heavy emphasis on a racial concept of themselves as a political entity. It permits no ready assimilation as citizens, 'others' of alien origin. While still uneasy about their Korean, and Burakumin minorities, the Japanese are relatively free of some ethnic issues that bedevil others, such as religious animosities. Nor do they have any linguistic issues of note. Being a Fleming in background, I am aware of the negative potentials of ethnicity defined by loyalty to language.

There are more subtle ethnic issues that lurk beneath the surface. 'Culture' as represented by food habits can lead to patterns of rejection. Smell as an 'ethnic' marker can define a Korean for the Japanese, or an Algerian for the French. Occupational specialisation may become related to ethnicity. In certain countries such as Indonesia, or in African states this has lead to bloodshed in the past.

I would like to make another point, related to what Ivan Hall was talking about: what are the units of analysis? Are we looking at the individual as a unit, at the family as a unit, at the community as a unit, or at the nation-state as the unit of analysis? If you look at *vitality*, the Chinese have a very peculiar form of *vitality*, because they have overseas Chinese everywhere who exist in communities and family units, not in national states. So in this case, how are we going to talk about such Chinese *vitality*. This unit of analysis is something that we have values about, and the American unit of analysis ideally is the individual, although this could be seen as rather spurious because there are no real individuals out there. On the other hand, the Japanese have the nation-state as the unit, and 5 per cent of the population are minorities which Nakasone and others won't admit exist in Japan. That's an ideological position, and in the US we equate this with individualism while in Japan they equate it with homogeneity. These are some of the things I think we should put on the table and talk about.

A. Clesse: Thank you, George De Vos. David Arase, would you like to add something to this?

D. Arase: Thank you, Dr Clesse. I'd like to make two points: one about a possible domestic dimension to explain Japan's *vitality*, and the other about a contextual or international dimension. First, on the domestic dimension, I remember speaking with Dr Clesse about moving beyond trivialities like the savings rate or why Japanese companies prefer growth over short-term profit. What about first causes, getting to real independent variables?

That brought to my mind an article, written in 1915 by Thorstein Veblen, entitled 'Japan's opportunity'. It was a very interesting essay because what he was arguing was going against mainstream Western social theory, by arguing that Japan's feudal - perhaps even primordial - values and forms of social organisation would actually facilitate Japan's modernisation and help implement the adoption of Western forms of modernity such as the company or the state. I haven't given this line of thinking a lot of thought, because in my own work I mostly look at the institutions, but as I look at institutions I realise that the cultural and societal factors are really important for explaining the current configuration of institutions and how they relate to one another. In particular, as one considers what might be the forms of successful institutions which have been incorporated into the modern Japan and facilitated its *vitality*, one looks at such structures as the *ie*, as described by Nakane Chie. It's very interesting because the functional analogy between the *ie* and the firm is to maintain the existence and the integrity of the household through time. One does what one has to do in order to do this; one doesn't chop up the firm and sell it off in bits and pieces as one finds Americans doing. More than this, if one looks at how households related to each other in traditional Japan, one finds so-called *doozoku*, or corporate groupings of households that are functionally interdependent and yet households still compete with one another within the village. Villages would be split up into these competing groups. It's very interesting because, if one had to explain corporate organisation in Japan, one could carry over the analogy: the firm is the *ie* and the way companies relate to one another in *keiretsu* is analogous to *doozoku*.

Why? What explains this and the behaviour which results? We need to consider not only corporate organisation and how firms relate to one another, but also in the way that individuals relate to society. Many commentators have noted that in Japan, unlike in Western societies, the crime rate is much lower and the individuals are integrated into the work place. This is curious, because according to Western social theory, as modernisation progresses, you would expect to have rationalisation, the prevalence of contract as the mechanism regulating relations between individuals, but in Japan we see that this legalistic form of social cohesion is not the preferred norm. What I am suggesting is that one way to approach this question of Japan's *vitality* would be to finally take seriously the cultural argument.

Let me point out the implications if one actually does this. One is that one might find that Japan really is different, and that, as the Japanese say, Japan is culturally unique and must be treated as such. Therefore, you can't expect us to negotiate *keiretsu* in SII, for example, because it cuts to the heart of Japan's culture. If we take this cultural argument seriously, its implications are that Japan doesn't really fit in with the West, and that we may have to negotiate a set of new understandings to take into account these differences.

The second point, about the external dimension which I'd like to mention, is the economic effect of alliance with the United States in the post-war period. This is very important because, as we leave the Cold War period and emerge into a tripoli world, the nature of strategy and alliance changes radically. Whereas in the Cold War, alliances only existed between unequal powers, between the US and dependent powers and the Soviet Union and its dependent powers, in the tripoli world, you have alliance flexibility. Alliances can be made and broken, and these are alliances between great powers. This can make critical differences, obviously, because the game is to avoid isolation. Now, what does this mean. At least theoretically, one has to consider the effect of a break-up in the alliance, and what might be the implications for Japan's *vitality*. In the Cold War period, what you saw developing, at least in my opinion, was a differentiation in terms of the orientation of the US and Japan. The United States focused on providing security; Japan focused on economic growth. Of course, the two could not have existed independently, and America's military protection can be considered an economic subsidy in two senses. One is that it saved Japan from spending on defence. Secondly, it allowed Japan to invest more in commercial development, thus increasing its growth.

Now, the problem in the post-Cold War period is that relations between the US and Japan are likely to become more difficult to resolve, simply because the Cold War has ended. It has less to do with racism than the deeper structural factors. Let's consider cooperation between Japan and the US and their utility curves. In an alliance structure, it's not just a zero-sum form of cooperation, but a positive sum, in the sense that if the US gives up a certain unit of utility, but Japan gains actually more than that unit in return, and since both parties are interested in minimising the sum of their utilities, the overall alliance is strengthened. With the end of the Cold War, such alliance reasoning disappears, and the area for compromise becomes much smaller in negotiating cooperation. Now, what happens in a situation of economic competition, where competitive relations prevail between the US and Japan? Let's assume that the proposal is to cooperate in developing a technology, but the technology will benefit the country that develops it first. Here, the US is willing to give up utility, but only if Japan is hurt more, in order to prevent them from developing it first. With a similar approach by Japan, there exists no zone of compromise for mutual benefit. There is direct conflict. With the end of the Cold War, the introduction of alliance flexibility, and the rise of economic competition, you are going to have a much tougher political agenda. Thus, those are the two factors, domestic and international, which might help us get at Japan's *vitality* and evaluate its prospects.

A. Clesse: Thank you. We will return to more of these considerations tomorrow morning. Now there are two participants who would like to comment. Professor Shinohara.

M. Shinohara: Thank you so much. Since this question goes back to past phenomena, let me go back and consider Japan's past dynamism. I think the *capacity or willingness to combine two heterogeneous factors* is very important. For instance, in behaviour, we maintain a high rate of savings, and this is a relatively conservative model of life. On the other hand, in the mode of investment, Japanese corporations are very dynamic, and this is explained by the term 'demonstration effect'. These are, in fact, opposite ways of behaviour. So in understanding Japanese economic dynamism, a combination of opposite tendencies seems to be very important. I have prepared a small paper with two statistical graphs to show this.

Another problem is that from the Meiji era, the Japanese adopted two different things. One was the developmental strategy, in which the government's role was very important. The other was that the Japanese tried to introduce market mechanisms. The two are very different, but their combination in the past has been very important. Of course, in the future, the government's role needs to decline, but we see once again the significance of two opposite things.

Another such dichotomy is the strength of Japanese companies in hard and soft aspects. On one hand, there is the development of hard technology. On the other, there is the strength of soft know-how in international trade, such as the marketing and intelligence-gathering capabilities of the trading companies.

This combination of hard and soft technologies has been crucial. Therefore, in an analysis of Japanese economic dynamism, an analysis of only manufacturing or only market mechanisms will not be enough. The interaction of two heterogeneous factors is important. Furthermore, we need to make an analysis of the players, not just the playground.

K. van Wolferen: As I listen to the variety of speakers this morning, I am trying to integrate what they said into a coherent picture. I thought I should try to tempt perhaps part of this audience to enter into my favourite frame of reference. As George said, *vitality* is a biological metaphor. The problem when you use this metaphor for a social/political use is that the question of intention does not get raised. In a biological entity, you can postulate that there was a creator at some point, or you can say that there was no creator, that the biological entity just exists. However, when you look at social/political organisation, if you do not ask the question of intention, I don't think you can say very interesting things. Now, what the problem is with the sociological approach to many societies, including the Japanese society, is that it tends to overlook the power currents that run through it. In the case of Japan, these are particularly surprising. As I was listening to Professor Inoguchi saying that it was a matter of learning and unlearning, taking the example of the gun, I was reminded of the ease with which you can see the visible connection between cultural borrowing and political intention. The gun was given up, it was unlearned, for political reasons. It was too uncomfortable for power holders to live with the awareness that commoners or rebellious samurai could have the means to overthrow them. You can go through the history of Japanese borrowing and see that Buddhism and many other things were borrowed for specific political purposes.

The *ie* that David Arase mentioned is sometimes presented as an original Japanese indigenous construct arising from some genetic or quirky root, but I think it is quite clear that, if you look at the history of the *ie*, it is a political construct. It was a means by which the Tokugawa rulers kept order in society. Of course, there were *ie* before then, but they didn't have the function that they received in the Tokugawa period. Here we have a political construct, at first relevant only for the samurai society, gradually filtering downward to merchants and being replicated in corporate organisation at the end of the last century. But there are power-holders at work with political intentions. So I propose that when we are discussing Japanese *vitality* as distinct from *vitality* in other places, especially, though not exclusively, *in the case of Japan vitality is politically based.* Unless you recognise these political dimensions, you won't understand it.

Moving on to what Professor Shinohara said, the market was used by the government, indeed. This was a very *vital* aspect of Japanese economic history. The market is a tool in the hands of Japanese power-holders and administrators, not something that is comparable to the concept of market in free market ideologies. Again, here we have a political use of something that is often described as cultural. This is one area where I disagree with David Arase; of course it's cultural, but by saying it's cultural, you're not really saying much, because the microphone I'm using is also cultural, as is the glass of water from which I just drank. We need to narrow it down, especially in the case of Japan, it is so very simple to see the political underpinnings of whatever you describe. From the conversations I've had with various people before this conference began, I think that what we are going to see is a division among the people who are going to talk about upbringing, child-rearing methods, psychological and sociological drives which bring forth the kind of Japanese who then participate in institutions and those people who focus on institutions, because Japan's institutions are obviously a formidable element of the *vitality* of the state. I could go on, but I think that this is enough for now.

G. De Vos: Just a brief note on what Karel has just said. In social theory, there is another basic discussion between Hobbes' concept of power and something that goes with the degree of 'internalisation' in a society. In other words, the degree to which people, in a sense, automatically submit themselves to a system or are so internalised that they are not in opposition to the system. I think that this is a very important characteristic to examine in Japan.

W. Wetherall: I'd like to make various comments regarding previous speakers and raise a couple of viewpoints myself. I have heard many people today talk about 'Japan is', 'America is', etc., and we seem to be reducing this to a concept of a single system, but I think that this may interfere with a more intelligent discussion of *vitality* in a complex, dynamic, diverse society or set of societies in cultures. In the idea of culture or Japan as a singularity, one must always ask, 'which Japan? Which culture are we dealing with?' I would like to defend the biological metaphor a bit more. I think Karel van Wolferen's point is well taken about the need to look at institutions and the source of intention, but then one must ask, 'Is this source of intention identifiable as a single element?' In other words, how many brains does this organ which we call Japan have? How many hearts does it have? Then, if we test the *vitality* of these internal organs, as we would if we were performing some sort of demonstration in a laboratory, we would obstruct an organ and see if what remains continues to live. We could then rank the *vitality* of these organs in terms of their importance.

How important is the imperial institution? I have written a short story that explores the idea that the Imperial Palace just disappears one morning; it takes a couple of weeks for this event to work its way out of the media, but life returns to normal, Japan continues, and the palace site becomes an event on bus tours, where the guide gets out, says, 'The palace used to be here,' everybody says, '*Naruhodo*' and gets back on the bus for the next stop.

But I would like to say that if we're looking at the *vitality* of organs like the LDP, and the Gaimusho (Foreign Ministry), which I think may be slightly more important than the LDP, there are more *vital* organs of Japan like the skin - the interface of Japan with the outside world. This is not defined by the Ministry of Justice or the Foreign Ministry, it is defined by the people of Japan who are diverse and represent many groups. That is why I say that one cannot claim that 'the Japanese' believe in homogeneity, because, in fact, only some Japanese do. The skin of Japan is becoming colourless, because of the concept of citizenship and participation in society that one does not realise if one only reads Gaimusho propaganda. In other words, if you are on the streets of Japan and out with the people, you realise that Japan has *vitality* because of the large, diverse geographical and demographic entities, not because of the small and fractured central nervous system which we talk about. I would like to introduce this variable of diversity and complexity beyond the concept of a single Japan which we are going to have to talk about.

K. Calder: I think that the perspective of Karel van Wolferen, with a focus on institutions in Japanese *vitality*, is certainly important. It seems to me, though, to note a couple of important things which are, in my understanding, implicit in his remarks. In the discussion of intention, for example, I certainly can agree that one has to look at that, but in thinking about the implications of that for Japanese behaviour, one has to look at Japan in the context of broader international forces and so on. The question really arises as to whether intention itself is determining, and I have always been a believer in the importance of institutional analysis. But in the broader context, we need to ask to what extent institutions themselves are determining.

The other point would have to do with the nature of political intervention and structuring that goes on. Needless to say, I think that's an important perspective for analysis, but can we assume implicitly that the intervention of politics itself is, in fact, strategic? I think that the thrust of a lot of Karel's own analysis is that the intervention of politics is not necessarily strategic, that fragmentation in the system as a whole, which he talks about in the lack of a state, the salience of the system, is the way that markets are configured politically. So, I think thinking carefully about the degree to which political institutions are strategic, the extent to which they function in terms of bureaucratic standard operating procedures, the extent to which they are clientalised, and the extent to which fragmentation across the society as a whole and the institutional structure prevents them from functioning in a strategic fashion are also important things to look at.

This interaction in the international system, then, is an additional variable in considering *vitality* as one moves from a period when the domestic system has been more determining in the past toward the 1990s. We can already see it in areas like finance and telecommunications. To what extent is the international system as a variable going to affect the *vitality* of Japan?

K. van Wolferen: I mean intention on a much more basic level: keeping order domestically, not only in the international context. Of course, also in the international context security is an issue. What I mean to say is that areas of life in many other histories of other countries left to their own resources have been very consciously used by Japanese powerholders for political purposes. I'm not saying that this has never happened anywhere else, but the extent to which it is the case in Japan is very striking. Also, I very much like the metaphor which Bill Wetherall said about the skin. I fully agree with him. But you have to ask the question, 'How do you translate this *vitality* on the basis of different peoples, their ideas and talents, into that which contributes to the political and economic life of a country?' There you have to look at the obstacles which make it difficult for a citizen to actually express himself as a citizen.

D. Hale: I just wanted to follow up on what Kent Calder said. If we are looking at *vitality* we need to begin to define our concept in different ways. First, in looking at Japan, we have to look at it as one of a group of non-European countries and how it responded to the consequences of the industrial revolution. In the 19th century, it was the only non-white society to escape domination or colonisation by European powers because it was able through a variety of changes in social and political organisation to move quickly in importing technology.

Secondly, moving into the modern period, we have to look at *relative and absolute vitality*. After World War II, there is no doubt that you could characterise Japan as having a high level of absolute and relative *vitality* because its growth rate was extraordinarily high, as a consequence of policies which not just Japan, but most industrial countries other than the US pursued after the war. Now, in the 1990s, Japan's absolute *vitality*, if we choose to measure it in terms of economic growth, is not that outstanding, because its capacity to catch up is limited, given the fact that it's now affluent. But it may continue to outperform the US in particular because of failures in the US economic system. So we could have, in absolute terms, much less *vitality* than before - say a growth rate of 3 or 4 per cent, but if America is doing 1 or 2 per cent, that could still have many of the consequences we've seen recently in terms of trade tensions, etc.

Somewhere in the economic discussion today or tomorrow, we have to consider not just the reasons for Japan's out-performance, but see it in the context of the economic upheaval that occurred all over the world except in the US that resulted in higher savings and investment. The US, because it escaped most of the damage of the war, did not have to go through that process of change, and now at the end of the 20th century has to address some issues other industrial nations, like Japan, addressed 40 to 50 years ago. We may then conclude that there is actually much convergence in the policies of Japan and other nations, while the real outlier is the US. If we approach the issue from that perspective, we may gain some insights to the current tensions; there is perhaps too much focus on Japan's uniqueness and not enough on America's uniqueness.

B. Keehn: I'd like to address some of these recent points, because there has been a lot of detailed talk about domestic factors of *vitality* and how they interact with the international context. I think it's worth remembering that *one sector of a nation's vitality can be harmful to that of another nation.* Ivan Hall alluded to this in his five factors earlier this morning. You can certainly look at this in the domestic and international contexts. Certainly you see this in the US-Japan trade context and increasingly in the Japan-EU trade relationship. We should differentiate between the kinds of *vitality* discussed by Bill Wetherall. There are serious institutional boundaries to *vitality*. What gives a great deal of *vitality* to bureaucrats, *keidanren* or manufacturers may not benefit some of the Japanese citizens Bill was talking about. Some sectors of Japanese society may suffer from the gains of others.

G. Fukushima: I wanted to make a couple of comments on what Kent Calder and Bill Wetherall said, and by implication what Karel and David Arase have mentioned as well. The first point is that when Kent mentioned the importance of the interaction with the international system, I think he is correct in pointing to the significance of that factor. In particular, the whole notion of *gaiatsu*, or pressure from abroad, is one of the sources of Japan's economic *vitality*, for it has been able to creatively use pressure from abroad to benefit Japan. We can find many examples of this, but from my own experience, the Structural Impediments Initiative is a good example of where the US administration asked Japan to undertake certain changes, based on the assumption that the Japanese system is like the US system. In fact, what happens is that Japan takes selectively some of the pressure and undertakes changes which will, in the end, benefit Japan. I think that this really is a source of *vitality* for Japan because of the ideological differences between the two countries and the lack of understanding by American bureaucrats of how the Japanese system works

The second point is what Bill Wetherall said about the separate factors or actors within each society. One of the ways in which I think that this is very important is that, for example, when Carla Hills comes in October of 1989 and meets with the Minister of Construction to discuss the issue of the Japanese construction market, she did not say, 'We have a problem between the US and Japan which we need to resolve, therefore let us resolve it.' What she did say was there was no economic problem as far as the administration was concerned, however the Congress and Democrats and private sector in the US want to close off the US market to Japan. We in the administration do not want this, and therefore we want a trade expansive solution. Therefore you Japanese open up your markets, at least on paper, so we can fend off the trade protectionists in the US. We are in the same boat, together fighting off the protectionists. This is an illustration of the interaction of the international system and the differences within each society which can impact Japan's *vitality*.

D. Arase: I want to concede Karel's point, and in fact in my remarks I said that I don't much favour cultural analysis, but that if we were to take it seriously, this is how we might do it. I don't believe wholly in the cultural argument because change in society is never affected by culture directly. It's always mediated by institutions, in particular the most important institution in modern society, which is the state, as Karel points out. If you wanted to find out what is the range of options for institutions to determine and legitimate what they do, then they might resort selectively to so-called cultural factors. I was suggesting that the use of cultural legacies actually worked out rather well, better than we would have expected, in the sense that these traditional elements didn't inhibit modernisation, but in fact complemented it. That was my point.

Y. Sugimoto: I am a sociologist, and I have been rather uncomfortable about some of the arguments which look at the question of *vitality* only at the level of nation-states. Japan, for example, is a collection of various subcultures and subsystems, and I think it is very important that we not lose sight of these. Other variables have been mentioned, and I think it is very important to connect some of these variables in some systematic way. I would venture to hypothesise that the high level of *vitality* of one section of a subsystem of a society would quite closely correlate with the absence or even suppression of *vitality* in other areas of society. I wonder if we can raise the question of *vitality* of Japanese housewives, for example. Are they really *vital*? How about the level of high school students' *vitality*? Or the agriculture sector of Japan? The labour movement? How about the level of *vitality* of part-time workers in this country in comparison with their counterparts in other countries? What is the level of environmentalists' *vitality* in Japan? Or minority groups? I would suspect that the levels of *vitality* of all these groups are rather low, and that there is some degree of correlation of this with the high level of *vitality* in the corporate sectors. There is a trade-off, as it were, between these two segments.

G. De Vos: I think his thesis relates to the ideas of the last two speakers. The question of political control has to take into account questions of coercion, who is coercing and how. Let us put it another way. The very singular thing about Japan is the relative absence of overt conflict in the society. Other countries have tried to have a political direction of economy, etc., and have failed at it. This is where I get to the point of culture again and I would say that one has to examine cultural patterns to relate them to political coercion. What is under the illusion of total harmony as an ideal in Japan does cover some cultural aspects that do have to be examined.

One other point about the housewives. I would say that they have a great deal of *vitality*, so let us not neglect that they are in charge of the children. If you are looking at cultural continuity, you have to see to what degree are women internalised about bringing up the next generation and to what degree are women leaving that kind of pattern in Japan compared, say, with the United States. So we have to look at the family unit and its continuity as a question of ultimate *vitality*. This is a cultural question, not an institutional one directly.

G. Berger: I have a very brief comment to make, which is that I think that trying to dichotomise the focus on institutions and the focus on cultures is somewhat like trying to dichotomise the chicken and the egg. That is to say that I think that the culture is a generator of political attitudes and of political institutions, just as they, as Professor De Vos has just observed, in turn are utilisers of that culture for political purposes. I do not think we should try to exert too much of our effort on trying to find a first cause in one or the other, since I think there is a kind of median loop relationship between the two which will frustrate us and have us running around in circles.

K. Calder: Very briefly, I think there is a level of analysis issue here. On a very broad level of generality, I would certainly agree with what you say. But if we look at the evolution of individual institutions, their roles in society and so on, what we find is what I think Chalmers Johnson showed rather nicely with respect to industrial policy in MITI. If you do not look at specific historical episodes, in particular the mobilisation, for example, in the Second World War and in certain ways, certain parts of the occupation itself where there is a lot one can not account for in public policy and social behaviour.

G. Berger: Indeed, I have given a great deal of my professional career to studying the mobilisation of Japan prior to the war and after the war, so I quite agree with Kent's observation. I also very much agree with the fact that there is a level of analysis issue, but we should be very much mistaken in assuming the priority of any given level of analysis. One can not understand the behaviour of the Japanese, who are the heroes of Chalmers Johnson's book, without understanding something of their personality and the culture from which they came. It is a median loop.

K. van Wolferen: Very briefly, I disagree with Gordon Berger. It looks like a chicken and egg question, but I postulate there was first a chicken in all these cases. I think you can see this very clearly in Japanese history. It is important to make that point because the nature of the animal depends on having first been a chicken. Political use of cultural elements is very clear and political manipulation of cultural elements is very clear. Of course, these things existed in some diffuse form earlier on, but they are shaped for political purposes. If you have a historical view over it, which I believe you do have, then you can hardly escape this discovery. I will leave it at that, but you see very clearly, especially in Japanese history, the political origins of cultural phenomena.

R. Cooper: I did not want to intercede in this discussion, but the problem I have with Karel van Wolferen's argument, not that I disagree with it, is that I do not understand it. Because it assumes that there is an autonomous political authority there which has objectives and is making decisions, and yet in most societies that is the thing which needs to be explained, that can not be taken as a given. There are some exceptions, where the political authority is imposed from outside, the Mongols on China, etc. But in general the political authority is itself an object that requires explanation; it is androgynous, to use an economist's term. Therefore, one needs to know when one is speaking about using religion, which was the example you gave for political purposes, who defined the political purpose? Since I suspect the answer to that question is very complex, what was the process by which the political use of Buddhism or of gun-making or of gun-unmaking got decided? Those are all androgynous, and so it really is a chicken and egg problem.

K. van Wolferen: It is not a complex thing at all. It is incumbent power-holders who want to hold on to power. They use these cultural elements in order to hang on to power.

R. Cooper: But even in Japan we have seen dramatic changes in power-holders. So one also needs to explain those episodes. Guns played a role, I gather, in changing the power structure and then the unlearning of the guns presupposed sufficient acquiescence or intimidation or some combination of the rest of society to live with that. That deserves explanation; it can not just be taken as a given. There were similar big changes in power in the mid-19th century not imposed from the outside. Then there was in the mid-20th century from the outside. It was, around 1930, androgynous. So one needs to explain those; they can not be taken as given. And the public's reaction to them, acquiescence and why acquiescence? It could be intimidation or genuine acceptance; all of those things need explanation. My only point is that the invocation of political purpose does not settle this issue.

S. Sato: It is true that all incumbent powerholders throughout the world, in any society, try to find cultural components which they can use. It is not a uniquely Japanese phenomenon. In Japanese history, there are many cases where the incumbent powerholder helped to mobilise the cultural factors; I can cite hundreds of cases.

A. Iriye: I shall be very brief. As a historian, I have listened to the discussion with great fascination and also with a slight sense of frustration. Because we are trying to, more or less, think in terms of historical periods, it has seemed to me that, when you talk about the notion of *vitality*, we need to keep in mind not only a discussion in terms of different segments of the population which are affected and are more *vital* than others, but also in terms of historical periods.

Which periods of Japan, or segments thereof, have been more *vital* than others and so on? I think there has been a tendency this morning to equate Japan's *vitality* with Japan's modernisation. That would be, I think, only one condition of *vitality*. One could argue that during the Meiji era at the end of the 19th century, if you define *vitality* as modernisation, Japan was a very *vital* country. But if you define *vitality* in terms of cultural creativity, intellectual innovation, and so on, then you really cannot make such a point.

In the 1930s, on the other hand, Japan may have been characterised by *vitality* in the wrong direction, in terms of its domestic totalitarianism and aggression abroad. It may have been culturally quite *vital*; I am interested to hear what Professor Seidensticker might say about that. It depends, I think, on which period we are talking about. And so I hope at some point we will raise that question, why is it that in a certain period of time a country is more *vital* in one aspect but not in others, and why in other periods some other aspects become characterised by *vitality*, while some lose *vitality*. It is not as if Japan has always been characterised by some kind of *vitality* throughout its history.

In response to another point, I have found the references to various historical points very interesting. I do wonder, however, if Meiji Japan, that is the end of the 19th century and the beginning of the 20th century, can really be characterised as a period of *vitality* in any sense except that of war-making. If you define *vitality* as the ability to wage and win wars, that was a very *vital* period. In other respects, in terms of industrialisation for instance, I do not think you can really say that industrialisation began in the 19th century. It takes two wars, three wars, before Japan really begins to industrialise. First of all, I am always struck by the fact, as I think economists can illuminate further, that even as late as the 1930s Japan was the poorest of the advanced countries in terms of per capita income. I can not really agree that there was any true economic *vitality* in that sense, in terms of industrialisation, not until we get into the post-war period in fact.

Japan was a very vital country in terms of war-making, going back to Professor Inoguchi's example of gun-making. If that is what is meant by *vitality*, that is war-making, armament, aggression, that it is fine. I am not sure that is the kind of *vitality* I would like to live with, but that is something else.

Economic Vitality

A. Clesse: Thank you, Mr Iriye. Let us turn now to the economic aspects, the evolution of economic *vitality* in the recent past and present. I hope we have some discussion and some description of this *vitality*. Professor Iida will speak; Professor Shinohara, we have your paper if you would like to come back with some remarks, and all the other economists here - Taggart Murphy, Professor Iwai, Professor Kihwan, and also Richard Cooper. David Hale will speak, and Glen Fukushima, perhaps again, when the session continues this afternoon. Professor Iida, please.

T. Iida: I think *the economic vitality of Japan over the recent years lies in an unreserved devotion to commodity making, manufacturing*. I do not know where it comes from, but anyway, the Japanese people have an

unreserved devotion to commodity making. That is the basic reason why
Japan causes economic frictions with many countries in the world. And I
feel that this devotion is somewhat inhuman, somewhat against the human
nature, so I believe that it will end in due course. I do not know how many
more years it will continue, but the end will come after all.

M. Shinohara: When the United Kingdom and the United States were
prosperous, there were no international criticisms. Therefore, they could
maintain for a long time, even for a century, a huge surplus in the current
account of payments. Their surpluses in the commodity and service trade
were huge and continuous. In Japan, at present, we are in a different
situation. Although, due to the temporary and business cycle reasons,
Japan's trade surplus increased last year, I think that it will be reduced
within the years to come. The Japanese government has now tried to shift
to a policy to expand domestic demand and further promote the quality of
life of the people. But one problem remains.

That is, the United States for instance, indulged in over-consumption -
between 1981 and 1987; on the one hand, there is a tremendous drop of
the personal savings ratio, even in absolute terms. During this period,
personal savings declined tremendously. On the other hand, the United
States' fiscal deficit increased tremendously during that period.

I think when a big country, or a superpower, declined in economic
power, there were two primary reasons. One is a macroeconomics cause
that is related to the over-consumption of the nation. Another is the rate of
decline of industrial competitive power. At present the Japanese
government emphasises the promotion of life style improvement as a target
and the Japanese decrease of the savings ratio for the coming ten to fifteen
years. In addition there is the political pressure from outside; I am afraid,
the present government policy attitude will be obliged to change to
something comparable to that of the United States and the United Kingdom
in the past. I think one big reason of the relative decline of big powers is
the over-consumption attitude, and within ten or fifteen years the Japanese
economy too may follow the same course which both the UK and the US
experienced.

K. Iwai: I think that Professor De Vos, in his listing of the four carriers of
vitality, forgot to mention one more unit of *vitality*: the corporation, or
organisation. In Japan, this seems to be the most important unit which
carries *vitality*. This single sector dominance implies that there is a trade-
off, that many other sectors may suffer, as Professor Sugimoto mentioned.
Why does this trade-off exist? It is in the nature of the corporation, and
more generally, in the nature of capitalism itself. Don't mistake me for a

Marxist, but I use capitalism as a system whose sole aim is to expand itself without any attention to other sectors of society. My thesis is that the Japanese corporation is the purest form of capitalism. Marx uses the individual as the personified carrier of this expansionist capitalist society. But in the case of the Japanese economy, those capitalists were replaced by corporations, at the expense of all individuals. This was a conscious policy decision after the Second World War.

Now, why did corporations become such an important carrier of this capitalist system? If you look at corporations, it is a very strange thing, because in classical textbooks, there is a very clear distinction between persons and things, between owners and property. But if you look at corporations and read commercial law, then corporations play a double role of property owners, without reference to specific individuals, and of things which are in turn owned by shareholders. The Japanese economy has used this structure to eliminate the influence of individuals, shareholders, etc. When you compound this by the ownership of corporations by other corporations, two corporations can become pseudo-individuals through cross-share holding. With cross-share holding on the level of *keiretsu*, the influence of individual shareholders, including foreigners, is eliminated. So this can explain one aspect of Japanese *vitality*, for corporations are not restricted by individual owners. This, however, is also a limitation.

D. Hale: Just two sets of comments. First, I would like to elaborate on what has just been said and discuss a paper written recently by Richard Koo that describes what is now a very intense debate in Japan about the structure of their corporate system and how it has developed certain behavioural characteristics in the modern period because of this unusual ownership structure. Let me just highlight the major themes, because anybody writing about Japan today really has to look at this issue; it's central to the whole evolution of the corporate sector and Japan's growth rate going forward. Providing institutional reasons, part of which reflects Ministry of Finance regulations on competition in the financial service area; that is, the law nurtured cartels and insurance and other service areas that control large shareholdings and therefore limit competition. We have effectively 60-70 per cent of Japanese corporate equity tied up in stable shareholding products that did not demand a high stock market return. For various reasons there was a high stock market return, but there was not the same kind of competition on the part of fund managers that we have in America or Britain or elsewhere to churn the account and demand immediate returns.

This system may now be breaking down for a variety of reasons. First, we do have financial de-regulation partly because of American pressure over five to ten years. There is now a capital market, as opposed to purely bank-driven finance. There's also an international capital market as money flows in and out, and therefore Japanese real interest rates are now high compared to previous years and converging with the rest of the world. In addition, we are going to have more competition now among fund management companies in the life insurance sector and elsewhere which could create more of a short-term investment focus.

Finally, this previous pattern of low capital cost and concentrated investment has created a situation where Japan now has just too many enemies. As the Richard Koo paper explains, because Japanese corporations have no real profit criteria, given their low cost of capital, their sole goal is to maximise sales, and the result has been an increasing collision with the rest of the world. Now you have both an internal change, a much higher cost of capital which will be allocating credit, and also this international trade pressure. I'd encourage all of you to read this paper. It will, I think, be dominating discussions about Japan over the next two or three years and provide an important test force over the next ten years about what aspect of Japanese behaviour is a function of straight economic price theory (with low capital costs and high investment grade, you can accept low profits in seeking market share) and what I would call more cultural or sociological, what is not price-driven but reflects a lot of unique historical features that might have evolved over time.

The real test here lies ahead in the 1990s. I could explain much of Japan's economic performance since the Second World War with just straight price theory; I don't need all the cultural things. Where I need these things is to go back to the Meiji period to understand why in the 19th century Japan was the only non-white society to be able to successfully launch itself on a try for industrialisation to escape European domination and to generally hold its own. I mentioned in the previous session that in the history of developing countries, the pattern has been that the later you industrialise, the greater the potential for the government to be actively involved, and to use non-market channels for allocating capital.

You would then have had Germany all through the second half of the 20th century held up as the example, not the Anglo-Saxon countries which dominated for a while or perhaps more recently Japan. Some of the similarities between the German and Japanese historical experiences of the late 19th century would be worthy of examination later on. I hope that in this afternoon's discussion of sociology, anthropology, and even psychoanalysis, we can get into some of these more unique aspects of

Japan and where it came from in the 19th century and how this reinforced the modern period. But, as this paper will explain, *much of the recent performance can be explained by straight theory - capital allocations, investment rates, and so on.*

A. Clesse: I will now proceed systematically from the list because there are so many who wish to speak. I would remind us that we should not forget the comparative perspective. Also, I was warned that it would be very difficult to maintain the distinction between description and explanation, and we now seem to be discussing more in explanatory terms. Hopefully, tomorrow morning, with Kenneth Courtis, we will return more to description. Now, Dr Kihwan Kim.

K. Kim: Thank you very much. I will try to bring out the comparative perspective to these questions as much as I can. Before I get to my main point, I want to make a few remarks about my framework. I listened to the discussion on what *vitality* is, and the Chair asked to discuss the manifestations of *vitality*, but I think the whole group this morning went right into the sources of *vitality* instead. I will also not try to define *vitality* extensively; to a simple economist like me, *vitality* is simply dynamism, and dynamism, in macro terms, means rapid growth. The period I want to talk about is the last 40 years. The unit I want to talk about is the nation.

What are the sources of Japanese growth in the eyes of an economist who lives in neighbouring Korea? Since I am not a mathematical economist, as Professor Iwai, I also tend to think very loosely, including the variables you might not call strictly economic. One important source to explain the economic dynamism of Japan over the last 40 years, or the last century for that matter, is the *strong desire on the part of the Japanese people to catch up with the West* and not be swallowed up by the West. I think this psychology was reinforced after the Second World War, in the *drive to recover from defeat and restore their respectability in the eyes of the world*. I think the same can be said for the Koreans, too. We lost a lot of time, and we wanted to catch up - first with the Japanese and then the rest of the West. The second important source of dynamism has to do with the special arrangement with the US for defence and security. When other countries had to spend 5 or 6 per cent of GNP, Japan spent 1 per cent or less for the whole period. Suppose you put only half of the difference towards investment, the investment ratio would be 2 to 3 per cent higher than the other; you could do a lot to promote your competitiveness with this.

The third variable I want to call your attention to is that both Japan and Korea, for the first time in many years, were given the opportunity to engage in trade with the entire world on a non-discriminatory multilateral basis. Both before the second World War were denied this opportunity. This opportunity to trade is very important when your resource base is so small. So this opportunity was an enormous advantage, and it was a result of the Cold War. The US, in its struggle with the Soviet Union, needed to promote such free trade through the GATT structure.

I wanted to note another important source of *vitality*. This is another result of the international structure which arose during the Cold War. I am referring to the *political stability* that Japan has enjoyed over the last 40 years. The LDP has ruled virtually without any interruption, and this has allowed businessmen to plan investment rather easily, because the future expectations are easy to make with political stability. There are different factions within the LDP, but they don't have different ideologies, just different personalities. This is somewhat similar in Korea, although it didn't have the same political stability as Japan over the past 40 years. But Korea devised its own kind of political stability on its own ingenuity, as it were. They invented an authoritarian government, which allowed economic prosperity.

The last variable I want to mention now has to do with the level of education. The Koreans and Japanese devote so much of their GNP income to educating people, and this kind of education has been very conducive to the kind of production and economic activities that the countries were engaged in. In catching up, all you really need is discipline and hard work, and the educational systems in these two countries provided precisely this.

R. Cooper: The working assumption this morning has been that Japan is a *vital* society. I would like to put that on the table as a question. In doing so, I do not mean to imply the opposite. I am not a specialist on Japan, and therefore I am really just posing a question. In order to do that, we need to know more precisely what *vitality* means. Several suggestions of definitions were given this morning. One which Fernand Braun offered coming out of the conference in Prague was it meant identity and viability to Eastern Europeans. But that then confronts the question which George De Vos put, what is the unit of observation? Identity of whom? Viability of whom? The people who use these expressions take it for granted that they know what the relevant unit is, but it is not at all clear as we see now in Yugoslavia, the former Soviet Union. Professor Inoguchi suggested it is the ability to deal with challenges, both internal and external. Well, I would say it is the rare society that fails at that, for human beings are enormously adaptable creatures and most societies through history have adapted to the challenges.

I will fall back on an empirical approach and take as my starting point one of the most clearly *vital* societies we've ever seen: classical Greece. Depending on how you count, this lasted for three to six centuries and had an influence on society that lasted far longer. Now what were the characteristics of classical Greece that made it a *vital* society? I'd say there were two. One was a burst of creativity in areas that could be put under the heading 'truth and beauty': a lot of plays, sculptures, poetry and so forth in a tremendous burst of artistic creativity and philosophy and mathematics in the realm of the mind. The second criterion was a very strong civic sense, an identification with the community, and an active participation in the community was seen as part of the civilised life and necessary for the first. You wanted a society which understood and was receptive to creative outpourings, etc. Thus, the existence of a civil society and activities of the mind, including all of the arts, were key.

This is not just classical Greece, and I will cite John Maynard Keynes, who considered economics and the functioning of economies as a necessary but not sufficient condition for civilisation. In other words, *economics is secondary to a vital society*. This doesn't mean it is not important, but it is not the end objective. The outstanding thing about modern society since the industrial revolution is that we - Europe, North America, Japan, and increasingly countries like Korea and Singapore - have actually solved the economic problem. The best measure of that is that we feed ourselves with less than 10 per cent of the population, and in the case of the US far less than that - 2 per cent of the population. We take that for granted, but we shouldn't. All we have to do is mentally scan the world and appreciate that in Sub-Saharan Africa and even China, it takes 70-80 per cent of the labour force to feed the population. That's the way we all were six centuries ago. So we've solved the economic problem in that sense, we've created scope for all kinds of other things, and the question we now have to ask is how does society use that new freedom?

This is all just background, so let me turn now to the economic side and suggest very strongly that *economic growth per se is not a sufficient indicator of vitality*. Let me give two examples. One is Kenya, which in the 1980s has grown in excess of 4 per cent, quite a respectable rate of growth and much higher than the US. But this is all due to population growth, and per capita income actually declined in Kenya. It has the highest growth rate in the world, in excess of 4 per cent. So we don't want to count that. The Soviet Union had very respectable growth rates in the 1950s and 1960s due to a tremendous rate of increase of the capital stock.

They deprived their public of consumption and force-fed the capital stock of the country, and for a period of time grew very rapidly. There is a strong component of that, as Professor Kim just suggested, in the total aggregate economic growth of Japan and Korea in the last four decades. So somehow we don't want to count that, or at least I don't want to count that. So if you want a quantitative measure of economic activity, you choose total factor productivity growth that abstracts from the growth of the labour force and from the growth of the capital stock. One has to admit at this point that any society which is growing rapidly for whatever reason is imposing on itself the need to change and adapt, so it's an interesting question how rapidly growing societies adapt to that growth, and I don't want to dismiss this altogether.

If we focus now on total productivity growth, there are three ways to increase it. One is to move more resources out of low-productivity activities into high-productivity activities, and that's what all of our societies have done in moving people out of agriculture. In Japan and Europe, 40 per cent of the labour force was still in agriculture in 1950, so there was a big reallocation of resources into more productive activities. Secondly, absorbing applied knowledge from the rest of the world - imitation for sure - is an important process in the growth of all countries. Historically, the growth of the United States, and Japan and Korea in the last 40 years has come from Europe and the US in terms of absorbing technology. Both of those processes are important for societies that haven't undertaken them. But both are historically limited, for obvious reasons. Once the labour force is used in the most efficient way possible at any given time, the scope for reallocating the labour force is limited. Once existing technology has been fully absorbed, the scope for that is limited. I don't want to minimise those, but once they are set aside with their limitations, one is left with the *ability to generate new technology*. That's the fundamental source in economic *vitality, increases in total factor productivity*.

Here I make an observation, though I don't have the answers, that one of the notable features about the US, with some exceptions, though they are exceptions that prove the rule, is that almost all new ideas come from individuals operating as individuals and small firms. It's true that the development of economic innovations often takes place by large firms, but often only after they see the possibilities or the threat of the new idea. This is a striking thing, well-documented historically, and it has been updated recently. There is a structural reason for that, that large institutions, corporations, etc., have a large stake in existing modes of operation. It has existing products, marketing techniques, and capital stock, each of which is potentially jeopardised by new ideas. So American corporations take on new ideas when they see that the ideas are going to take place anyway, so the question is not whether, but who does.

The interesting thing about Japan, as I understand it, is that the sources of innovation seem to be large organisations, quite different from the US. Again, there are exceptions, but they tend to prove the rule. One of the things the rest of the world can learn from Japan is how to mobilise large-scale collective behaviour in a way that is innovative. The question for us to address tomorrow is, 'Can it last, or is it temporary?' Is it really a by-product of the catch-up phase which will atrophy once the catching-up is done? I don't pretend to have the answer to that question.

Another notable feature, again with a few exceptions, is that most of the Japanese innovations, at least in the studies which have been done, suggest that these are incremental in nature rather than fundamental in nature. Well, that's got to be true in general for the world. But when one apportions ratios, there are many more fundamental ideas coming out of Europe and the US relative to incremental ideas. And so again, for the future, in this Japanese corporate mode of innovation is there a bias against fundamental innovation, which is likely to be crippling in the long run? I pose this as a question, because there are exceptions to this, but the issue is: can the exceptions become the rule?

I come back then to my initial question. Is Japan a *vital* society? I think it is worth posing the question by these two criteria. I have a sense that in Japan while many activities, one might even say most, are communal in nature, at least for the majority male, Japan is not a civil society like that of ancient Greece in the sense that the Japanese actively participate in their own governance. There's an *extraordinary degree of acquiescence* here, as seen by an outsider. Now maybe one reason to acquiesce is that things are going so well, so why raise any complaints? Anyway, I think that this is a question that needs to be addressed. The second one is this issue of creativity. I am in no position to judge what is happening in the artistic world, but I don't have the impression that Japan is enormously creative in the most general sense. Then we come back to economic innovations, where, as I say, there is this very interesting feature that Japan seems to have mastered, at least for a certain class of innovations, a collective structure to achieve them, which I think the rest of the world would do well to understand better. But I leave the question as to whether that mode of organisation is sufficient to generate the fundamental innovations which would be the hallmark of a *vital* society.

Another thing I should have said earlier in response to George De Vos' very important intervention on who it is exactly we're talking about.

Again, if we are using Greece as the model, there is no question that the unit of observation, which we call the individual, really means the family. It is the family unit, in a collective enterprise, but nonetheless it is the family which is civically minded and creative. It is the interaction of this and the society. Using those standards, I again raise the question about whether or not Japan is a *vital* society. If those are not the appropriate standards, then we should be very clear what the alternative standards are.

T. Murphy: There have been a number of references to the Cold War during the course of the session, and the discussion and my identification as an economist lead me to recall a story from the Cold War. Apparently sometime during the 1960s, when Soviet military might was still very much at its height, there was the semi-annual May Day Parade through Red Square. This was at the time when Leonid Brezhnev was the head of the Soviet Union, and he and his generals were standing on the balcony overlooking the troops marching by. Brezhnev's chest swelled with pride as he saw rank upon rank of missile, troops, and armaments. Then he saw one man with a briefcase walking all by himself, and he turned to one of his generals and asked, 'Who's that?' The general responded, 'Oh, that's an economist! You have no idea the damage they can cause.'

In any case, considering the concept of *vitality* and how it relates to Japanese economic performance, *vitality* is one of those words which has entered into the Japanese language as *gairaigo*, often used by personnel departments. I remember being at a dinner with a chairman of a major Japanese financial institution, and he was talking about the qualities they looked for in coming recruits. He mentioned that *vitality* was the most important quality they were looking for. This peaked my interest, so I looked up some of the literature. *Vitality* seems to mean, in the Japanese context, a kind of great energy, though without any particular purpose, as with the ideal recruits. Obviously, in the economic sense, it would only take one chart parading Japan's GNP over the last 40 years vis-à-vis those of the OECD countries to show Japan's *vitality*. I'm not sure that in and of itself is therefore all that relevant. But if we consider the biological metaphor of *vitality* mentioned this morning, the point of *vitality* is to keep the creature alive. So, is the economic behaviour we see from Japanese corporations and the Japanese state likely, in the end, to preserve both Japanese corporate interests and the long-term economic interests of Japan as a whole?

This is where I have some question, and I know that Professor Cooper this morning said that he was not actually sure if we had answered the question of whether Japan has sufficient *vitality*. I would like to contribute to that question by posing it in another way. I am concerned specifically about the economic activity of Japanese corporations. Are they provoking the very ends that they seek to avoid? That is, is their expansion of market share so rapid that it triggers hostility and protectionist reactions to Japanese industry in other countries? Would it not be a greater sign of *vitality* to have a higher level of political consciousness on the part of major Japanese corporations which flood foreign markets with products, thereby inducing anti-Japanese political reactions? I guess I can make these statements now without being accused as a racist Japan-basher because it has now entered public dialogue in Japan, as well - most importantly in Morita Akio's article in *Bungei Shunju*, where he has raised these questions. It has now become part of the general discourse in Japan.

Concerning the trends and directions in Japan's external accounts, one more time you see that Japan is beginning to accumulate an enormous current account surplus. This time, however, it is not being accompanied by the capital exports which in the 1980s avoided a balance of payments crisis. Again, if Japan tries to export its way out of the current recession, a likelihood exists that the global balance of payments system will simply not be able to accommodate. This could bring about the kind of breakdown in the global trading and financial systems which would make it impossible for Japan to accomplish its goal of exporting its way out of the recession.

The current debates that are going on in Japan are very bitter about the appropriate level of interest rates. The leading politician, Kanemaru Shin, has actually called for the resignation of the governor of the Bank of Japan, Mr Mieno, because he's refusing to lower interest rates. One consideration which one does not hear as part of the Japanese debate is the effect on Japan's external relations. Japan now, as a country that accounts for 20 per cent of global GNP and was in the 1980s (and will again be in two years) the world's principal source of investment capital, no longer has the freedom to make economic decisions in isolation because it affects the entire planet. But one does not hear that element in the debate.

I saw in the paper this morning that the *shunto*, the annual ritualised negotiation for wage increases by what are called labour unions here, finished with an agreed wage increase that is effectively the lowest in something like 20 years, in percentage terms. Again, the effect on the global economy, when one of the significant problems is the lack of Japanese consumer demand, suggests that there are questions outstanding about the *vitality*, as it were, of economic debates and economic processes in Japan. I just simply throw these out as questions, not as any solutions.

M. Shinohara: In relation to the corporation, let me add one more problem. In the decision making for corporations, Mr R. Ballon of Sophia University, Tokyo has said that Japanese business leaders - the president or chairman - are just the followers, not the leaders. 95 per cent of decision-making is conducted by little people, and therefore there has to be negotiation in the middle groups. This takes time, and so sometimes the decision-making of Japanese companies is described as slow in decision, but quick in action. Once the direction of the decision is determined, not only is the conduct quick, but it is dynamic because there is such consensus. In Japan, the investment ratio in these is much higher than in the US. Secondly, the Japanese investment pattern was very dynamic, especially before the oil crisis, as discussed in my paper.

In the Japanese decision-making system, the consensus system has the biggest problem of who takes responsibility. All of the people in the corporation try to act very dynamically, as seen in the very large amplitude of Japanese investment ratios. This difference in investment behaviour with the US can be traced in part to the mode of decision-making in the two countries. But also, in the case of the Japanese labour market, people are hired out of school into a system of lifetime-employment. This allows the corporation to educate them successfully. This kind of thing will not occur in the US and Korea because there is a higher level of mobility. This is another reason for Japan's high growth rate. Japanese business behaviour is not top-down, but middle- (or bottom)-up, and the resulting sense of joint responsibility and a spirit of collective commitment allows the company staff to forge ahead with their work.

K. Iwai: I will only make a brief response to what Professor Shinohara was trying to say. He is talking about the peculiarity of Japanese corporate decision-making. I don't want to make the concept of corporations a cure-all, but I may be able to explain part of what he said. In the 1930s there was a treated discussion about modern corporations, and it said that the decision-making shifted from the shareholders to the management. But when we ask who controls corporations in Japan, my answer would be neither shareholders nor management. This is a caricature, but what Japanese management is doing is carrying out the 'will' of the corporations. In this way you can explain why top management doesn't have to take responsibility and can delegate the decision-making to middle management, because their decisions are always in the name of corporations. This partly explains what Professor Shinohara was saying.

G. Fukushima: I would like to make the comment that in thinking about the *vitality* of the Japanese economy by the measure which Professor Kim said, in terms of growth rates, one of the conclusions I've reached based on my dealings with many Japanese and US corporations and their governments is that the relationship between competition and cooperation, as alluded to by Professor Shinohara earlier, is an important difference between the US and Japan. To put it in simplified terms, in the US there is a tendency to have a great deal of faith in the market and let the chips fall where they may, with the notion that that will be the best outcome for the consumer. The notion is to protect competition, not competitors. In Japan, it has been my observation that the notion is that you don't trust the market, that you set the goals and parameters in advance and, as Karel van Wolferen said this morning, use the market in order to produce certain ends. In the case of post-war Japan, I think these ends were to benefit the producers. So the notion is to *protect the competitors rather than competition per se.*

The basis on which the Japanese Fair Trade Commission operates versus the American Anti-Trust division of the Federal Trade Commission is a good example. I won't go into details, but if you talk to the individuals involved, you will note quickly that the notion of competition is considerably different. I think in many ways the *Japanese combination of the competition and cooperation has contributed to the vitality, or at least the growth, of the nation.* By the same notion, in both the US government and corporations, there is a tendency to think of competition and cooperation in dichotomous terms, and in American companies' relationship with each other or with Japanese companies, they tend to classify the others as friends or adversaries, and strategic alliances accentuate this. Japanese firms, in my opinion, are more able to make different determinations based on the particular context as to whether another company is friend or adversary. I think this extra complexity in the Japanese companies' relationships is a factor in the *vitality* of Japan.

On Professor Cooper's comments this morning, while I agree that in the Western classical-derived sense of *vitality* there are required attributes, I also think that they are Western-based notions that emphasise process and the individual. The Japanese example has set in many ways a challenge which up till now has been a passive challenge, but it will be increasingly an active challenge to these Western notions. This challenge is more in a very goal-oriented, results-oriented purposeful way of thinking about *vitality*, with more emphasis on groups and organisations and corporations, as opposed to the individual.

T. Inoguchi: I'd like to bring up a case which demonstrates Glen's point about different views of the markets quite starkly. In the World Bank, there are disputes over the lending policies, and one of the Japanese executives in the World Bank has somehow been successful in publishing one big study on industrialisation in South Korea and India. The thrust of the study is that not only the market mechanism but also appropriate and effective government interventions are indispensable in pushing successful economic development. In the study the different views are well revealed. In previous and current World Bank lending, the policies have been basically the US belief in the market mechanism. But this recent study counters that orthodoxy, and it has been put forth in written form, even if it is restricted to internal use. I think that this is going to be a very significant debate, and the Japanese view of the market is that you have to tame the market and discipline the economic actors, both of which can be very wild. This debate will emerge very sharply, especially in the international institutions like the World Bank. Related to the concept of *vitality*, however, I cannot say which way in this debate is superior, for it depends on circumstances, habits, etc.

G. Fukushima: I only mentioned this because if we take Dr Kim's definition of *vitality* as economic growth rates, then it is very relevant to what extent government intervention or full faith in the market contributes to economic growth. I really believe that there is a real challenge to the orthodox University of Chicago view of the world, with real policy implications for not only the World Bank, but countries like the US and its trade policies.

T. Inoguchi: I understand your point and its ongoing relevance, but in my earlier presentation I did not intend to praise Japan's *vitality*, but only to present my own very elementary view of the *vitality* of nations in very general form. I have not said anything to confirm the past or present *vitality* of Japan in any area, and I even am concerned about the wisdom of debating the *vitality* of nation-states when it is so unclear if nation-states are going to continue to be the primary unit of global organisation. Therefore I would like to see more discussion of *vitality* in general terms before we focus on any area or country like Japan.

G. Fukushima: My understanding was that we should approach this inductively, drawing on case discussions to form broader conclusions, but you are working the other way. Perhaps the chairman can help direct us in the proper direction.

A. Clesse: Of course, the term 'nation' does not mean nation-state in this context. It is a very broad term, referring above all to societies in a general sense, but this morning it was the aim to start with some general perspectives and, from there, proceed to more specific analysis and discover correlations. For example, one that was mentioned during the lunch break was a possible dissociation in time of the economic *vitality* and economic success of Japan. If that were true, it would be an intriguing phenomenon. I hope we can have more discussion on this kind of questions. I think Richard Cooper would like to say something.

R. Cooper: I would just like to say something on the earlier discussion. I think what is called the 'American position' in the World Bank is a caricature of the American position which is unfortunately made credible by the fact that the Reagan Administration offered a caricature of the American position. There are not many Americans who would disagree with the proposition that markets can sometimes be erratic, and therefore you need a regime to influence them, and certainly that market participants must be subject to a set of conditions - that is not a difference between the US and Japan. What is a difference is, as Fukushima mentioned, that, if it's true, Japan protects the competitors while America protects the competition. That would be a fundamental difference, but I wonder if the generalisation is true about Japan, because there have been a number of competitors that have been allowed to fail - to be sure with state aid in a phasing out. That could be an empirical question here. But certainly, if as stated, that would be an important difference in the points of view of the two. I think that the American view is that it is necessary, in a system that relies on private initiative for progress, that failure be allowed. My impression is that the Japanese system also allows for failure, just in a different way.

A. Clesse: To maintain our intellectual *vitality*, I think we should soon switch to other aspects and return tomorrow morning to these economic aspects. Philip Windsor.

P. Windsor: What I would like to do, and this might provide some transition to other aspects, is to ask some kind of question about my understanding of how the Japanese economic system might be working and what consequences this might have in the short term. I am emphatically not an economist, but these might be somewhat at variance with what Mr Hale discussed this morning.

My first contention is not that Japan is not economically *vital*. That would be a bit silly to say and of course cheeky for anyone who comes from the United Kingdom. But the contention would be that it is a *very peculiar kind of economic vitality*, and it might be *more vulnerable to changes in the world order*. It depends on a relationship between banks, corporations, and stock markets, which is a very strange kind of relationship. In the past, banks have not been making much money, if any, from their main lending activities because their competition was the market share. What this led to was a growth in the money supply which exceeded the nominal growth of the GNP, and therefore the excess liquidity flowed into the asset market. The asset inflation was quite staggering, if you consider that the land value of Japan is five times that of the United States, which is 25 times bigger than Japan in sheer territory. Nonetheless, if the stock market kept rising, the banks could adjust their level of current profits by realising capital gains on their huge equity holdings, so what you have then is not making money on the lending but rather on the equity holdings. This rising market in turn allowed the corporations to raise funds cheaply through equity financing, and therefore cheap funding strengthened international competitiveness, especially in commodities. So this means that the level of the stock market in Japan seems to be *vitally* important, and as the markets declined, it has created a near crisis of capital adequacy. No wonder the Bank of Japan doesn't want to reduce interest rates. This all leads to the danger of a recessionary spiral with a marked decline in capital investment.

In these circumstances, it seems to me likely that the government will try to sustain nominal growth by expanding the money supply and by deficit. That, as I understand it, would lead to inevitable inflation, but this time not asset inflation, but Consumer Price Index inflation.

Now, the poor old Japanese society - family structures and all the rest of it - have already taken enough of a battering from the asset inflation. Are they now going to have to face the kind of CPI inflation which would also threaten the way that society functions, the assumptions on which it works, the traditional values, and so on? All those non-*vital* elements of society, which Professor Sugimoto mentioned this morning, become extremely import in this context. In other words, the social context of Japan is going to be changing and affect the economic future of Japan in a way in which, up till now, has not been the case in Japan. At the same time, Japan is going to be much more vulnerable to international pressures than it has been before. I think in that sense, the economic question is turned into a whole bunch of social questions.

S. Sato: I'd like to go back to the very interesting argument related by Professor Cooper in the morning. I quite agree that the essence of economic *vitality* is the growth, the ability to raise productivity. There are three ways to do so, as elaborated by Professor Cooper. For the world right now, the third factor, technological innovation, is the most important factor. He pointed out two Japanese characteristics, that the technological development in Japan is more incremental than in the West and that most is done by the large corporations. Let me explain the reasons for these. Japan's incremental approach is a function of its stage in economic development. First Germany, in the 19th century, and later America, were also both primarily incremental in their research because they were catch-up countries. So this was normal for Japan also.

M. Kohsaka: Let me say something about the meaning of *vitality*. To me, *vitality* is nothing more than an idea or biological energies. Therefore, when I listen to some of your remarks which describe the Japanese economy now as *vital*, I am a little confused. The Japanese economy now may be powerful, but *the society is not as vital as it was 40 or 50 years ago*. There is a historical precedence here, England in the middle of the 19th century was less rich than the England of the 20th century. But apparently, the England in 1850 was more *vital*. At the same time, as Marx described, the England in the mid-19th century was full of problems, as was the United States at the beginning of the 20th century, with social troubles, strikes, etc. So *vitality is accompanied by a kind of violence*. That is my first point.

When I listen to words like *vitality*, I go back to the second half of the 1940s, when both the labour unions and management were strong. As a result, there was much disturbance and conflict, not at all like today's mild, calm negotiations. Also, look at the black market. It was a bad thing, but it was full of *vitalities*. Everything which was not constrained by governments was considered as democratic. That kind of energy must be channeled into some systems, and I think we did that in the 1950s. We produced a system, but a system, by definition, channels and restrains energies. Institutions and organisations have their own inertia, which restrain energies and bring problems. These are the problems we may now face, and I think the Japanese are not so *vital* now. My point is that *any institution restrains human activities*. It is necessary, but it can become a yoke.

Another thing is that *vitality can be grown into fruits by historical accident*. Japan was able to create the Japanese system only because of the stability provided by the occupation by American troops after the Second World War. That was a historical accident, and such accidents in history are quite rare. Even in Eastern Europe today, I sometimes hope that they could be occupied, but they are not.

A. Clesse: I shouldn't be biased, but these were very interesting comments. I think you have raised some very important questions, even with regard to the general project on the *vitality* of nations, questions which have not been raised in previous meetings about the channelling of *vitality*, what it implies, and the role of historical accident. Professor Sato.

S. Sato: I have a violent proposal. Let us confine our discussions to economic *vitality*, not to biological or cultural *vitality*. Of course, there are many issues which play a part in economic *vitality*, but the definitions involved with the other *vitalities* are too vague. According to the Prague meeting, in which I didn't participate, the essence of *vitality* is the maintenance of resiliency and identity. In the pre-industrial period, the Chinese and Indian societies were two of the most *vital* societies in the world. They had successfully maintained their identity, their system for 2000 years. But is this appropriate in the age of industrialisation, where technological innovation is so rapid? The main interest why we are interested in the *vitality* of nations is that we are now living in an age where innovation is a matter of fact, where the level of rapid technology development promotes rapid changes in the centres of production throughout the world. That is the reason why an increasing number of people are interested in the *vitality* of nations. If that is true, then we had better confine ourselves to economic *vitality*. Otherwise our discussions will lose focus.

A. Clesse: So Professor Sato, if I understood him well, wants to confine the discussion only to economics.

S. Sato: No, my point was that if you want to explain economic *vitality* we need to consider all the other aspects of society, cultural and political, but we should not discuss the *vitality* of music or family life. We cannot define these, like why 18th-century Germany produced such *vital* composers. If we discussed that kind of thing, it is beyond our capability.

Social and Cultural Vitality

G. De Vos: I think we concentrate on the present and don't look at what was going on in the so-called 'pre-modern' period before and during the Meiji Restoration. In addition to Japan's strong early roots in Confucianism, with its emphasis on internal self-development, another interesting transformation happened when the samurai were displaced at the end of the Tokugawa period. They became the educators and the entrepreneurs. We understate the idea of entrepreneurship in Japan; there were many entrepreneurs during the Meiji period. Some of them were of merchant background and some of samurai background, but you certainly had people reading Horatio Alger and Samuel Smiles in Japan as they modernised. We don't find anything comparable in China or Korea. So the Japanese were rather unique in what they were doing in the Meiji period. You must consider the historical dimension when we talk about where the *vitality* was coming from.

The samurai ethic became universalised. It became the backbone of education. The Imperial prescript of education ironically enough was based on the work of a Korean Confucian scholar, not a Japanese scholar. The rescript was promulgated in the schools. There was universal conscription, whereas in the pre-modern period the samurai did the fighting, the modern period had a development in which the military service was universalised by the government.

The government looked around, and they were very wise. Who had the best army? The Germans did, so they brought in German advisers. Who had the best navy? The British did, so they brought in British naval advisers. Who had the best railways? The British again, railways went into Japan relatively early compared with most parts of Europe. Railway development and electrification easily took place fairly early on. Japan didn't just suddenly appear and modernise; they were modernising while Europe was modernising, all of this is overlooked. So let me say again that the Japanese had a modern bureaucracy potentially in place. If you go to Africa or other places that are trying to accomplish economic development, they have no educated bureaucracy to carry the weight of a complex modern system. The Japanese had a government administration in place, and it was deliberately conscious of what was going on in Europe.

Again, on innovation, let's take a look at Honda. Honda started out with a bicycle shop. This is a typical American success story: he went from bicycles to motorcycles, and now he's got the Honda Accord as a car selling in the tradition of Henry Ford in the United States. So all of these things show that the mentality of the Japanese was entrepreneurial, and they inherited this from what was going on in the pre-modern period. They had a very active, adaptive merchant class. They had a bureaucracy in place. They had all the necessary personnel for modernising in place during the Tokugawa and Meiji periods. So this does have to do with culture, because you can't explain this only by institutions.

You have to explain - and this is my final outrageous psychological statement - that the Japanese produced the *most successful Confucian mothers*. That is, the Japanese women internalised Confucianism and acted it out; they were relatively educated and they educated their children. The men didn't educate the children, the women did. If you look at modern societies, and I heard this from the Egyptians discussing their fight with the Israelis, they said, 'We don't have educated women like the Israelis.' So some of the strength of the nation lies in its educated women. So I'll get on that outrageous topic and quit right there.

A. Clesse: Thank you, George De Vos. Let me also encourage participants from other Asian countries to join the debate. We have some from China, Hong Kong, India, and elsewhere. First, perhaps Gordon Berger will add to what has been said.

G. Berger: I wanted to add two things briefly to what Professor De Vos has said, both to further what he has said and to question it. The first was that another very prominent feature of the Tokugawa period was diversity. That is to say that each of the 268 or 270 *daimyo* domains in Japan tended toward conforming to norms established by the Bakufu or the Tokugawa government, and it was more often the case towards the latter end of the period that what these tended to conform to was successful policies initiated in one or another of these domains. One of the most successful innovators of the Meiji period were indeed the same administrators of local *daimyo* domains who in previous years were successful in this way. So the *diversity* in Japan at that point was an extremely important part of the dynamism and *vitality* of the Tokugawa Japan.

Now the question I have, and I don't know if we'll have time to get back to this today, but I have every intention of talking about mothers. I want to suggest the possibility that the education of Japanese children by mothers is a phenomenon that comes after the Tokugawa period rather than before. It is my understanding that what was sought out as being a good woman in the Tokugawa period was being a good wife, and it was only after the Meiji period begins, actually with studies of Western families, that the idea of good wife and wise mother comes to describe the paradigm of the ideal Japanese woman.

S. Sato: I don't mean to disagree with anything that Professor De Vos has said, but it should be pointed out that, as in Thailand and South Korea, rapid growth and industrialisation can occur with various cultural backgrounds without the strong Confucian influence.

G. De Vos: Well, one very uncomfortable thing for the Koreans to admit is that they had 45 years of a Japanese educational system, and although it was very disparaging to them, it was still the same educational system that was developing in Japan. Secondly, the Koreans have Confucian mothers, as do the Chinese. The Chinese merchants took over Confucianism when the Mandarins disappeared. You find there was an emulation of the higher class, and Confucianism became very important in the merchant class, even though it was a despised class. We find the same in Korea. If you are emulating the elite, they educated their daughters with flower-arranging and even literacy to some degree. So there was in the wealthier merchants and farmers the idea of preparing her well so that she could marry into some higher position. One of the great dynamics of Japan which is hidden by some people that think these classes were so rigid is the fact that there was tremendous social mobility within the classes, the merchants and the samurai. Hideyoshi is an exemplar of this. So, within the Japanese system, there was a *great deal of energy associated with social mobility patterns emulating the elite*.

S. Sato: Just a quick response: I don't know how important the Confucian mothers are for the *vitality* of a nation, and I don't know just how Confucian Japanese mothers are based on my own experiences. But having said that, the Japanese rule over Korea was very short - only 35 years - so it was quite different than modern British rule over India. The Japanese failed to establish a modern bureaucratic position in South Korea. But without such conditions, South Korea did develop, and more quickly than the Japanese did.

A. Clesse: I would like to let someone from Korea respond.

K. Kim: Well, I do not wish to defend or characterise Korean mothers. The reason why I raise my hand is to endorse the suggestion made by Professor Sato earlier, that we should talk about *vitality* with reference to a challenge. Without a challenge or a threat to an organism, the *vitality* question never comes up. Professor De Vos' exposition on the history is relevant to Japan's ability to meet the challenges of that time, namely modernisation. But we are here to talk about the *vitality* of a nation, not its modernisation. We are here to talk about the ability of Japan to make a successful adjustment to new opportunities which arise. So we need to talk about the nature of the challenges facing Japan today. Otherwise this will be only a course in history, but the reason why so many of us from different disciplines are here is to talk about whether or not Japan is going to make a positive contribution or role in the development of mankind.

A. Iriye: I agree with the statement just made. *There is a tendency to confuse vitality with modernisation,* and once we do that we get into all sorts of problems about why some countries have modernised more successfully than others. I think this is a mistake. This conference is more about the *vitality* of nations in the current situation, not comparative modernisations. What matters is how countries contribute to global well-being and *vitality*. Is there anything in today's Japan that can contribute to that, to the further *vitalisation* of mankind? I'm not very optimistic about that, because once you ask that question, then the discussion ceases to be purely economic. Japan may continue to trade with nations, but will it promote global *vitalisation*? It seems to me that it has to be in the cultural sphere. Sato said that we should not be talking about culture in terms of music and literature and the like, but I think that this is the only area where we can talk about *vitality*, cultural *vitality*, if we are focusing on the contemporary world. What can this country produce culturally that can add to universal *vitality*? I think that there is a great deal of scepticism about that around the world.

Y. Sugimoto: I just want to return to some of my earlier points in the context of what Professor Kim called the challenge to Japanese society and the global community. I would like to make three random observations. The first is the question of the interconnection between what may be called aggregate or corporate *vitality* on the one hand and individual *vitality* on the other. I venture to hypothesise that in present Japanese society there is a definite negative correlation between those two factors. There is very little question in my mind that there is a great deal of corporate *vitality*, but when you look at the life conditions of individuals, the level of *vitality* would be relatively low. The *level of individual exhaustion or fatigue* is the complete opposite to what one would expect. There are a good number of corporate soldiers who have died because of overwork. They are not living anymore; they are not *vital* at all. So the first suggestion is that it might well be the case that there is a *very strong negative correlation between corporate and individual vitality*.

My second point relates to the rather useful dichotomy that Richard Cooper brought up in the distinction between the economic and the civil. Here I would suggest again that in Japanese society there may be a very strong negative correlation between economic and civic *vitality*. Richard Cooper suggested that economic *vitality* may be a necessary but not sufficient factor for national *vitality*. I would suggest that *perhaps economic vitality Japanese style might be an impediment to civic vitality*. It is not difficult to observe some of the *vital* areas in the Japanese civic community. You can look at popular culture and female office employees, and consider the extent to which individuals are free from corporate and economic constraints might be positively correlated to the degree of civic *vitality*.

The third point relates to what Glen Fukushima made some brief reference to, the possibility of a conceptual bias which might be built into our way of looking at the question of *vitality*. I think he raised a rather interesting point in that. Although there is no question that Japan is an economic superpower, it is still situated in a cultural periphery in the global context. We are still living in the age of Anglo-Saxon dominance, we are discussing these things in English, US television networks are very dominant factors in our perception of what is happening in the world. I would like to see sometime in the future the emergence of Japanese cultural *vitality* in the international context. However, I am quite puzzled about what kind of civic or cultural model Japan can offer the international community. We have heard much about the adoption by other societies of the Japanese management practices, industrial relations practices, etc. in the economic sphere. But is there anything that Japan can offer as the civic model of this society to the outside world?

E. Seidensticker: We're talking about *vitality*, but we don't really know what it means. *Vitality - vital* - comes from the Latin word for life. However, we don't really know what life means. I got out lots of books from libraries and read about it, and the conclusion is that nobody knows what life is. You can write about the attributes of life, that it grows and ceases, etc., but these are all just attributes. So here we are talking about *vitality*, which means essentially the existence of life, and we don't even know what the most fundamental word means. So really, and this is an awful thing to say, but we don't know what we're talking about. I suppose we're talking about a kind of grasshopper life, hopping all over the place stomping on others and being stomped on, and certainly that is a kind of life. But we still don't know what we mean.

Nor do we know if *vitality* is necessarily good or not. Common sense may tell us that it is not necessarily good, that it is neutral. Some kinds of *vitality* are good and others are not so good. I am sure that the Spanish buccaneers and small pox germs absolutely overflow with *vitality*, but do they do anybody any good? I think there has been an assumption in our discussions that *vitality* is good, but it is a neutral quality which we must judge by what it is aimed at.

My chief subject is Japanese popular culture. Here I think we have an instance of a kind of *vitality* that has gone very badly wrong. Japanese popular culture is very *vital*; there's no question about that. The number of people who are addicted to the latest *aidoru*, the Japanese expression for a television celebrity, runs into the millions. The number of *manga* magazines that are sold runs into the billions. These indicate *vitality* and the grasshopper aspect of it - an awful lot of jumping around. But if we compare Japanese pop culture today with 150 years ago, in the *bunka-bunsei* era, I think it would be awfully hard to deny that there has been a

dreadful falling off, that it once was good and now is not. So you see it
goes on having this neutral attribute, *vitality*, but it was once much better
than it is now. The Tokugawa period had Japanese classical music, which
was very good music, at least in the sense that it was subtle, complex,
good music. Japan had the geisha. Japan had a very lively, varied
literature. Japan had the *ukiyo-e* colored print. If we look at the successors
to all of these things, they are all of them vastly inferior.

The successor to the *ukiyo-e* is the *manga*, isn't it? Now, I think I'll limit
myself to this because I am running out of time. The *ukiyo-e* was a
popular and vulgar form. It was vulgar in almost every sense of the term.
It was vulgar in the sense that the plebeian audience liked it and in the
narrow sense of the term, for much of it was pornographic. But the
essential thing about it is that it was good. When it reached Europe in the
latter half of the century, it was in a very vulgar fashion. It was used as
packing paper, the Japanese thought so very little of it. Very important
European artists, particularly in France, retrieved it, were deeply
impressed by it, and it played a very important role in the transition of
European art from the three-dimensional to the two-dimensional. Even
when *ukiyo-e* is pornographic, it is still good art. It is a very difficult
balancing act when something, which in its subject matter is ultimately
gross, is still good art. Even when they were giving us openly erotic work,
they did not lose their sense of line and colour. Now, what are we to say
about the *manga*, except that it is awful? Nobody could call it good art.
There is nothing really distinguished about it. It is the successor to *ukiyo-e*.

There are many other examples that could be introduced, but the main
point is the same. Japanese popular art has declined dreadfully in the past
two centuries. Now the best thing that can be said for it is that it's bad; the
worst thing that can be said is that it's nauseating. But it vacillates between
the two. So what can Japan contribute to the world? What Japan has
contributed is not very promising in artistic terms. It has contributed three
items: that awful thing that young people put in their ears so they live in a
constant din - what's it called? A Walkman? The *manga*, that is the second
thing. And the third thing is *karaoke*. Now, what is one really to say about
karaoke, except that it's the absolute pits. It's bad music badly sung. You
can't really go much lower than that. If this is what Japan has to contribute
to the world, I think we can say that Japan has contributed nothing. The
prospect is sort of bleak, isn't it?

W. Wetherall: As a student of popular culture, both past and present, I
share some of Professor Seidensticker's opinions. However, some of the
vulgar *ukiyo-e* of the Edo period also disturbed the authorities, and they

censored it. It was then thrown out as wrapping paper, and, like a lot of our so-called 'high culture' today, it was rediscovered. The vulgarity of the *kabuki* also angered the authorities, who banned it due to its elements of prostitution. Today, interestingly, the P.T.A. and local communities are trying to control or censor the content of *manga*. So perhaps in two centuries our descendants will be taking *manga* out of our trunks as collector's items and have a different view. I don't basically disagree on his comments on the *manga*, but there are elements which are similar in the way these features of popular culture are regarded by contemporary authorities.

E. Seidensticker: Well, not being a prophet, I can't say what will happen to *manga*, and as a historian after a fashion of literature, I am perfectly aware of the impossibility of saying what is good about what is good and what is not good about what is not good. It is really next to impossible, but you can have a very strong feeling about which is which.

I. Umezu: I would like to touch upon one or two things related to culture in general. First of all, on the so-called education-related role which the Japanese mother plays: now it may be that in former days the Japanese mother played a very confucianistically-important role as an educator, but now I must confess that I'm one of those Japanese husbands who leave almost all the education-related responsibility to their wives, but the major part of the Japanese mothers' responsibility is to get their kids to go to a good prep school, or *juku*, so that it's less substantive. This causes a difficulty, though, as the whole education system is coming under debate now. Certainly education played an important role in Japan's modernisation, but it is becoming a bit of a problem-area in keeping up Japanese *vitality* and, more broadly, in terms of what Japan can really contribute to international society.

My main topic relates to the corporation which has been mentioned quite often today. Certainly this is an economic factor overlapping with the cultural issue, and the element of organisation in economic *vitality* is a very cultural thing, I think. I often recall when an American friend of mine said, 'I have many good Japanese friends, but I just don't understand the mechanism by which such thoughtful people become part of the organisation, an anonymous entity, and party to the sometimes ruthless decisions which are made in the name of the organisation.' This is a mystery which is often taken up in the discussion on the Japanese mentality. As was pointed out earlier, there is a trade-off between this organisational discipline and regimentation and the strengths and dynamism of each individual. We can argue in positive and negative ways about this. Certainly, this organisational strength has been the source of Japanese economic development. But, on the other hand, it is a difficulty in the process of Japan becoming more internationalised and acquiring the art of getting along with the rest of the world.

Now, on the positive side of this organisation, the individual can have a sense of fulfillment in playing a role that you're required to do within an organisation. Many Japanese don't mind being unsung heroes; they can find some sense of fulfillment in this. On the other hand, there are some negative things. This tendency of the Japanese becoming totally mindless in the name of the organisation is that perhaps there is a conventional wisdom in Japanese society that to follow in the majority opinion would be the safest way of dealing with the world. So this is quite contrary to the American society, where the squeaky wheel gets the grease.

This is a very important point in the context of what Professor Kim pointed out; when we discuss the kind of challenges that Japan faces, how we can reconcile the positive strengths of this corporate behaviour and the negative side of the corporate ethic which is embedded in most Japanese. I do not have an answer and would like to hear your opinions on this.

A. Iriye: I have to miss tomorrow morning's session, so I wanted to make a few comments on the very interesting statements so far. In my view, two things have emerged in this afternoon's discussion. One is the great difficulty in defining *vitality*. The second theme which seems to have emerged is that Japan may have begun to lose its historical *vitality*. Both of these generalisations are, I think, going to stay with us throughout the conference. I think one way to get at that would be to deal with *vitality* not in the abstract, but in some comparative framework.

In any given moment, which country or countries could be characterised as more *vital*, or driven by this sense of *vitality*, than other countries? It is in this comparative sense that Japan has been characterised as driven by *vitality* at the end of the 19th century, though I don't think it was in absolute terms like rate of growth, per capita income, etc., where the US and Western Europe were far ahead until the 1960s. But compared with other Asian countries, it cannot be disputed that Japan was making more rapid economic progress. In that context, however, I have to take exception to the very useful statement by Mr Hale when he talks about Japan as the only non-white Asian country to retain its independence; Thailand did, too. I think that in making an exception out of Japan, one might be somewhat distorted in looking at Meiji history. In looking at this, Japan may not have been that much different from other Asian countries, it may just have been lucky. Of course, with the samurai tradition, it was able to organise its military more quickly and effectively, but I am not so sure it was that far ahead in terms of culture, religion, and economic performance. It may even have been behind Korea and China until about 1900. China was the most advanced, economically speaking, in the world until about 1800. So it really depends which time period and which countries you are comparing.

But we also need to compare different aspects of *vitality*. I and a few others have begun to discuss the cultural aspect of *vitality* as distinct from economic *vitality*. That is very important. A country could be economically characterised in terms of *vitality*, but culturally it could be very stagnant. What Seidensticker pointed out, and I think we all agree, is that *Japan's cultural vitality today is either nil or negative compared to the past, even though its economic vitality still seems prominent*, although it has lost its momentum for some time as seen in relative growth rates with the other East Asian countries except the Philippines. I don't know when the cultural downturn began. The only area which I know is in terms of scholarship, and of course other experts might disagree with me, but in my own field of inquiry, the history of international relations, I think there was a tremendous creative energy in Japan around 1960. Most of the important works were published between 1960 and 1963, and that's now 30 years ago. Why is it then that in some areas *vitality* may linger on but in others it is lost?

This brings me back to question education. To the extent that cultural *vitality* has declined in Japan, why is it? It seems to me that education has to be one basic answer here. It would seem to me that the United States, in terms of education, is far more characterisable as *vital*, as well as the United Kingdom and most other countries, in fact. The fact that far more foreign students wish to study in the United States or the United Kingdom than in Japan says something about their cultural *vitality*. The stress on information and conformity may have created the kind of situation where there is not much creativity going on.

This leads to my next and final point, the question of global *vitality*. One question I can raise is, to the extent that *vitality* is a good thing, where is the cultural and economic *vitality* the world will need going to come from? Put another way, is there anything Japan can contribute to global economic and cultural *vitality*. If I may be permitted to confine myself to the cultural aspects of this, it would seem that in today's condition *there is not that much one can expect from Japan in playing a role in vitalising the world*. This would have to be related to contemporary problems of the environment, global telecommunications development and consequent cultural vulgarisation of individual creativity. All of this is going on, and we need to ask if Japan is prepared to play such a role in *revitalising* the world's culture.

W. Wetherall: There has been a tendency in recent comments to separate culture from economics in terms of *vitality*, but I don't think that is really the case. If the economic *vitality* results in an increase in pathology in the family, then you are going to find in the future a feedback. This could also be argued for the culture. Let's look at the content of the economic activity which is producing the vulgar culture and the environmental destruction. One cannot separate these issues; they have to come together. In fact. if one anticipates consequences, then one must come up with a non-neutral concept of *vitality*, because, as Professor Kim said, it is a question of being able to accommodate and survive the challenges of the future. These challenges are various forms of pathology within our human societies and between our human societies and the larger ecosphere.

S. Vishwanathan: As we saw in the economic aspects, there is a tendency to define *vitality* in economic terms only. I would rather take over from what Professor Kim said about a nation's ability to respond to a challenge. I have problems here with the comparative perspective. What are we really comparing? Can we compare India and Japan? As national units, of course, they can be compared, but will I not encounter over-generalisations in this, and thus coming to the wrong conclusions? Professor Iriye discussed the timing of such comparisons, but the variables in each nation are so different. So even when I talk about India and Japan, the differences are so many. For example, it is generally said that Indians try to escape coming to proper conclusions by talking about their multi-ethnic society with its various cultures, etc. But this is really an important thing, because from this perspective, Japan is very small, very easy to organise, and thus comparable more to one of the ethnic communities in India. So when I have to make a generalisation about India with regard to economic *vitality*, there may be no meaning. But if I compare a community, for example, if I analysed the community that really prospered after the partition of India and Pakistan, there are so many factors similar to the way Japan has developed its own nation. Therefore, if I make a generalisation from the results, only the GNP, per capita income, and income distribution, etc., I will run into a lot of difficulties. So the way a particular country responds to particular challenges, including the enormous internal challenges faced by a country like India, shows *vitality*. So, from Japan's point of view, a multi-ethnic society like India might appear to have not *vitality*, but weaknesses. This is a broad question, applying to countries other than India. We must consider differences other than culture, like the geophysical situation, the historical development, and social organisation. *Everything is so different that the parameters which we use to define Japan's vitality might not even apply to India's vitality.* So even comparing two countries' *vitalities* at the same historical time on the basis of certain elements would bring us again to the problem of putting societies in a hierarchical scale, or a scale with two different categories (like Confucianist and non-Confucianist cultures), and then trying to deal with that.

So if the purpose of our discussions is to understand Japan better, then I agree that we have to know how their organisation works and in what ways they have been able to respond to challenges. But we should not necessarily come to the conclusion that that is the only way in which they could have responded.

This brings me to my last point. I have a *feeling that the Japanese, with their homogeneity, have a certain in-built weakness of not being able to really interact and work in unison with societies which have different cultures or with other cultures.* This has to be started within Japan itself, as is now being talked about as internationalisation, but also with developing new ways of interacting with cultures within Japan, so that they may be able to develop, if I may say so, compassion or a sense of understanding of the problems of other nations with a different geophysical placement and historical development. I hope this conference addresses itself not only in placing nations in a scale of *vitality* which contributes to the economic development of the nation, but also various other factors which would help nations to find means to coexist and help each other in the development of nations in the developing world, not just the 'new dragons'.

Y. Muhaimin: I think this conference has some confusion about the definition of *vitality*. I know we are just brainstorming, but without any clear or strict definition, the discussion will be rather messy. For example, if we consider *vitality* as a function of viability, or survivability, then even nations like Greece or China need to be included here. But we seem to focus on primarily Europe, Japan, and the US.

Also, is there any cultural pattern which makes a nation *vital*? I don't think there is, because if you compare Japan and the United States, they have almost completely different cultural patterns. Japan stresses collectivity, harmony, and hierarchy, with more personal interaction in society, while the US is quite different. So if we include a cultural element in the foundation of *vitality*, then there should be some kind of general pattern. Yet, even with other Asian nations with similar cultural patterns as Japan, there was different development. So we must be careful with this cultural element.

If it is not so important, then we have to include other elements, maybe social structure, maybe history, as discussed by Professor De Vos, or maybe political system. This is my question for the participants.

A. Clesse: Vitality is a very complex and elusive notion. We can only come nearer to some kind of a definition, but there will never be a monolithic and very precise definition of *vitality*. We are only seeking a working notion of *vitality* to allow us to do further work. As Seidensticker has said, it is a neutral notion; it has the quality, in a sense, of an independent variable. It leads to certain materialisations and phenomena. Even after all these meetings for the project, we should not try to come up with a very precise definition. It is intriguing to some, though perhaps to others it is not easy to live with this intellectual uncertainty, but I think it is quite productive intellectually.

T. Li: What is the *vitality* of Japan which we are discussing? There are a lot of studies on the topic, but I think we have to deal with the problem from two aspects, from the cultural side and the economic side. First, viewed from the cultural point of view, Japan has been under the influence of Confucius, with the tradition of an oriental culture. After the Meiji Restoration, Japan introduced the Western civilisation and advanced technology from the West. I think, the fact that Japan succeeded to bridge these two cultural traditions is one of the foundations of its *vitality*. Viewed from the economic standpoint, the high level of education, corporate spirit, the cooperation with the public sector, and the fierce competition in the private sector have all contributed and enhanced that *vitality* of Japan.

We do have some similarities between Japan and China, but the starting point of the economies are quite different. As to the economic policy, China had adopted the planned economy, so there was no competition among private enterprises. So we had a hard time trying to develop our economy. Chinese enterprises, frankly, lacked *vitality*. After the '80s, China introduced its policies of reform and openness, with various pluralities in the economic system so that the market economy will be introduced gradually to the private sector, thereby allowing private competition. The combination of the planned economy and market economy is the characteristic of China.

A. Clesse: Perhaps Professor Lai can say something about the comparative *vitality* of Hong Kong.

F. Lai: The *vitality* of Hong Kong is the complete opposite of China because we have absolute laissez-faire. In order to build upon what has been discussed, let me first summarise what I have heard today. The concept of *vitality* seems to be in four areas, or with four definitions. One is the more focused definition of economic productivity. The three other definitions are broader: one is activeness that is basically neutral, which can be good or bad depending on the situation. Another one, which is definitely positive, is the capability to excel in certain areas, be it cultural, military, creativity, or innovation. The third general definition is the ability to meet challenge and regenerate or survive. So participants may build on any one of these definitions.

When I first came across this concept of *vitality*, I think I responded more to the last definition. I don't have a ready answer, but it evoked a long term research interest of mine. In a comparative context, it would be interesting to examine political corruption because in studying Third World development, political corruption almost always brings about the collapse of the system. In Japan we see a lot of political corruption, but the system seems to survive. Thus, it would be interesting to consider the cultural and social aspects and how they relate to the ability to meet a challenge such as that of political corruption.

W. Wetherall: Perhaps I could say some things that could help bridge today's discussion to tomorrow's. I would like to comment on Dr Cooper's comments. It may be overly romantic to use the model of ancient Greece, but perhaps the only two traits which are really recognisably human are our mental activity and our civility. If we consider these throughout history, we see remarkable changes and directions which we could even define as universal. I feel that mental activity - philosophy, ideas, and technology as by-products - is essentially stateless. Regardless of political boundaries, technology has essentially molded us all together over the millennia, and this is why we do share so much today. The problem is the civil mind. It is possible to argue that this is culturally relative, and yet I see in the histories of all communities, including Japan, a history of civility. So the question is, to lead to tomorrow's discussion, how do politics relate to the civilisation of a country internally, the transition of a country from a lesser to a more humane civil state. I'm talking about a process of reaching an improved civil state internally, in the ways which we relate to each other, and also internationally.

Let's look at US-Japan relations today, just to focus, although you could look at any of Japan's international relations. We are seeing a tremendous amount of descriptive radicalisation. If we go back and ask questions, as

Dr Hale did, about the condition of Japan in the Meiji period and its - as several participants today have put it - its status as the only non-white nation, that viewpoint was possible because the US and Japan at that time and up to 1945 both incorporated fairly racist self-concepts into their formal policies, despite fairly civil constitutions which provided for citizenship despite ethnicity. But today I think the non-white versus white-descriptive nomenclature is counterproductive. Japan is not a non-white country; it is a citizen-state, and I think we have to talk about each other in these civil terms. If we talk about countries based on a racist concept, we exacerbate our civil relationships, which results in hate crimes and violence, as we see, in both, the US and Japan. In an economic context, when Japanese corporations go overseas and we talk about their identity - are they Japanese or not? - and examine who they have hired in the US, they have tended to avoid so-called minorities and treated their local employees in a way which probably would not be accepted in Japan. This overseas context also includes a double standard with environmental laws, where Japanese corporations abide by rigid standards at home but pollute abroad with impunity.

I would suggest in terms of practical politics that the Foreign Ministry take some responsibility for this pattern of radicalisation of the image of Japan, because it uses the word 'race' in much of its distributed material. Here again we find that a lot of the misunderstanding of Japan does not originate from outside Japan but from the inside. As journalists and scholars, I think that we also need to contribute to the civilisation of Japan, of the rest of the world, and of the relations among these countries. And as the first step towards such civilisation we should deracialise our own images of these countries. That is all I will say now.

A. Clesse: I think Professor Shinohara wants to say something about the emphasis on Confucianism in today's discussion.

M. Shinohara: Yes, in today's points there has been some discussion of Confucianism's strong role in Japan, but I think there is also an effect of Buddhism. I think in Japan there may be in fact a mixture of horizontal and vertical society. There may be a problem with this type of discussion. As to the vertical, there seems to be a decidedly Confucian influence. As to the horizontal, it is a Buddhist influence, and this emphasises *wa*, or harmony, over hierarchy. Therefore, in understanding Japanese society, I feel it is very important to combine these two different influences. In the Japanese industrial system, there is a vertical structure called *keiretsu*, but there is also within each business group a big corporation with very loose communication, and this is more of a horizontal system. So there is rigidity as well as flexibility.

A. Clesse: We will give the last few minutes to Gavan McCormack.

G. McCormack: Well, I've been waiting for people to become so fatigued that anything I say they will be receptive and uncritical towards, so I hope that state has been reached. I wanted first to make the observation that it's almost 30 years since I first came to live and work in Japan, and I've spent quite a lot of time here during that period. It seems to me that neither in 1962 nor in 1992, i.e. today is Japan a place that I would describe with the adjective '*vital*'. In fact, the adjective to describe the mood of the Japan in which I am living today would be quite the opposite. It would include the words '*exhausted*', '*tired*', '*stuffed*'. These are the words that come to mind for most of the Japanese people I have contact with. If we are using the word '*vitality*' to imply economic productivity and successful resolution of the problems of expanding GNP, then that's another matter altogether. The point that Professor Sugimoto made that we need to disaggregate the structures within which this multiplication of GNP has been achieved is a very important one. There are two problems about the degree of expanded productivity which has been achieved. One is that, in my subjective judgement, it has not brought prosperity to the Japanese people. The massive production of certain durable types of commodities and the non-satisfaction of other material needs points to a severely distorted economic structure, even before we consider the relation of economic considerations to the other elements of society at large.

Also, the Japanese state today seems near a state of exhaustion: total bankruptcy of ideas, as seen in the fact, on the Japanese side, there was really nothing brought forward as a proposal for the Bush visit. There was an intense sense of fear and intimidation before the Bush arrival, but there was really no feeling that Japan had any sense of where it wanted to go. *So long as vitality implies exuberance, that quality is notably lacking in Japan today*.

The last set of comments I wanted to make relates to the question of culture and the peculiar roots of what should be described as economic mobilisation, rather than the expression of any *vital* spirit. It seems to me that following on some of George De Vos' earlier comments, the structures of Edo society and their influence on cultural patterns and views since then are essentially the product of the failure of the Tokugawa family to impose unification on the country at the end of the 16th century. That failed attempt had the fortuitous result of a pattern of tense and continuing confrontations of the regions and the Edo Bakufu itself. This produced essentially feudal institutions - decentralised institutions relying heavily on the patterns of personal loyalty and rivalry. These, as we know, are sets of values which apply themselves very well to the development of capitalism. So, ironically, the Tokugawa family's effort to impose a completely stable pattern on its society froze, for a time, the patterns of structured contradiction and tension, but it was those patterns which created the possibility for the successful resolution of the problems which Japan would face in the late 19th century.

So far as its economy is concerned, I accept that Japanese corporations have the dynamic capacity to produce goods, but they have created a highly charged, mobilised system. Some expressions of that mobilising energy include students efficiently mobilised into schools and then into the workforce, workers mobilised to serve and to produce, consumers mobilised to consume endlessly with, it seems to me, less and less satisfaction. But the system which has this highly developed capacity to produce goods has a much lower capacity to satisfy the basic human needs of housing, leisure, work satisfaction, or environmental amenity. Instead, the effort of mobilisation to achieve the very limited purposes which have been achieved has seriously deteriorated the basic amenities of social life, especially the environment, while rendering ever-more frenzied the processes of production and consumption. The quality of contemporary consumerism seems to have almost a fetishistic quality about it. So *this vitality, in other words, has bloated corporations, 'enervated' the people, and petrified the state.*

My second point is that this mobilisation, since I prefer the word 'mobilisation', is a successful adaptation of the substance of the feudal samurai tradition in the first instance, the pre-war military tradition in the second, and in the third those *ie* and *dozoku* kinds of vertical social institutions which demanded loyalty and service and gave in return protection, a sense of belonging and pride. But, at the same time, they diminished the horizontal or popular traditions of village cooperation in traditional Japan. This division into fiercely competing rival units has undoubted dynamism, but its flaw has been the suppression of the community, the interests of the real social whole, and the *vitality* of the people.

My third point, however, is that these are conjunctural rather than fixed cultural patterns. If you concentrate on only the two most conjunctural phases, which today I will refer to as Edo and post-1945, the political-social order of both of these was designed to adapt perfectly to the circumstances of the origin. Both adapted so well that flexibility was missing, and as the circumstances changed, the pattern served less and less well the original purposes. The former, which I would call designer feudalism, and the latter, Cold War capitalism, were both designed to meet specific conditions. The design was successful, but overtime, the operation, in an ironic historical dialectic, emptied out the structures and began to grow within them the chrysalis of a new social form. This post-1945 state, which I think is essentially a Cold War state, pursued the maximisation of conditions for corporate accumulation under the central bureaucratic state, and pursued them obsessively. The Cold War was the overall structure in which Japan was licensed to develop these capacities. But as the external conditions that Japan responded to have collapsed, the limitations of the system have become clear. The obsessive, almost fetishistic pursuit of market share has brought nothing but market share.

Fourthly, the malaise now evident in this society as a whole seems to me to be deeper than at any period that I have known it in the past. It is interesting that one now hears voices from quite central and powerful positions within the system calling for radical restructuring of the two central institutions of the post-1945 system: the centralised bureaucratic state and the corporation. On the one hand, a very influential commentator, Ohmae Kenichi, in his recent article in *Gekkan Asahi*, is calling essentially for a dismantling of the bureaucratic state. On the other hand, Morita Akio of Sony is calling for at least a very radical restructuring of the corporation. And of course, there are many others. There is a deep debate rising out of the sense that the institutions of the Cold War Japanese system have reached very near the end of the road.

I am not as gloomy as Karel van Wolferen in his writings about the capacity of the system to *revitalise*. But in that process, what are the forces that I look to? I look first of all to the forces and energies of the citizen groups in the society, the *shimin undo*, the community groups in which the ethos of cooperation, the democratic commonwealth, has been developed in microcosm: environmental movements, consumer movements, women's movement, anti-nuclear movements, and so on. These are the movements in which the values of traditional village society, rather than the values of samurai or *ie* or *dozoku* society, it seems to me, have been preserved. Secondly, I look to the cultural energies which are evident in those aspects of cultural expression which are least controlled and mobilised. Here, although I understand very well what Ed Seidensticker was saying yesterday, I dissent fundamentally in that I believe *manga* and possibly even *karaoke*, though they may be at a very early stage of development, nevertheless are forms which allow a high degree of free expression. My third point is that the liberating potential of the technical attainments of the Japanese post-war system is enormous. Their potential to meet the human needs, not only of the Japanese people, but the demands of the people of the South, is very high. In other words, the demand that Morita Akio talks about for more goods more cheaply is one which in a much more liberalised, humanised, Japanese system would have an enormous liberating potential.

G. De Vos: I am going to change hats and talk a little bit like a sociologist. I would say to follow up what you have said that there is malaise. But the interesting thing about the Japanese is that you have *malaise without breakdown*, so far. If you look at social indices of Japan compared with other modern countries, it has a very low rate of crime and delinquency, the suicide rate has dropped, and there is a low rate of divorce and family disruption. So if you consider these social indices which are usually used, there is not much social or personal breakdown in evidence. Of course, if we look at *karaoke* and things like that, these are release mechanisms like drinking in Japan. Again, if you look at patterns of alcoholism compared with the Soviet Union, US, Sweden, and other places, you find that the Japanese get drunk, but they appear at work the next day. Drinking, so far, has not interfered with work and with these collective activities. So the individual may be under stress, but it has not reached the breaking point.

There was some mention of the educational system, and we should take a look at that. If you compare the Japanese system with the American system, there are some interesting differences. The Japanese system works up to a point, and if you look at education in terms of adaptation, Japanese children do learn science and mathematics, and they learn it well. But if you turn this around and look at Tsukuba, you see its failure, because Tsukuba's intention was to be an international university, and this has not happened. If you compare the American system, the graduate education is superior, but our primary and secondary education is breaking down. Let me give you one statistic: at MIT, in the entering class three years ago, 20 per cent were Koreans. So there is a kind of a perpetuation of a pattern in the US, but it depends on immigration and the bringing in of new people to the system to keep it going because we are not reproducing, you might say, educationally within. We are still functioning, but it depends on bringing in specialists. The Japanese have the opposite problem; they cannot bring in specialists, *they cannot enrich themselves in some kind of educational community because they cannot digest foreigners*. Therefore, you do not have a dynamic education system on the graduate level in Japan. There is *something constrictive and non-functioning and bureaucratic*, as Karel points out, because why is Tsukuba not working? There is no way to bring in foreigners because they are outsiders with absolutely no decision-making power within a Japanese system. This doesn't only happen in education, it happens in business and everywhere.

Now, inside the family - this is where I become more psychological - you can consider the effects of the corporate dedication as the *Sorcerer's Apprentice*: nobody knows how to turn it off. It is going and going, and there is very little family life for many individuals, like the so-called *gozen-sama*, because they come early in the morning. On the weekends, they have a weekend neurosis; they don't know how to relax. The Japanese can't feel comfortable if they are not working. Thus, in the family with an absent parent, there is the danger which has not been realised yet that the mother may work, too. We have reached this in the United States, and it is becoming a real problem in the breakdown in our family system. So one measure of positive *vitality* for the Japanese is that their family is still intact, although there are tensions there of a very severe nature. Other institutions which we won't have time to look at are functioning well in a comparative perspective, including the police and the courts.

So there are some processes for rectifying problems. For example, here in Tokyo the air is now very clear, unlike the 1960s when the police in some areas were wearing gas masks. So when these problems are resolved, we tend to forget about them. The remarkable thing I would say about the Japanese society is that there is a tremendous amount of malaise, but it has not reached the breaking point, and we are not seeing very overtly some of these symptoms of breakdown. The question is, then, will there be an alleviation before these symptoms start to appear to a greater degree?

A. Clesse: Thank you, George. Several people want to respond to the points you've just raised. Richard Cooper is first.

R. Cooper: I actually wanted to emphasise something that Professor McCormack raised. It seems to me that he threw out a challenge for Japanese participation in a most acute form, and I didn't want to let the opportunity pass to ask the Japanese around the table to respond. He said, essentially, that the Japanese post-war system has delivered the goods physically, but that the quality of life has deteriorated, and I wanted to hear the opinions of the Japanese here. I am an economist, and what is most impressive by economic standards in Japan is that per capita income has risen enormously over the last 40 years. The outstanding thing about this is that it permits individual choices which become possible only at a high level of income, so the question is whether the choices for the Japanese are being constrained by the system in such a way that they cannot enjoy their now very high levels of income.

George De Vos also threw out a challenge focused on the educational system. I would like to make an intellectual distinction between education and training. My observation is that the Japanese educational system is unrivaled in training, but I would again like the Japanese to respond to this question of training. I do so by making a pointed remark, which also applies to Koreans. At Harvard, like MIT, we have many students from Japan and Korea. From a technical point of view, they are superbly trained. The problem comes when they finish their courses and turn to writing their dissertation. I will tell a story which is not a caricature, when the Japanese and Koreans would come to me in that frustrating period which every student goes through in the months after completing their general examinations when they must find a dissertation topic. They would come and say, 'Please tell me the most interesting unsolved problems in the field, and I will solve them.' In other words, it is a high-level setting of an examination question. They have the technical skills to solve a problem, but what they are saying is they don't know how to pose a problem. Some Japanese students, I would say about half in my experience, surmount that problem, and the other half don't. Although this example is overly concrete, I consider that a failure of an educational system if its very brightest students cannot pose the interesting problems that face society. I would be interested in a Japanese response to this issue, with the future in mind.

A. Clesse: Thank you, Richard. I suggest that first Karel van Wolferen and Dr Kim Kihwan speak, and then any Japanese participants who are willing to take up the challenge.

K. Kim: I am not Japanese, but I think I have something to say about the subject of education. I really fully endorse what Professor Cooper and Professor De Vos have said about the educational condition in Japan and Korea. I fully agreed with the very pointed observation by Professor Cooper that Korean students, and to perhaps a lesser extent Japanese students, after their qualifying exams and after their degree, have great difficulty writing original articles. The educational systems in Japan and Korea suffer from a lack of creativity, and one reason is that the educational systems are so nationalistic. They were designed to meet the national needs of nation-state building in an effort to catch up with the West. But now, this catch-up task has been fully achieved in Japan and Korea. This does not contradict what I said yesterday about the role of education in these countries' dynamism, but the educational systems are now exhausted.

The other issue is the psychology of this catching-up. Especially for Japan, which has not only caught up but surpassed the GNPs of the West, there is now a need for Japan to redefine itself. This will have to include its new role in international affairs. This will have to accommodate the loss of two of Japan's key advantages: it must now share the burden for the security which it received freely from the US during the Cold War and its open market access to the economies of the West can no longer be taken for granted as the world's tripartite trading blocks emerge in Europe, North America, and Asia. Furthermore, the advantage of Japan's political stability will be lost with the need to be reformed as Japan's responsibilities in the world grow. The fact that politics has reached its limit is so evident, for the legitimacy for the lone rule of the LDP has been seriously undermined by a series of scandals involving its leaders and the nation's financial establishment. So I wouldn't say that Japan really faces malaise, I don't think the problem is that serious, but it will face the challenges that I have just outlined.

G. Berger: I simply want to add something, in looking at the issue of *vitality*, related to the psychoanalytics of what makes Taro run? The issue of motivation comes very strongly to the fore in my thinking about this subject. This leads me to look at the dyadic relationship between the primary caretaker and the infant/child growing into society, because it is in that relationship that human personality is formed, capacities are formed, and motivations are formed. One of the things that has struck me is how the quest for security, safety, seems to be a powerful motivator, whether it is the wish for greater market share, the quest for greater military defence, as a metaphor for greater security. But it strikes me that in Japan this quest for security is virtually unending, and it is the unendingness of it which is of particular interest. It's almost like the person who has been exposed to starvation, and thereafter can never eat enough, never feel safe, and never feel that there is enough food. The value system which it seems to me that most Japanese children come away from their primary caregivers stipulates, as Professor De Vos elegantly stated a long time ago, that they achieve. Achievement-orientation is not unusual to Japan either, but what is particularly interesting in achievement-orientation in Japan to me is embodied in the expression *issho kenmei*, which doesn't just mean you have to work hard, but you have to work hard all of your life - *issho*. To me, that really summarises the dilemma faced by the individual Japanese as addresses the system that Karel talks about, or society or the corporation. He or she is obliged, in order to have even the chance of a positively-toned sense of himself or herself, to strive all of their lives. You never reach home-base until it's all over. 'You only score one run in Japan' is the way I think of it. This makes life difficult, but it's always pushing the Japanese forward. In this way, it is the source of the *vitality* that is brought to all of the various organisations which we have talked about.

I. Hall: I would just like to make a few points about universities and schools. We have a whole educational sector, either evidence of *vitality* or the lack of it, and we also have the institution which creates it and transmits it and so on. One point is on the educational system as a response to challenge, and I would like to suggest that the *Japanese university* is perhaps an *example of what has now become an ossified response*. There was a tremendous rush in the early Meiji period to all kinds of schools, and it was such a drain on the economic resources that the government narrowed the gate of access to higher education very sharply. Two things happened which even now a hundred years later continue and represent perhaps a response that has outlived its usefulness. One is the very clear emphasis on applied learning as opposed to fundamentals, the so-called *oyo-kagaku*. The other one was the fear at the time that the Japanese universities, if they kept their foreign staff too long, might follow the path of colonial universities. Laws were introduced to keep the foreigners out of the tenure system. Those laws were changed ten years ago, but there is still in the elite national universities, which would be like the 20 best universities in the US and Europe, only one tenured foreign scholar. He's an American at Tokyo University. What happened was that the universities themselves promptly set term limits to the period of time that foreigners serve basically as an ornament.

For the real scholarly interchange and particularly for the ability of the Japanese to give of themselves to the outside world requires an interlocking and interfacing that is not there at the moment. What is striking is that this pattern has continued now for over a century. Both of these points were alluded to by Dr Erwin Baelz, the German who founded the Tokyo Medical School and contributed to its development, in his farewell speech at the turn of the century. On the first point, he suggested that the Japanese were too eager to simply take the fruit of the tree of knowledge, the final product, without considering the root. This is the difference between incremental and fundamental learning which we dealt with yesterday. He also said that for the true development of knowledge, it would require a more easy-going acceptance of foreign staff as human beings, not simply as the bearers of the fruit baskets, the final products of knowledge.

My own experience in universities is that the students tend to come rather exhausted from their period of cram education to get into the best slot in the sorting mechanism that the universities tend to provide for the Japanese society. It is a brief spell of three or four years before they go into another sort of fixed slot. Personally, I can sympathise with their desires to explore themselves and to do other things, to relax and develop athletic and social activities, but I find it very odd, looking at it from the outside, that on the intellectual and academic side, there is almost a reluctance to shine too much or be outstanding. I think there is great awareness that the corporations would prefer to have a student who is not too very *vital* in any provocative sort of way, but can be retrained and reoriented. I believe that there is a certain consciousness that real education starts again in the corporation. So you have here in the education system a real lack of emphasis on the types of things which Professor Cooper mentioned as the legacy of Greece: individual self-expression and individual political responsibility.

With this sort of lack of *vitality* in teaching, the professors are driven into a corner where teaching is even lower on the list of priorities than it is in our universities. Instead, they devote themselves to research, but again, there is not the sort of tenure system pressure there, where lifelong employment is virtually automatic. So there is not the peer-pressure nor the publish-or-perish pressure, and you have a certain lack of *vitality* in this. In the national universities, you have a very heavy-handed administration in the bureaucracy which exists with a kind of force and presumptuousness which we would not know in the West. A full professor ranks in the national service's career system as the equivalent of a section chief, a *kacho*. I've known senior professors who absolutely quail and quake to go into the Ministry of Education to ask for anything. So I would simply like to add that footnote and echo Professor De Vos' remarks about Tsukuba, for it was the university that had all of the financial backing of the government, the Ministry of Education, the ruling party, and so on, and yet it failed to create a lively intellectual and international atmosphere, in part because the foreign professors who had been qualified to join the Japanese ranks had been thrown out: a German, an American, a Chinese, and a Korean.

S. Sato: I'd like to respond to the challenges presented by Dick Cooper and the others. There are a lot of frustrations by the Japanese people to many aspects of Japanese society, and I myself have many criticisms vis-à-vis the society in which I am living. Having said that, I was really amazed when Gavan McCormack, who has unfortunately left and I don't want to criticise someone who is not here, said that Japanese society fails to provide for the basic human needs.

Of course Japanese society is not 100 per cent successful in providing for these basic needs, there's no question about that. But one of the good measures of a society's care for its people is the average life span, and the Japanese life span is among the longest in the world: 81 or 82 for women, 78 or 79 for men. How can the people live so long in a society where basic human needs are not provided? I have not gotten an answer from people like Gavan McCormack about that.

He also pointed out that after the Second World War Japan has been a Cold War state. But I don't think the end of the Cold War will necessarily be a bad thing for Japan because Japanese influence has been confined primarily to economic aspects, so once the Cold War ended, there is a golden opportunity for Japan to increase its international influence. This is not a terribly bad thing for Japan. Secondly, the decline of the ideologically oriented parties, including a new change among the opposition parties, especially the Socialists, to change its basic policy directions. So I would not be surprised if in the very near future the Socialists' policies are not so different from the LDP's. That will trigger a fundamental realignment of the constellation of political parties, and the continued domination of political power by the LDP will end. That is my prediction and hope.

My third point is about education. I quite agree with Dick Cooper that the Japanese education system has succeeded in training people but has failed in educating them to think independently. That is one of my deepest criticisms against the Japanese school system. Again, though, there are some interesting signs of change at all levels of the Japanese education system. In the elementary schools, boys and girls are being less obedient to their teachers, and so the teachers' influence has declined. And that's good. Secondly, a growing number of the Japanese younger generation have experienced not only visiting foreign countries, but are also staying there. They have returned, and their attitude is conspicuously different. Their numbers are growing, and that is a completely new development in Japanese society.

The final point is that in the higher education, the worst parts are the humanities and social sciences. Engineering is not too bad, and it is producing excellent, very creative people. Moreover, there is an effort among private universities to create a new kind of university. They are more flexible than the state universities, and there is a fierce competition now among Japanese universities because of the expected sharp decline in university students. So many will be forced to change their systems, or they will not survive. That is my hope.

K. van Wolferen: As I was listening to various comments about the education system, legal system, protest movements, and so on, I am trying to find causes for the phenomena that are described, which I mostly agree with, and I wonder if there is some way to tie it together. Maybe we should start with the legal system. Now, I didn't think that I would disagree very vehemently with George De Vos today when he says that we've got a very good working legal system. Well, that is true in that it's a wonderfully well-oiled system, well controlled by the Secretary of the Supreme Court, and it has everything well under control, including the judges. If a judge passes judgement that is not to the liking of the Secretary, the chances are that they will be moved to a far away place where they don't want to go. There are very few exceptions. *We do not have in Japan an independent judiciary.* There was one for a very brief time after the Occupation period, and it has been studied by very few people. We have a judiciary that is very, very small. It is very difficult to find a lawyer in Japan, and he is very expensive. *Litigation is not really an option*, unless it be for reasons of principle, like to clear your name.

Compromise is always suggested at every stage in legal proceedings. It is almost forced upon you. Most who enter the legal process are not even aware that they have an option. I could go on and on about this, but let's just establish an important fact: *Japanese society and its political and economic systems are not ultimately regulated by law.* Here you have an important mechanism which exists in the European and American industrial systems that force powerholders to explain what they are doing and their motivations and intentions. What is everything for here in Japan? *Why is this vitality channeled into the corporate system, and why is it doing nothing else that is visible except unlimited industrial expansion?* Intention is a question we should continue to ask here, and of course it is the crucial question when you consider the future and international relations.

Passing from the legal system to *protest movements*, I can say that yes, they do exist. They are not as difficult to start as you might think, in fact they are emerging all the time like mushrooms. But when a protest movement becomes large enough to be noticed, to become an irritant to the administrators, a very interesting mechanism begins to work. It is a mechanism to encapsulate and in some way undermine it, to embrace it and make it disappear as a potential seed for sustained political opposition. So you see compromises when it is accompanied by violence, as it usually is, but it gradually becomes an extension of the various administrative bodies which it is protesting. This works well, to some extent, as with the woman's movement, for example, the *fujinkai*, was very active in the 1950s and 1960s on behalf of consumers. These were responded to by the bureaucrats; a number of the things they wanted they got, and subsequently, they stopped being an engine of the consumer's movement. In fact they became the eyes and ears of the administrators that wanted to stop such movements. It works beautifully, it is really a wonder to behold.

The *education system* has been sufficiently criticised here, but let's also say how well it functions for a certain purpose. It selects on the basis of *stamina and memory*, as seen through 'examination hell'. This requires pupils to memorise trivia facts, with little coherence between what must be memorised. The result is that the graduates of the universities with the best reputation go into the highest levels of government and corporate offices, and they have tremendous memories and incredible stamina. The result is this whole system selects a certain type that is very useful for what the administrators try to accomplish. But I know many Japanese who seem extremely talented in some way, and these people end up not even in a high school with a good reputation. Thomas Rohlen wrote a beautiful book, *Japan's High Schools*, on this. He compared the elite schools with those for the failures, and it's a very telling and moving book. So we have a system which on the outside seems remarkable because the students score so high on mathematics test, and this is an obsession especially for American observers who say that because Japan has a successful economy it must have a successful education system. Indeed, the students do very well on mathematics tests, because the students have been trained to pass tests, and the easiest tests to pass are mathematics tests.

The education system in Japan is not even beginning to educate, if education means bringing forth the powers of the mind. Many powers of the mind are, in fact, systematically discouraged, because they may be a potential problem for the authorities. *You do not want*, for example, *creativity*. I spoke to a group of teachers and school administrators in Osaka just last week, and they asked me to tell them what should be the priorities of education reform in Japan, because they felt it is not going anywhere. I told them that originality is one of the greatest gifts that is given to mankind, and it is so very systematically discouraged in their schools. We discussed this, and they agreed, but they responded, 'How can you deal with children who are too original, because you can't keep order?' There is no way that the authorities in the Ministry of Education have ever thought about this problem. I could talk about this for an hour, but I won't bore you.

We ultimately must come back to this question of *answerability*. We have a nation that is doing very well economically, but it doesn't seem able to deviate from the course of industrial rebuilding and then unlimited economic expansion that it was set on after 1945. You never hear it discussed anywhere in the Japanese political system whether this should be continued forever. Of course you hear a lot of discussion about whether the economy should grow a little bit more or less, all the technical details to keep the ship on course. But the ultimate goal is never discussed. There is no mechanism for discussing it. The Diet, which supposedly consists of representatives of the Japanese people, does not discuss this thing. The politicians have sometimes discussed important issues of education and defence, but not anything related to the economy, which is the central, most important, unformulated, and unstated, but de facto national policy of Japan - unlimited economic expansion.

Where is the centre of accountability in all this? Who is answerable to whom? Where can foreign leaders and business go to find explanation of what the Japanese are doing and, if they want, discuss it with them? Where can Japanese citizens go to ask why are we doing this, and for what? This is to me the focus of the main problems that come up in the domestic and international Japanese situations; *there is no central political accountability*. Now, institutions that in other countries remind the potential centre of accountability of the fact that it is a centre of accountability, like the newspapers and academia, do not function in this way in Japan. We have seen Professors Inoguchi and Iwai, who have very good minds and do benefit students, but I think they are exceptional.

I think it is especially since the demise of Marxism in Japanese universities that the *very notion of opposition has begun to disappear*. Part of the problems in the education system is the result of the demise of the Teachers Union. It's only in the last three or four years that this has become evident. The war between the Education Ministry and the Union that lasted for several decades is over, and the Ministry won. The result, which may surprise George De Vos and others, is a state of war in some schools in some prefectures where it is no longer possible to keep order. What happens? The students are subjected to very arbitrary and silly rules, like the length of your socks or the colour of your underwear. These are purposeful to impress upon the students the need to obey, regardless of the logic behind it. Stricter rules have prompted more unruly behaviour, especially in areas where the Teachers Union has lost all influence. This unruly behaviour is responded to by stricter and more arbitrary rules. So we are entering this vicious circle.

I am glad that Gavan McCormack is back, because he said that he is less gloomy than I am about change, but I can report that I am now also less gloomy. I have met more and more Japanese who are concerned about these things, who are meeting and trying to do something. I have realised that there are many more Japanese who do not follow the *shikata ga nai*, or 'it cannot be helped' formula. *There is also a potentially very vital civil society out there*. The problem is that the Japanese don't participate in the discussion about Japanese political or economic problems on any level in or outside of Japan. We only know about them because we happen to come upon them, otherwise we would not know about these people.

So when we talk about *vitality*, who are we talking about? Let me close on this point. We are talking about a *system with large corporations that work extremely well and have sucked all potential vitality into their uses, but this is at the expense of the vitality of many causes of the Japanese life*. This is a subject we should pay most attention to, because this is connected to everything else.

A. Clesse: Thank you, Karel. We will return to this afternoon and talk about the strengths, weaknesses, and limits of Japanese *vitality*. We have to move on soon to political aspects and institutions. Philip Windsor, please speak first.

P. Windsor: This is all pitched at a very high level of generalisation, but I am trying to draw some considerations together from this morning's very fascinating discussions and put it into some kind of context of continuity. There is a kind of legend in the West and the Western press that Japan has always adapted successfully to the outside world, but *I think that Japan has always adapted the outside world to its purposes*, right from the time that it imported Buddhism, as Karel was saying yesterday, to the economic system of now. That includes also, by the way, isolation as a form of settling this adaptation of the world for a certain period, and this was very successful in its own terms. This process of adaptation has always been done in a context which has been imposed externally, in which every threat has become a model: the threats of China and Korea, the successive waves of European imperialism, the collapse of the European system in the Axis onslaught. In all these moments, it was the threats which became the next stage of the model for the development of Japan. Even at the end of the Second World War, defeat and occupation were absorbed in a new success in the context of the Cold War, and in this context it really worked very well, as Gavan discussed.

But in a sense, this successive series of adaptations of the world to Japan has enabled both a myth and a psychology of an unchanging nature and essence of Japan, itself, to be perpetuated. That has two consequences. Mishima has a lovely phrase about this essence of Japan, he says 'its savage serenity'. These two consequences have the real meaning that Japan is still really and willfully isolated. It struck me recently because, though the Japanese did not invent the game of baseball, foreigners are not allowed to see the high school baseball championships at Osaka because they wouldn't understand the Japanese spirit. The fact that you can see them on television doesn't make any difference. In that sense, this *kind of isolation is still a very strong feature of Japanese society*. The second consequence, picking up on what Karel said earlier on, is that it makes it very hard to leave the group. Just as in the Tokugawa period you couldn't leave the country, today it's very hard to get out and voice Wagner's divine discontent or whatever, as in the story of the women's movement. It affects this nature of the system being ultimately not regulated by law. It is this whole thing, from which you can't get out, that regulates the system and perpetuates the positions of people within the system.

These internal problems, it seems to me, are reflected now in international problems. There is one very straightforward reason for this: there is now no external context for Japan to operate in; there is neither a threat nor a model. In those terms, Japan might have to do things like make decisions, and the whole system - socially, psychologically, and educationally - makes it very difficult indeed for Japan to make decisions. Even to be an intermediary in making decisions in international relations is very difficult for Japan. This brings to mind an interview I had with a very recent foreign minister at the time of Eastern Europe's emergence. I asked, 'What do you think Japan might wish to do in these circumstances of rapid change in Eastern Europe?' He said, 'Japan will abide by the rules of the London Club and the Paris Club.' I rest that case.

Political Vitality

J.A.A. Stockwin: A number of people have touched on political issues already this morning, but I want to discuss the situation of the political system here more generally. I would preface my remarks by two general points. The first is that the nature of the issues related to politics in this country is tremendously complex, and it is very important that we should avoid stereotypical thinking or particularly rigid theorising, because there is a considerable degree of openness about how things may develop hereafter. The second general point is that I believe politics are important in this country. Politics and the political system are not an epiphenomenon; they are something which must be taken very seriously.

Let me take a look at the external context of the Japanese political situation at the moment. Since the late 1980s the world has changed very radically, and what I find fascinating about this is that whereas revolutionary situations have developed in Eastern Europe and the Soviet Union, in East Asia generally that has not happened. Here we find incremental change - change indeed - but at a slower pace and, from some points of view, more productive than has taken place in Eastern Europe. However, so far as Japan is concerned, the breakdown of the Cold War, as a number of speakers have mentioned, is going to create problems, particularly of potential exacerbation of relations between the United States and Japan. That I see very broadly as the external context.

So far as the political system of Japan is concerned, it has been stated to the point that it is now a cliché that Japan has a first rate economic system but a third rate political system. In a way this is not entirely true; the system has brought a *degree of stability and predictability* enabling long-term planning in certain areas, especially the economic growth field, as Professor Kim discussed yesterday. I think that although there are positive sides to the long predominance of the LDP, there are also some very severe problems. The apathy and lack of interest on the part of the electorate are definitely a result of one party being in power for a very long time. Of course, there have been other systems, like Sweden, which have shown that this is not an immutable situation. In Japan, as in Sweden, it is possible for the electorate to vote such a party out of power.

The next point is that Japan has for a long time had a candidate-centred constituency patronage system which provides a form of popular input into politics because local people can obtain benefits for their own areas from the system. But this is a particularly narrow kind, leading to *corruption* and, indeed, *nepotism*. We have a large number of Diet members in Japan who are sons or sons-in-law of previous Diet members. This arguably also leads to a great limitation on policy choices.

Another point is that the LDP runs *a seniority system*. Essentially, the LDP has become very like a ministry of the Japanese bureaucracy. You do not get a cabinet position until you have been elected six times to parliament, and then virtually everybody gets a cabinet position. Promotion is by merit from then on, in the sense that only a proportion go on to have more senior cabinet positions. The multi-member constituency system notoriously leads to corruption. It is not the only factor in this, but in that it exacerbates political factionalism, it undoubtedly leads to a considerable degree of corruption. Some people say corruption doesn't matter; there is a very famous article by Chalmers Johnson about Tanaka Kakuei arguing that corruption is not something that matters in this system. I believe that it does matter, and there is considerable evidence at the present time because the government is in great trouble as a result of public and media reaction against corruption.

The present situation relating to decision-making is very interesting. There has been much discussion over slow decision-making in Japan over the Gulf Conflict. What few people point out, in the foreign press at least, is that a prime reason for that is that the government does not have a majority in the Upper House, which has very important veto powers

What are the prospects here? One is the continuation of *very poor governability* in the system. Another, which Professor Sato touched on, is the *possibility of radical party realignment*. I do not have time to go into this in detail, but I think there are possibilities for such a radical realignment. The present developments with the Rengo Federation, combining several of the opposition parties, are extremely interesting, as are the possibilities of a split in the LDP and some recombination of parties across the Left-Right divide.

I also believe that it is crucial for Japan to reform the electoral system. I think that the Kaifu government's approach to this was along the right lines, whereas the present government has not pursued the same course, but some combination of reforms would make a better electoral system. The electorate needs to have more of an input, to force the system to respond more on real issues. Japan, I believe, has a *talented bureaucracy which performs extremely well*, but it *needs much better political leadership* and direction. I think therefore that it is necessary to keep a very open mind about the immediate prospects and possibilities for the development of the Japanese political system. I personally am highly critical of the present system but not without optimism about the prospects for change. It is time for Japan to develop not a third rate, but a first rate political system by radically reforming its institutions. Finally, I believe that the culture of Japan has changed since the war sufficiently to permit this. It is only the rigidity of certain aspects of the present system that holds back real and important change.

A. Clesse: There are several participants who wish to speak, after which we will then move back to economic aspects with Professor Courtis, Akio Mikuni, Glen Fukushima, and others. One thing that has struck me this morning and yesterday is that we have looked at many of the deficiencies reported here, but many of these criticisms also apply to institutions and mechanisms in Europe, as for example in education. So, one possible danger is that we are too one-sided in our critique. We should perhaps relate these to deficiencies in our society. I speak now of European societies, of course, but I think we should keep this in mind. We should also not forget to relate all of this to the question of *vitality*, the strengths and weaknesses of a certain institution or phenomenon can have quite a diverse impact on *vitality*. The correlations are extremely complex and often very difficult to establish. So we should not lose sight of such possible relationships between general phenomena and the question of *vitality*.

D. Arase: Professor Stockwin mentioned that Japan was relatively fortunate because its regional context was free of the sorts of crises that are plaguing Eastern Europe and the former Soviet Union. What I'd like to say is that that is an overly optimistic assessment of the region, because I think other countries in the region are facing the problem of dealing with the political consequences of rapid economic growth and structural transformation. That is to say, with the emergence of better educated and more cosmopolitan middle classes, there is a pressure for political liberalisation and democratisation and also the demand for more respect for human rights. In this context, I think Japan does have an important opportunity and role for demonstrating *vitality* in the sense that a *vital* nation is expected to contribute to the resolution of international problems, especially among its neighbours.

Here I want to point to a few troubling trends in Japanese foreign policy, because I think they demonstrate some of the problems Japan has in demonstrating *vitality* in this area. That is to say, *Japan seems to lack the values or the internal gyroscope that will help it orient its policy after the end of the Cold War*. I have not heard anyone at this meeting mention any values of any universal significance that motivate Japan. The only value that I've heard mentioned here is nationalism, and of course that has limited universal appeal. I'd like to say that this is actually manifesting itself in Japan's foreign policy today. If you look at Japan's performance or the ability to use its considerable weight, especially with its foreign aid, in addressing issues of democratisation in Asia or human rights, Japan is in a position to move events in the region in the right way, but it isn't taking nearly as active a role as it could. Of course, I merely mention the cases of China and Burma, for example, where Japanese policy diverges considerably from those of other democratic advanced countries.

As for the pernicious effect of nationalism and its persistence - and of course, every nation has a right to be nationalistic - but the lack of countervailing values or orientations allows Japan to have its foreign policy course or behaviour skewed in destructive or non-constructive directions. For example, if you look at its orientation in the GATT, clearly Japan has a role to play there, and its inability to make a decisive contribution there has something to do with the perception that Japan is just being pushed around by the Western countries. It could also be more forthcoming in promoting trans-Pacific economic cooperation, as Dr Kim has already mentioned. To end my comments, I'd like to say that Japan actually does have an important agenda in the region, it does have a role to play in demonstrating *vitality* and leadership, but I think for reasons that others can offer Japan hasn't really done what it could do in these areas.

H. Takeuchi: We are talking about *vitality*, and I was very impressed by the definition given by Professor Kim, the ability to face challenges. Maybe one of the problems for Japan which the people in the streets may not realise is that we have a challenge to take. It's obvious if you go down to Roppongi at 7:00 or 8:00 in the evening and talk to young people, they are essentially happy living in rabbit hutches with a terrible transport system. So this might be one of the factors we have to take into account.

Another point is that I was in the administrative side during the Gulf Crisis, and if I had to summarise my impressions from the crisis, it would be that the Japanese people deserve a better government. Someone talked about the joint responsibility of the economic cooperation yesterday, but as a witness I would have to say this is joint irresponsibility. So we have to have a better system to cooperate in this kind of crisis management.

Another point is that one of the challenges we face is how to translate our economic points to the political arena. This is very easy to say but hard to realise. The way that the system works in this country, and few have mentioned this, is that everything is done in an incremental manner, and the word of the game is pragmatism. So those two things are far from dramatic, and in politics you need to have a dramatic element. That is to say that economics is, by its very nature, anti-dramatic. You have to wait for five or ten years of sustained effort to see if one fiscal or economic policy succeeds or not. That is essentially not dramatic. So our friends in Eastern Europe have experienced the fall of the Berlin Wall, which is dramatic, but the hard work of economic recovery requires long, sustained efforts, which are of course not dramatic.

Finally, we have been talking about Japan, but Dr Clesse is quite right that some of those points are peculiar to Japan, but many problems are part of democracy in general. The Cold War is over; democracy seems to have won, but it is facing a new reality with a whole new set of problems.

If we have to talk about the *vitality* of a nature, maybe one day we will have to talk about the *vitality* of democracy as well. Thank you.

R. Cooper: I simply had a question for Professor Stockwin. In his presentation, he outlined the serious possibility of a realignment of the political parties, among both the opposition parties and a splitting of the LDP. My question is how can that be reconciled with what we heard earlier about the very strong personal loyalties which Japanese have to their organisations, which provide a sense of security and so forth? Or do these loyalties not apply in the political domain the way they do in the corporate domain? Isn't there a catch-22 situation, where a realignment of parties would be, in the context of party loyalties, an inconsistent and radical change?

J.A.A. Stockwin: I think this is a crucial point. Taking the British example, which is completely different from the United States, a party in parliament is sustaining the government in a way that a party in Congress does not. That is a very important difference, and in Japan you have essentially a Westminster model system. I think that the loyalty to party in the Japanese system has an element of cultural loyalty in it, but it also has a great element of pragmatism. It simply makes a lot of sense for a Liberal Democratic Party member to stick with his party, because he'd be out in the cold should he desert his party. If, however, the possibility for a different alignment leading to a different set of parties should emerge, then the premises of the situation radically change. I think you will find people moving around and scurrying in different directions.

K. Kim: Just one sentence on this possibility of realigning the politics in the face of strong loyalty. I think loyalty, from the point of view of an economist, is also made of incentives. In Japan, in order to get elected you need financing from the party, from the interest groups which are sponsoring you. If the money in politics could come from elsewhere - let's say the financing could come from the government - then loyalty could be reduced.

G. Courtis: I am an amateur in this field, but let me just say this. The three pillars of the LDP are the three groups in society that don't pay tax: the farmers, the shopkeepers, and the doctors. They vote systematically for that party. The average age of farmers is 57 at the moment. The average age of mom-and-pop shop-owners is 59.2 years. They are demographically condemned. The LDP has to change, or whatever party is going to be in power has to create over the next decade a new electoral base. As was just said, the financing of power is going to change. It was interesting in the last election, because for the first time in history the main contributor to the LDP wasn't the construction industry or the *Nokyo,* it was the car industry followed by the electronics industry. That is the change that is coming.

Professor Sato said before he left that there could be a great upheaval in Japanese politics. Of course there is going to be a great upheaval because the base of the government for 40 years, which has had the tax system and regulations tailored in its favour, has developed a tremendous vested interest in the status quo, but its electoral power is now going to be atrophied. So the government party, whichever it may be, is going to have to build a stable, urban, conservative coalition to stay in power. That is going to have to mean, of course, tremendous changes in some of the trade-offs which have been at the centre of the political system for the last 40 years, like the trade-off between producer and consumer, land-owner and land-consumer. This will force the government to address issues of fundamental land reform and tax reform that will set in place a dynamic of change that has to be very carefully managed if the LDP wants to stay in power. That is why the situation that develops after this July becomes so interesting. It is not anything as esoteric as cultural loyalty or sociological traditions; it's based on reality, and that reality is one of power.

After the July elections, it will be necessary for factions in the LDP to sow together some type of new arrangement with some opposition groups that go beyond their original battalions like Komeito, and they'll have to buy into some type of coalition with what is left of the Socialist Party. That is what is driving change, not that people are becoming less loyal or these other cultural things. I think it is fundamental sociological demographics on one side and economic interests on the other.

K. Calder: Anything in this world can be summarised in three points, so I would like to present my discussion of political issues related to politics and broader Japanese political economy. The first point has been touched on, but I think it is critical to re-emphasise it, namely the functional role of politics in the broader Japanese political economy. Essentially, its role has been stabilising, to try to create some degree of predictability in the system as a whole. Of course, that generalisation pertains particularly to the post-1945 system. Particularly for those who argue that politics are unchanging, one needs to look at the significant transformations that have occurred in Japanese politics over the post-war period. One-party dominance, for example, has existed just since 1955, and in that period there have been major nuances also within the political ranks themselves, with two major prospects of political splits in the LDP in 1960 and 1974, for example. Broadly speaking, it is important to look at the role of politics essentially as one of stabilising larger parameters that have allowed the economy, large firms in particular, to operate with some degree of autonomy. Of course, we have a very strongly segmented system, with a lot of important exceptions including the small business sector, agriculture, and many of the areas which are heavily centralised and operate in a different fashion. Coalitions based particularly on these groups are moving increasingly towards groups in the urban area because of the structural changes in the political economy which Ken Courtis alluded to. So there is some degree of change there. But the main point to think about is that politics are a stabilising mechanism to minimise the intrusion of politics into a broader range of areas, apart from some rather explicitly politicised sectors that are clientalised like agriculture, coal, and non-ferrous metals with significant employment.

On the issue of *vitality*, this suggests that the heart of Japan's *vitality* in an economic sense has really been a private sector operating largely autonomously. I do differ with Chalmers Johnson on that point to some degree. If one looks at the state up-close, even the bureaucracy and MITI have been considerably more fragmented than the picture that is presented there. For instance, on the issue of the Bank of Japan and the emergence of overloans, if one looks at how that process occurred, there was tremendous surge of investment during the Korean War, and in response to that reactively the Bank of Japan began to move into a system of overloans. But this was not strategically dictated, and the Japanese bureaucracy has been generally risk-averse. Even in the sector of computers, the bureaucracy did not promote industry adventurously, until there was a strong overseas threat on the horizon. So the *heart of Japanese 'economic vitality' lies in the private sector*, both in small group industrial organisation, particularly in plant-level organisation, and in certain risk-diffusion mechanisms like *keiretsu*. This, then, is one result of the function of politics.

The next point I would like to make has to do with *discontinuity in the Japanese political economy*. Here I agree with a range of people, including Arthur Stockwin and Sato Seizaburo who made this point. I would like to say a word about the dynamics at work there. The first aspect is that historically the Japanese political system has been considerably more dynamic. It has changed greatly, much in reaction to economic forces. The conservative merger of 1955 came about as the debt-equity ratios rose very rapidly during the Korean War, and the private sector began to bear considerably more risk with cash flow, particularly with the recession right after the war. It was business pressure which created the conservative merger which had not existed previously. There have been major threats of a break-up in the party, and there are strong internal pressures in the party related to the nature of the electoral system, which is unusual in the internal competition and personal rivalries of the five major factions of the party.

But in terms of the discontinuity, I would go first to the economic forces. I feel strongly that there is more autonomy to economic forces, and they present more pressure for discontinuity than we have generally discussed here. You have externally huge mobility in the factors of production in some areas like finance, and in sectors like telecommunications there are great pressures for change. Politically, there are many international pressures like we have been saying. The internationalisation of Japanese business in the last five years, in terms of approvals, the level of investment offshore have risen almost five-fold between 1985 and 1990. In some sectors imports have risen rapidly. There are important pressures in the demographic shifts which Ken Courtis alluded to, including much of the LDP's own base. Much of the scandals, as Karel van Wolferen has said, have led to rising frustrations. Finally, pressures on the LDP resource base, in which traditionally the LDP has been very based on compensation politics: construction, agriculture, and so on.

But there are counter-claims rising, especially with the ageing of society, pressures for broader international commitments in the area of foreign aid and the issue of defence. The internal catalyst is the factor which Arthur Stockwin alluded to, the rise of *rengo*, and factional divisions within the LDP itself. And there are external catalysts as well.

The last point is that politics has to do with the political structure of Japan's international role. Here I would emphasise the structural. On the one hand, there are a range of economic forces, with the rise of international economic commitments, which create pressures for a broader role, particularly for heavy overseas investment. On the other hand, there are certain structural impediments which make it difficult to become proactive. There is no central executive, a small foreign ministry, very limited intelligence capabilities, and a fictionalised role of the LDP in foreign policy. So, it is difficult to be proactive.

But in conclusion, I do think that the Japanese political system has certain reactive capabilities. We've seen some of this, as Glen Fukushima pointed out, in Japan's ability to respond to foreign pressure, although this has certain obvious problems with it. Given the interdependence of Japan, a nation with over 300 billion dollars in international trade and the role of the multinational business in the political economy, it seems to me that those things, apart from what others have suggested, could be agents in the system for change over time.

B. Keehn: I will speak a bit about the bureaucracy and a topic given me by Frances Lai yesterday, political corruption. First, on the bureaucracy, I'd like to go back to Professor Inoguchi's comment yesterday, that the Japanese approach to economy is taming the market and disciplining economic actors. Of course, when you talk about these two factors, you are talking about the bureaucracy. It is generally believed, certainly by many Western scholars, that the power of the Japanese bureaucracy has greatly decreased as a result of losing some of its formal licensing and approval authority. But the *keidanren*, for example, points out that 41 per cent of all the total value-added manufacturers in Japan are covered by extensive ministerial licensing and approval, and this is certainly a fairly large chunk of the economy. So I think we should be a little cautious in talking about the demise of bureaucrats in Japan. They remain extremely powerful not just in the economic sphere, for there is an unfortunate tendency to think only about MITI and MoF, but the power of the bureaucracy goes far beyond that. For example, in the *Japan Times* yesterday, I noticed the recent decision to keep out the birth control pill, yet again. So there is a lot of power which has nothing to do with economic forces for high technology industries, that directly affects Japanese society.

Is there a link between bureaucrats and political corruption, two spheres which are usually kept quite separate in most analytical discourse? We could reflect on the Nomura-Shoken scandal, in which bureaucrats must have known well in advance what was going on. There is now a more recent scandal, which Tag Murphy knows a lot about, the Tobashi scandal. It is almost impossible to imagine that the bureaucrats don't know what was going on. And so I think it is a bit unfair when you talk about corruption to lay it all at the feet of the LDP. Certainly bureaucrats play an implicit role, at least through simple economic cueing activity, providing incentives for corruption through over-regulation. With such extensive licensing and approval powers, it can be far more effective and economical to bribe your way through the system than to work through formal channels.

But there are other factors about corruption in Japan which need to be kept in mind. There is the whole issue of timing and sequence of institutions. People who work on Europe have long pointed out that when there was a bureaucracy which preceded the legislature, you often get corrupt, patronage-oriented parties seeking to establish some sort of voter base in response to bureaucratic power. Japan would seem to fit this example.

On the societal level Harumi Befu has written extensively about the problems of money and corruption in a gift-giving society. This is an area where culture and institutions collide quite interestingly. The other great developed nation with a history of corruption is the US. Pat Choate's book, *Agents of Influence*, is often misunderstood, in this context it is first and foremost an important expose of American influence peddling.

There is also the question of what corruption means in the Japanese political system. Marubushi Tetsuro has written about *Kozo-oshoku*, structural corruption. In the Showa Era alone there were almost 200 major corruption scandals affecting politics. I think it is safe to say that this is not necessarily a new phenomenon and it plays a fundamental role in Japanese politics.

Now, I'd just like to skip a little bit to some of the comments that were made about party reform, because it is impossible to talk about changing the Japanese political system by talking simply about party reform. In my view, this is like trying to put a band-aid on a cancer. You have to bring the bureaucrats more into line, and create courts that are more proactive and willing to decide against the government in a whole range of cases, not just individual rights cases. It probably means doing away with a great deal of the informal power that bureaucrats have, of which administrative guidance is just one example. Informal control over information is another example.

Rather than discuss party reform, the subject should be government-wide reform. It is trying to create a political party that is much more interested in leadership. It is trying to create a bureaucracy that is more responsive to leadership. It is trying to create a judiciary that plays a more independent role in the governmental system in general.

F. Lai: Actually, I want to respond to yesterday's challenge, to discuss Japan's *vitality* in the comparative context with Hong Kong. At first I thought that Hong Kong is too small to take under consideration, but then I decided that the case of Hong Kong is a good footnote or anecdote to our discussions here, because in our search for commonality, there is a great tendency to ascribe certain stereotypes of *vitality*. Hong Kong offers a very contrasting model of *vitality*. I think a lot of people would agree with me that Hong Kong is of high *vitality* as a small colony that has survived more challenges than any other government. But they have survived in a very different way. In contrast to the strong government in Japan and the other NICs, the government in Hong Kong takes a very minimal 'positive non-interventionist' role in economic development, providing a neutral and rather free environment for an entrepreneur to operate.

In Japan and South Korea, the role of big corporations is very major, as we discussed yesterday. In Hong Kong's case, we don't have big corporations, only small and medium-sized firms. This is one major way we differ from other countries in the region, for the *vitality* seems to lie with the individual entrepreneur. Small businesses have the flexibility to meet challenges, overcome them, and regenerate. Sometimes new developments emerge without grand government planning, and are a making of all these private individual entrepreneurs. For example, 1997 is a source of a great lack of confidence, but we look at the books and find that 70 per cent of the total foreign investment in China has come from or through Hong Kong. This is a contradicting situation, for the crisis of confidence is still there.

In addition, the outflow of capital was expected to be an alarming problem, but what has happened is that it has actually helped the small and medium-sized firm to enlarge and internationalise their operations and management. Thus, in a real way, it has enhanced the foundation and structure of the private businesses. These are some of the examples how the *vitality* of Hong Kong has emerged without strong government, planning, or big corporations. Of course this does not mean that Hong Kong is without its problems, but it is an interesting footnote that maybe there is not a fixed model of *vitality*, and maybe we need to search a little deeper for its meaning.

A. Clesse: Thank you. I think it would be interesting after what has been said to hear what the Japanese participants have to add to this. I am also looking for some balance. Perhaps Professor Inoguchi, Shinohara, or Iida would like to comment. Takashi Inoguchi.

T. Inoguchi: Extremely briefly, I would like to comment on bureaucracy and corruption because Barry mentioned my remark on the role of bureaucracy in the context of the World Bank lending policy. With respect to the bureaucracy's discretionary power, I have been writing on these things in a number of newspapers. Basically, three factors have to be kept in mind. One is that another important role of the Japanese bureaucracy is to monitor reality, like the market.

They are quite good at monitoring so many things (Americans like to say 'intelligence', but we say monitor or surveillance, in the IMF sense). They do not tend to trust in explicitly stated laws; Japanese laws tend to be very broad and general. This is because Japanese bureaucrats do not necessarily believe in this sort of thing, and they rely on their discretionary power.

With the rise of the private sector *vis-à-vis* the public sector over the last two decades or so, I think the private sector naturally uses politicians because they are naturally superior to the bureaucrats in terms of the Constitution and all the constitutional structures. Politicians are naturally interested in meeting the wishes of the private sector, because politicians need money. They also have power to put pressure on the bureaucrats to change some discretionary decision, like to change some land classification from agriculture to commercial. Then the whole system changes; taxes go up, prices go up, and those who bought these agricultural lands become extremely rich overnight. So this rise of the private sector and the tandem rise of politicians sometimes is the second factor.

The third factor is the general public. They - or perhaps I should say we - tend to view politics in a different way. The bureaucrats are viewed neutrally, with their broad and general powers, but the world of politicians is like a special world. Many view them as a *water business* - you know, like journalism and securities houses which are considered like water business. As long as the bureaucrats' work is not too much influenced by the politicians' corruption, as long as the economy keeps growing, then the political corruption is tolerated. As long as policy formation functions relatively well, then some politicians' intervention is tolerable. When Japan was a small power, the international prestige of Japan was not affected negatively by small issues of corruption and scandal. When you compare the scope of corruption to Japan's GNP, it's nothing in the public perception. So this corruption can be tolerated, as long as it doesn't harm the general growth, as personal excesses. As long as the politician seems repentant, at least in his expression, the public's negative reaction will go down. So the bureaucrats have the real role in maintaining the organisation, reproducing it, and enhancing it.

Now, another point which I think is important for us now and for the editor of this conference's report is that another perspective on these issues of *vitality* is the *vitality* of humankind. The book could be organised under that perspective as the possible role of Japan in sustaining it, with three sections on comparability, competitiveness, and contributions, and the conclusions can be written by someone. I thought that I should throw out this perspective to the conference. Thank you very much.

A. Mikuni: First I'd like to touch on the role of the administration, looking into the financial scenes. I had a very interesting experience in Davos last January, where Mr Akio Morita was on a Japanese panel discussing how

Japanese industry is working. At one point he mentioned that Japan has excessive competition within Japan, that we have eight auto companies, whereas an ideal number of manufacturers might be two or three. So Japanese companies have two kinds of threat to use. In the domestic market, they use what we call a *takemitsu*, or a fake bamboo sword. In the overseas market they use the real sword on competitors. In Japan, you think that some companies are going to be belly-up, but they usually recover like phoenixes. Whether or not the throat is slit is really up to the Japanese banks and the Japanese administration. For example, the major Japanese manufacturing companies are not easily bankrupted because they are supported by the main banks, which is due to the fact that the MoF controls interest rates very exactly and asset prices. Also, the MoF can avoid the bankruptcy of banks, so banks can support industries.

The second point is related to the point brought up earlier. What is the purpose of Japan's unlimited economic expansion for ever-greater market share? I think the ultimate purpose is quite clear; it is production capacities. I was reading a paper by Professor Kim Kihwan when I came here. On page six, he said that Japan should waste no time in confronting its past history. I am a little sarcastic, but I don't think Japan has wasted any time confronting its past history. After the Meiji era, Japan spent much effort in building up its military. After the Second World War, Japan spent much time studying why it was defeated. The reason was our lack of production capacity *vis-à-vis* the US production capacity. So the main game after the Second World War has been to create efficient production capacities. If we try to maintain these, the main issue is whether the export market can take the products. As long as the export market can absorb our products, we can expand our capacities to produce. For these, we need the roles played by the administration and *kikan ginko* (producer-linked) banks.

Finally, there is a very interesting system of how the financial market is to be administered. In Japan we have almost complete intermediation in the financial market. This means that household savings are almost totally intermediated by banks and licensed financial institutions. Thus, it is easy to control interest rates under the administration of the MoF. So this is how our system works.

Whether or not the system can be changed in the future is another question. I think Karel believes that the Japanese system is not easy to change, and this may be true. But we had a very interesting scandal last summer involving major brokerage houses. From January 1 of this year, the new securities act provision came into effect. The compensation arrangements are now subject to criminal offence, and when the Diet discussed this, the Ministries of Finance and Justice validated the law's change based on the principle that the manipulation of market prices is to be incriminated. But this is a very, very new idea in Japan, because the job of the administration is the manipulation of price.

K. van Wolferen: I am very pleased with what Mr Mikuni has just said, because he and Professor Inoguchi have been taking the words right out of my mouth. The difficulty that I have had with this conference is that there is an attempt to separate political from economic matters. Japan's *vitality* is the one subject where unless you consider these two realms as coinciding with one another, you will never understand what you are talking about. So, to start with an audacious proposal, I would invite you to imagine that Japanese administrators have accomplished something that we have long believed was impossible. Anybody who is interested in world politics or economic affairs concluded that you cannot merge private and public sectors, and the command economies of the Soviet type proved it. Now I propose that what Japanese authorities have accomplished is virtually to erase the line of demarcation between private and public sectors. Of course, in order to make you believe me I would need much more time, so I am going to jump from subject to subject, trying to incorporate some of the things which have been said earlier.

First of all, let's take account of the political scenarios. As I was listening to Professor Stockwin, I agreed with everything he said except I kept wondering what difference does all that make? There Professor Inoguchi is closer to the mark when he says this is the *mizu shobai*, the water trade. I characterise the goings-on of the LDP as a *soap opera*; it is very interesting to see who is going to do what to whom in order to determine the next prime minister. But it is almost totally irrelevant to the affairs of Japan. Now, suppose that there was a coalition government, that the LDP somehow lost power to the Socialists, what would happen if the Socialist politicians replaced the LDP politicians? In the 1950s and 1960s this would have made a difference, but by now I do not think that Socialists formally governing Japan would have much power to do very much that is different from what is going on now. Why? Because their formal power means very little. Their informal power is most important. The world which Mr Mikuni has described is a completely informal world. It is a political world in which banks and companies belong to the same family, own each other. As Professor Iwai so very brilliantly laid out yesterday, large companies own each other, and therefore what they do and their effect are different.

One element in this system has not yet been mentioned, and I think that it is an important one. Like the *keiretsu* system, it developed its current shape only after the war. It is the industrial associations which exist in every sector. These are the two main post-war contributions to economic history. The *keiretsu* system in which ownership is so amorphous that it allows for a large degree of external interference in the company's policies. This external influence does not just come from government agencies - and Kent Calder is quite right, that the direct influence of these agencies is not the crucial factor. It is the indirect influences that go through the industrial associations. They are supposedly interest groups representing the members of the corporations operating in a particular sector. In actual fact, they are as much an extension of the bureaucracy. These *associations have tremendous extra-legal powers*. If you want to operate as a manufacturer in Japan, you must belong to one and adhere to what they consider is good for you and the collectivity. Depending on influence and status of a particular sector, these associations come to life. Interestingly enough, there is absolutely no literature about them at all, except for their own self-serving and propagandistic publications.

I consider the *industrial associations* to be half the story, and the *keiretsu* are the other half. Together they have, for all intents and purposes, *eliminated the line of demarcation between private and public sector*. This is connected with everything else that we have been saying here. While the ability of corporations to mobilise the energy of the nation, to make the education system and the press subservient to its aim, the 1920s was a model of laissez-faire. This is really a post-war phenomenon, not rooted in ancient culture, even though some have made use of the proclivities, the traditions of subservience and dependence. When needed, they can come up with traditions at the drop of a hat.

A very important aspect of all this needs to be mentioned. It is very important to understand, if you agree with me that the *law does not ultimately regulate Japanese society*. What means do you have, then, to keep order? First of all, *maintaining order* is not just a concern of the Japanese authorities like it is of the authorities in any other country. *It is an obsession*. The notion that they could perhaps at some point lose control over outcomes is horrifying to them. A great deal of behaviour is explicable from these motives. *Informal controls have become more important as* time passes. Formal controls are gradually being replaced by these, for informal controls are far more effective. An element of this is *intimidation*, and this has not yet been mentioned.

Let me give you one example to illustrate this. What Ms Lai was saying about entrepreneurism among small businessmen in Hong Kong still exists in Japan today. Although you can consider this part of the private sector, in Japan these smaller companies are usually in some subcontracting relationship to the big ones. They are very dependent. When an entrepreneur becomes big, as in the recent example of Kyocera, it becomes in the opinion of its peers and so-called competitors (who, as Mr Mikuni put it, use bamboo swords) too big for its boots, showing that it does not know its place. So all of the sudden, the officials at the Ministry of Health discovered that Kyocera had not applied for the proper permission to market one of its products, ceramic bones. These were in use all over Japan, and they had never been found defective in any way.

It is the nature of bureaucratic control over Japanese industry that although you try not to control so much, you must have as much leverage at any given time. So they forced the CEO of Kyocera to go before the nation and apologise publicly. Everybody in the system knows what's going on, and everybody pretends that it is an issue of following the rules, but it is in fact the mandate to behave.

So I just mentioned an instrument of coercion that exists throughout the political and economic system and it is very important to keep it together. It is true as Kent Calder says that the *bureaucracy is reactive*, that the bureaucracy is *risk averse*. If there are any people in the world that are risk averse, it is the Japanese. And it is very true that they *hesitate to apply strategy*, and I wouldn't even call it a strategy, I think that Japanese bureaucrats in all areas, are *masters at tactics*. They understand a certain situation and changes in the situation and they are able to adjust that situation to themselves, as Professor Windsor very interestingly noted this morning, or, to do the kind of thing that will maximise their advantages.

They play it by ear a great deal. They can do this because of *phenomenal institutional memory* which is coupled to an institutional motivation of a kind that I have not found in the West. Maybe the US Marine Corps - you are more than a soldier if you're a member of it, you are a member of something that has a legacy. It has a purpose that goes far deeper than what soldiers usually feel. But it is not a good comparison. I don't know of any good comparison except perhaps a proselytising new religion. These bureaucratic bodies and corporate bodies cooperate with each other, although there is conflict between them also, but they depend on each other, at least while Japan does things directed outward like unlimited industrial expansion. These bodies do not operate from a blueprint that has been laid out way into the next century; they play it by ear. But the important thing about them is that they can't stop what they're doing. The important thing about them is that *there is no mechanism to turn them around; there is no mechanism for them to re-shift their priorities*. And that, of course, in the long-run is a problem that Japan will be facing because it is highly questionable, as Mikuni just said, that the world markets can continue to absorb ever-more products produced by ever-larger production facilities.

K. Kim: The comments I want to make relates to Karel's mention of the demarcation between public and private sector, the rise in corruption mentioned by Professor Keehn, and the rise in informal controls emphasised by Karel, and the increasing use of the instrument of caution. I think all of these are just different manifestations of the same phenomenon, the *privatisation of the Japanese government over the past 40 years*. Why has this taken place? Because for the past 40 years the government didn't have any unique role to play. The most important role for any government is that of defence, and that external threat is gone. So when you have samurai with no wars to fight, then they get in the way of civilians. When you have a bureaucrat without *vital* functions to perform, they get into the private sector and want to have part of it, resulting in corruption and informal controls with coercive power. So these are all just manifestations of the same thing.

My second point is about corruption. The question of whether it is serious or tolerable depends on what the government does. If the government's charge is to provide defence or define the future directions of the country, then corruption matters. But when government itself is in private business, then corruption is just some extension of the market mechanism. To me, corruption is the employment of a market mechanism in an area where the market mechanism should not be used.

A. Clesse: George De Vos, one sentence.

G. De Vos: One thing which is not being addressed about corruption is that the game becomes different when public opinion gets involved. Also, I have been watching over the last few years the increasing cynicism of youth with respect to these processes being discussed. In other words, as long as these things do not disrupt the illusions that people have about authority and its legitimacy, it has no serious effect. But once this becomes something that youth get a hold of, you have a generational problem emerging in what is going on, and that has to be addressed.

A. Clesse: It's getting late. If you agree, we will have lunch now. After this, we will hear an economist, Ken Courtis.

Future Vitality

K. Courtis: Thank you very much, Dr Clesse. I would like to thank the Institute for the kind invitation to be here. I would like to look at two or three issues, which have been raised by others, but from a perspective which happens to be mine. I'd like to set what is going on now in a context and look very briefly at what is going on, where it is leading the country economically, and what I think are the issues it raises.

My vision of Japan is that it is in a cycle that will last about 15 years. The cycle was triggered by the Plaza Accord, which was really a decision to throw the Japanese export machine out of gear. Japan had to order its priorities strategically, and its first priority was to reposition the economy to compete not at 190 or 200 yen to the dollar, but at 115 or 120 yen to the dollar. To do that, they had to have disciplined labour and oceans of cheap cash so companies could effectively make that type of investment to reposition themselves. In a simple sense, that is the story of this economy as it expanded from 1986 to late 1991. By making money free, which is essentially what the bureaucracy did - I remember my company in 1989 helping industry to raise money at less than 1 per cent after tax cost, and with 2.2 per cent inflation, people were actually being paid to borrow money in real terms - the investments were being made. To sum it all up, the numbers are fantastic. From 1986 to 1991 this economy invested $4.2 trillion in research and development, new plant and equipment, and investment abroad, for an economy that is $3.3 trillion. We have never seen anything like this before.

In the MITI study released in January of 18 600 companies, the break-even point on exports is now 123 yen to the dollar. But if you just take the top 100 companies which represent 72 per cent of exports, it should be no surprise that the trade surplus is exploding and is running at about $10 billion per month. Their break-even point we calculated as 118.3, and the yen is now at 133, and it will get weaker before it gets stronger again. So that strategic repositioning of the economy has largely been achieved and accomplished.

When money is free, people become extremely creative, and you don't realise how creative until the money stops being free, and some of the investment projects can't pay for themselves. Then you have to clean things up, and that's what is going on now. The economy is in a sense being purged of the excesses of the 1980s. It's being cleansed and toughened up again. This process is happening in a very interesting manner. During the funny money period of the 1980s, the *keiretsu* were able to raise virtually free money from the stock market and used it to reposition strategically and to deliver, to write down their debts. They have today the best balance sheet in four decades. The small and medium-sized firms, not having access to the stock market, had to borrow from miserable institutions like mine. As they borrowed, they bought land, and then they came back to see us. We lent them more money, they invested some of that in the stock market, and things went up and up and up. These companies have set themselves up with the worst balance sheets in decades. So you have a dualisation of the Japanese economy like never before. In this purging, the small and mid-sized overlevered producer is being pushed to the wall, and the big *keiretsu* companies are coming in to pick up the pieces. The *keiretsu* are becoming even stronger as we speak.

At the same time, in the banking system we also have a fundamental transition occurring. The mid- and small-sized banks through the 1980s, when it became obvious that there would be deregulation, should have known - and probably most of them did - that they would have to restructure to survive. But like most institutions, these liked to stay independent, and on aggregate, most came to the conclusion that to bull their way through the transition, they would have to bloat up their balance sheets. So they went out and lent massively to these small and medium-sized companies, and they now have balance sheets that are overskewed to the riskiest part of the market. So there is tremendous pressure as bankruptcies increase, and bankruptcies are already at a record high. This is directly impacting on the balance sheets of the mid- and small-sized banks; they are in a very weak position. At the same time, they have pressure from the Bank of International Settlements to build up their capital base, they've got the threat of new competition from stock-brokers, who will try to move into the juiciest part of the banking industry, and they've got tremendous pressure for interest rate deregulation. Their margins will be squeezed further. So we see a major restructuring also occurring in this sector. We could see through the second half of this decade a quarter to a third of these mid-sized and small banks disappear. At the end of this cleaning-up transition period, we will see a stronger banking system that is rationalised and competitive as never before. Mikuni-san said that the banking system never operated according to the laws of competition in the past; I submit that it will in the future.

As Japan's repositioning so quickly after the Plaza Accord changed the international economic balance of power, it is once again, through extraordinary *vitality* and dynamism, repositioning itself. This leads to the third part of the 15 year cycle, a new phase in the mid-1990s of explosive growth driven by partly some of the pressures on the political system, which are affected by the relative demographic decline of the agriculture and key clientele of the LDP. The new clientele is going to demand more infrastructure investment, so you kill two birds with one stone - you satisfy the Americans and build up your new constituency. It will require some increase in consumption as a proportion of GNP. The main motor for growth in the late 1990s will be the explosive markets between Tokyo and Jakarta, where America is in retreat and Europe is not sufficiently present. Japanese companies, with this toughened base, are repositioning themselves for strategic control by default and design of the mega-markets of the next decade. So they will get tremendous volume increases, which will allow them to keep going down the cost curves. If this continues, *10 or 12 years from now this economy will be the size of the American economy.*

What are the issues that this raise? One is what are Japan's economic, and therefore political, relations going to be with the rest of the world? There is a debate that started with this about different models of capitalism. It seems that this debate is in fact a very important one. One part is being driven by those companies that can only be investing the way they are investing if they suppose continued free access to the world market - the Sonys, the *keidanren*. How is their relationship to the world market going to change over the 1990s? Their exports are running $320 or $335 billion, only 9 per cent relative to GNP, which is in fact the smallest of the G-7. Exports will increase over the 1990s to perhaps $550 billion, but that will still be 8 per cent or 9 per cent of GNP.

The real change that is coming can be seen in the numbers the Japanese government puts out. They predict Japan will run a current account surplus of about 2 per cent a year over the next decade. That's a trillion dollars, equal to the GNP of France, and that will obviously cause one debate. But of course that money will be recycled, reinvested, and Japanese direct foreign investment, which is now about $200 billion, will be $500-$600 billion. So Japan's stock of total direct foreign investment around the world will be close to three-quarters of a trillion dollars.

A. Clesse: Thank you. Now, Professor Sato will make some comments about the future.

S. Sato: When the United States was an underdeveloped country, isolated from the European continent by the Atlantic Ocean and protected by the British Navy, the Americans could afford to have such a divisive structure. But as a superpower, the only superpower in the world, it is very dangerous. We need a more integrated system in the United States. But take just one example, the IS Negotiations between the US and Japan: Americans criticise the Japanese' performance as not so brilliant; I quite agree. But no one talks about the American performance. Americans have done nothing about this agreement, about which they promised. The reason is simple. There is a lack of leadership on the part of Washington. The Japanese situation is no better than the Americans'; we are in about the same state. But now that, as I said, Japan is facing a great age of transformation, we need much stronger leadership. So it is a good time for Japan to try to have an excellent pilot. I am not so sure that we can do that. I do know how difficult it is for a big democracy like Japan. But I do think that it is a challenge we are now facing.

There is no need for Japan to have the single excellent pilot, providing that there is a consensus for a common development in Japan. After the Second World War to the 1960s, there was a national consensus so everybody was heading in the same direction, without any pilot; that was okay. But *there are no clear-cut ideas of which way, how, and how quickly Japan should move - then we need someone to pilot this course.* That is my first point.

The second is again a matter that was touched upon by van Wolferen and Glen Fukushima. That is the demarcation between the public and private sectors. In any society, the demarcation is not so clear as some Americans tend to believe. Even in the United States, the demarcations between the public and private sectors are not so clear-cut. But, I believe that the demarcation is broader in Japan than both in the United States and Europe. The reason is very obvious. In the United States, from the very beginning, the separation between the public and the private has been a part of the basic ideology. In Europe, especially after the Second World War because of the Socialist influence, there is a public sector owning a lot of factories, whereas in Japan, there are very few factories or companies owned by the government. Glen used one word to describe this; I prefer the word *'interpenetration'* to describe the relationship *between the public and private sectors. That makes the Japanese society extremely effective and also makes the size of the Japanese government relatively small.*

Many people criticise the Japanese government with regards to its activities in the private sectors of Japan. But if you look at the total number of government officials and the size of the government's budget, Japan's government is among the smallest in the world, in terms of its GNP and its population. The secret of that is this interpenetration between the public and private sector. And that is okay as far as Japan was in the stage of catching up.

But now the scope of Japan's participation with the rest of the world has been broader, especially in terms of the economic activities, including service industries. So we have to extend much more effort to harmonise our practices with those in the outside world; that is the challenge we are now facing. If we fail, then Japan will face a serious problem.

When we discuss the present state of Japan, we should not depend too much on anecdotal episodes. I am very informed of the activities in some parts of Japan and am critical of that. The motivation of people who spread particular opinions through anecdotes as a good excuse is that they foolishly think that is a way to protect their vested interests. For example, on the issue of lawyers, some have said that they believe themselves to be government employees, but I think that is ridiculous. Therefore, we should not be too dependent upon the anecdotal episode.

A. Clesse: I think Gordon Berger would like to briefly raise a question for Professor S. Sato. Professor Berger.

G. Berger: I want to clarify what seems to me to be an interesting parallel in your comments. On the one hand, pointing out that the distinction in Japan between the public and the private is not as clear as it is in America has a lot to do with ideology. And yet in the issue of the lawyers, where the question is whether they are defined as being public or private, I do not yet know where they are situated in Japan. Are they somewhere between public and private, like the corporate?

S. Sato: That is very clear; they are in the private. I would say that 99 per cent of the Japanese lawyers would consider themselves to be in the private sector, no question about that. But they have the control, and each district has at least one bar association. And all attorneys-at-law are organised to belong to these associations; otherwise, they are not allowed to practice law. That is just a clarification - so the bar association in Japan has a special status, but they are not paid by the government, except during the first two years as a 'trainee' association.

G. Berger: But since the public and private sectors are not that clearly distinguished in Japan, how can we say that the lawyers are irrevocably in the private sector? That is the confusion I was referring to.

S. Sato: What I said is that almost all, maybe with some exceptions, lawyers are members of the bar association and do believe that they are not public servants. Maybe the person who talked used the word *komuin* - that is too much. I would never consider that accurate because it is against the legal provisions; *komuin* means 'government employees'. That is absolutely wrong. I think that most lawyers in Japan do know better about the legal system in Japan.

G. Fukushima: If I could just clarify for a minute. It was a Ministry of Justice official who explained to me that, in their view, Japanese lawyers are fundamentally servants of the state, public servants, and therefore, it would be contrary to the national interest to allow them to be under the supervision of a foreigner. That was the main point. But I would say also that it seems to me that Gordon raises an interesting and important issue because I think you probably will concede that the Japan Federation of Bar Associations' relationship with the Ministry of Justice is a very complicated and very interpenetrated relationship, if you will, compared to the relationship between the American Bar Association, on the one hand, and the US Federal or state governments. So I think there is a much less clearly defined delineation between those two.

S. Sato: That I do not argue against. But, as far as civil servants and government employees are concerned, there is a very clear difference. Anyone who receives money, a portion of authority from the government, is regarded as a government employee. The employees the Japanese Government actually employs according to Japanese regulation - they are also government employees. There are several different categories of government employees, but lawyers are categorically not among them.

G. Fukushima: He was not using this in a very strictly legal way; he was using it in a looser fashion in terms of what kinds of interests they should represent. That was the important point.

S. Sato: It is an analogy.

G. Fukushima: Yes.

S. Sato: And a foolish analogy to make.

G. Fukushima: Probably. I would like to make one additional point, which is that I can understand that Professor Sato would not want us to draw conclusions from anecdotes or circumstantial evidence. I would say that, having studied about Japan for eight years in graduate school at Harvard and then having spent five years in the US government, I have learned that specifics and anecdotes are a manifestation of reality, as opposed to deductive theories.

S. Sato: As long as you put these anecdotes into context.

I. Hall: I would just like to say that this argument, on the lawyer's side, is an exact parallel to the law which has been going on for many years against the participation and tenuring of foreign professors in national universities because national university professors are civil servants, which they are. The interesting argument was that, as civil servants, Japanese professors take part in the formation of the national will and therefore, participation of foreigners would not be appropriate. That law was changed ten years ago, but to no practical effect. So I think the psychological implications, whether anecdotal or systematic, are very pertinent to the question of Japan's fuller participation in the outside world through the permission of fuller participation in Japan. I would say that this also reflects the overlap, the interpenetration, of the public and private sectors in areas and that we would certainly consider lawyers and professors to be in the private sector. As an activity, not part of the political system and otherwise.

K. Calder: I think it is important, as we look at the question of where the market should be dealing, or in fact is doing adjustments, or where public policy should be doing this sort of thing, we make some distinctions across sectors. This has come up as people cite different examples for their purposes. We have not really been making this explicit, but many of the highly regulated sectors, traditionally law has been regulated for example, you could take power, you could take banking, you could take insurance. But then, on the other side of the coin, you can also find a lot of other sectors like, for example, most of electronics, most of the automobile industry, a lot of the most basic manufacturing sectors, where the issues are really somewhat different and where the dynamics of public and private interaction are also greater.

To me, this echoes the importance of a point that was made by Professor Kohsaka earlier, about the importance of markets as a fundamental mechanism for adjustment here. If we expect too much of the political process in Japan's relationships with the world, not only are we going to be frustrating market forces that have considerable power in many sectors and the ability then to subvert intention of these sorts of global forces, but at the same time will overload the political system, a political system which is having difficulties in the short run and is in a process of transition.

Then finally, I think, we can look to the point Ken Courtis made and I would agree with totally, which is that over the long run we have *some very important emerging lines of cleavage in the political system, and a certain part of the business world that is going to have increasingly important international stakes*. We can already see this, for example, in policies in the agricultural area, and in *Nihon Keizai Shimbun*, with major parts of the business world which have been pushing for liberalisation.

So, in conclusion, I think it is important to look at a lot of the sectorial distinctions and not overgeneralise too much.

A. Clesse: Taggart Murphy, related to what Kent Calder said, and Karel van Wolferen, too. Please be as brief as possible.

T. Murphy: Yes, I will be as brief as possible. What I hear in discussions of lawyers, discussions of university professors, and discussions of the economic problems are reflections, I think, of something very fundamental. Those fundamental points are also not raised because they are difficult to see, but they have an implication for certainly the economic and for the overall theme of this conference, the theme of *vitality*.

Let us start with our anecdotal example of lawyers. The conception of the legal profession in the West is that a lawyer is a servant of justice in an attempt to arrive at the concept of justice. This assumes a fundamental concept that such a thing as justice exists as a transcendental reality.

Also, if we look at the case of university professors: The underlying assumption in the West is that the functions of intellectuals are involved with the search for truth. This presupposes that a transcendental concept of truth exists.

If you look at the concept of economic well-being and the governing rules of an economy, or the governing fundamental concepts of an economy, in the West they are fundamentally, in the philosophical tradition in which it is rooted, to achieve the greatest good of the individual consumer.

Now, what we are hearing coming out here is that the fundamental presuppositions which are often not raised in the Japanese context are fundamentally different. That is to say that university professors, to quote Ivan Hall, exist to a certain extent in the formulation of the national will. If that is the case, then why is there only one tenured foreign professor in the Japanese university system?

S. Sato: There is no use of talking and discussing very wrong ideas. It is unfair to base an argument on one or two very small examples.

T. Murphy: Whether the argument is fair or unfair - certainly I would accept the fact that in the West indeed the whole idea of transcendental concepts of truth and justice and good have been under attack.

S. Sato: This is basically the same in Japan.

T. Murphy: They have been under attack from both the cultural left and Marxism, so there is no intellectual agreement even in the West. But the fundamental philosophical concepts are there and when we ignore those, we ignore those at our peril because it goes towards explaining a lot of the contradictions in, for example, a country where, as we have said earlier today, the basic economic assumption is the protection of competitors rather than the protection of competition. The fundamental problem that the world has now is that the world liberal economic system is predicated on a set of concepts which do not necessarily apply in the Japanese context. Unless we address that fundamental issue, I think the rest of it will continue to be on an anecdotal level.

S. Sato: There is no fundamental difference. I was really amazed to listen to that kind of argument, that Japanese scholars are not servants for the truth. Of course, they are not so loyal, in many cases, as many Western scholars are. And are Japanese lawyers servants of justice? Of course. If you were to raise that question, that would be the response from the members of the bar associations in Japan. And many of the members of the bar association are strongly anti-government. I can cite many examples to support this.

T. Murphy: I am sure they are, but why then was the argument used that Japanese lawyers could not work for foreign law firms?

S. Sato: You should not confuse everything. That is a completely different argument than the concept of justice.

T. Murphy: I do not follow.

S. Sato: There is an agreement needed for the lawyers to work in some countries, so that if all of the American states, all 50 states, accept the Japanese lawyer as a lawyer without any bar examinations, then the Japanese Bar Association will accept American lawyers to practice law here in Japan. Or, if the American lawyers take the bar examinations in Japan, and to pass the examination is very difficult unless the Japanese language has been mastered, but it is not impossible. Some Koreans have already passed the Japanese bar exams and are practising law in Japan. Also, many Japanese lawyers have passed the American bar examinations and are practising law there.

T. Murphy: Maybe I should clarify.

A. Clesse: Yes, but first, Ambassador Matsunaga.

N. Matsunaga: I have no intention of intervening in this very stimulating discussion, but let me just say a few words about what I am feeling about the problem we are discussing at this table. Yesterday, in my opening arguments, I said that the three basic principles, of freedom, democracy, and market economy, which I strongly believe that we should continue to uphold and strengthen, are now facing a world-wide challenge, whether these basic principles would prove to be successful in the management of world economy. That is particularly the case for Japan.

Now, regarding these fundamental principles, which in my view were originally created and emerged in Europe, and then were introduced to the United States, and a while later, were introduced to Japan. Therefore, we have been learning from European experience and from American experience and we are still on that course. That is one thing I want to say.

Now, regarding the question of lawyers, of the Japanese Bar Association: I myself feel very strongly that Japanese lawyers, that the Japanese Bar Association, are extremely closed and conservative. I think we have to make many efforts in order to make them open-minded and open the door to foreign lawyers, as well as foreign enterprises. However, and this is what I would like to point out here, this does not mean that the bar association in the United States or the law system in Europe are really the only ones which should be governing in the society of law. That is another thing, another question.

There are some legitimate fears on the part of Japanese lawyers that if they open the door entirely, they will then be immediately dominated by powerful foreign lawyers. They have, in my view, their own legitimate reasons to fear that. However, again I must stress that this does not mean that the system should be kept in the present form.

A. Clesse: Thank you. This discussion, of course, unfortunately takes us away from the main topic of the conference, namely the *vitality* of nations. It is important to focus, since everything, in a sense, is related to the *vitality* of nations. Now the polemics launched by Taggart do not have a very strong cognitive value, but this is not a criticism. However, we should not engage too much in polemics. There are enough polemics at many other conferences, academic or not, and we should remain somewhat placid.

T. Murphy: The attempt is not to be polemical; the attempt is to get at something fundamental. The attempt is to be general and to be fundamental and to talk about the long-term limitations of Japan's *vitality*, which is, I thought, what you wanted to discuss this afternoon.

A. Clesse: Yes, that is the objective of the meeting. But when it comes to means, of course one may discuss them. I see so many hands. First, very briefly, perhaps Karel van Wolferen.

K. van Wolferen: I will also try to go down to fundamentals and that will inevitably take me back to ground that has already been covered. But before I do that, I have to respond to Professor Sato's points.

Naturally, the argument is very familiar to me, when you say there is no central political accountability in Japan, which is, I believe, a fundamental problem. The question then is, who is the pilot in the United States? All right. Obviously, other countries show characteristics that remind you of the Japanese situation. And obviously, the Japanese situation reminds you constantly of flaws in other market economies and in other democracies, obviously because the Japanese are human beings and we share these things. However, by singling out certain things, you single them out for a purpose. And by saying there are similarities, you should not take the next step and say they are the same, because there is a fundamental difference.

Let us compare the American President with the Japanese Prime Minister. Saddam Hussein invades Kuwait. The American President has to make a decision. Is he going to make a fuss, or not? Is he going to make clear to the world the United States will remain a forceful order in the world, or is he going to let this pass and decide he will do nothing at all? He has a decision to make, and he makes a decision. Three days after Saddam Hussein's invasion, this decision was made.

The Japanese Prime Minister, interestingly enough, was scheduled to go on a tour of Middle East capitals in August. And as far as we know, he wanted to go even though this invasion had taken place. Kaifu wanted to go. The Foreign Ministry told him that he could not go. Why not? Well, they did not explain that to the rest of the world. But I understand that Kaifu actually insisted and the Foreign Ministry maintained that he could not go. To explain the cancellation of the trip, the Foreign Ministry said that Japan had not made up its mind yet.

What I believe happened is that the Foreign Ministry officials were afraid that Kaifu might say the wrong things. They feared amateurish encroachments on what they considered their turf. The Prime Minister of Japan, at that point, is not the centre of political accountability of Japan. He is not the person you want to deal with if you want to deal with Japan. The Prime Minister of Japan, at that point, becomes totally invisible as a diplomatic entity. What Kaifu could have done is to go to the Middle East capitals; he would have been the first official leader of a major country to do so and make the right noises, and put otherwise unobtainable proof in the hands of the American President, to use *vis-à-vis* Congress, that Japan is indeed an ally. That would have been pretty good for Japan; it would have been a great advantage for Japan had that happened.

Nothing of the sort took place. But the interesting thing is that the Japanese public was very perturbed by this. The Japanese public, as came across from my conversations with people in the street and with many correspondents who wanted to find out, almost to a man, was perturbed by this, that the Japanese government could not have a presence in the world. And it was puzzling to Southeast Asians, including Lee Kuan-Yew, that a country so dependent on oil from that region could not do something or say something to make clear where it stood.

That is what I mean by a centre of political accountability. Now we can go on for a long time with what happened afterwards and there have been many rationalisations. I can give you those rationalisations before Professor Sato does. There have been many. *The important point is that, at such a moment, Japan does not exist in the world and it is not clear what Japan is all about at such a moment.*

Okay, the United States has a problem with its leadership. We can talk about that for a whole evening. On purpose, power in the United States is spread out over a lot of entities. It is spread out geographically over different states. It spread out over courts, over legislature, and so on. . .

A. Clesse: Karel, I would like Kenneth Courtis to say a few words; he must leave very soon. Perhaps you can come back to this.

K. Courtis: I see we have heard that the role of historians is to relate the past to the present to the future, and Professor Iwai very eloquently said that we need to do more work in that area in this country. My sense, to take on the issue that Professor Kohsaka set out for us, is that the role of the government is to represent the future to the present. And to sort through the options and set out the choices, and Kohsaka Sensei set out the difficult choices. Then we went on to discuss that one of the ways that Japan adapts to these extraordinary changes that are coming internally and internationally that are both, as Professor Iwai said, the result of Japan's success and partly the result of others' failures, the failure of leadership elsewhere to use the market mechanism itself. It seems to me that is one of the major political challenges, to have the political vision and leadership to allow the market to work. In other words, cut through this structure of regulation that puts into question, obviously, huge political interests.

Professor Sato told us earlier that Japan in the past had sort of been on automatic pilot because the environment was so stable. *We were on automatic pilot because the environment was stable, but also because there was a social contract that was vital*, in a sense, and *that was extremely efficient in performing*. That was a social contract that implied an *implicit guarantee of full employment, in return for modest* consumption, moderate social welfare, constant increases in productivity, with the value added going largely to the corporate sector so that it could invest at a much higher rate than other leading countries. So the companies could provide the implicit guarantee of full employment. The success of that model is without contest. And I guess it would not matter if Japan was, say, my country, Canada. It is irrelevant to the overall scheme of things.

But in a country that is this large and is operating with a model that is different and that may now mean that the democratic basis of that social model seems to be put into question. My sense is that the question of leadership becomes extremely important. Perhaps that can serve as a post-face to what I said earlier and a not very eloquent preface to Karel van Wolferen's remarks.

A. Clesse: Thank you, Professor Courtis. Karel van Wolferen would like to go on - perhaps Professor Sato would prefer that you dwell on the German example instead of the US example.

K. van Wolferen: Fine. The point is this. The United States had made fairly clear what it is about and what it wanted. The United States has, after the Second World War, said to the world that it intended to contain the Soviet Union and was going to make sure that Communism did not spread. That was the main international aim - did you want to join them or not? The United States, of course, at this moment is in a period of transition because the world has changed and it is true that it is not very clear what role it is going to play. But I think most people who have had experience with the United States are not worried about the United States. I think most people do not think that the United States is going to be a problem for them.

Now Japan may be one hundred per cent benevolent as far as the rest of the world is concerned, but the rest of the world does not know that yet. And Japan is expanding at an incredible rate. Ken Courtis just left - his favourite example is that, in the past four and a half years of the current growth cycle, Japan has added to its economy a volume that is equal to the GNP of France, and the momentum continues. And, as we heard before, perhaps in the next dozen years or so, Japan will pass the United States as the strongest economic force in history, unless somebody throws a wrench into the works.

But the point is that *Japan is an incredible power and it is a political power because its economic presence has very grave political repercussions*. So it is a political problem unto itself and for the rest of the world and it must be addressed. You cannot say, as Professor Kohsaka says, 'Leave it to the market', because we have just ascertained that the market at best in Japan has a subsidiary role. It is a tool in the hands of people who use it for a certain end, but it is never allowed to ultimately determine outcomes. So you cannot leave it up to the market.

Also, I think that you cannot say as, with all respect, Ambassador Matsunaga says, that this is a democracy and a free market economy and that Japan, together with all the other democracies and free market economies, has to pool resources and create a better world, because it is a question whether Japan is all these things.

As long as we cannot come to grips with these issues, as we cannot find a civil society in Japan where the Japanese discuss these things amongst themselves, we cannot hope as foreigners to discuss them with the Japanese, except with a few private individuals over cups of sake, as I have done very often. When you do that, you will find that your Japanese friends, over a bit of sake, will agree that this is a problem, that a Japanese democracy is there potentially; it has got all the mechanisms and all the instruments. But as long as the Japanese population cannot influence political outcomes, you may have a democratic system, but it is not a true democracy. And as long as the market will not ultimately determine the economic outcomes, you do not have a free market.

Finally, and this is fundamental, because you have to address fundamental incompatibilities. *The future of relationships between Japan and the rest of the world will be determined by whether or not we can address fundamental incompatibilities.* The most fundamental problem is what I started saying, that is that you do not have a centre of political accountability because, and this is, Professor Sato, what I mean by it, the right to rule, the question of who has the right to rule in Japan, has never been settled. *Who has the right to rule* - the Japanese Prime Minister? Obviously not. A group of politicians - no; they do not determine what happens in Japan economically. MITI or the Finance Ministry - maybe we are coming closer, but not. They do not run the whole show. Who then does? Which order, which body, which person, which group has the right to rule and can therefore rule in effect? This is a very essential, basic problem.

The response to this is usually that Japan is run on consensus, but I do not believe that consensus can ever be a substitute for what I am talking about, because you cannot have consensus over things that have yet to happen. And you must have a government, a central political accountability, that can cope with an immediate situation.

If another Gulf-like crisis should develop, then at that point, perhaps, Japan's administrators will know how to respond since they have experienced one before. In cases where there is experience, they could perhaps respond. But as the world is developing now, it is full of unexpectedness. *And in this world of unexpectedness, I think this is the problem - how do you cope with it if you have not given the right to rule to any particular person or any particular body?* This is an essential problem.

Again, I think that as long as Japanese intellectuals publicly do not try to come to terms with these problems, there is not going to be a useful dialogue between Japan and the rest of the world on any but technical or ritualistic matters. I hope that this conference could perhaps address some of these problems.

A. Clesse: Professor Kohsaka, but first Professor Sato. Perhaps we Westerners, if I may say this, should also try to be somewhat self-critical and not be ethnocentric. Ethnocentrism, or Eurocentrism, is always a danger in such debates or analysis.

K. van Wolferen: I hope you are not implying that I am Eurocentric in any way, because I do not like that. I hope you are not implying that.

A. Clesse: No, I am not referring to any specific participant. It is simply a general remark. Some people may refer to a certain ideology and examine all sorts of phenomena in order to point out how imperfect, or less perfect, other societies are. This is just a very general, almost epistemological remark, but it is perhaps useful to keep it in mind. Professor Kohsaka.

M. Kohsaka: I do not believe in fundamentals too much, because fundamentals can mean several things and can be very dubious.

S. Sato: In order to avoid misunderstanding, I would like to repeat what I have said several times since yesterday. I have been extremely critical of the conservative nature of many of the Japanese organisations which serve to protect their vested interests, and especially against the Japanese Bar Association. Having said that, we should not make too clear-cut a contrast between Japan on the one hand and the so-called 'Western' world on the other.

Just one example: van Wolferen said there is no single body in Japan invested with the right to rule over the country. I do not know that there is any democracy in the world in which a single person or single organisation has a right to rule over all aspects of activities in the society. That is a dictatorship.

K. van Wolferen: No, you are distorting my argument. But go ahead.

A. Clesse: Perhaps, Karel van Wolferen, you should not interrupt.

K. van Wolferen: But this is a distortion; it is clearly not what I am saying.

A. Clesse: You can explain your position in a minute. You will get a chance to reply, but whoever is speaking really should not be interrupted. Professor Sato.

S. Sato: I do not think I misunderstood what Karel van Wolferen said. I have read many of his articles and believe that my understanding of his position is correct. He made a very simplistic contrast between Japan and the Western world. As he said, the Japanese are human beings - and Japan is a democracy. If you say that Japan is not a democracy, I would like to know the definition of a democracy. You said that the Japanese people cannot have any influence on the Japanese politics; that is a ridiculous argument to make, that Japanese politicians should be elected in campaigns. Of course, you can say that they can mobilise voters under any democracy but, in the case of the United States Congress, around 95 per cent of the Congressmen who run again will be reelected. Then are you ready to say that the United States is not a democracy?

N. Matsunaga: I shall be extremely brief. First of all, let me say that Professor Sato and Professor Kohsaka, whom I respect wholeheartedly, are most sophisticated and far-sighted professors and who are trying to convince the Japanese people to move ahead in the right direction. But having said that, I would just like to repeat what I said. Japan is moving ahead, and in the right direction. I am not saying that Japan has nothing to do; there are still more things to be done. However, you would be wrong if you say that Japan has been doing nothing. Japan has been doing quite a lot, particularly when you look back to 10 or 20 years ago - then Japan has put forth quite a bit of effort in order to make Japan compatible with the international society.

I would say that the Japanese people as a whole are not fully aware of the responsibility, of the role, of the burden, which Japan and the Japanese people are expected to assume. That is because Japan has reached this high level of economic development so quickly, and it was not only a surprise for the world community, but for Japan as well. And I think that fact has been causing the delay in the awareness of the Japanese people becoming reality.

And that is precisely what we have seen in the case of the Gulf War. During the Gulf War, you may recall that at the beginning of the war, more than 70 per cent of the Japanese people believed and felt that the Gulf situation was happening far away from Japan, and so we have nothing to do with that. But in the later stage, public opinion, as gathered in a public poll, demonstrated very clearly that 80 per cent of Japanese people started to feel that the regional conflict of the Gulf War was connected with the world community, in which Japan has to play its own role and has to assume its responsibility. In that sense, the Gulf War gave a very good lesson to the Japanese people. I think that Japan is moving ahead.

As I said about the Bar Association, here again we have been making some improvements, but I admit that there is certainly much more to be done. In particular, *Japanese society should become compatible with international society*, and that is what we have to do in the future. I am looking forward to this; I am not very pessimistic about that.

K. Iwai: I will try to be very brief. We have been listening to a lot of interesting explanation and anatomy of Japanese political, cultural, and economic systems; it has been a revealing experience. What the Japanese have been taking for granted is brought to the surface by the observations of the foreign analysts. As our discussion is moving towards the future aspects of Japan's *vitality*, I would like to touch upon important points that have been made by various people, that where Japan has to adjust or change in order to sustain its *vitality* so that it can really meet the challenges that it is facing in the future. This is going to be just a partial summary resulting from the discussion of the past two days.

Now, I think there are, broadly, two problem areas. One is institutional; the other is non-institutional, or spiritual, or psychological, or societal. The first is the institutional area, and *here bureaucracy is the biggest problem area*. On the basis of my experience in government, bureaucracy is certainly a problem in terms of the haggling in which each ministry engages itself. That results not only in *a delay in the decision itself, but also in the vagueness of the decision* which the government as a whole comes up to as a final result. This is never more true than in the field of foreign policy. As far as the Foreign Ministry is concerned, perhaps you may know that there has been a lot of discussion as to how we can strengthen the capability of foreign policy formulation. Within the Foreign Ministry now, there is much heated discussion regarding a reorganisation of the Ministry so that it can have a very powerful office, which can formulate foreign policy from a comprehensive point of view. As for this haggling process of each ministry, it is often said that each ministry is mindful of its own interests rather than national interests. It will be very difficult, and it will take time to improve the situation. One hopeful sign is that many of our colleagues in the economic-related ministries are very much aware of the kind of problem this is causing and, individually and privately, they support the idea that they should work together for the national benefit. But once they become an official at a desk, they become very much loyal to their own ministry's interests, as they are trained. But somehow they have to be changed in this.

The second problem area in this institutional aspect is, of course, the political leadership and much has been discussed about the lack of political leadership. There is *a lot of demand on the part of the bureaucrats for the political leadership*, perhaps as a result of their own inability to come up with a strong, decisive policy formulation. Hopefully, many politicians are clearly aware that the people are fed up with the present political situation. I hope that this will work towards a better mindset for many of the politicians and there are some good politicians, who have a very sort of 'right' mind in viewing this issue. For example, Ozawa can be a very strong leader in the future, in Japanese external relations as well.

I think perhaps I will move on to a non-institutional aspect of Japan. There are two things which deserve special mention. One is something which relates to the corporate ethics that I mentioned yesterday. The Japanese people have got to develop the kind of independent thinking, the kind of independent frame of reference on which they can base their judgement. Some time ago, I chuckled to read a letter in the 'Reader's Column' of one of the Japanese monthly magazines. In the letter, a young man in his late twenties was talking about the merits of the 'lone wolf' lifestyle. At the end of the letter, he proposed the establishment of an association of 'lone wolves'. This is the kind of individuality that may come to the minds of the Japanese in the future. But I think there are good signs.

Perhaps the area we need a lot of effort in would be to raise the substantive-oriented discussion or debate, the kind of debate which took place for two days in this conference room. This is vitally necessary because *Japan needs some kind of broad consensus in foreign policy*. There has been too much of a split in the public opinion with regard to foreign policy, so that resulted in some form of an inefficiency perhaps in the policy formulation. And I think there is a sign that the Japanese people's awareness of international affairs is rising. For instance, just yesterday, as I was watching the television news, there was the result of a further fall in support of the Miyazawa cabinet. There were three top reasons given. The primary reason given was the lack of leadership in international affairs - 11 per cent felt this. This clearly shows that the people are expecting very much of the leadership in international affairs, that the people's awareness is there and increasing, I hope. Well this is something that perhaps we have to promote - an *understanding of the other countries, compassion, and a sense of involvement*. Now this prospect will take time because it will involve a wide range of adjustment and changes that have to take place. But, hopefully, since the source of *vitality* of the Japanese is their ability to learn and adjust, I think this quality will work for their improvement.

K. Calder: In the interest of time and because I do want to hear Professor Iriye at length, I would just like to make one point - the importance of thinking more systematically. This is for our research agenda now on, about the international forces that are building for change against the Japanese system, probably particularly broad economic forces and then, conceivably also, certain international political contingencies that could have an impact on Japan's global role.

G. Berger: I would love the opportunity to speak as an historian, but I think that with Akira Iriye waiting in the wings, that I will only say that I have been struck by the way in which the experience of the Second World War, the Pacific War, hovers in some unspoken way over much of what has been said today and yesterday and, as well, over much that has gone on in the last 47 years in post-war Japan. As Mr Mikuni told us today, the growth of market share is motivated by a desire to have productive capacity this time, so that Japan will not suffer the indignities that were experienced in the middle of the 1940s. And for many of those who have been critical of a Japan 'out of control', I think that the debate has been very much informed through a concern that Japan might once again go out of control, that there was a heedlessness about the politics of the 1930s that might be replicated in a much larger and more powerful form. So those were a couple of observations I had as an historian.

I want, finally, to bring us back to the level of the individual Japanese and his mother - to send us all off with good thoughts - and to say that the discussion we've had about public and private is one that, although as I've made very clear, does not begin in culture or institutions; it begins temporally, for each Japanese, in the crib. The Japanese are simply not raised with the sense of the legitimacy of privacy, when privacy is defined as independence of mothers' concerns or the well-being of the child or, more particularly, of the family. *The child is obliged from the very beginning to assume a public status which obviates much of the development of the private self in Japan and leaves the individual in need, indeed, of opportunities to develop a private self later in life, which are not always afforded to it.*

One of the hopes for change in the future is in this particular limited area. I cannot speak about the megaconcepts that others are so well-equipped to discuss, but in this small area, Professor Iwai has noted that

Japan may be subjected to the view of what women should be and what families should be, by the return of people from overseas who have very different and subversive ideas about that sort of thing, that as the role of women in society is redefined and women find more meaningful ways of themselves being public figures than simply as the producers and educators of children, they may back off a little bit and allow their children to develop the private selves. This is not something which can take place in the absence of sweeping institutional changes as well; I realise that. But I do think there are opportunities for micro-changes here which can have mega-effects on the larger scheme of things in Japanese life.

A. Clesse: The next historian and perhaps the last participant to speak at this meeting is Professor Iriye, from Harvard University.

A. Iriye: I think an historian is poorly equipped to end a conference with any profound statement - I do not have any profound statement to make. But listening to all the discussion, which has really been quite fascinating, I think it has become more and more clear to me, in any event, that we have been discussing Japan's *vitality* and then comparing Japan's *vitality* to the *vitality* of Korea, and various other countries, the United States, and Europe. And I think we seem to be ending with internationalising it. In other words we seem to be talking more and more about international *vitalities*, the kinds of *vitality* that the world requires of each country, including Japan. I think that is the right direction to go so long as we realise that, when we are focusing on just one country's *vitality*, questions cannot be thoroughly explored. We are talking about Japan in the world, which means *what kind of vitality do we need from Japan*.

That leads us to the question of *what kind of vitality does the world require today*? It seems to me that, if my reading of the events of several decades, if not centuries, is at all relevant, perhaps what the world required was an economic kind of *vitality*. That is, the world, particularly since the 1970s, has required a great deal of economic restructuring and economic *revitalisation* and so on. In that kind of a situation, Japan may be said to have played a significant role and will probably continue to do that. But I think it is becoming more and more clear, from the discussion and in my own mind, that *vitality of a purely economic kind is not going to be sufficient because the world of the 1990s is going to encounter not only economic issues, but many other questions*. There may be issues of a more cultural nature, ideological nature, and many other emerging social issues - the question of protecting the environment, refugees, human rights, those sorts of questions. And it seems to me that, to the extent we are facing a world in which this kind of *intellectual vitality* is going to be required, the question would be whether Japan is in any position to contribute to that kind of world environment in which intellectual *vitality* is going to be one of the key issues.

This fits in with the discussion that took place earlier, before the coffee break. I listened with rapt attention to the exchange between van Wolferen, Murphy, and others on one side and some Japanese participants on the other. Throughout the distressing spectacle, I thought it indicated that Japan is not quite ready to play a role in the intellectual *vitality* requirement. That is if the Japanese continue to remain so defensive, if they remain so concerned with their own interests and so intellectually narrow-minded, I think it does not quite argue well for the requirements for a new age. I do hope that something can be done.

I agree with Professor Iwai there, to the extent that *some kind of intellectual vitalisation is absolutely crucial, that intellectual engagement, openness, and interchange will be very crucial.* Therefore, I will conclude, at least from my understanding of the discussion, that it seems that to make Japan, as Ambassador Matsunaga said, compatible with international society - the *key question is to develop a mentality of openness in Japan.* I think, in this sense, Glen Fukushima is right, and various other people as well. Van Wolferen and Murphy were absolutely right in pointing to the absence of fundamental universals. To say that there are no universals and universals don't count is not the way to stop. If nothing else, I do hope that engagements of this kind will force the Japanese to accept the fact that you do have to start with absolutes. You do have to start with absolute and universal concepts of justice and equality.

Let me say that, in the American context, I am viewed as one of the more reactionary academics, because many American academics do not believe in universal truths anymore - but I do. At least that should be the starting point; *vitality is a very important concept and I hope that this can be put into some kind of an intellectually vitalising formula, which would be very important, not just in the Japanese context to open up Japanese minds and so on, but because that is what the world requires as well in the 1990s.*

A. Clesse: Thank you, Professor Iriye and all of you. As I said at the beginning, this was just a brainstorming meeting and it should form a satisfactory base for future endeavours, following also what Professor Iriye said. We hope that we will stay in touch with all of you about this project, about future meetings; we will certainly write to you. We hope that we can produce a book after this conference; it might also be a source of satisfaction for all of us who have been here, to provide further development for our intellectual endeavours.

To all of you, of course, I wish a very nice evening and a good journey back. I wish to thank very warmly once more the Japan Institute of International Affairs for its intellectual and logistical support for this meeting, especially its director, who has also been contributing intellectually to this meeting, Itaro Umezu. I would also like to thank all of his staff, who have devoted a lot of time in setting up this meeting. Thank you very much.

I. Umezu: On behalf of Ambassador Matsunaga and the Japan Institute of International Affairs, we would like to express a sense of appreciation and congratulations, and we wish a safe journey home for all of you. Thank you very much for your cooperation.